The Book of
God and Man

The book of God

THE UNIVERSITY OF
CHICAGO PRESS

CHICAGO & LONDON

AND MAN

A STUDY OF JOB

BY ROBERT GORDIS

THE UNIVERSITY OF CHICAGO PRESS, CHICAGO 60637
The University of Chicago Press, Ltd., London

© 1965 by Robert Gordis
All Rights reserved. Published 1965
Fifth Impression 1978. Phoenix Edition 1978
Printed in the United States of America

International Standard Book Number: 0–226–30410–8
Library of Congress Catalog Card Number: 65–25126

Foreword

"O F THE MAKING OF MANY BOOKS there is no end," declared an ancient Hebrew sage, who had himself magnificently aggravated the situation he was decrying. His observation is particularly true of the Book of Books, and above all of its crowning masterpiece, the Book of Job. He who would add to the vast library of interpretation and analysis to which Job has been subjected must therefore be prepared to justify his action.

Some years ago an American scholar declared that just as the humblest actor harbors a secret ambition to play Hamlet, so every biblical student nurtures the hope of some day writing about Job. The truth is that Job is a perennial challenge to every reader and biblical scholar. This "Mount Everest" of the human spirit continues to defy even the most intrepid and confident of climbers and probably will never yield all its secrets. For every aspect of the book poses problems that each reader and student must solve for himself. There is not, nor can there be, universal agreement on such major issues as the structure, the unity, and the basic meaning of the book, or even on such relatively minor questions as its style, date, and origin. Aside from these general considerations, the complexities of the book's language necessarily intrigue the commentator as he tries to interpret each word and passage in the text.

It is no wonder then that each reader creates a Job in his own image.

Throughout the ages, the unsophisticated believer and the recondite philosopher, the rationalist and the mystic, the skeptic and the existentialist, have all been fascinated by Job. Each has found in it a matchless expression of his own temperament, some striking illumination of his own problems. No "definitive work" on Job is possible while man continues to live and remains free to ponder the human situation.

Nonetheless, while unanimity on Job is not to be expected, the possibility of achieving steady progress in our understanding of the book ought not to be ruled out. We may hope for a growing measure of agreement on its content and meaning—in broad outline and in specific passages. The ever richer resources available in Hebrew and Semitic linguistics, including parallels from cognate literatures, shed increasing light upon the idiom, vocabulary, and syntax of the biblical masterpiece. Archaeological discoveries and, above all, the elucidation of newly found literary texts of the ancient Near East, are highly significant in understanding the material and cultural background from which the Book of Job emerged. The extent to which a commentator utilizes this material in large measure determines the quality of his work.

Much more, however, is required than technical knowledge. Like the practice of medicine, exegesis is an art resting upon a foundation of science. The truly gifted interpreter of a literary work is one who possesses a creative imagination of a high order, an empathy for the subject and the hero of the work, and a capacity for penetrating to the spirit of the author. It is these gifts, which are the results of temperament rather than training, that give him insight into the meaning and intent of the text. One has only to compare any two works on Job to see how scholars of equal competence may produce constructs of the same book that differ radically in coherence and cogency. Like the mathematician who follows in the footsteps of God, the great interpreter thinks the author's thoughts after him. In revealing what he finds, he creates what he discloses.

The tremendous literature on Job continues to grow steadily; no man can hope to read it all—let alone master it. This fact explains in part the practice of some scholars of ignoring the names of predecessors in their area of research. All too often we find commentaries and other scholarly works that set forth the views of their authors as though the ideas were newly conceived, when in fact they represent the conclusions and insights of generations. In one of his passionate outbursts against his antagonists, Job sarcastically declares, "No doubt you are the people that count, and with you all wisdom will die!" Frequently, modern writers act as though all wisdom were born with them.

The rabbis of the Talmud were keenly aware of this human weakness characteristic of scholars and tried to overcome it by declaring, "He who cites a statement in the name of its author brings redemption to the world." To consign a scholar to involuntary anonymity may give his successor the appearance of originality, but the moral and intellectual cost is high. It deprives the scholar, who shuns delights and lives laborious days, of even the modest immortality of being remembered for his contribution to learning. Moreover, all genuine progress in research depends upon reckoning with the work of earlier students; whether their results are accepted, rejected, or modified, they are invaluable guidelines to those who come after.

I certainly have not exhausted the scholarly literature on Job, but I have sought to cite what I believe to be most valuable in the extant literature. It is true that I have often had occasion to blaze a new trail for myself on fundamental issues and on questions of detail. When this has happened, I have tried to set forth the earlier views with my reasons for diverging from them. This arduous procedure has been more than an act of piety toward the earlier generations of scholars— Jewish and Christian, traditional and critical—who have labored lovingly over this complex masterpiece. It has been my hope that explaining the grounds for the positions I have taken would commend them to the reader. At the same time, I have tried to put him in possession of all the data necessary for evaluating the various views and for making his own decision.

The present work, however, is not simply, or even principally, a compendium of the research of other scholars. I believe that I have arrived at a new conception of the meaning of the book as a whole. This is derived largely from my recognition of its architectonic structure and its inner unity. In ever greater measure, my view of Job has deepened with the passing years. I should like to feel that the experiences life has brought me have induced a deeper faith in God and a more mature insight, at once wiser and humbler, into His ways with man.

The translation I have prepared for the present volume cannot claim to possess a tithe of the passion and power of the original. I have, however, striven to transmit the content and spirit of Job in a version which seeks to be faithful to the original text as well as vigorous and intelligible to the modern reader. The introductions to each section will help to orient the reader to the book as a whole and to the meaning of each individual passage. In many instances I believe I have been able to achieve a new understanding of the text. The full apparatus justifying my views is reserved for a projected commentary. In the interim, the interested student may refer to the *Vorstudien* that have appeared in various journals here and abroad, a list of which will be found in the bibliography. These contain the results of much of my research. Unless otherwise noted, I have prepared my own translations of the biblical and post-biblical passages cited in this book.

In great measure, this book represents the fruit of my teaching of Job for over a quarter of a century. During this entire period, I have derived stimulation and challenge from my students at the Jewish Theological Seminary of America, where I serve as Professor of Bible, and from those at Union Theological Seminary in New York, where I was privileged to serve, more briefly, as Visiting Professor of Old Testament. For the opportunity to study and teach at these great institutions I am deeply grateful to Dr. Louis Finkelstein, Chancellor of the Jewish Theological Seminary, and to Dr. Henry P. van Dusen, former President of Union Theological Seminary. This book also owes much to another great leader in higher education in America, Dr. Robert M. Hutchins, President of the Center for the Study of Democratic Institutions of the Fund for the Republic. Impelled by warm friendship and true generosity of spirit, Dr. Hutchins invited me to spend the academic year 1960–61 in Santa Barbara. As a Consultant to the Center I shared actively in its basic task, which is the exploration of the problems of a free society in a modern world. Going far beyond these terms of reference, however, he graciously provided the encouragement and the conditions for me to write the first draft of this book during my period of residence in Santa Barbara.

I cannot sufficiently express my gratitude to the thousands of men and women in my congregation, Temple Beth-El of Rockaway Park, New York, to whom I have ministered for over three decades and who, out of their love and understanding, have provided me with the security and peace of mind required for scholarly work. Nor would I wish to overlook the large number of intelligent laymen, in my congregation and throughout the United States and Canada, to whom I have expounded the content and meaning of Job as I understand it.

I am grateful to my son David, with whom I discussed many issues in Job and who brought a fresh and independent viewpoint to these problems. I am also grateful to Neal Kaunfer, a student at the Jewish Theological Seminary, who served as my research assistant. He read the manuscript and suggested many improvements in style and corrections in substance. The detailed index is the labor of love of my honored and learned friend, Dr. Abraham I. Shinedling, who also carried through the arduous task of proofreading with his characteristic accuracy. My devoted and capable secretary, Marjorie Deutsch, has labored with exemplary care and skill over the many revisions of the manuscript.

That I have been able to produce this book in spite of the unending demands of an active community career is a tribute to the boundless love and understanding which my dear wife has lavished upon me through the years. The extraordinary courage with which she has surmounted physical trials and with God's help emerged triumphant expressed itself also in a single-minded insistence that I let nothing prevent the completion of this work.

Finally, I am humbly grateful for the privilege of standing in the presence of transcendent beauty and truth. May this work, for all its imperfections, prove a worthy thank offering on the altar of God.

Contents

Part One

A STUDY OF JOB

I

On Reading Job

A Noble Book; all men's Book! It is our first, oldest statement of the never-ending Problem,—man's destiny, and God's ways with him here in this earth. And all in such free flowing outlines; grand in its sincerity, in its simplicity; in its epic melody, and repose of reconcilement. There is the seeing eye, the mildly understanding heart. . . . Sublime sorrow, sublime reconciliation; oldest choral melody as of the heart of mankind;—so soft, and great; as the summer midnight, as the world with its seas and stars! There is nothing written, I think, in the Bible or out of it, of equal literary merit.[1]

NO LESS FERVENT is the tribute of the historian Froude, who describes Job as "towering up alone, far above all the poetry of the world."[2] Carl Cornill, a modern biblical scholar possessing a fine literary sense, has characterized Job as "one of the most marvelous products of the human spirit, belonging like Dante's *Divine Comedy* and Goethe's *Faust* to the literature of the world."[3]

These sweeping tributes to the Book of Job have been echoed by untold readers and scholars who have recognized in it one of the supreme human masterpieces. Its influence on literature and art has been widespread. Goethe used the narrative of God's wager with Satan, described in the opening chapters of Job, as the model for his prologue to *Faust*. Blake found scope for his unique artistic genius in his moving illustrations for the Book of Job. After World War I, H. G. Wells adopted the framework of the dialogue of Job for his treatment of the same basic problem in his novel, *The Undying Fire*. A decade and a half after World War II, Archibald MacLeish, in his drama *J.B.*, used the biblical tale and text of Job as a means of grappling with the problems confronting man in an affluent society.

3

The greatness of Job is heightened by the fact that it belongs to a unique literary genre, without parallel before or since its composition. It is literally the only book of its kind. Some few scholars have described Job as an epic, comparing it with the work of Homer.[4] Many more have been tempted to place it in the category of drama. One distinguished author has treated Job as an authentic tragedy on Greek lines, complete with chorus.[5] The truth is, however, that it bears little resemblance to the classic Greek drama of Aeschylus, Sophocles, or Euripides. In the ancient Greek drama, little action took place on the stage, it is true, the spectators being kept informed of the march of events by the chorus and messengers. Yet the plot develops as the play continues. Job, on the other hand, is characterized by a total lack of plot. After the events narrated in the prologue there is no further progress in the action, although scholars have attempted to find a development in the thought patterns of the protagonists. The fact is, however, that there is no progression in the views of the Friends as the debate proceeds from the first cycle of speeches to the second and the third. It is only the emotion of the speakers, notably Job's passion, that grows more intense as the debate continues; the same basic positions continue to be maintained by all the speakers throughout the dialogue.

It is clear that Job is also poles away from Elizabethan and from modern drama, in which intermediaries are dispensed with and the entire action is presented on the stage in full view of the audience. In Job there is no plot from the opening of the debate until its close, with the final appearance of the Lord from the whirlwind and Job's reconciliation with his Maker.

Nor may the debates in Job be compared with the *Dialogues* of Plato. The widely held view that there was a total dichotomy and lack of contact between Hebrew and Greek civilizations is yielding to the recognition of a long-standing relationship between the two cultures. Recent research has demonstrated the existence of these contacts and affinities, not only during the Greco-Roman period, but also during the classical age of Hebrew Wisdom, the "heroic age" of Homer, and the early history of Israel.[6] Nonetheless, the differences between these two great seminal cultures of the Western world, ancient Hellas and Israel, are far-reaching. Nowhere are they more strikingly highlighted than in the contrast, in both spirit and form, between these supreme embodiments of the creative genius of the two peoples.

Plato's *Dialogues* are the expression of an incisive yet sensitive spirit, seeking to establish the proper norms of human conduct through the exercise of reason. In Books I and II of the *Republic* an effort is made to analyze the meaning of justice by discarding false notions, thus arriving at a true understanding of the concept. The same theme preoccupies the author of Job. But what a world of difference in temperament and method as well as in the mode of expression and in the conclusions reached! Nowhere in Job does the author undertake an analysis of the nature of right and wrong. What the Greek philosopher sought to discover through logic, the Hebrew poet knew through instinct. It is not merely Job's antagonists in the debate who are certain that right is right and wrong is wrong: Job himself never differs with them on the nature of righteousness.

The ancient Hebrews believed that only sinners who were seeking to confuse and mislead their fellows would raise such questions:

> Woe unto them that call evil good and good, evil,
> That change darkness into light and light into darkness,
> That change bitter into sweet and sweet into bitter!

> [Isa. 5:20]

For honorable men the truth was clear: "It hath been told thee, O man, what is good and what the Lord thy God doth require of thee, to do justice, to love mercy, and to walk humbly with thy God" (Mic. 6:8). Man knows the good because God has revealed it to him —and justice and mercy are recognizable by their presence or absence in human affairs.

After two millennia of Western civilization, it should be clear that each viewpoint is inadequate in and of itself: each is indispensable as a corrective to the other. The Hebrew attitude has all too often been invoked as the basis for an absolutism in morals that has imperiled true morality, while the Greek approach has been the seed from which various schools of relativistic ethics have developed. The moral crisis of the mid-twentieth century bears tragic testimony to the perils that ethical relativism has spawned.[7]

But these reflections are not directly germane to our theme. Suffice it here to note that the far-reaching differences between Plato and Job, in both content and temper, are reflected in a striking variation of form. The Greek *Dialogues* are inspired prose; the Hebrew dialogue, exalted poetry. Each work is supreme in its own field.

Having noted the vast differences between Plato and Job, we

should not ignore the affinities, recognizing, however, that what is primary in one is likely to be secondary in the other. It would be a grave error to underestimate the deep emotional drive underlying the ostensibly cool analyses of Plato's Socratic *Dialogues*. It was the poet in Plato that led him to banish poets from his Republic, for he knew the strength of the irrational, the power lodged in the creative aspects of human nature, which brook no discipline and confound the neatest blueprints of the future. The entire structure of Platonic ideas is a creation of the poetic faculty, a myth that seeks to interpret the nature of reality. To ignore the emotional drive behind the Platonic *Dialogues* is fatal to a true understanding of their nature.

Equally disastrous is a failure to recognize the strong intellectual content of the Book of Job. The trial of Job, the heart of his tragedy and triumph, is, to be sure, expressed in passionately emotional terms, but it is an intellectual experience as truly as it is a moral challenge. If Job did no more than raise the issue of "the prosperity of the wicked and the suffering of the righteous" in a world created by a just God, its value would be immeasurable. To ask the right questions is the height of wisdom, for on ultimate issues only the questions endure; the answers are transitory. But Job does more. It offers a positive approach to the problem of evil in terms that give promise of being perennially valid.

Job enriches our thought in another direction as well. Aside from its positive contribution to the content of religious faith, it illustrates the process of religious growth. How is a man nurtured by the teaching of the past and living in the realities of the present to resolve the conflict between them as he faces the future? Job points the way to the solution of this problem: the contradiction between the accepted tradition of the group and the personal experience of the individual. It is this tension, painful as it is, that serves as the sharp growing-edge of the human spirit. When the challenge is not ignored, minimized, or denied, but creatively resolved, new truths emerge, deepening man's insight into life and ushering in a new and fruitful stage in religion.

The greatness of Job becomes even more evident when it is compared, not with such lofty expressions of the human spirit as classic Greek drama or the Platonic *Dialogues*, but with the literary products of the ancient Near Eastern culture, from which Israel and the Bible emanated. With their penchant for unearthing literary parallels, scholars have called attention to such fragments of Near Eastern

Wisdom literature as the Egyptian *Complaint of the Peasant* and *Dialogue about Human Misery*, or the Babylonian *Pessimistic Dialogue of a Master and a Slave*, which are also concerned with the problem of justice and its deserts.[8] Some scholars have ventured to dub these poems the "Egyptian Job," the "Egyptian Ecclesiastes," and the "Babylonian Job."

These literary documents reveal the framework of oriental Wisdom literature, of which biblical Hokmah literature is an integral though highly distinctive element.[9] But, as will become clear, these poems and laments bear little resemblance either to the biblical Job or to Ecclesiastes. Any direct relationship or dependency is out of the question, as virtually all scholars agree.

If Job is neither an epic nor a drama, it must, according to the classical distinctions, fall into the category of either lyric or didactic poetry. Actually, Job partakes of the nature of both, but only in a very special sense. It is didactic, being concerned with teaching truths about life, and thus occupies an honored place in biblical Wisdom literature. At the same time it is lyrical, being characterized by deep emotion. In Job, logic and passion, emotion and thought, are fused in the crucible of genius. Yet the dialogue cannot be described simply as lyric poetry, for it contains the conflicting utterances of various protagonists. Finally, the poetry is set within the framework of a prose tale, which is itself a superb example of narrative art. In sum, the author of Job has not only written a masterpiece but, in the process, has created his own literary genre.

The literary greatness of Job is only one element, and perhaps the less important element, of its universal appeal. Job's enduring significance lies in its theme, for it is concerned with the most agonizing issue confronting men—the mystery of evil. This central issue in the Hebrew Bible has remained the great stumbling block to faith for men through the centuries. A universal genius with all-embracing sympathies, the author of Job was able to give fair and eloquent expression to the accepted religious doctrines of his day concerning the problems of human suffering and divine justice. But being an original thinker as well, he was able to reveal the inadequacy of these views, challenging them with unequaled passion and depth.

The author does not content himself with criticism, however. He succeeds in resolving the conflict between the accepted teaching of traditional religion and the existential tragedy of Job's suffering. His insights and attitudes, when properly understood, constitute a fundamental and perennially valid contribution to a mature religious faith. While the simple believer has found consolation in the prose narrative of "the patience of Job" being rewarded by his restoration to prosperity, the poetry of Job has continued to intrigue and stimulate the more sophisticated scholar and philosopher. It is no wonder that two such distinguished exemplars of rational thought as the medieval philosopher Moses Maimonides and the eighteenth-century thinker Immanuel Kant utilized the ancient book of Job as the springboard for their own philosophical reflections on the tripartite problem of God, man, and evil in the world. Where piety found the warmth of faith, reason discovered the light of truth—and both were right. For in Job, poetry and philosophy, passion and truth, are united in one of the supreme achievements of the human spirit.

II

The Enigma of Job

THE STORY OF JOB is generally familiar in its broad outlines. It is imbedded in a prose tale which is divided into a prologue (chaps. 1 and 2) and an epilogue (42:7–17). Between these two sections lies the poetic dialogue (3–42:6) which is the heart of the book and for which the narrative serves as a framework.

The prologue is a masterpiece of narrative art, written in terse, vivid, rapidly moving prose unsurpassed in the Bible or in ancient literature generally. The tale is divided into five scenes, which alternate between earth and heaven. The action opens on earth where Job is a chieftain whose life is marked by integrity and piety. He has long enjoyed prosperity, universal respect, and the warm companionship of his family.

A popular misconception about Job needs to be corrected at the outset. In both tradition and popular thought, Job is generally pictured as a "patriarch," a man advanced in years. This impression is totally mistaken and has not the slightest warrant in either the prose or the poetry of the book. In the folk tale his sons and daughters are unmarried, nor is there any mention of grandchildren when calamity comes upon Job's family. Since the story is laid in the ancient East, where marriages took place early, the implication is that his children were relatively young. After his restoration, Job is still vigorous enough to beget a large family. The poetic dialogue bears out this

9

view. In his complaint, Job refers to the fact that in the period of his prosperity even the aged stood up in his presence. Eliphaz, with poetic exaggeration, declares that he and the other Friends are older than Job's father.[1] Finally, the passion and energy of Job's response to his undeserved suffering and the misunderstanding of his friends are more appropriate for a man in his prime than for one whose life is largely spent.

The second scene of the drama takes place in heaven. Satan, the prosecuting angel, has returned to the divine court and taken his place among his peers, the heavenly beings or "sons of God" who surround God's throne. When the Lord, with legitimate pride, refers to His loyal servant Job, on earth, Satan charges that Job's piety is motivated entirely by the ample rewards he has been receiving from God. The Lord enters into a wager to test the depth and sincerity of Job's piety by giving Satan permission to bring whatever calamities he wishes upon him.

The scene then shifts back to earth. A series of four disasters, alternately man made and natural, comes upon Job's family and possessions. Marauding Sabeans carry off Job's cattle, followed immediately by a fire from heaven that devastates his sheep. Chaldean bandits then fall upon his camels, and the final blow takes the form of a hurricane from the desert which destroys the house and kills Job's children, who are gathered there for a family feast. As reports of these disasters reach Job, he tears his garment in mourning, but he submits to the will of his Maker. "Naked I came from my mother's womb, and naked shall I return. The Lord gave and the Lord has taken away. Blessed be the name of the Lord."

The fourth scene is again situated in heaven. God questions Satan on the results of the experiment, and Satan proves a hardy adversary. Still unprepared to concede the disinterested character of Job's virtue, Satan now cites a familiar proverb: "Skin for skin! All a man has he will give for his life!" Only if Job is made to suffer in his own person will the test be conclusive. God then gives Satan permission to inflict a loathsome disease on Job.

The fifth and concluding scene takes place on earth. Job has been smitten with an affliction akin to leprosy. Only his wife remains at his side. Unable to bear the sight of his agony she urges Job to curse God and die. But Job reproves her rather curtly, saying, "You talk like an impious, foolish woman. Shall we accept good from God and not accept evil?" And Job permits no sinful word to cross his lips.

It seems less than kind of Augustine to describe Job's wife as *adiutrix diaboli*, "the assistant of Satan." Actually, as the Midrash recognizes,[2] her reaction is dictated by her love and loyalty to her husband. This theme is elaborated with some touching details in the apocryphal *Testament of Job*,[3] which gives her a name, Sitides, and relates that she sells her hair to support Job. In her final appearance she goes in rags to Job's friends to plead with them to search the ruins of her house for the remains of her children. These embellishments are lacking in the biblical text, but they are not out of harmony with its essential spirit. Thus far the story as told in the prose narrative.

At this point, three of Job's old friends—Eliphaz, Bildad, and Zophar —who are evidently princes of dignity and importance in their respective tribes, hear of the calamities which have befallen him. They arrange to meet and go to comfort him. When they enter Job's presence, the horror of his position impels them to silence. After seven days the much tried sufferer breaks into a lament, cursing the day of his birth. As yet he has uttered no complaint against his Maker; he laments only the destiny that gave him life, and contents himself with a description of the peace that awaits him in the grave (chap. 3).

In an effort to console him, Eliphaz, the oldest and most respected of the Friends, begins a reply. He takes it for granted that Job needs only to be reminded of the basic religious beliefs by which he has hitherto lived in order to overcome his bitterness and despair. It is these universally accepted truths about sin and suffering that Eliphaz sets forth with tact and consideration. Job, however, has undergone a profound transformation under the impact of his undeserved suffering. He responds with mounting fury and indignation to Eliphaz, in whose words he sees a thoroughly unjustified accusation against himself. The other two friends enter the fray and the debate increases in intensity through three cycles of speeches (chaps. 4–27).

The three friends restate the accepted religious doctrine of the time, ringing countless changes upon it. It is their fundamental belief that in a world created and governed by a just God, suffering is the result, and by that token the sign, of sin. It therefore follows that Job, who has suffered, must be a sinner. Job has no well thought out doctrine of his own with which to counter this accepted teaching. In his agony he knows only that it is false, and he is therefore driven to deny the righteousness of God. Job calls for the God of Justice to protect him from the God of Power, who has persecuted him. Unable to persuade his friends of his innocence, Job ends with a tragic soliloquy (chaps. 29

and 30), climaxed by a moving protestation of innocence, in which he sets forth the code of conduct by which he has lived. His final words are a plea to God to answer him directly (chap. 31).

A new personage now appears on the scene, unheralded and apparently unwanted. He is a brash young man called Elihu, who castigates the ineffective defense of God by the Friends even more vigorously than he decries Job's assault on God's justice. After a lengthy apology for his intrusion among his elders (chap. 32) he presents his views on the subject under debate (chaps. 33–37) and then subsides into silence.

As Elihu's words come to an end, the Lord himself appears out of a whirlwind. These speeches of God rank with the most exalted nature poetry in all of literature. Can Job comprehend, let alone govern, the secrets of creation? Earth and sea, cloud and darkness and dawn, snow and hail, rain and thunder, snow and ice, and the stars above—all these are wonders beyond Job. Nor do they exhaust God's power. With a sensitivity born of deep love and careful observation, the poet pictures the wild beasts, remote from man, yet precious to their Maker—the mountain goat, the wild ass, the buffalo, the ostrich, the untamed horse, the hawk—all testifying to the glory of God. Despite their variety these creatures have one element in common—they are not under the sway of man, nor are they even intended for his use (chaps. 38; 39; 40:1–2).

Job is overwhelmed by God's omnipotence and admits his own weakness. But God ignores Job's surrender and with torrential force continues to hurl His challenge at His human opponent (chaps. 40:3–41:26). Were Job able to destroy evil in the world, even God would be prepared to relinquish His throne to him—a moving acknowledgment by God Himself that the world order is not perfect! (40:6–14). Then follow exultant descriptions of two massive beasts, whose power is depicted with poetic hyperbole and mythological overtones. These animals—Behemot, the hippopotamus, and Leviathan, the crocodile—are far from beautiful, but they, too, reveal the creative power of their Maker. When God has finished speaking, Job again voices his submission (42:1–6) and the poetic portion of the book comes to a close.

The book ends with a prose epilogue in which God condemns the three friends for their words. They are told to offer a sacrifice for forgiveness, and Job is asked to pray for them. His trials are over: he is restored to his earlier prosperity; his wealth is doubled; a new family of sons and daughters is born to him. Job lives twice the normal life-span, passing away "old and satisfied with days."

There is almost no aspect of the book on which there are not far-reaching differences of opinion. Because of its patriarchal setting, the old talmudic tradition ascribed it to Moses;[4] yet there have been scholars who have attributed it to the First Temple period, to the age of Solomon, and to that of Hezekiah.[5] Most scholars, however, attribute Job to some period between the sixth and second centuries.[6]

The existence of the Hebrew text has naturally persuaded most scholars that the author was a Jew who wrote in his native tongue. However, the opinion has also been expressed that he was an Edomite[7] or an Egyptian.[8] The suggestion was advanced long ago that the book is a translation, on the ground of its difficulty—a theory that does not stand up under examination.[9] Voltaire thought the author an Arab, a suggestion made by Carlyle as well, on the "objective" ground that the book is too broadly universalistic to be Hebrew.[10]

These technical questions of language, and time and place of authorship might perhaps be ignored by the general reader since they do not materially affect his understanding of the book. There are, however, other debatable issues that are definitely germane to its significance and intent. These cannot be bypassed if we are to arrive at any real understanding of Job.

The unity and authenticity of the various sections of the book constitute a complex of major problems. As we shall see, the prologue and epilogue differ greatly in substance and style from the poetic dialogue. Only one instance need be cited here. One of the most familiar of phrases is "the patience of Job," which occurs in the Epistle of James (5:11). Yet this epithet stands in sharp contrast to the bitter and rebellious Job who dominates the poetic substance of the book. The traditional image of the patient sufferer applies only to the hero of the prose narrative in the two opening chapters. Are we, therefore, to regard the prose and the poetry as the work of independent writers? If so, which came first, and what relationship exists between them?

The prose tale itself appears clear and straightforward to the uninstructed reader. Some scholars, however, have been led to suspect its integrity. They have found in it two distinct and totally independent narratives, and for good measure, have assigned new roles to some of the characters.

The authenticity of the poetic dialogue itself has been questioned, and chapters 3 to 41 have been atomized, with countless passages deleted as glosses. It has even been suggested that there was originally only a single cycle of speeches followed by one monologue of Job,[11] while some have rejected all the speeches of Job and the Friends![12]

Perhaps the largest measure of agreement among scholars concerns the deletion of the whole of the Elihu speeches (chaps. 32–37).[13] Some students have divided the words of Elihu among several authors.[14] Only a few scholars, particularly of late,[15] have ventured to defend their authenticity. Yet here again, the proposed remedy proves, as we shall see, to be worse than the malady.

An even more fundamental question is raised by the magnificent God speeches (chaps. 37–41) which constitute the climax of the book. What precisely are the relevance and intent of the Lord's words, if, as many commentators presume, they emphasize the power of God as manifested in nature? What Job demands from God is justice; His power he has conceded from the very beginning. Why should Job "repent in dust and ashes" after God has spoken (42:6), seeing that his cry for justice has been ignored and only the divine might has been reiterated?

A number of scholars have cut the "Gordian knot" by simply denying the authenticity of the God speeches and deleting them from the text.[16] This simple solution suffers from one major defect—it leaves the book a shambles, or, if you will, a torso. It also produces a number of minor problems. These include the difficulties of elucidating the "original" theme of the book and of discovering the reasons for subjecting it to such extensive expansion.

Conscious of the weakness inherent in treating the God speeches as irrelevant or unauthentic, many modern interpreters have adopted another approach. They suggest that the speeches constitute a favorable response to Job's plea that God Himself answer: "This is my desire: that the Almighty answer me!" (31:35). Thus when God finally breaks His silence and directly addresses Job, He is assuring Job that He is with him in his affliction.

This existential interpretation of the God speeches appears attractive at first glance. It does not, however, stand up under analysis. It is not to experience an "encounter with God" that Job pleads with the Lord to answer him, but in order that God Himself may judge his claim to righteousness. He calls for more than the "existential" experience of meeting God face to face; what Job demands is a vindication of his complaint that he has suffered unjustly. Moreover, when God finally appears out of the whirlwind He does *not* assure Job of His protection and love for His suffering creature. For that theme we must look elsewhere in biblical and extra-biblical literature. Here it is the divine transcendence, the majesty and mystery of God, far removed from man and his concerns, that finds expression. The entire thrust of the God speeches undermines the anthropocentric view of the universe, presupposed by Job's challenge, by insisting that the universe and all it contains do not revolve around man and his interests. Finally, if God's reply represented a victory for Job, he should have responded in triumph rather than in contrition.

> Behold, I am of small account;
> How can I answer You?
> Therefore I abase myself
> And repent in dust and ashes.
>
> [Job 40:4; 42:6]

It seems clear that the interpretation of these speeches, and consequently the meaning of the book as a whole, lies elsewhere. What is required is a recognition of the organic relationship between content and form, substance and style in the book. This insight is basic to an understanding of the meaning of Job, both as a work of art and as a contribution to religious thought.

In sum, what is generally proposed as a solution to the enigma of Job substitutes an even greater mystery. The assumption is made that a conglomeration of separate documents, unrelated and at times even opposed to one another, were either haphazardly or deliberately manipulated to produce a masterpiece.

This tendency to atomize the book belongs to the "age of analysis" in biblical scholarship. It reached its apogee in the years before World War I in the Higher Criticism of the Pentateuch, particularly in the Documentary Hypothesis of the Graf-Wellhausen School.

The single most important cause for the change of attitude in biblical studies in general was the impact of archaeological discoveries in the lands of the Fertile Crescent—Egypt, Palestine, Syria, and Iraq. These placed the Hebrew Bible within the framework of ancient oriental civilizations, the various aspects of which gave new credibility at a thousand points to the content of Scripture. A vast array of ancient law codes, epics, hymns, incantations, and narratives emanating from the non-Semitic Sumerians, Egyptians, Hurrians, and Hittites, and from the Semitic Akkadians, Canaanites, and Arameans, have come to light. They have illumined countless passages in Israel's ancient literature and helped to clarify our understanding of the genesis and character of biblical literature. It should be added that the direct impact of archaeology upon the study of Job is far less significant than upon a study of the Pentateuch or the historical books. Its value is limited largely to details of prosody and mythological allusions, yet the importance of these should not be underestimated.

In the period following World War I a marked shift of emphasis and approach took place in the field of biblical scholarship. This shift was induced by a variety of factors, not the least of which was a reaction against the hypercritical analysis of sources, which had previously been carried to extremes.

Though the change in the climate of opinion is still far from complete, contemporary biblical scholarship is becoming increasingly aware of the truth trenchantly expressed by the Greek scholar H. D. F. Kitto:

> The attribution (of the *Iliad* and the *Odyssey* to Homer) was accepted quite wholeheartedly until modern times, when closer investigation showed all sorts of discrepancies of fact, style and language, both between the two epics and between the various parts of each. The immediate result of this was the minute and confident division of the two poems, but especially the *Iliad*, into separate layers of different periods, appropriately called 'strata' by critics, who imperfectly distinguished between artistic and geological composition.
>
> The study of the epic poetry of other races, and of the methods used by poets working in this traditional medium, has done a great deal to restore confidence in the substantial unity of each poem; that is to say, that what we have in each case is not a short poem by one original 'Homer' to which later poets have added more or less indiscriminately, but a poem, conceived as a unity by a relatively later 'Homer' who worked over and incorporated much traditional material—though the present *Iliad* certainly contains some passages which were not part of Homer's original design.[17]

In the case of Job, the Higher Criticism's "analysis of sources" has largely been replaced by several other techniques, less extreme in scope, for dealing with the linguistic and exegetical difficulties in which Job abounds.

The first of these methods is the wholesale use of emendations. One may be certain that an ancient text, however well preserved, must have suffered some error in transmission through the centuries. This is particularly true of a difficult text like Job, which must often have been unintelligible to copyists. Yet the observation that there is scarcely a verse in the book that has not been subjected to conjectural emendation gives one pause. Although it is unlikely that the book suffered no errors, it is equally unlikely that it was exposed to corruption in virtually every line. This conviction is strengthened when one contemplates the type of "emendation Hebrew" which is proposed as an improvement on the Masoretic text. One often has the uncomfortable feeling that the self-assurance with which a given emendation is proposed is in inverse ratio to its plausibility.

When passages seem inappropriate to the context, it is frequently assumed that extensive glosses and interpolations were made by ancient readers. It is argued that when orthodox readers encountered heterodox sentiments in the original text, they proceeded to "correct" or supplement the text by more conventional verses that were in harmony with their views.

Widespread as this assumption is in some scholarly circles, it is open to serious doubt. One may well question why antagonistic readers would go to the trouble of interpolating pious sentiments into a heretical text when it would be simpler to consign the book to oblivion by ignoring it completely or placing it in an ancient *Genizah*. It was once a popular assumption that Ecclesiastes was a heterodox text which had been worked over by conventional glossators.[18] Deeper insight into the contents and style of the book has made this assumption unnecessary because it has revealed an inner unity and coherence. Frequently the advocates of deletion excise most of a given text (as in Job, chap. 4, 12, or 13). When these alleged interpolations are eliminated, "the breaches are more extensive than the remaining ramparts."

True scientific method would suggest that passages that are not understood would be the very last to be tampered with. The old canon of textual criticism, *difficilior lectio praestat*, "the more difficult reading is to be preferred," still remains valid. For although it is understandable that an originally difficult text might be simplified by a well-meaning scribe, it is unlikely that a clear, straightforward reading would be changed into a difficult one.

Another technique is frequently suggested. Some scholars delete stichs or entire verses on the basis of metrics. Now far too little is known of biblical metrics to justify excisions in the text on this basis alone. Metrical considerations constitute an appropriate tool for the textual critic, but only when there are other, independent factors that call for modifications of the text.

Finally, some commentators on Job have proposed large-scale transposition of passages, reassigning sections from one speaker to another. Frequent rearrangements of the accepted text argue an enviable omniscience on the part of modern scholars. They assume that the thought processes of the ancients were identical with our own. Moreover, they often betray a failure to reckon with the radically different emotional timbre of the Oriental: the rapid rise and fall of emotion, the ebb and flow of passion, the shifting tides of faith and despair, indignation and entreaty. Only as a last resort, and preferably where there are strong objective criteria pointing in that direction, should the transposition of passages be undertaken.[19] What is really required in the Prophets, the Psalms, and Job is a genuine capacity for *Einfüllung* and identification with the biblical poet.

This critique of the textual procedures widely adopted by commentators on Job is not intended to deny that some passages give evidence of error and corruption. But the power of diagnosis often outstrips the ability to heal. At times we are in a position to repair the injury; at others, we find that our present knowledge of biblical Hebrew is inadequate, particularly in view of the rich vocabulary of Job. All too often the plethora of emendations, deletions, and transpositions indulged in by commentators gives evidence of ingenuity rather than insight, testifying to cleverness rather than to understanding. When one reads the text of Job as "revised and improved," one encounters a work of collaboration between an ancient genius and a modern "rewrite man." One can sympathize with the desire of a modern scholar to share in the composition of a masterpiece like Job, but one may doubt whether the ancient writer would have invited the partnership!

What is required is a patient and humble study of every facet of the book, utilizing as wide a knowledge as possible of the various disciplines that are basic to biblical scholarship. These include all branches of Semitic grammar and philology, comparative religion and anthropology, archaeology and ancient history, textual and literary criticism. And beyond all these resources, the interpreter of Job must possess the elusive ability to penetrate to the spirit and intent of a work of genius. The book is too profound and complex an achievement to yield up all its secrets easily; but if we approach it with knowledge, humility, and insight, we may be able to enter the precincts of this noble temple, sacred to beauty and truth.

III

The Cultural Background:
The Law and the Prophets

N^O MATTER HOW GIFTED the creator, every supreme achievement of the human spirit, whether in art, music, literature, or science, necessarily builds upon the work of predecessors. It is they who have laid the foundation of the tradition and worked out the techniques utilized by their successors. The pioneer finds his reward in a breathtaking glimpse of new and unsuspected vistas, but he almost never attains the highest level of perfection. That experience is reserved for the later practitioners of the art or science. Hence masterpieces tend to appear at the end and not at the beginning of movements. When we encounter a great work that seems to have no forerunner, like the Homeric epics, we would do well to heed the wise words of Koheleth: "There may be something of which a man says, 'Look, this is new!' It has already occurred in the ages before us. For there is no recollection left of the earliest generations . . ." (Eccles. 1:10–11).

The Book of Job is no exception to this rule. In spite of its universal significance it is the product of a specific time and culture. In spite of its antiquity, it is the end result of a long process of development. It can therefore be fully understood only against the background from which it arose.

At a later point in our discussion we shall set forth the grounds for believing that Job was probably composed in the early years of the Second Jewish Commonwealth, roughly between the sixth to fourth centuries before the Christian Era. The book represents the culmination of long, many-sided, and fruitful intellectual activity in ancient Israel. The Hebrew tradition of Wisdom was itself the embodiment of an older literary and cultural development characteristic of the entire Near East.

In ancient Israel there were three principal intellectual and spiritual currents. They are clearly referred to by the Hebrew prophets Jeremiah and Ezekiel, who foretold the destruction of the Temple in Jerusalem and the downfall of the Jewish state (587 B.C.E.), and who lived to see their prophecies come true. Jeremiah speaks of foes planning his destruction because "instruction is surely not lost to the priest, nor counsel to the sage, nor the word to the prophet!" (18:18). Ezekiel declares that in the day of doom men "shall seek in vain a vision of the prophet, and instruction shall be lost to the priest and counsel from the elders!" (7:26).

Here we have welcome evidence of the lively intellectual ferment in ancient Israel, expressed in the distinct activities of the priest, the prophet, and the sage. They have left an imperishable record of their respective functions and goals in the three sections of the Hebrew Bible: Torah, the Law, Nebiim, the Prophets, and Ketubim, the Sacred Writings.[1]

The first and most authoritative type of spiritual leadership in ancient Israel was *torah* (instruction, teaching, law), of which the preserver and interpreter was the priest (*kōhēn*). The center of all this priestly activity lay in hallowed shrines and temples like those at Shiloh, Beth-el, Gilgal, and later, the Temple of Solomon in Jerusalem. In time, the Solomonic Temple took precedence over these older and lesser sanctuaries, but it never succeeded in superseding them completely. Fundamentally, the priests were the keepers of the sacred shrines and the officiants at the temple rituals.

But they did much more. As the only educated group they became the custodians of culture. The literature and science of ancient Egypt and Mesopotamia were almost exclusively the work of the priesthood. In Israel, during the days of the First Temple, the priests were medical authorities, judges in civil and criminal cases, and arbiters of all religious problems, as well as guardians of the ancient historical traditions of Israel's past. These narratives included accounts of the Creation, the Garden of Eden, and the Flood. Originally part of Israel's Semitic inheritance, they were transformed by the alchemy of Hebrew religion into matchless vehicles for universal truths about God and man. They also contained detailed descriptions of the lives of the patriarchs who had wandered up and down the land of Canaan sanctifying the ancient shrines that dotted the landscape. Most important, they encompassed the epic account of the enslavement of the Israelites in Egypt and their miraculous deliverance by God through Moses. By that unforgettable event, the Lord had demonstrated His universal sway over history and established His suzerainty over Israel. The Covenant at Sinai had sealed a permanent compact and established an unbreakable relationship between the people and their God.

Important as the preservation of these historical traditions was, even greater practical significance lay in another function of the priests. As the legal experts, they were the custodians and interpreters of many, short, written and unwritten, manuals of law. The most famous of these codes was the Decalogue. In these "Ten Words" proclaimed at Sinai (Exod. 20; Deut. 5), the fundamental principles of conduct governing man's relation to his God and to his fellow man were set forth.

But the Decalogue was only one code among many. The Bible contains many other, briefer *torot*, or legal manuals, more specialized in content, that were necessary to the functioning of the priesthood. Such are the *torot* of the leper, of forbidden foods, and of the various sacrifices, all set forth in Leviticus. Also included were more comprehensive legal and moral codes of great antiquity. As was characteristic of most Semitic codes, these documents combined ritual enactment, civil and criminal law, moral exhortation, and legal procedure. They include the Book of the Covenant (Exod. 21–23) and the Holiness Code (Lev. 17–26), now imbedded in the Pentateuch.

In II Kings, chapter 22, we read of an even more elaborate code discovered during the reign of King Josiah (621 B.C.E.). Repairs had been undertaken of the Temple buildings in Jerusalem and this torah was found buried in the foundations or hidden in the walls of the sanctuary—a common means of preserving important documents in the ancient world. The code is generally identified today, in whole or in part, with Deuteronomy, the fifth book of the Torah. Doubtless, there were many other *torot* of briefer or more extensive compass which have not reached us, especially those of local sanctuaries. The prophet Hosea seems to be referring to such codes when he says, "Though I write him ten thousand *torot*, they are alien to him" (8:12).[2]

The patent of authority for the priest, which constituted the basis for his status in society and for his activity in the Hebrew cult and culture, was derived from the divine revelation to Moses. It was Moses who had spoken "face to face with God" and received the Torah for Israel. That immediate confrontation between the Lord and His servant was attested to by every section of the Torah, which traced its enactments back to the great Lawgiver: "The Lord spoke to Moses, saying. . . ." It was Moses who had ordained the priesthood through the line of his brother Aaron, thus conferring the stamp of legitimacy upon the priestly role.

The process by which the various narrative traditions and individual codes were combined and ultimately united in the Five Books of Moses was highly complex and may never be reconstructed in all its details. Undoubtedly, the creation of the Torah took place at an earlier period and was less complicated than the Higher Criticism of the late nineteenth and early twentieth centuries maintained. Recent scholarship now recognizes that the concept of "the Torah of Moses" is not a figment of the imagination and surely not a "pious fraud" perpetrated by later scribes. Contemporary research makes it increasingly clear that there is a central and significant core of Mosaic material in the Pentateuch, even though it is difficult to reach a consensus as to its exact extent and contents.

Whatever the origin and early stages of the Torah, it may be regarded as certain that its final compilation took place during the Babylonian Exile. The conquest of Jerusalem in 587 B.C.E., which destroyed the Judean state and exiled the people, was accompanied by the destruction of the Temple, the center of public worship. The Babylonian Exile, therefore, threatened the extinction of the people and of its faith. In this critical period the priests, who were the guardians of the national tradition, ritual, and legal codes, felt impelled to create one large, integrated torah that was to be preserved against the day of national restoration. This was the Torah of Moses, its basic material emanating from the great Lawgiver himself, while all of its contents derived their sanction from his luminous and numinous authority.

The material included in the Torah certainly did not originate in the Babylonian Exile. It emanated from earlier ages, the core going back to the Mosaic age, the remainder to different periods following that of Moses. One can sense the difference between the older material in the Torah and a law code written during the Babylonian Exile. The prophet Ezekiel created his own utopian law code (chaps. 40–48), intended for the new commonwealth whose restoration he envisioned. Here the symmetrical and mechanical lines along which he plotted the future state and temple demonstrate that he was drawing principally upon his own ideals and aspirations, rather than upon genuine earlier sources.[3]

The collapse of the Babylonian Empire and the rise of Persia in its stead gave the Jewish people a new lease on life. Cyrus was magnanimous and farsighted in his policy toward subject peoples. He permitted those Jews who so desired to reconstitute their community life in Palestine by granting them religious and cultural autonomy. The Torah now proved an indispensable instrument for uniting and governing the Jewish community. Three-quarters of a century after the Return, Ezra, who was a priest by birth and a *sofer*, or "scribe," by calling, inspired the struggling Jewish settlement in Jerusalem to accept the Torah as its constitution for all time.

Nor was this all. Though a priest himself, Ezra carried through a unique peaceful revolution that stripped the priests of their religious and intellectual leadership, leaving them only in charge of the conduct of the Temple ritual as prescribed by law. Instead of a hereditary priesthood, which all too often exhibited the marks of moral corruption and degeneracy, the spiritual leadership of the people was now vested in the scholars. Being recruited from all classes, they represented a non-hereditary, democratic element. The ritual ministrations of the priests in the Temple went on unimpaired, according to the explicit imperatives of the Torah granting them exclusive rights.[4] But the dynamic, creative impulse in Judaism was henceforth centered in a less pretentious institution, the synagogue, in which all Jews were equal and which was at once a house of prayer, study, and communal assembly.

The importance of this revolution, unparalleled in ancient religion, can scarcely be exaggerated. The Talmud gives Ezra little more than his due when it declares, "Ezra was worthy of giving the Torah to Israel had not Moses preceded him."[5] Ezra and his scholarly successors are to be credited, in large measure, with the democratic character of normative, traditional Judaism. The fact that religious leadership in Christianity and Islam today is personal, not hereditary, is indirectly due to the crucial decision of Ezra, who placed his influence behind the scribe rather than the priest.

Ezra's successors, the *soferim* and the rabbis, not only preserved the Torah but gave it new life. By their painstaking study and interpretation of the biblical text they endowed the Jewish tradition with some of its most noteworthy characteristics—its protean capacity for growth and its fusion of realistic understanding and idealistic aspiration. Their activity made the Bible relevant to the needs of later generations confronted by new problems and perils. Thus they contributed in no small measure to the survival of the Jewish people during two millennia of dispersion. But their influence was not limited solely to the household of Israel. The Christian world, too, owes them a debt of gratitude. These nameless scribes helped create the background from which Christianity arose, for they formulated many of the basic teachings shared by Christianity and rabbinic Judaism.

After the return from the Babylonian Exile, the written Torah was complete. There was nothing to be added or removed. Henceforth the oral Torah, the product of the rabbinic "houses of study" or "academies," would carry the growth and development of the Jewish religion forward. But this development belongs to a period later than that of our present concern.[6]

The second kind of spiritual activity in pre-Exilic Israel was that of the prophet, who proclaimed the vision ($h\bar{a}z\bar{o}n$), the burden ($mass\bar{a}'$), or the word ($d\bar{a}bh\bar{a}r$) of the Lord. Like so many other aspects of Israelite life, the role of the prophet represented a unique Hebrew development of elements common to all the Semitic peoples.[7] There are grounds for believing that the primitive Semites possessed a single functionary who performed all the existing religious roles, functions that were later divided between the priest and the prophet. Thus the same Semitic root lies at the base of the Arabic $k\bar{a}h\bar{\imath}n$, "seer of a spirit or djinn," and the Hebrew $k\bar{o}h\bar{e}n$, "priest." We have briefly traced the role of the latter as the officiant at the ritual and as the custodian of Torah. The peak of the other line of development is represented by the Hebrew prophet. In its origins, prophecy was, however, infinitely less exalted than in its culmination, as represented by an Isaiah or a Jeremiah.

The priesthood, hereditary in nature, attached to a given sanctuary, and charged with the performance of a carefully prescribed ritual, was highly formalized. Side by side with the priest, and often in competition with him, was a considerably less formal type of religious leader, the diviner, soothsayer, or "seer." His functions were not restricted to foreseeing the future; it was believed that he could also shape it. In other words, being "a man of God," he was a wonder-worker as well as a diviner. Not being assigned to a sanctuary, and without a fixed locale, he had to depend upon the resources of his own personality for subsistence and position. Under the influence of trances or ecstatic spells he would mutter or shout his message from God. Self-hypnosis was induced through dances, rhythmic swaying, music, ceaseless repetition of the divine name, or self-laceration. The diviner was feared because of his connection with God and despised as a cross between a beggar and a lunatic.[8] The Semitic soothsayers, who remained on this primitive level, unquestionably had their counterparts in ancient Israel.

In the Bible, however, this type of functionary plays an insignificant role. In fact, he is not encountered except for a few stray allusions during the periods of Samuel and the early monarchy.[9] This is due to two factors. In the first instance, the Bible was written from the incomparably higher vantage point of the great prophets, who despised these lowly practitioners of doubtful arts. In the second instance, in the biblical period this primitive functionary had largely evolved into a higher type, the *nābhī'*, or prophet. Other titles by which the prophet was known were *rō'eh* or *hōzeh*, "seer," *'īš hā'elōhīm*, "man of God," and *'īš bārūah*, "the man possessed of the (divine) spirit."

The Hebrew prophet lacked both the status and the emoluments of the priesthood and was supported by voluntary gifts. His patent of authority lay in his conviction that he was a direct communicant with the Deity: his words were not his own, but those of his God. His utterances were often prefaced by the formula, "Thus says the Lord," or concluded by the phrase, "The word of the Lord." The prophet's contact with the Divine was not derived from a past tradition, but was direct, immediate, overpowering. The Book of Jeremiah, for example, contains many deeply moving passages in which the prophet rebels against his tragic lot as a man of strife and contention to all the earth. Yet he finds that he cannot be silent because God's word is "as a fire pent up in my bones, that cannot be contained."[10]

Even among the prophets there were various levels to be distinguished. Humbler practitioners were consulted by the common folk who were troubled by personal problems. Better known prophets were attached to the royal court, serving as counselors and convenient instruments of royal policy. Both types naturally tended to echo the conventional ideas and prejudices of their day. By their lights, and those of their contemporaries, they were decent, well-meaning, respectable purveyors of the divine word. By the standards of the biblical writers, however, most of them were "false prophets," pure and simple. The Bible records varying explanations of their activity. Thus the ninth-century prophet Micaiah ben Imlah declared that his adversary, the false prophet Zedekiah ben Kena'anah, was being misled by "a spirit of falsehood" emanating from God (I Kings 22:20 ff.). A century and a half later the prophet Micah went even further, stigmatizing the popular seers of his day as charlatans who were impelled by greed: "Thus the Lord says concerning the prophets, who lead my people astray, who call for peace when they have food between their teeth, but whoever does not feed their maws, against him they proclaim war!" (Mic. 3:5).

The great prophets, whose words have reached us in the prophetic books and whose ideas permeate the Law and the historical books as well, served no master but their God.[11] They came from every social stratum: from the level of the lowly farmhand and cattleherd like Amos; from the farmer class like Hosea; from the priestly class like Jeremiah and Ezekiel; and even from the royal household, to which Isaiah was probably related. They were not "professionals" and could neither be bribed nor silenced. Fired by a vision of the Kingdom of God in which injustice would give way to brotherhood and oppression would yield to freedom and peace, they weighed society against their ideals and found it wanting. They were outraged at the perversion of the pure worship of God, on both religious and ethical grounds, which for them were indivisible. They were scandalized by the widespread identification of the Living God of Israel with the popular Baal cults which glorified fertility and sought to induce it through sexual rites. They were bitterly scornful of the spectacle of punctilious ritualism going hand-in-hand with moral depravity and callousness to human misery.

The Hebrew prophets poured out their indignation in passionate utterances preserved to us in the pages of Scripture. Later generations found the messages uniquely relevant to their own times and conditions, but the prophets directed their words primarily to their own contemporaries. And here they failed tragically to make any genuine impact. On the contrary, since they were rebels against the political, social, economic, and religious status quo of their day, they were generally regarded as enemies of the people, "troublers of Israel."

It was not until centuries later, when a decimated people returned to their homeland after the Babylonian Exile, that the prophets attained recognition. This great catastrophe had demonstrated that Amos and Hosea, Isaiah and Jeremiah, were right and that all the "respectable" elements—the royal court, the military leaders, the upper classes, the priests, and the popular prophets—were abysmally and fatally wrong. Now a chastened people turned to the writings of the earlier, pre-Exilic prophets and to the living word of their contemporaries Ezekiel and Deutero-Isaiah, the prophets of the Exile, for reproof, hope, and guidance.

The prophets were vindicated by events, to be sure, but their grand visions were not fully realized. The return from the Babylonian Exile was a triumphant fulfilment of the prophetic faith that God would not totally abandon His people and that they would be restored to their own soil. That much had taken place, but little more. The period of the Second Commonwealth, which followed the Return, was well described as "an age of small things," with little to stir men's hearts either to ecstacy or to wrath. There was neither stimulus nor need for the grand prophetic vision. The unyielding insistence of the prophets upon righteousness as the basic premise of national well-being was now an accepted element of Jewish thought, but it was no longer particularly novel or especially relevant to the problems of the hour. Faith in the triumph of God's cause and the establishment of His Kingdom became integral to Judaism. However, there was little prospect of Jewish national greatness and power either in the present or in the foreseeable future.

The Second Commonwealth in Palestine was a tiny, modest, and insecure Jewish island in a welter of foreign peoples—Samaritans, Edomites, Moabites, Ammonites, Philistines, and later, Greeks. The small Jewish settlement, far from representing the triumphant Kingdom of God, was a tributary of the great Persian, Ptolemaic, Seleucid, and Roman empires, which arose in succession and held sway over Palestine for the last five pre-Christian centuries. The glorious Maccabean War (167–142 B.C.E.) was followed by the period of independence (142–63 B.C.E.) which proved only a brief interlude. It ended with the surrender of the Jewish Commonwealth to the Romans by the degenerate descendants of the heroic Maccabees who had sacrificed their lives in the struggle for freedom.

The masses of the people, ground by poverty, fleeced by taxation, chafing under the foreign oppressor, nevertheless held fast to their trust in the righteousness of God. They could no longer believe, however, that this fulfilment of His will would take place in history through the normal processes of human activity and struggle. Only a supernatural cataclysm could rout the forces of evil and usher in the good. Hence, Hebrew prophecy was driven underground, from whence it emerged in radically altered form as apocalyptic, purporting to "reveal the hidden things." A new literature came into being which proceeded to describe the ultimate war between the forces of God and Satan, the hosts of light and darkness, and to foretell the inevitable triumph of good over evil. In maintaining a faith in the victory of righteousness, the apocalyptists were preserving, though in strange and distorted guise, the unshakable prophetic faith in the moral government of the world. But there was a crucial difference. Their patience strained beyond endurance by rampant unrighteousness everywhere triumphant, the apocalyptists were not content to wait indefinitely for "the end of days." The End-Time, when the Kingdom of God would be established, had to be now—the cosmic struggle and the triumph of God's cause must surely be imminent. It behooved men to lay aside all lesser concerns and prepare for the great day by repentance and self-purification.

Apocalyptic literature was generally frowned upon by the official custodians of normative Judaism. They were aware of the dangers of such mystical and extravagant hopes and of the despair likely to arise in the wake of unfulfilled expectations. By and large, the apocalyptic writings originated with and were cherished by smaller fringe groups, whose attitudes toward the official religion varied from acceptance of rabbinic Judaism, in whole or in part, to indifference, and even to violent antipathy. What all these groups shared in common was a passionate concern with eschatology, "the last things."

The apocalyptists nearly always envisaged the advent of God's cause through the triumph of His supernatural messenger, a Messiah or anointed king, who, by his physical power or spiritual might would destroy "the kingdom of arrogance" and usher in the "Kingdom of Heaven." In this respect, too, apocalyptic represented the preservation of a basic prophetic ideal, transposed, however, into a supernatural key. The pre-Exilic prophets, notably Isaiah, had foretold the advent within history of a just ruler, a scion of the house of David. He would be imbued "with the spirit of wisdom and knowledge, the spirit of counsel and might, the spirit of knowledge and the fear of the Lord" (Isa. 11:2), and would usher in an era when "man would do no evil and work no destruction on all God's holy mountain, for the earth would be filled with the knowledge of the Lord as the waters cover the sea" (Isa. 11:9). This concept of a righteous king from the dynasty of David who would rise to redeem his people and establish universal justice and peace was echoed by Micah, Jeremiah, and Zechariah.

As time went on, however, the objective conditions in the Second Commonwealth period seemed less and less propitious for the emergence of such a leader in the natural order of things. The messianic faith did not die; it was transformed. In increasing measure the Messiah became a supernatural figure whose advent awaited the "proper hour" (Hebrew, *qeṣ*; Greek, *kairos*), when men's hearts would be prepared and their lives regenerated. Then God would send His anointed from on high to destroy the hosts of evil. Ultimately, the doctrine of a supernatural Messiah became the faith of pharisaic or normative Judaism.

This faith was the cornerstone of belief and action for the various apocalyptic groups. The most influential among them were the Essenes, a semi-monastic order of holy men revered for their piety, generally living apart from the cities and the hamlets of the land. In recent years our knowledge of these Essenic groups has been tremendously augmented and complicated by the discovery of the Dead Sea Scrolls. For the first time we are able to read their own words and thus to penetrate the lives and aspirations of these dreamers and warriors for the establishment of God's Kingdom.

There were other messianic sects whose hopes for a supernatural deliverance grew stronger as the tyranny of Roman rule became increasingly intolerable. Among them were the Judeo-Christians, who began as a Jewish sect but who differed from other Jewish groups principally in their recognition of Jesus of Nazareth as the heaven-sent Redeemer. In rabbinic Judaism, the leaders generally looked askance at this tendency "to hurry the End" or even to compute its date, particularly by mystic activity or ascetic exercises. Yet even here there were key figures, like Rabbi Akiba, who were caught up in the messianic vision and hope.

Thus, classic biblical prophecy lived on after the Babylonian Exile on two levels. On the surface there were the written words of the great prophets preserved in the Bible and available to all people. And on a deeper level there was the submerged drive of the prophetic faith, finding new expression in esoteric circles as an "apocalypse," a revelation of hidden mysteries.

In the period of the Second Commonwealth both the Law and the Prophets had become Scripture, a sacred corpus of authoritative books to which the entire people looked for guidance. The Five Books of

Moses attained a transcendent position as the repository of the Law of God. Like its divine source, the Law was eternal and capable of universal application. Hence the canonization of the Pentateuch marked not its petrifaction but the commencement of a new era of vital interpretation that was to produce the Talmud at the end of a thousand years.

Almost equally sacred was the second section of Scripture, the Prophets. This section, which had two divisions, included the historical books from Joshua to Kings and the great collections of prophetic utterances bearing the names of Isaiah, Jeremiah, Ezekiel, and "the Twelve." These books, too, served as the starting-point of an elaborate process of interpretation which continued for nearly a millennium. This literature comprises such radically different works as the Pesharim or commentaries on the prophetic books by the Dead Sea sectarians; the treatises of the Alexandrian philosopher, Philo; the Gospels and Epistles of the New Testament; and the varied and innumerable rabbinic Midrashim.

We have traced, albeit briefly, the origin and development of two mighty spiritual currents in the life and thought of the Hebrew people. In the period of the Second Commonwealth, which followed the return from the Babylonian Exile, no Jew could be immune to the power and influence they exerted. The author of Job was no exception. The basic ideas and attitudes of the Torah and the Prophets had an important role in molding his spiritual growth and outlook. The specific evidence of his familiarity with these classic sources of his people's faith will be considered later.[12] But he himself was neither a priest nor a prophet, neither a scribe nor an apocalyptist. For the author of Job, the decisive influence came from the third intellectual current of ancient Israel, that of *Hokmah* or Wisdom. This third strand in the pattern of Jewish religious and cultural creativity must now engage our attention.

IV

Wisdom and Job

A S WE HAVE SEEN, the Law, which was the province of the
priest and later of the scribe, and the Vision, which was the
experience of the prophet and later of the apocalyptist, did not exhaust
the range of spiritual activity in ancient Israel. A third strand was
supplied by Hokmah (Wisdom), which was cultivated by the sage
(*hakam*) or the elder (*zaken*). This discipline was more inclusive and
more concrete than is suggested by the honorific and rather abstract
term, "Wisdom."

Hokmah may be defined as a realistic approach to the problems of
life, including all the practical skills and technical arts of civilization.
The term *hakam*, "sage" or "wise man," is accordingly applied in the
Bible to all practitioners of the arts. Bezalel, the skilled craftsman who
built the Tabernacle and its appointments in the wilderness, and all
his associates, are called "wise of heart" (Exod. 28:3; 35:31; 36:1).
Weavers (Exod. 35:25), goldsmiths (Jer. 10:9), and sailors (Ezek.
27:8; Ps. 107:27) are described as *hakamim*.

Rabbinic Hebrew undoubtedly preserves an ancient usage when it
applies the term *hakamah* to the "midwife," upon whose skill life and
death depend. The women skilled in lamentation (Jer. 9:16) and the
magicians and soothsayers with their occult arts are similarly described
as "wise" (Gen. 41:8; I Kings 5:10–12; Isa. 44:25; Jer. 9:16). Skill
in the conduct of war and in the administration of the state (Isa. 10:13;

29:14; Jer. 49:7) are integral aspects of Wisdom, for the successful management of affairs—in war and in peace, at the royal court and in the confines of the individual family—requires a realistic understanding of human nature, the exercise of practical virtues, and the avoidance of at least the major vices.

Above all, Hokmah refers to the arts of poetry and music, both vocal and instrumental. Song in ancient Israel was coextensive with life itself. Harvest and vintage, the royal coronation, the conqueror's return, courtship and marriage, all were accompanied by song and dance.

This relationship between song and Wisdom was so close that often no distinction was made between the two. Thus, in I Kings (5:10–12) we read: "Solomon's wisdom excelled the wisdom of all the children of the east, and all the wisdom of Egypt. For he was wiser than all men, than Ethan the Ezrahite, and Heman, and Calcol, and Darda, the sons of Mahol; and his fame was in all the nations round about. And he spoke three thousand proverbs; and his songs were a thousand and five."[1] Ethan and Heman are the eponymous heads of the musical guilds mentioned in I Chronicles, chapter 15, verse 19, to whom Psalms 88 and 89 are attributed. First Chronicles ascribes these guilds of singers to the Davidic age and traces their genealogy back to Korah, the contemporary of Moses.[2] Today the tradition is no longer dismissed as an unhistorical, artificial "throwback" of a later institution to an earlier age. There is growing evidence in Ugaritic sources of musical and other guilds connected with the temple cult.[3]

Since improvisation was often the rule, no line was drawn between the composer and the poet, the instrumentalist and the singer: all were part of Wisdom. Thus, in Psalm 49 (vss. 4 and 5) we read:

> My mouth shall speak Wisdom,
> My heart shall meditate[4] understanding.
> I shall turn my instrument[5] to a parable,
> I shall begin my riddle with the lyre.

All the material aspects of Hokmah, as embodied in art, architecture, and the manual crafts, disappeared with the destruction of the physical substratum of ancient Hebrew life. All that has remained of Wisdom is its incarnation in literature, which has survived, only in part, in the pages of the Bible. The Wisdom writings are concerned not only with the practical arts of living, but also with the development of a sane, workable attitude toward life as a whole, without which proficiency in the technical skills will avail men little. To convey the truths of Wisdom, a specific literary genre came into being, the *mashal*, or (less frequently) the *hidah*.[6]

The term *mashal*, derived from a Hebrew root meaning "represent, resemble, be similar," develops a variety of related senses. Its most common meaning is "proverb," a short, pithy utterance expressing some observation on life and human nature. Reasoning from the known to the unknown, the *mashal* frequently depends on analogy to make its point:

> As a door turns on its hinges,
> So does a sluggard on his bed.
>
> [Prov. 26:14]

The term is also applied to somewhat lengthier literary compositions such as the allegory, parable, or fable. It also refers to more extensive collections of proverbs[7] or poetic utterances,[8] in which poetic comparisons or philosophical reflections are common.

The *hidah*, or "riddle," is a term which appears much less frequently and is more restricted in meaning.[9] In several passages where it occurs it is defined by some scholars as "an enigmatic, perplexing saying."[10] A more satisfactory rendering would be "an utterance on a mysterious theme." This would explain its application to oracles or psalms dealing with such ultimate issues as the fate of the cruel Chaldean foe, the suffering of the righteous, or God's ways with His people.[11]

These literary techniques were not ends in themselves. Basically, Wisdom was an intellectual discipline, concerned with the education of upper-class youth in Israel. It is highly probable that the *hakam* was a professional teacher[12] whose function was to inculcate in his pupils the virtues of hard work, zeal, prudence, sexual moderation, sobriety, loyalty to authority, and religious conformity—all the elements of a morality aimed at achieving worldly success. When necessary, Hokmah did not hesitate to urge less positive virtues on its youthful charges, such as holding one's tongue and distributing largesse as aids in making one's way. In brief, this practical Wisdom literature represented a hard-headed, matter-of-fact, "safe-and-sane" approach to the problems of living.

The discovery and elucidation of ancient oriental literature has made it clear that Hebrew Wisdom was not an isolated creation in Israel. On the contrary, it was part of a vast intellectual activity that had been cultivated for centuries throughout the lands of the Fertile Crescent—Egypt, Palestine, Syria, and Babylonia. Everywhere its basic purpose was to prepare youth for success in government, agriculture, commerce, and personal life. These branches of oriental Wisdom were older than biblical Hokmah, the Fertile Crescent countries having attained political and cultural maturity long before Israel. Naturally there are many adumbrations of biblical Wisdom in oriental literature, as well as many illuminating parallels. These similarities have been noted by scholars who, flushed with the natural excitement of discovery, have sometimes displayed more enthusiasm than caution in postulating borrowings. While the extant remains of Babylonian and Egyptian Wisdom rarely reach the level of Hebrew Hokmah, they are invaluable in supplying a general background and in shedding light on particular details.

The Hokmah of the biblical sages, unlike the Torah of the priests or the Vision of the prophets, usually made no claim to being divine revelation. It was, of course, self-evident that the source of Hebrew Hokmah, as of every creative aspect of man's nature, was God. Thus when Isaiah described the ideal Davidic king who would govern in justice and wisdom, he sees "resting upon him the spirit of the Lord," which is defined as "the spirit of wisdom and understanding, the spirit of counsel and might, the spirit of knowledge, and the fear of the Lord" (Isa. 11:2).

Nevertheless, some of Wisdom's more fervent disciples went even further. They sought to win for Wisdom a status almost equal to that of Torah and Prophecy by endowing her with a cosmic role. In composing hymns of praise to Wisdom, the Hebrew sages were able to draw upon motifs found in Semitic mythology.[13] Thus a Mesopotamian text of the late second millennium B.C.E. describes the goddess Siduri Sabito as "goddess of wisdom, genius of life." Albright, in calling attention to this reference, suggests that she was a prototype of a Canaanite goddess of Wisdom. In the Aramaic *Proverbs of Akiqar*, emanating from the sixth century B.C.E., a passage reads:

> Wisdom is from the gods,
>   And to the gods she is precious,
>   Forever her kingdom is fixed in heaven,
>   For the lord of the holy ones has raised her up.[14]

Passages such as these inevitably suggest comparison with Hebrew poems. In the Book of Proverbs, Wisdom is pictured as dwelling in a temple with seven pillars (9:1) and as declaring,

> Ages ago I was poured out, at the first,
> Before the beginning of the earth.
>
> [Prov. 8:23]

The present Book of Job contains a magnificent "Hymn to Wisdom" (chap. 28), in which Hokmah is endowed with cosmic significance and is virtually personified.[15] Ben Sira (Ecclesiasticus), in the first half of the second century B.C.E., also personifies Wisdom:

> I have come forth from the mouth of the Highest,
>   And like the vapor I have covered the earth;
> I have made my abode in the heights
>   And my throne on a pillar of cloud.
>
> [Ecclus. 24:3-4]

The Book of Enoch pictures Wisdom as homeless among men and therefore returning to the abode of the angels (42:1-2).

But the similarity in language, interesting as it is, is far less significant than the fundamental difference between the Hebrew poets and sages, on the one hand, and the pagan writers, on the other. For the biblical and post-biblical authors the personification and glorification of Wisdom is mythology, not religion; it is poetry, not truth. To heighten the vividness and power of their compositions they utilize the resources of their Semitic inheritance, as Dante, Shakespeare, and Milton invoke the gods of Greece and Rome; but like the later writers, they do not believe in these echoes of a dead past.

In their most lavish paeans of praise to Wisdom, the Hebrew sages do not attribute to her any independent existence, let alone the status of a goddess or a divine being. She is indubitably the creation of God, His plaything, His companion, His delight, perhaps even the plan by which He fashioned the world, but nevertheless, completely God's handiwork, as is the entire cosmos:

> The Lord created me at the beginning of his work,
>   The first of His acts of old.
> Ages ago I was poured out, at the first,
>   Before the beginning of the earth.
> When there were no depths I was brought forth,
>   When there were no springs abounding with water.

Before the mountains had been shaped,
    Before the hills, I was brought forth;
Before He had made the earth with its fields,
    Or the first of the dust of the world.
When He established the heavens, I was there;
    When He made firm the skies above,
When He established the heavens, I was there;
    When He drew a circle on the face of the deep,
When he made firm the skies above,
    When He established the fountains of the deep,
When He assigned to the sea its limit,
    So that the waters might not transgress His command,
When He marked out the foundations of the earth,
    Then I was beside Him, as His ward.[16]
I was daily His delight, frolicking before Him always,
    Rejoicing in His inhabited world and delighting in
        the sons of men.

                      [Prov. 8:22–32]

All wisdom comes from the Lord
    And is with Him for ever.
The sand of the seas, and the drops of rain,
    And the days of eternity—who can number them?
And the height of the heaven, and the breadth of the earth
    and the deep—who can trace them out?
Before them all was Wisdom created,
And prudent insight from everlasting.
    The root of Wisdom, to whom has it been revealed?
And her subtle thoughts, who has known them?
    One there is greatly to be feared,
The Lord sitting upon His throne;
    He Himself created her, and saw, and numbered her,
And poured her out upon all His works;
    Upon all flesh, in measure,
But to those who love Him, without limit.

                      [Ecclus. 1:1–10]

    In Palestinian Judaism, where the study and interpretation of the Torah ultimately produced the Mishnah and the Midrash, Wisdom was equated with the Mosaic Law. This idea is clearly set forth by Ben Sira, who indites another extended "Paean to Wisdom" (chap. 24) and then cites verbatim the verse in Deuteronomy (33:4):

> All these are the book of the covenant of the All-high God,
> The Torah which Moses commanded to us,
> The inheritance of the congregation of Jacob.
>
> [24:23]

The same identification of Wisdom and the Torah is expressed in the apocryphal Psalm 152, long known in a Syriac version.[17] The Hebrew original has now been discovered at Qumran and may emanate from the same period as Ben Sira.[18] In rabbinic thought the equation became virtually axiomatic and is part of the Jewish liturgy to the present day.[19]

In the Diaspora, outside of Palestine, where Greek ideas were more influential, Wisdom was given a more philosophic interpretation. In the apocryphal Wisdom of Solomon the spirit of the Lord and Wisdom are explicitly identified and are taken to encompass both the creation of the natural world and its moral government (1:6; 7:24).[20]

In some circles, the earlier personifications of Wisdom were taken literally and served as the point of departure for a complex development. Of the various forms which this concept assumed, the most notable was the Philonic doctrine of the *Logos* or the Divine Word, which became the demiurge or instrument by which God creates and governs the universe. It is only a further step to conceive of the Divine Word as the intermediary between God and the world, even as a distinct "person" or "aspect" of the divine nature.

Thus the process has come full circle. The independent god or divine being who first appears in an early though far from primitive mythology, reappears, in vastly transformed guise, in a later, highly sophisticated theology. But for all the writers of the Hebrew Bible, whether priest, prophet, or sage, such doctrines were totally outside their purview. Had they been able to conceive such ideas at all, they would have rejected them as vitiating the Unity of God. In any event, it must be remembered that these later developments took place long after the Book of Job was written.

To revert to biblical Wisdom, it is to be expected that in an ancient society in which religion permeated every aspect of life, the effort would be made to give Hokmah a supernal position in the divine plan. Thus it could claim a status not too markedly inferior to God's revelation embodied in the Torah or His communication with the prophets. Basically, however, the claim of biblical Hokmah to authority rested on its pragmatic truth. The teachers of Wisdom insisted that the application of human reason and careful observation to all the problems of life "worked," that it brought men success and happiness. Its origin might be in heaven, but its justification was to be sought in the lives of men on earth:

> The Lord by wisdom founded the earth;
> By understanding He established the heavens;
> By His knowledge the deeps broke forth
> And the clouds drop down the dew.
> My son, keep sound wisdom and discretion;
> Let them not escape from your sight,
> And they will be life for your soul and adornment for your neck.
> Then you will walk on your way securely and your foot will not
>   stumble.
> If you sit down, you will not be afraid;
> When you lie down, your sleep will be sweet.
> Do not be afraid of sudden panic
> Or of the ruin of the wicked when it comes;
> For the Lord will be your confidence and will keep your foot
>   from being caught.
>
> > [Prov. 3:19–26]

> I have counsel and sound wisdom;
> I have insight; I have strength.
> By me kings reign
> And rulers decree what is just.
> I love those who love me,
> And those who seek me diligently find me.
> Endowing with wealth those who love me
> And filling their treasuries.
> For he who finds me finds life
> And obtains favor from the Lord;
> But he who misses me injures himself;
> All who hate me love death.
>
> > [8:14, 15, 17, 21, 35, 36]

The Bible regards King Solomon as the symbol of Wisdom and attributes to him the books of Proverbs and Ecclesiastes, as well as the Song of Songs. Though this tradition is not to be taken literally, neither can it be dismissed as valueless. It reflects the established historical fact that King Solomon's reign was marked by wide international contacts and internal prosperity which contributed to the flowering of culture in general and to the intensive cultivation of Wisdom in particular.

The roots of Hokmah, as the extra-Hebraic parallels make abundantly clear, are pre-Solomonic. The Bible has preserved some precious examples of early Wisdom literature. The unforgettable "Parable of Jotham" (Judg. 9:7 ff.), which compares the would-be king to a sterile thorn bush, must go back to the primitive democracy of the age of the Judges.[21] It could not have emanated from a later period, when the monarchy was well established and regarded as legitimate. In I Samuel, chapter 24, verse 13, David quotes "an ancient proverb" (*meshal hakkadmōni*), "Out of the wicked cometh forth wickedness, but let not my hand be upon thee." The prophet Nathan's moving parable of the poor man's lamb (II Sam. 12:1 ff.), with which he indicts his royal master, David, constitutes another valuable remnant of ancient *mashal* literature.

A particularly significant passage for the development of Wisdom is to be found in II Samuel, chapter 14. Here we have a "wise woman" (*ʾishāh ḥākhāmāh*) whom Joab calls, and probably pays, to present an imaginary case to King David. She possesses dramatic skill as well as literary inventiveness. Thus she prepares herself for the role of a mourner (vs. 2) and then presents her suit for the king's decision. When David pronounces judgment, she confesses that her fictitious case was a *mashal*, a parable of the king's relationship to his son Absalom, the murderer of Amnon. Finally, she climaxes her appeal for the king's forgiveness by a reference to the melancholy brevity of human life, thus going beyond practical Wisdom to its more philosophical aspect: "For we must surely die and be like water poured out on the ground, which is not gathered up and which no one desires" (vs. 14).[22]

The Book of Kings preserves another parable which is post-Solomonic—that of Joash, king of Israel, in which he contemptuously dismisses Amaziah of Judah as a thistle by the side of a cedar (II Kings 14:9).

The various collections in the biblical Book of Proverbs emanate from different periods. Yet it is being increasingly recognized that the individual apothegms, which often cannot be dated, are largely derived from the First Temple period, and in part, at least, may go back to Solomon's reign, as several headings indicate (Prov. 1:1; 10:1).

As we have noted, the Babylonian Exile and the Return witnessed the decline and disappearance of prophecy and ushered in a new phase of oral interpretation of the Torah. It was then, in the early centuries of the Second Commonwealth, that Wisdom reached its golden age, largely because of a basic shift in the primary concern of religious faith and thought.

While the Torah and the prophets were divergent in substance and temper, they were agreed in placing the nation in the center of their thinking. Both were concerned with the weal or woe of the entire people and called for the fulfillment of God's will, which the priest found embodied in the Law, and which the prophets saw expressed in the moral code. To be sure, it was the individual who was adjured to obey, but only as a unit of the larger entity, his destiny being bound up, indeed submerged, in the well-being of the nation. This concern with the group was a fundamental aspect of traditional Semitic and Hebrew thought.

The individual, however, could never be completely disregarded. His personal happiness and success, his fears and his hopes, were by no means identical with the status of the nation. The people as a whole might be prosperous and happy while an individual was exposed to misery. On the other hand, even if the nation experienced defeat and subjugation by foreign masters, the individual would still seek to adjust himself to conditions and to extract at least a modicum of happiness and success from his environment. This recognition of the individual plays an enormous role in the Torah. Being a practical code of life it necessarily had to deal with man's problems and conflicts, as its civil and criminal ordinances abundantly attest.[23] Increasingly, too, the prophets, whose basic concern was the ideal future of the nation, became concerned with the happiness of the individual: "Say of the righteous that it shall be well with him; for they shall eat the fruit of their doings. Woe to the wicked! It shall be ill with him; for the work of his hands shall be done to him" (Isa. 3:10–11). With the later prophets, Jeremiah and Ezekiel, the problem of individual suffering becomes a central and agonizing element of their thought.[24] Fundamentally, however, torah and prophecy remained concerned with the group, its present duties and its future destiny.

It was the decline of faith in the fortunes of the nation, coupled with the growth of interest in the individual and his destiny, that stimulated the development of Wisdom. Wisdom was not concerned with the group, but with the individual, with the realistic present rather than with a longed-for future.

Wisdom's eminently practical goals for success in the here and now appealed principally to those groups in society which were least dissatisfied with the status quo—the government officials, the rich merchants, the great landowners, whose soil was tilled by tenant farmers. These groups were concerned less with the will of God than with the way of the world. This was true even of the high-priestly families among them, whose prestige and income derived from their position in the hierarchy of the Temple. The goal of upper-class education was the training of youth for successful careers. These needs were admirably met by the Wisdom teachers who arose, principally, if not exclusively, in Jerusalem, the capital city.

Nearly two decades ago I called attention to the striking resemblance between the Wisdom teachers and the sophists of classical Greece, who performed a similar function for the upper-class youth of Athenian society, teaching them the practical skills needed for government and business.[25] There were, of course, far-reaching religious and cultural differences between Greece and Israel. These differences dictated different roles for the Greek sophists and the Hebrew *hakamim*. For example, while the art of public speaking was intensively cultivated in Greece, it was not a conscious discipline in Israel, at least so far as extant sources indicate. All the more striking, therefore, are the similarities between the two groups. The semantic development of the Greek *sophia* closely parallels that of the Hebrew *hokmah*. The basic meaning of the Greek word is "cleverness and skill in handicraft and art"; then, "skill in matters of common life, sound judgment, practical and political wisdom"; and ultimately, "learning, wisdom, and philosophy."[26] The adjective *sophos* bears the same meanings, as descriptive of sculptors, and even of hedgers and ditchers, but "mostly of poets and musicians."[27] The substantive *sophistes*, "master of a craft or art," is used in the extant literature for a diviner, a cook, a statesman, and again for poets and musicians.[28] From Plato's time onward, its common meaning was that of a professional teacher of the arts.[29]

The most illuminating parallel lies in the division of the Wisdom teachers into two numerically unequal groups, a process evident everywhere in Egypt and Babylonia as well as in Israel and Hellas.[30] Most of the exemplars of Wisdom were hard-headed, realistic teachers of a workable morality, intent on helping their youthful charges attain successful careers. Among the oriental Wisdom teachers, however, were some restless spirits who refused to be satisfied with these practical goals.

In the relatively extensive remains of Egyptian Wisdom, which bear the name *sboyet*, "instruction," two literary types are included:

"discourses on worldly prudence and wisdom intended merely for schools"; and "writings far exceeding the bounds of school philosophy."[31] Babylonian Wisdom exhibits the same division between "practical maxims" and "meditations on the meaning of life."[32]

In Greece, too, a small number of thinkers were unwilling to limit the scope of their thought. Though they derived from the sophists, "the wise," they adopted the less pretentious name of "lovers of wisdom," or "philosophers," with perhaps a touch of Socratic irony. Their contempt for the sophists (with whom, however, they had many affinities) parallels the rejection by the Hebrew literary prophets of any identification with the popular prophets from whom they emanated, as in Amos' scornful denial, "I am no prophet nor a member of the prophetic guild!" (Amos 7:14).

In Israel, both types of Wisdom are clearly marked. From the practical-minded teachers of youth emanated the short maxims of the Book of Proverbs, as well as the longer essays of Ben Sira, who makes explicit reference to the bet hamidrash, or "academy," in his call, "Turn to me, ye fools, and tarry in my house of study" (Ecclus. 51:23). These two books are the principal Hebrew repositories of the "lower" Wisdom, practical in goal, conventional in scope.

For a few bolder spirits within the schools of Wisdom these practical goals were not enough. They had been trained to apply observation and reasoning to the practical problems of daily life, but the more fundamental issues intrigued them: the purpose of life, man's destiny after death, the basis of morality, the problem of evil. When they weighed the religious and moral ideas of their time by these standards, they found some things they could accept, but much that they felt impelled to reject as either untrue or unproved. Hence the higher or speculative Wisdom books are basically heterodox, skeptical works, at variance with the products of the practical school.

As well as we can judge, no violent antagonism existed between the teachers of practical Wisdom and those who ventured into uncharted waters. In part, at least, the reason lies in the fact that these more original thinkers continued to pursue the calling of professional teachers of practical Hokmah. That conditioning would affect their style and thought ever after. In sum, both the conventional and the unconventional teachers of Wisdom spoke the same language, reflected the same environment, and shared a common outlook. The epilogue in Ecclesiastes (12:9 ff.) testifies to this conventional activity of the unconventional author of the book.[33]

In seeking to penetrate the great abiding issues of suffering and death, these rare Wisdom teachers were unwilling to rely on tradition and conventional ideas. When they insisted on applying observation and reason to the ultimate questions, they courted tragedy—but achieved greatness.

Like so many rationalists since their day, they found unaided human reason incapable of solving these issues. Some, no doubt, finally made their peace with the traditional religion of their time. But others, tougher-minded, refused to take on faith what reason could not demonstrate. Consequently, their writings reveal various degrees and types of skepticism and heterodoxy. Several of these devotees of the higher, speculative Wisdom were able to transmute the frustration and pain of their quest into some of the world's greatest masterpieces, notably Job and Koheleth (Ecclesiastes). Smaller in compass and frequently enigmatic in content is the fragment imbedded in the Book of Proverbs and ascribed to Agur ben Yakeh (Prov. 30).[34]

Koheleth, the skeptical observer of life and man's pretensions, was keenly aware of the problem of injustice in society. He reacted far more strongly than one might have expected in view of his upper-class orientation. Primarily, however, his malaise was intellectual in origin: he was troubled by man's inability to discover ultimate truth—the real meaning of life and the purposes of creation.[35]

The author of Job, on the other hand, though by no means inferior in intellect, possessed a far deeper emotional nature and a greater capacity for involvement in the joy or misery of his fellow men. He was roused to indignation, not by man's intellectual limitations in a world he had not made, but rather by man's suffering in a world into which he had not asked to be born. The result was a work of grand proportions, the writing of which probably spanned his lifetime. He attempted to grapple with the crucial questions with which the psalmist, prophet, and poet alike had wrestled for centuries and which remain the greatest stumbling blocks to religious faith: Why do the wicked prosper and the righteous suffer? Why is there evil in a world created by a just God?

The Book of Job represents the supreme achievement of Hebrew Wisdom. In form and approach, as well as in background and content, its affinities with both conventional and unconventional Wisdom teaching are striking.

When the full scope of biblical Wisdom is kept in mind, it is clear that by virtue of its literary form Job belongs in this category. It obviously qualifies as a branch of Hokmah, since it is given over to the discussion of a basic problem in the form of a great debate. All the resources of argument, as they were undoubtedly practiced in the Wisdom academies, are found here. While a detailed analysis of its style will be set forth later, we may note here such forensic features as the *argumentum ad hominem*, the personal attack upon one's opponent (including the citation and refutation of contentions by the other side.) The book is marked by the frequent use of the *mashal*, the characteristic literary genre of Wisdom, which appears in metaphoric, proverbial, and other forms.

The recent discovery in Babylonian and Egyptian literature of complaints by individuals about their suffering at the hands of gods or men[36] has injected a new element into the discussion. Some scholars have argued that the Book of Job belongs to the literary genre of elegiac complaints rather than to Wisdom.[37] It is true that Job begins with a lament on his tragic lot (chap. 3) and ends with a soliloquy describing his former prosperity and his high standard of rectitude (chaps. 29–31). Job's pain breaks out time and again during the course of his replies, while the Friends offer him, however woodenly, both comfort and hope. In addition, there are hymns praising the creative power of God imbedded in the speeches of the Friends (e.g., 5:19 ff.) and in the words of Job (9:4 ff.; 12:14 ff.), though given in a radically different spirit.

Nonetheless, it is clear that the bulk of the book does not consist of these literary "complaints." Nor are the hymns independent compositions. Both the complaints on man's suffering and the hymns extolling God's power are introduced as means to an end—to illumine the agonizing problem of the suffering of the righteous. This is discussed in accordance with the rational canons of Wisdom thought, here heightened by the passion of the poet.

Moreover, even if the book is atomized into these components, it still testifies to the Wisdom character of Job. For as we have seen, poetry in general, and lamentation in particular, constituted an important segment of the Wisdom activity which was carried on in ancient Israel by the *hakhamim* and the *hakhamot*, "men and women skilled in the arts of composition." Thus the Book of Job, in its constituent parts and in its structure as a whole, belongs to Wisdom by virtue of its form.

The authentic Wisdom character of Job is even more strikingly attested by its approach to the basic theme. All the protagonists in the debate—Job, his friends, Elihu, and the Lord—seek to establish the validity of their respective positions by using the methods of logical argument, the observation of reality, and the evidence of experience. Thus Job calls attention to the manifest inequity in the world, while the Friends counter by invoking the longer experience of the race to demonstrate the triumph of justice and underscore the undeniable fact that all men are imperfect. It is true that in one moving passage (4:12–21) Eliphaz declares that he has been vouchsafed a revelation in a dream from on high. The content of that revelation, however, the idea that all men are sinful when compared with the moral perfection of God, is eminently defensible by the canons of rational thought and indeed is not disputed by Job. When the Lord speaks, following the dialogue of Job and his friends, He does not seek to demonstrate the truth of His position by invoking some supernatural faith beyond the canons of reason. Nor does He offer an escape from evil by flight to a mystical refuge, open only to the elect and denied to the generality of men. The author of Job makes it clear that the question of man's suffering in God's world cannot be fully answered by the application of human reason, experience, and observation, but only because the problem is cosmic in scope and it would be senseless to expect a solution with instruments of lesser compass. As an exponent of Wisdom, the author of Job might well have approved the words of a modern believing skeptic, "It is not wisdom to be only wise." For the poet, faith goes beyond reason, but does not negate it, and to believe the absurd would be the height of absurdity.

Finally, the integral place of Job within Wisdom literature is amply demonstrated by its content and background. By its very nature, Wisdom, assiduously cultivated throughout the ancient Near East, was broadly human rather than rooted in a specific national milieu. This supplied an ideal vantage point for the author, because the mystery with which he was concerned had no root in class or nation. In choosing Job, a non-Jew, as his hero, the author underscored the universal significance of his theme and was, incidentally, able to bypass the problems of the observance of Jewish ritual law, which loomed so large in the religious consciousness of the post-Exilic community. Job is a man of integrity and piety who fears God and eschews evil. No more need be said.

The upper-class orientation of Wisdom literature emerges at many points in Job.[38] Whether the author himself was born a member of these affluent groups or merely identified himself with them is impossible to determine (as is the case with Koheleth). What is significant is the author's choice of an upper-class figure as his hero. In order to exhibit the tragedy of human suffering, the poet has selected a man of great prosperity who is hurled to the lowest depths of misfortune, rather than a member of the lower classes who has suffered a lifetime of poverty and misery. It may, of course, be argued that this contrast between Job's earlier prosperity and his later calamities makes for a more dramatic plot. Nevertheless, the fact remains that the Book of Job poses the problem of evil in the form most likely to confront a member of the upper classes. And the evidence goes much further. We have perhaps the only reference in later biblical writings to a multiplicity of wives in one family in the passage, "his widows will not weep for him" (27:15).[39] Polygamy was always restricted to the rich, who alone could afford the luxury. In Job's moving Confession of Innocence (chap. 31), which represents the code of conduct of a Jewish gentleman, it is obviously a patrician who speaks. He takes pride in the consideration he shows the poor, the widow, and the orphan. Unlike the crasser members of his class he is deeply sensitive to the truth that both he and his slave are fashioned alike by God. Nor has his wealth ever tempted him to arrogance. Job reveals a wholly admirable quality in his insistence:

> Have I ever concealed my transgressions like Adam,
> Hiding my sin in my bosom
> Because I stood in fear of the crowd
> And the contempt of the masses terrified me—
> So that I kept silence and did not go out of doors?
>
> [Job 31:33 f.]

Yet in this moral courage and scorn for the mob there is at least an echo of the pride of the wellborn and well-circumstanced.

At every turn, the author himself, and not merely his hero, gives evidence of an upper-class environment. The poet's wide familiarity with various geographical locations—mountain and desert, sea and plain—points to his being widely traveled, an activity possible only for the rich in ancient times. His reference to the papyrus ships (9:26) and his colorful descriptions of the hippopotamus (40:15 ff.) and the crocodile (40:25 ff.) do not prove that the author was an Egyptian,[40] but they do show that he had visited the land of the Nile. Similarly, his vivid depiction of hail, ice, and snow, suggests a knowledge of the north.[41]

Because of his knowledge of agriculture and medicine, astronomy and anatomy, mining and warfare, Pfeiffer concluded that "the author was the most learned ancient before Plato."[42] This range of knowledge and experience, which recalls that of Shakespeare, is, of course, a tribute to his curiosity and intellectual powers, but it would have been denied him had he been poor.

It is in the area of religious thought that the poet's upper-class orientation is particularly clear. In this regard, the use of divine names is highly instructive.[43] In Egyptian and Babylonian Wisdom the individual names of gods do not totally disappear, but they yield increasingly to general descriptions of "God" or "the Gods." The names of individual deities are generally retained only in traditional apothegms or in contexts concerned with the attributes of a specific god.[44]

The use of divine names in Hebrew Wisdom is similar. In the lower Wisdom books like Proverbs, JHVH, the national name of the God of Israel, occurs exclusively in the oldest collections (10:1–22:16; 25–29), which are probably pre-Exilic. Yet even here, when JHVH does occur it is often in stock phrases like "the fear of JHVH," "the blessing of JHVH," "the abomination of JHVH," "the knowledge of JHVH."[45] The later collections in Proverbs use JHVH much less consistently. In Ben Sira the general term, 'ēl ("God"), is used in half the cases. The use of JHVH here is apparently to be attributed to the author's identification of the God of Israel with the world creator, so that the specific national name has become divested of any particularistic character.

In the higher Wisdom books the name JHVH is avoided with such consistency that it cannot be accidental. In Koheleth, 'elōhīm is the exclusive designation of the Deity.[46] In the poetic sections of Job, the specific name of JHVH is almost completely rejected in favor of the general terms, 'ēl, 'elōah, 'elōhīm, Šaddai.[47] Only in the prose narrative, which is a recasting of an ancient folk tale, does the traditional name JHVH occur. In avoiding local or national divine names in favor of the general designations, the higher Wisdom writers were seeking to express their concept of God in the broadest and most universal terms.

The upper-class orientation of Job emerges again in the treatment of the book's basic theme—the problem of suffering. Fuller consideration will be given to this issue later. Here it suffices to note that Wisdom writers could not shut their eyes to the inequities of the present order. At the same time, as representatives of the affluent groups in society, they did not find the status quo intolerable.

The lower classes, ground by poverty and oppression at the hands of domestic and foreign masters, were tormented by the prosperity of the wicked and the suffering of the righteous. Holding resolutely to their faith in God, they were nevertheless unable to see divine justice operating in the world about them. Their solution to this agonizing problem was the espousal of the doctrine of a future world where the inequalities of the present order would be rectified. Thus, the idea of life after death became an integral feature of pharisaic Judaism and of Christianity.[48]

The teachers of Wisdom, on the other hand, felt no need to adopt these new views. The sages of the conventional Wisdom schools continued to maintain the old view of collective retribution here and now, where the sins or virtues of the fathers determine the destinies of the children.[49] The idea of a future life is not so much as mentioned in Proverbs, probably because the material is comparatively early. However, by the time of Ben Sira, in the second century B.C.E., the doctrine of an afterlife had achieved such wide currency that it could no longer be ignored. The sage therefore explicitly negates this belief (Ecclus. 10:11): "When a man dies, he inherits worms, maggots, lice, and creeping things."[50] His grandson, who translated the book into Greek, gives the passage a pharisaic interpretation by having it affirm judgment after death: "Humble thy soul greatly, for the punishment of the ungodly is fire and worms."

The unconventional sages, the authors of Job and Koheleth, are too clear sighted and too sensitive to overlook the manifest instances of undeserved suffering and undeserved prosperity in the world. Yet neither of them accepts the pharisaic solution of a life after death, although both are familiar with it.

Koheleth dismisses the idea of an afterlife with a shrug of the shoulders:

> Furthermore, I saw under the sun that in the place of judgment there was wickedness, and in the place of righteousness, wrong. I said to myself, "Both the righteous and the wicked, God will judge, for there is a proper time for everything and every deed—over there!" I said to myself concerning men, "Surely God has tested them and shown that they are nothing but beasts." For the fate of men and the fate of beasts are the same. As the one dies, so does the other, for there is one spirit in both, and man's distinction over the beast is nothing, for everything is vanity. All go to one place, all come from the dust and all return to the dust. Who knows whether the spirit of man rises upward

and the spirit of the beast goes down to the earth? So I saw that there is nothing better for man than to rejoice in his works, for that is his lot, and no one can permit him to see what shall be afterwards.

[Eccles. 3:16 ff.]

Whatever you are able to do, do with all your might, for there is neither action, nor thought, nor knowledge, nor wisdom in the grave towards which you are moving.

Though man does not know his hour, like fish caught in an evil net, like birds seized in a snare, so men are trapped in an hour of misfortune, when it falls upon them suddenly.

[9:10, 12]

Job lacks the tough-mindedness of Koheleth. He cannot pretend to be indifferent to the hope for an afterlife. He wishes he could accept it as true, but he sorrowfully comes to the conclusion that the renewal of life after death is not given to men:

For there is hope for a tree—
If it be cut down, it can sprout again
And its shoots will not fail.
If its roots grow old in the earth
And its stump dies in the ground,
At the mere scent of water it will bud anew
And put forth branches like a young plant.
But man grows faint and dies;
Man breathes his last, and where is he?
As water vanishes from a lake,
And a river is parched and dries up,
So man lies down and rises not again;
Till the heavens are no more he will not awake,
Nor will he be roused from his sleep.

Oh, if You would hide me in Sheol,
Conceal me until Your wrath is spent;
Set a fixed time for me, and then remember me!
If a man die, can he live again?
All the days of my service I would wait,
Till my hour of release should come.
You would call and I would answer You;
You would be longing for the work of Your hands.
For then You would number my steps;

You would not keep watch over my sin.
You would seal up my transgression in a bag,
And You would cover over my iniquity.

But as a mountain falls and crumbles
And a rock is moved from its place,
As waters wear away stones
And a torrent washes away the earth's soil,
So do You destroy man's hope.

[Job 14:7–19]

It is in their reaction to the problem of evil that the social background of the authors of Job and Koheleth is most clearly revealed. The fact that they did not accept the nascent idea of life after death has usually been attributed to the general conservatism of the Wisdom writers. This explanation is, however, totally inadequate, for we should then have expected to find in Wisdom an adherence to the older doctrines of the "day of JHVH," as expounded by Amos, Isaiah, and Jeremiah, or the conception ot the "End-time," as developed by Isaiah, Jeremiah, and Ezekiel. Actually the Wisdom writers, whether conventional or not, accepted neither the older nor the newer views that ran counter to their group associations. Neither the hope for a Messianic era on earth nor the belief in an afterlife is echoed in their writing. Nowhere in the entire literature do we find the prophets' faith in a dynamic world. The Wisdom teachers are pre-eminently guides to the status quo, in which they anticipate no alteration. Whether they accept contemporary society as fundamentally just, as do the conventional Wisdom writers, or have doubts, as does Koheleth, or are passionately convinced that justice and truth are trampled under foot by God and man, as does Job—they do not contemplate any serious change in the structure of society.

The clear-cut social conservatism of Wisdom literature as a whole sheds light on several hitherto unexplained characteristics of Proverbs, Koheleth, and the Wisdom Psalms.[51] Our present concern is with Job, which reflects the same point of view, indirectly but unmistakably. In the dialogue, the Friends frequently give extended descriptions of God's power (5:9 ff.; 25:2–6; 26:6–14).[52] In response, Job also gives elaborate pictures of divine power, but with a significant difference: while the Friends stress the beneficent and creative functioning of the Almighty as revealed in the gift of rain (5:10), the discomfiture of the wicked (5:12 ff.), the glories of the heavens (26:2–3), and the mysteries of creation (26:5 ff.), Job emphasizes the negative and destructive manifestations of God's power:[53] God moves the mountains, makes the earth tremble, and shuts up the sun and the stars that they give no light (9:5 ff.).

The same spirit permeates Job's description of God's might in chapter 12: God destroys beyond rebuilding and imprisons men so that they cannot escape; he withholds water to cause drought and pours it forth in flood; nations are exalted only to be destroyed (12:14, 15, 23). The rest of Job's description is to be understood in the same light —as evidence of God's destructive power:

> He leads counselors away stripped,
> And of judges He makes fools.
> He opens the belt of kings
> And removes the girdle from their loins.[54]
> He leads priests away stripped
> And the mighty ones He confuses.
> He deprives counselors of speech
> And removes the discernment of the elders.
> He pours contempt on princes,
> And looses the girdle of the strong.
> He reveals deep secrets from the darkness,
> And brings the blackest gloom to light.
> He makes nations great, and then destroys them.
> He enlarges nations, and forsakes them.
> He removes understanding from the people's leaders
> And leads them in a pathless waste astray.
> They grope in the dark without light,
> And He makes them stagger like a drunkard.
>
> [12:17–25]

There is a striking contrast in spirit between Job's picture of social transformation and the descriptions found elsewhere in the Bible of God's power to transform conditions so that the proud are abased and the humble exalted.[55] These hymns are intended as paeans of praise:

> Those who were full have hired themselves out for bread,
> And the hungry have ceased (to starve),
> While the barren woman has borne seven,
> And the mother of many has languished.
> The Lord makes poor and makes rich;
> He casts down and raises up.
>
> [I Sam. 2:5, 7]

He raises the poor from the dust
And the needy from the dung-hill,
To seat him among the princes,
The princes of his people.

[Ps. 113:7–8]

Job's description has nothing in common with such pictures of social change. The salient difference lies in the fact that the psalmists
who praise God's greatness depict both aspects of the change—the fall
of the mighty and the rise of the lowly. Similarly Eliphaz, who extols
God's power (5:11): "He sets the lowly on high, and the afflicted are
raised to safety." Job, however, describes only half of the picture—the
decline of the powerful—because he is arraigning his Maker as a destructive force.

Nor is Job's attitude similar to that of the prophets. They saw in the
collapse of these elements of society the deserved punishment of a sinful
people (e.g., Amos 6:1 ff., 7 ff.; Isa. 3; Mic. 3) and the necessary prelude to a reconstructed social order (Isa. 1:24–28; 5:8–17; and often).
But for the author of Job, as for the Wisdom writers in general, a
transformation of the social and political status quo meant catastrophe.

In conclusion, we have seen that Hebrew Hokmah is one element in
the cultural and spiritual activity of the Hebrew genius during its most
creative era. The Book of Job represents the high-water mark of
biblical Wisdom, embodied in a unique literary genre of extraordinary power and originality. The author's roots lie deep within his
people and his class; yet the specific *locus standi* of the poet impugns
neither the truth nor the relevance of his insights for every manner and
condition of men. For his masterpiece is endowed with two qualities
which know no limits of time or space, nation or class—a sensitivity to
human suffering and a love of truth.

V

Job and Near Eastern Literature

W E HAVE BRIEFLY TRACED the history and development of the three principal strands in the pattern of ancient Hebrew religion and culture. Two of them, the Law and the Prophets, undoubtedly constituted important elements in the background of the author of Job. Basically, however, it was the third, Wisdom, with which he was most closely identified and to which he contributed his unique life work.

It is clear that he was familiar with the lower Wisdom, which was concerned with practical success in life. The sages expressed their realistic teachings principally through the *mashal* or proverbial utterance. They also used rhetorical questions to buttress their ideas with analogies from practical life. Both these literary forms are found in Job, where they are utilized by all the disputants in the argument.[1] As is the case with the other great exemplar of unconventional Wisdom, Koheleth, it is not always possible to determine whether the author of Job is citing an earlier saying or creating an original utterance.

Basically, however, the Book of Job belongs to the category of higher Wisdom, which was speculative in temper, unconventional in approach, and concerned with ultimate issues. High if not highest on the list was the problem of man's suffering in a world created and governed by a good God. This was an issue of universal human importance, and Job was not the only one in Israel, nor the Israelites the only people, to agonize over the mystery of evil.

That the Book of Job has deep roots in the Hebrew tradition has long been taken for granted. But that the Hebrew heritage itself has roots, as well as countless points of contact, in the culture of the ancient Orient, is a modern discovery.

Until a century and a half ago the Bible was virtually the only remaining document of its world and time. Since Napoleon's expedition to Egypt, however, oriental archaeology has, with rapidly increasing momentum, brought to light thousands of artifacts in Egypt, Palestine, Syria, and Mesopotamia. We now possess tangible evidence which enables us to reconstruct much of the life of the Fertile Crescent before, during, and after the biblical era. Even more important have been the discovery and the deciphering of various languages and literatures of the ancient Near East—Egyptian, Sumerian, Akkadian, Canaanite, Hurrian, and Hittite. As a result, the Bible no longer stands in splendid isolation. Yet the investigation of the religious, ethical, and legal literature of the ancient Near East has set into bolder relief the greatness of Israel's achievement. At the same time, a knowledge of the background from which Israel sprang, and against which it lived and created, has served to illumine untold aspects of Hebrew life and thought.

This is particularly true of biblical and non-biblical Hebrew Wisdom literature.[2] As we have noted, Wisdom is the least national and the most broadly universal element in the cultural heritage of ancient Israel. Unlike the Torah, it is not interested in the preservation of the historical traditions of the Jewish people or their particular forms of ritual. Unlike prophecy, it is vitally concerned, not with the national destiny of the Hebrew nation, but with the individual, his hopes and fears, the pitfalls he encounters along the path of everyday life, and the qualities he needs for success. These issues were no different for the Hebrew than for the Egyptian, the Syrian, or the Babylonian.

In each of these culture spheres there were a few searching spirits troubled by the ultimate issues—the purpose of existence, the destiny of man, the uncertainties of life, the problem of suffering, the nature of death. Here, too, the divergence among men would tend to be rooted in varying temperaments and personal experiences rather than in national differences. More than any other phase of Hebrew culture, biblical Hokmah was rooted in its oriental milieu.

It must be confessed, however, that the complex relationship between Israel and its neighbors has often been misconceived. As a modern thinker has pointed out, "the history of ideas is to be understood in terms of a dialectical development in which men react against the views held by their predecessors and correct any one-sidedness in these views by going to the opposite extreme that, alas, is equally one-sided."[3] As a natural reaction against the previous isolation of the Bible, and under the impact of the wealth of discoveries of modern archaeology, scholars have all too often gone to the opposite extreme, tending to see in every instance of similarity, real or alleged, an example of Hebrew borrowing from Babylonian, Egyptian, or Ugaritic sources. This is, of course, highly questionable methodology. The mere existence of similarities does not prove dependency unless there is an unusual sequence of thought or some striking and exceptional feature common to the two documents being compared. These conditions do obtain with regard to the Egyptian *Maxims of Amenemope*, which is dated from the tenth to the seventh centuries B.C.E. The work bears a striking resemblance to an entire section in the Book of Proverbs (22:17–24:22) and is accordingly regarded by most scholars as the direct or indirect source for the Hebrew work.[4]

In general, however, no such clear-cut evidence of relationship can be established. In the first instance, it must be kept in mind that Hebrew Wisdom drew upon the same ancient sources and fundamental concerns which agitated the sages of Babylonia and Egypt. Moreover, these basic human concerns would tend to produce similarities in outlook, mood, and form of expression. Finally, and most important, this common oriental heritage was subjected to a far-reaching process of "creative assimilation." The Hebrew genius adopted those elements in the surrounding culture which it found valuable, modified what was potentially useful, and rejected what it recognized as fundamentally alien. Hence, the similarities are often illuminating with regard to details, but it is the differences that go deeper and are more significant. A balanced study, therefore, of the extra-biblical parallels to Wisdom literature must reckon with the elements in common as well as with the divergencies that set Hebrew Wisdom apart from, and above, its oriental counterparts.

Since Job belongs to the higher, speculative Wisdom, we are not concerned with the more extensive remains of the lower, practical Wisdom in Egyptian and Babylonian literature.[5] To be sure, the organic connection between the two aspects of Wisdom means that each can shed light on some feature of the other. Thus the Egyptian *Instruction of Ani*, written toward the end of the Empire, is of interest because of its dialogue form: a father gives advice to his son, who answers respectfully, expressing the fear that he cannot measure up to the father's high standards.[6]

In the higher speculative realm, Egyptian literature contains several meditations and complaints against suffering, whether induced by the gods, or, more commonly, caused by the cruelty and oppression of men. To this genre belongs the *Admonitions of Ipu-wer* (end of the First Kingdom, circa 2300–2050 B.C.E.), which consists of six poems depicting the collapse of the established order and the transfer of power and wealth to upstarts.[7] The approach here is "prophetic": a scribe apparently musters up courage to charge the king with the maladministration of justice. This theme, as we have noted, reappears in biblical Wisdom as well and is particularly prominent in Job.[8] *The Dispute With His Soul of a Man Tired of Life* also reflects the despair induced by the breakdown of society.[9] The most popular work in this genre is the highly rhetorical *Complaint of the Peasant*, which narrates an alleged tale of oppression and fraud perpetrated upon a salt-field dweller in the Wadi Natrun, west of the Delta.[10] The moving *Song of the Harper* (Middle or New Kingdom) is concerned with the transitoriness of existence and urges the enjoyment of life. It is written in a rhythmic form and in a spirit that recalls both the Hebrew Ecclesiastes and the so-called "Babylonian Koheleth,"[11] though no direct relationship exists.[12]

With regard to Babylonian Wisdom literature, it cannot be determined whether it was originally less extensive than its Egyptian counterpart or whether the fewer remains are purely a matter of accident. Nonetheless, even these fragments exhibit both aspects of Wisdom—practical instruction and philosophical "laments."[13] Lambert categorizes them along slightly different lines as "practical advice on ethics and works dealing with intellectual problems."[14]

The first category of practical guidance is exhibited in various proverb collections which stress experience and common sense almost exclusively.[15] On the other hand, several works blend religious and ethical motifs with practical considerations, like the biblical Book of Proverbs. To this group belong the so-called Babylonian *Book of Proverbs*,[16] which goes back to the third or second millennium B.C.E., and the much later *Ahiqar Romance*, which was one of the most popular and widely diffused books in the ancient Orient.[17]

Again, our present concern is with writings in the second category, that is, complaints on the limitations of life, which fall into the sphere of the higher Wisdom. The first work in this genre is the poem *I will praise the Lord of Wisdom*, which has been called the "Babylonian Job."[18] Lambert argues forcefully that this epithet is a misnomer: "So long as knowledge was restricted to the second tablet such a description was justified. Seen now in a more complete form, it will not bear the title so readily. Quantitatively speaking, the greater part of the text is taken up by a description of Marduk's restoration of his ruined servant, and only a small part with an effort to probe the reason for the suffering of the righteous."[19] In the poem the author describes the ills he has suffered and complains of the misfortunes which have come upon him though he has been innocent of wrongdoing. He has violated no rituals and has been punctilious in paying honor to the gods. The interpreters of dreams and oracles have been unable to help him. He is driven to the conclusion that man cannot know the designs of the gods, and to an even more radical surmise—that man's conception of good and evil differs from that of the gods! The Babylonian poet declares:

> What man thinks good, for god is evil!
> What in his heart is wrong, for his god is good!
> Who can learn the will of the gods in heaven?
> Where has purblind man learnt the way of a god?
>
> [Tablet II, ll. 34–37]

Then comes a description of his physical suffering, followed by a sudden transition to confidence, to which we shall return:

> My ill-wisher heard it, and his countenance shone (with joy);
> They brought the good news to the woman who was my
>   ill-wisher, and her spirit was delighted.
> But I know the day when my tears will come to an end,
> When among the protecting deities their divinity will show
>   mercy.
>
> [Tablet II reverse, ll. 52 ff.]

After several unclear lines and a lacuna, the text describes the sufferer's restoration to health and divine favor.

A particularly intriguing example of Babylonian Wisdom is afforded by the *Pessimistic Dialogue of a Master and a Slave*.[20] The text consists of a series of paragraphs in which the master declares his intention to follow a given course of action, like visiting the palace, taking a meal, going hunting, facing his enemy, or building a house. In each case, the slave obediently agrees that it is wise. Then the master abruptly announces the decision to do the opposite and the slave again encourages his lord in the new activity. Finally, the master announces that since the same fate overtakes the public benefactor and the self-seeking individual, he will kill both his slave and himself. Again the slave seems to agree by recalling either man's incapacity to understand the world or, more likely, man's inability to escape the world and the universal law of mortality.

> Who is so tall that he can reach up into heaven?
> Who is so wide that he can embrace the earth?

But when the master modifies his plan and decides that only the slave must die, the latter gives an ironic and decisive answer:

> "No, slave, I will kill you and send you ahead of myself."
> "How indeed would my master survive me for three days?"

Prior to 1954, virtually all scholars regarded the text as a serious presentation of a pessimistic outlook on life. Yet they were struck by the "playful fashion," the "burlesque tone," and the "low irreverence" reflected in the composition.[21] Bohl therefore suggested that it was a skit written for the Babylonian "Saturnalia" and describing a reversal of social status, which, he assumes, took place on a day during the New Year festival.[22] Sutcliffe makes the plausible suggestion that it was not intended to be a serious discussion on the absence of values in life, but rather "a parody or jocose presentment of the obsequious slave," who agrees to every whim of the master except that of his own (i.e., the slave's) demise.[23]

Lambert, on the other hand, suggests that "the writer was in earnest, but owed his outlook to his emotional state. The whole atmosphere of the text, he believes, is reminiscent of contemporary Western adolescents, particularly those of high intelligence. Extensive study has revealed that many bright youths have sudden changes from exuberance to brooding depression and that suicide is often in their thoughts, though rarely acted upon."[24] I do not find this theory convincing. There is no warrant in the text for this alleged alternation of moods from exaltation to depression. Moreover, according to this view, there is no real need or function for the slave, who is in fact given the last and decisive word in the dialogue. I therefore prefer Sutcliffe's interpretation of the composition as a humorous presentation of an obsequious slave. It remains a striking fact that the *Dialogue* is a highly effective piece, though its precise meaning is unclear—very much like some examples of contemporary literature!

A third composition (fifteenth or fourteenth century B.C.E.), which has been described as the *Complaint of a Sage over the Injustice of the World,* is today generally referred to as a *Dialogue about Human Misery.* It has aptly been called the "Babylonian Koheleth."[25] The poem is an acrostic preserving the poet's name, a practice not attested in the Bible, but frequent in medieval Hebrew poetry. It is written in the form of a dialogue between the sufferer and his friend, thus recalling in rudimentary fashion the structure of Job. Unfortunately, the text contains many lacunae that make it difficult to follow. The themes treated apparently include such ideas as the following: death destroys love and joy (ll. 12 ff.); even the rich and the powerful cannot presume upon the abiding favor of the gods (ll. 60 ff.); the decrees of God are incomprehensible (ll. 80 ff., 220 ff.); murder and violence are triumphant in human affairs (ll. 215 ff.). The author urges joy (ll. 21 ff., 246) and closes with a petition to the gods for help. Here, too, the speaker protests that he has presented the prescribed sacrifices. Perhaps the boldest thought in Babylonian Wisdom is the idea—on which both the sufferer and his friend agree—that the injustice of the gods makes men prone to lie and to oppress their fellows.[26] In his bitterness he threatens to surrender his piety:

> Let me forget the votive gifts of the god, trample upon ritual
> prescriptions.
> Let me *slaughter the bullock* . . . eat. . . .
>
> [ll. 135–36]

This brief conspectus of Egyptian and Babylonian higher Wisdom is sufficient to indicate that biblical Hokmah did not arise in a vacuum. Even without this concrete evidence, the high level of achievement represented by its major works, Job and Ecclesiastes, would suggest a long period of gestation and development. A masterpiece emerges not at the beginning of a movement, but at its culmination.

There are many points of similarity between Job and these extrabiblical writings: the exposure to illness and other misfortunes, the mystery of the suffering of the pious, the uncertainty of life, the unknowability of human destiny, the lack of correspondence between virtue and well-being. All these are universal elements of human experience, however; their presence in two distinct literary compositions does not necessarily prove a relationship of dependency.

It is noteworthy that such stylistic features as the presence of dialogue, the citation of proverbs, and the use of quotations in debate are met with in oriental as well as in Hebrew Wisdom. They constitute part of the literary tradition of oriental Wisdom as a whole, and again, do not constitute evidence of direct borrowing.

One of the most famous passages in Job needs to be discussed in this connection. After pleading with his friends for pity and voicing a passionate wish to have his words permanently engraved on a monument, Job cries:

> For I know that my Redeemer lives,
> Though He be the last to arise upon earth![27]
>
> [Job 19:25]

No matter how the enigmatic second line is interpreted, it is striking that the formulation of the first has two analogues in the extant extra-biblical literature, in Ugaritic and in Egyptian. In a Ugaritic liturgical text which has described the death of the god Aliyn Ba'al, the worshiper triumphantly announces the rebirth of his god:

> And I know that the powerful Baal lives;
> Existent is the prince, Lord of the earth.[28]

The idea of a dying god coming back to life is obviously appropriate to the Canaanite worshiper.[29] For the Hebrew poet the notion was totally meaningless, since his God was not a nature deity whose life fluctuated with the seasons, but a God who ruled over nature and stood above it. Job is contrasting his own brief and tragic life, in which he has found no vindication, with the Eternal God at whose hands he will ultimately be justified.

In the Babylonian poem, *I will praise the Lord of Wisdom*, the poet describes the hatred of his foes and then calls out:

> But I know the day when my tears will come to an end,
> When among the protecting deities their divinity will show
> mercy.[30]

Here we have the sudden change of mood from despair to confidence which is particularly striking in the passage we have cited from Job. Unlike the Babylonian poet, however, Job looks forward to his moral vindication, not to his physical restoration. Moreover, the Babylonian poet does not invoke his god as do Job and the Ugaritic worshiper.

The biblical passage thus shares points of similarity and of difference with the Ugaritic and Babylonian texts. What all three literatures have in common is the triumphant affirmation: "I know." Whether the usage existed as a fixed liturgical form or is simply coincidental cannot be determined. In any event, there is no likelihood of direct borrowing by the Hebrew poet; at most, we have here another element common to the ancient oriental culture sphere.

Of much greater significance than these similarities of detail are the far-reaching differences between Egyptian and Babylonian Wisdom writings, on the one hand, and the books of Job and Ecclesiastes, on the other. Basically, they reflect the divergence between the pagan outlook of the oriental world and the ethical monotheism of Hebraism. For the ancient world, the gods were primarily personifications of the forces of nature or of human instincts. Undoubtedly the "great gods" of Egypt and Mesopotamia developed ethical attributes, but these remained secondary to their role as nature deities. In oriental religion, therefore, human suffering was often attributed to the intervention of evil spirits, against whom incantations were to be invoked. Frequently a man's misery was attributed to the unexpected caprice or the incomprehensible anger of the gods. Their hostility could be aroused by envy, by lust, or by simple *Schadenfreude*, the impulse to cruelty.

Whether the Mesopotamian gods are described as amoral or immoral may, perhaps, be a matter of semantics. What is clear is that they are far removed from the uncompromising moral character of the God of Israel. Hence, even in the most sophisticated examples of oriental Wisdom, the ethical motif was secondary, when it was not altogether lacking.

As we have seen, some Babylonian thinkers who wrestled with the problem of evil enunciated the idea that there was a lack of correspondence between the moral standards of the gods and those of men. While this early and highly original adumbration of the doctrine of the relativity of ethics may be congenial to some modern thinkers it was utterly out of the question for the Hebrew sage, for whom the ethical character of God and the ethical imperative for man were indivisible. The Hebrew world view was unforgettably expressed by the prophet Micah, "He has told thee, O man, what is good, and what the Lord your God requires of you, to do justice, to love mercy, and to walk humbly with your God" (Mic. 6:8, 9).

Similarly, it would be impossible for a Hebrew thinker to conceive of the idea that God is responsible for man's sinfulness or even his proclivity to sin. That man is free to choose the right is the bedrock of biblical ethics. The lawgiver in Deuteronomy enjoins: "Behold I have placed before you today life and the good, and death and the evil. . . . Life and death have I placed before you, the blessing and the curse. You shall choose life, so that you may live, you and your children" (Deut. 30:16–19; cf. 11:26 ff.). This thrice-repeated injunction is echoed throughout the Hebrew Bible by prophet and sage alike.

In Job, Eliphaz denies that God's world order is the source of evil and places the blame squarely at the door of man:

> Indeed, misfortune does not come forth from the ground,
> Nor does evil sprout from the earth.
> It is man who gives birth to evil. . . .
>
> [Job 5:6–7]

In all his bitter denial of the Friends' position, Job never contravenes the moral responsibility of man. It is only that he demands the same standard of his God.

For the same reason the oriental Wisdom writers indite complaints of their suffering but do not hurl challenges to the gods in the name of justice. The ringing cry of Abraham, "Shall not the Judge of all the earth do justice?" (Gen. 18:26), which might well serve as the motto for the Book of Job, and in somewhat muted form for Ecclesiastes as well, finds no echo in Egyptian and Babylonian Wisdom. The burning conviction that man's suffering in the world is an affront to the goodness of God was possible only to a Hebrew. For him alone, the essential nature of God resided in His ethical character. Indeed, the Hebrew saw both nature and history through the prism of ethical consciousness.

It has been noted that Mesopotamian literature reveals a philosophy of history. Not unlike the biblical historians, the *Weidner Chronicle* ties the weal or woe of various rulers to their loyalty or disloyalty to the gods. The differences from the prophetic philosophy of history are, however, far more striking than the similarities. For the Babylonian chronicler, the success or failure of the rulers depended upon whether they provided or failed to provide fish-offerings for the Esagil temple in Babylon.[31]

Another striking illustration of the deep chasm separating the Hebrews from their Semitic kinsmen may be seen in the varied interpretations of the ancient Semitic tradition of a primordial flood. According to Babylonian mythology, the flood was brought upon humankind because men made so much noise on earth they disturbed the repose of the gods. Utnapishtim, the favorite of the gods, is ordered to build a ship "when their heart led the great gods to produce the flood." He is instructed to deceive his fellow men about his plans and to lull them into inactivity with fair promises:

> Ea opened his mouth to speak,
> Saying to me, his servant:
> "Thou shalt then thus speak unto them:
> " 'I have learned that Enlil is hostile to me,
> So that I cannot reside in your city,
> Nor set my foot in Enlil's territory.
> To the Deep I will therefore go down,
> To dwell with my lord Ea.
> But upon you he will shower down abundance,
> The choicest birds, the rarest fishes.
> The land shall have its fill of harvest riches.
> He who at dusk orders the husk-greens,
> Will shower down upon you a rain of wheat.' "[32]

The biblical account attributes the flood in Noah's day to the moral corruption of the human race:

> And the earth was corrupt before God,
> And the earth was filled with violence.
> And God saw the earth,
> And behold, it was corrupt;
> For all flesh had corrupted their way upon the earth.

> [Gen. 6:11, 12]

It is characteristic of the Hebraic ethos that rabbinic legend declares that Noah's long process of building the Ark was intended to arouse his sinful contemporaries to repentance before disaster struck.[33] Nowhere is there any suggestion that Noah attempted to deceive his sinful contemporaries. Like every page of the Hebrew Bible, the account of the flood is drenched in morality.

This profound difference in outlook leads to other important divergences between biblical and non-Hebraic Wisdom. The Egyptian and Babylonian writers protest their innocence of infractions which are primarily ritual in character. This is true even of the Egyptian *Book of the Dead*, which reveals a high degree of ethical sensitivity.[34] In Egyptian religion, before a deceased man is admitted to the realm of the blessed, he must declare his guiltlessness by reciting a long catalogue of offenses from which he is free. These include murder, sodomy, theft, dishonesty in business, and other ethical sins. But the protestation of innocence in the *Book of the Dead* also includes many ritual infractions.

In Job, on the other hand, violations of ritual law play no part whatever. As the argument waxes hot, Job is accused by his friends and passionately defends himself against charges of *ethical* misconduct. His *apologia pro vita sua* reaches its crescendo in the great "Confession of Integrity" (chap. 31), which is significant not only for its ethical sensitivity and for the sins it includes but also for the ritual transgressions it omits.

In sum, it is clear that oriental Wisdom literature is invaluable in supplying the background for Job and in shedding light on countless details of the book. There is, however, no direct contact between Job and the earlier exemplars of oriental Wisdom; Job remains unique not only in Hebrew literature but in the literature of the world.

VI

The Tale of Job

THAT THE BOOK OF JOB is cast in a unique literary form is obvious at first glance from the prose tale which serves as the framework for the poetry. The first two chapters of the book, which describe the series of calamities that befall Job, serve as a prologue to the poetic dialogue, which itself contains several sections. Following the debate by the various protagonists, the prose narrative is resumed (42:7–19): Job's fortunes are restored and indeed increased. After the passion and the agony, all ends in serenity and peace.

Since the Book of Job is part of the Bible, it was taken for granted by both the Jewish and the Christian traditions that the hero was a historical figure. Only two talmudic sages, one anonymous, the other the well-known third-century rabbi, Resh Lakish, ventured to declare that "Job was never created, nor did he ever exist, but is simply a parable."[1] Even this utterance was transmitted with a slight textual variant to read, "Job was created solely to serve as a parable."[2]

Apart from this dissenting voice the historicity of Job was not questioned. Since the tradition possessed no authentic recollection of a man named Job, a variety of dates was proposed, all based upon slight verbal similarities between passages in Job and other biblical works. The dominant view among the rabbis was that he was a contemporary of Moses.[3] Other rabbinic views assigned Job to the age of the patriarch Jacob (making him the husband of Jacob's daughter Dinah), to the period of the Judges, to the era of Solomon, and to the age of the Persian king, Ahasuerus.[4]

Christian tradition largely followed the same pattern. Luther declared Job to be historical but did not argue for the accuracy of the details. Thus his view coincided, probably by accident, with one version of the opinion of Resh Lakish, according to which Job actually existed, although the calamities described never befell him.[5] Today it is universally recognized that the Book of Job is a work of creative imagination.

It is, however, a striking fact that in both the natural and the historical sciences, old and discarded theories are sometimes resuscitated and found acceptable when set forth in a new light. Recent trends in research strengthen the likelihood that there originally was a historical figure named Job who became the nucleus of a folk tradition which was later utilized by the poet. Increasingly, contemporary research in folklore and literary history attributes a high measure of credibility to the nucleus of fact underlying such epics as the *Iliad* and the *Song of Roland*, and such legendary figures as King Arthur, Robin Hood, and Dr. Faustus. Thus it is noteworthy that virtually all the proper names which occur in the book are associated with the lands lying east and south of Palestine. The term *B'nai Qedem* (1:3), "sons of the East," is a general designation in the Bible equated with the Amalekites and the Midianites, roving tribes of the Arabian desert.[6] In the Egyptian *Tale of Sinuhe* (twentieth century B.C.E.) the hero leaves Egypt to go to Kedem and then moves on to Retenu or Palestine.[7]

The "Land of Uz," from which Job hailed, has been equated by scholars with northern Mesopotamia,[8] with a district in Arabia,[9] and, less plausibly, with a territory in Syria.[10] It is most probable, however, that Uz is to be identified with Edom, since most of the proper names in Job are drawn from the genealogy of Esau in Genesis,[11] or have analogues with it. The land of Uz is a poetic synonym for Edom.[12] Eliphaz occurs in Genesis as the oldest son of Esau. The name itself seems to be a metathesis of Phasael, which occurs as the name of the son of King Herod, who was of Edomite stock.[13] Teman, given as the district from which Job's Eliphaz hails, is the son of the biblical Eliphaz. Bildad does not occur elsewhere, but it consists of two elements, the first of which has analogues in such non-Hebrew biblical names as Bilhah, Bil'am, and Bilhan, who is a descendant of Esau.[14] The second element occurs in the names of Eldad and Medad, the mysterious figures who once broke into prophecy in the wilderness in the days of

Moses (Num. 11:26 ff.). The name Bildad would seem to mean "Bel loves." Zophar has the same consonants as Zippor, the father of the King of Moab.[15] Moreover, where the Hebrew text in the genealogy of Esau now reads "Zepho," the Septuagint, by the change of one letter, renders "Zophar" (Gen. 36:11). Naamah, the territory from which Zophar comes, is the name of a female descendant of Cain, who is the eponymous ancestor of the wandering tribe of the Kenites (Gen. 4:22). It is also the name of an Ammonite princess, one of Solomon's wives.[16]

On the basis of these Edomite parallels and on other grounds, some scholars have argued that the book is of Edomite origin.[17] Several of the names, however, suggest an Arabic provenance. Shuah occurs as the son of Abraham by his concubine Keturah and was possibly also the name of an Arab tribe.[18] Sheba, whose hosts attacked Job's possessions, is the name of a well-known Arab kingdom. The Kasdim, who also robbed Job, are rendered "Chaldeans" in our English Bible. This tribe, dwelling on the lower Euphrates and Tigris rivers during the entire period of biblical history, is included with Uz and Buz in the genealogy of Abraham's Aramean kinsfolk.[19]

Elihu ben Barakhel (32:37) is the only authentically Hebrew name among the dramatis personae of the book. His name is identical with that of the prophet Elijah, and his patronymic has its analogue in several late biblical names.[20] The occurrence of this lone Hebrew name in Job has been used to support the view that the Elihu chapters are an interpolation from a later hand. I shall seek to assess the significance of the name below.[21]

With regard to the name of Job itself, Ewald has suggested that it is derived from the Arabic Awab, "he who turns to God." The name has its analogue in A-ja-ab, King of Pella, mentioned in the Tel-el-Amarna letters.[22] Meyer identifies Job with Jobab, a name that also occurs in the genealogy of Esau (Gen. 36:33) and is used for the protagonist in the apocryphal *Testament of Job*. The most probable view is that Iyyob is a Hebrew folk etymology of a previously existing Semitic name, being a passive participial noun from the verb 'āyab, "to hate," hence, "the hated, persecuted one."[23]

That neither the locale nor the protagonists of the book are Israelite is not strange. Literary works often have a foreign background for the *mise en scène*. The Homeric epics arose not among the Achaeans, who are its heroes, but among the Ionians and the Aeolians. The

Niebelung cycle developed not among the Burgundians but among the Franks.[24]

Moreover, the poet found available for his creative use more than the dramatis personae. Like the great Greek dramatists who were his contemporaries, or Shakespeare, Milton, and Goethe, who were to come centuries later, the author of Job did not invent his own plot. He chose instead a familiar folk tale concerning the tribulations of a righteous man named Job. A priori, one would expect the traditional story to have undergone much alteration before reaching its culmination in the Book of Job; but only recently has it become possible to reconstruct with some assurance several stages in its evolution.

As a point of departure we may take the only other biblical reference to Job outside the book bearing his name.[25] The sixth-century prophet Ezekiel, in one of his stern calls to repentance, warns his generation that its iniquity is so great that even if the three righteous men, Noah, Daniel, and Job, were living in the land, their signal righteousness would avail to save them personally from catastrophe, but not their children, let alone the land as a whole: "If these three men, Noah, Daniel, and Job, were in it, they would save only themselves by their righteousness, saith the Lord God. . . . As I live, says the Lord God, they would save neither son nor daughter; only they themselves would be delivered, but the land would be devastated."

The reference to Noah was, of course, clear. Noah was a "righteous man in his generation," whose virtue availed to save not only his own life but that of his wife and children when the Flood descended. The reference to Daniel in Ezekiel, however, always proved troublesome to the commentators. In the biblical book bearing his name, Daniel is a wise interpreter of dreams, but there is no suggestion anywhere about his saving his children or even of his being married. The key to this long-standing enigma was unlocked with the discovery of Ugaritic literature at Ras-es-Shamra in Syria. In 1930 and 1931 French excavations discovered three tablets, with possible fragments of a fourth, constituting an epic about a youth named Aqhat.[26]

The outlines of the story are tolerably clear. It tells the tale of a king of Hermon named Dan'el, who rules an elaborate court with his wife Dnty. As their names, which mean "justice," indicate, they are virtuous and hospitable, but they are unhappy because they have no son. The extant material begins with Dan'el's prayers, rituals, and supplication. Finally the prayers are answered and a male child is born to them, named Aqhat, which may mean "obedience, filial piety." The boy receives the gift of a bow from the god Kothar vaKhasis, the craftsman god of Ugarit. The bow, however, arouses the envy of the war goddess 'Anat, who offers to pay for it either in precious ore or with the gift of immortality. When all her offers are rejected, the wrathful goddess has the lad slain by an assassin, Ytpn. The heartbroken father weeps for seven years for his dead son. Finally, Aqhat's sister, Paghat, avenges the murder. At this crucial point, as is so often the case in the remnants of ancient literature, the tablet breaks off. All indications suggest, however, that the slain lad is restored to life because of the pity of the god El and the remorse of the goddess 'Anat. It is now clear that it is the Ugaritic Dan'el and not the biblical Daniel whom the prophet Ezekiel places in the company of Noah, as one who was able to save his son from death.[27]

From the Ezekiel passage it is possible to reconstruct the oldest form of the Job narrative, and by inference, several succeeding stages. In the form in which it was familiar to Ezekiel's contemporaries of the sixth century B.C.E., the tale doubtless told how the righteous Job, because of his piety, had been able to save his children from death as Noah did, or had brought them back from the nether world as Dan'el had. In the earliest version of the tradition to which Ezekiel refers, it is probable but by no means certain that Job's suffering was a test, like the one to which Abraham was subjected in the sacrifice of Isaac (Gen. chap. 22) and from which both father and son emerged unscathed. In this form of the story Satan had no part.

Another stage, perhaps the next in the development of the tale, is marked by the introduction of Satan into the narrative. This stage must belong to the Persian period, when Jews came into contact with Zoroastrianism and its doctrine of "two forces" in the universe—Ahriman, the god of darkness and evil, and Ahura-Mazda, the god of light and righteousness.[28] This dualism had a powerful effect on popular religion for two reasons. First, it offered a simple answer to the problem of evil, freeing God from the onus of responsibility by attributing evil to a malevolent spirit. Second, in assigning to men a crucial role in the cosmic battle between good and evil, it underscored their responsibility to fight the forces of darkness and bring about the triumph of righteousness.

This sensitivity to evil and faith in the ultimate victory of good were highly congenial to the Hebrew spirit. Unfortunately, dualism was dangerous—because it impugned the unity of God, the cornerstone of Hebraic religion. Because of this ambivalent impact of dualism upon biblical religion, it was both attacked and condoned by the authentic teachers of Judaism. Wherever the concept of the universal sway of God was compromised, it was opposed. Thus, the great prophet of the Exile boldly declared:

> I form the light, and create darkness;
> I make peace, and create evil;
> I am the Lord, that does all these things.
>
> [Isa. 45:7]

Where Persian dualism offered a less direct confrontation the Hebrew tradition accommodated itself to the concept by creating the figure of Satan as a quasi-independent symbol of the forces of evil. Nevertheless, the idea made its way slowly in Hebrew thought.

Satan first emerges as a well-defined personage in the tale of Job. Yet here Satan is still a common name with the definite article *"ha-Satan,* the prosecuting attorney" in the heavenly court. He occupies a special place among the heavenly beings who are called "the sons of God," but he is still one among them. In succeeding years he becomes Satan without the definite article, the source and personification of the evil that men found it difficult to attribute to God. The process can be seen clearly with regard to the incident described in the Book of Samuel, where we are told that "the wrath of the Lord" burned against Israel and "incited" King David to take a census of the people. In the post-Exilic Book of Chronicles the incident is modified significantly: "Satan rose up against Israel and seduced David into counting Israel."[29]

In later apocalyptic writings, as in the Dead Sea Scrolls, dualism became a cardinal doctrine, far more prominent than in normative Judaism. "The Book of the Wars of the Sons of Light" is a vivid description of the cosmic war between the forces of good and evil, which ends with the victory of the right. In apocalyptic and messianic circles, including that of the Judeo-Christians, Satan or Beelzebub becomes the Devil, the cosmic Adversary of God, who contends with God for dominion over the world and the souls of men.

It is, of course, entirely possible that there were intermediate stages and variants in the long evolution of the Job tradition that have left no trace behind. We cannot, for example, tell when the idea of the wager between God and Satan was introduced. What has reached us is the final version of the tale, which is imbedded in the prose chapters of the present book—in the prologue and the epilogue.[30]

The attentive reader is struck at once by some marked differences between the prose tale (particularly the prologue) and the poetic dialogue. To be sure, some of these differences are easily explained. In the prose tale Job's suffering is no mystery; it is the direct result of Satan's wager. In the dialogue, on the other hand, it is essential that neither Job nor the Friends have any inkling of the source of Job's misfortune, since the very theme of the debate is the mystery of human suffering. This same consideration would explain why Satan is not invoked in the poetry as the source of evil. For the ancient Hebrews, who could not conceive of God's existence apart from His governing the world, to attribute evil to any other power beyond His sway would be tantamount to a denial of God.

There are other contradictions between the prose and the poetry which may perhaps be disregarded as minor in character. For example, in the prose tale Job's family is totally annihilated, as is his entire household of slaves. In the poetry he complains of the estrangement he feels from his wife and kinsfolk and of the contempt and disrespect visited upon him by his slaves.[31]

There are, however, fundamental discrepancies that cannot be so easily dismissed. In the poetry there is no vestige of the patient Job of the prose narrative. On the contrary, throughout the dialogue he is in flaming revolt against God, whom he bitterly accuses of injustice. The prose tale and the poetry also differ radically in their conception of God. In the prologue the Lord is depicted as an earthly king who can be "seduced" by the wily Satan so as to afflict his creatures. In the poetry God is described in exalted terms as an all-powerful spirit who is at the same time the moral governor of the universe. The most concrete difference lies in the names for God employed in the text. In the prose, JHVH, the characteristic national epithet for God, is employed, together with the generic term 'Elōhīm.[32] JHVH is all but totally absent from the poetry. Instead, general terms like 'Ēl, 'Elōah, 'Ēlōhīm, "God," and Shaddai (commonly rendered "the Almighty") are used throughout.[33]

Moreover, the vocabulary and style of the prose are of classic simplicity, superb examples of the "Golden Age" of Hebrew literature. The dialogue, on the other hand, employs a very rich and complex vocabulary which often draws upon Semitic linguistic resources known to us from Arabic. Even more striking is the frequent use of Aramaisms, a basic trait of the "Silver Age" of biblical Hebrew, when Aramaic was widely used throughout Western Asia as a *lingua franca*, ultimately displacing Hebrew as the spoken language of the people.[34]

These contradictions between the prose and the poetry have led some scholars to believe that they represent two distinct and independent sources. As for the relationship between the parts, every possible variation has been suggested.[35] It has been proposed that the dialogue was written independently of the prose tale.[36] This view is highly unlikely since some prose background for the dialogue is essential. Besides, as we have seen, there are witnesses to the existence of an earlier Job tale. Some have held that there was an altogether different prose tale, but of this alleged narrative we have no trace.[37]

A theory that has attracted considerable attention and some degree of support is that of Albrecht Alt, who divides the prologue and epilogue into two tales, one earlier, one later.[38] The earlier tale (chap. 1 and 42:11–17) constitutes, as it were, an outer framework; the later tale (chap. 2 and 42:7–10), an inner layer surrounding the dialogue. On this theory, the Friends originally urged Job to blaspheme God and therefore were castigated by Him in the epilogue: "For you have not spoken the truth about Me as has My servant Job" (42:8).

Upon critical examination, this theory of two prose tales proves entirely unacceptable: it destroys the dramatic architecture of the five scenes in chapters 1 and 2; and it leaves the first narrative hanging in the air at the end of chapter 1, beginning the new tale with chapter 2, which then opens abruptly without an introduction. If this theory is to be accepted, it must be assumed that parts of both alleged tales are missing. In addition, the role of the Friends becomes superfluous, since Job's wife has already urged him to "curse God and die." What is most significant, God's comment in the epilogue that the Friends' speech is "not right" is entirely inappropriate to this theory: had they been urging Job to blaspheme his Maker, far stronger language would have been used against them.[39]

A widely held view suggests that the narrative in Job is a folk tale repeated in its original form by the poet, who utilized it as the framework for his poetic dialogue.[40] But the prose narrative which has reached us is no naïve, unsophisticated story. With its well-wrought delineation of character, its subtle touches of irony, its five scenes alternating between heaven and earth, and its swift narrative pace, it is a masterpiece of storytelling. It bears all the characteristics of literary craftsmanship of the first order. At the same time, the authentic Near-Eastern names employed, the many antique touches in the narrative, and the naïve spirit in which the relationship between the

Lord and His prosecuting angel is depicted, make it clear that the author utilized an already existing narrative.[41]

The most plausible theory is that the poet saw in the traditional tale of Job an excellent framework for the great theme which concerned him. He therefore retold a familiar story in his own manner, keeping its principal features of style and content unchanged. It is characteristic of Semitic literary usage that the writer keeps his traditional sources intact, even if there are obvious discrepancies between them. Thus, where modern practice would relegate to a footnote one or another of two contradictory sources, Hebrew and Arab writers did not hesitate to retain the variants cheek by jowl in the main narrative, without attempting to harmonize all the details. Instances of this literary procedure are common in oriental literature.[42] The wide diffusion of the familiar Job tale in ancient Israel would militate strongly against any changes in the well-known and well-loved narrative.

Having decided to utilize the traditional folk tale for his purposes, the poet then found it necessary to effect a transition from the prose prologue to the poetic dialogue and from the dialogue to the prose epilogue. This he achieved by adding two brief jointures, one at the end of the original prologue (2:11–13), the other (42:7–10) before the epilogue. In the first connecting passage the poet introduced the protagonists of the debate by name and told of their going to visit Job to comfort him. Following the extended poetic dialogue, which ends with the God speeches and Job's submission, the author added the second link. That this section does not belong to the original folk tale, but originates with the poet, is clear from the fact that the Lord upbraids the Friends: "The Lord said to Eliphaz the Temanite: 'My wrath is kindled against you and against your two friends; for you have not spoken the truth about Me as has My servant Job.'" This critical sentiment could emanate only from one whose sympathies were with the much-tried Job rather than with the Friends, who have tried to defend God but have done so inadequately and unconvincingly.[43] For the poet, as for countless other sensitive seekers of the truth, "there lives more faith in honest doubt . . . than in half the creeds."[44]

In the jointure preceding the epilogue, Eliphaz and his two friends are commanded to offer sacrifices for forgiveness and to plead with Job to pray on their behalf. This is done and they are forgiven, not because of their own merit, but because of Job's intercession. Job is restored to his former position and receives double all his previous possessions (42:9, 10).

There is a subtle irony at this point which was surely not missed by the ancient Hebrew reader. When Job was in the lowest depths of misery, Eliphaz had loftily assured him that if he, Job, would repent of his sins he would be restored to God's favor and would even be able to rescue evildoers through his own merit:

> Put yourself in harmony with Him and make peace,
> And thus you will attain to well-being.
> If you return to the Almighty, you will be rebuilt;
> If you remove iniquity from your tent
> . . . God will be your true gold,
> And your real treasure of silver.
> When you issue a decree it will be fulfilled for you,
> And light will shine upon your ways.
> When men are brought low you will say, "Rise up,"
> And he who has been humbled will be saved.
> Even the guilty will escape punishment,
> Escaping through the purity of your hands.[45]
>
> [Job 22:21 ff.]

Eliphaz' prognostication has been fulfilled, but not quite as he expected, for it is he and his friends who are now dependent upon Job's righteousness.[46] At this point the connecting passage ends and the epilogue takes up the strands of the original folk tale, describing Job's restoration.

Our present text preserves convincing evidence that the jointures in the prologue and the epilogue emanate from the poet. With regard to the jointure in the epilogue, it is easily apparent that 42:10 is distinct in origin from 42:11. The two verses read as follows:

> Then the Lord restored the fortunes of Job, when he had interceded for his friends; and the Lord doubled all of Job's possessions.

> Then there came to him all his brothers and sisters and all his former friends, and they ate food with him in his house, commiserating with him and consoling him for all the suffering that the Lord had brought upon him. Each man also gave him a piece of money and a golden ring.

Read consecutively, as they appear in the present text, the two verses are redundant, anticlimactic, and even contradictory. After Job has been restored to his previous estate and indeed been given everything in double measure, there is no point in his relatives coming to comfort him and give him a small coin to help restore his fortunes! Moreover, the theme of Job's being granted double all his previous possessions is spelled out in detail a few verses later.[47] It is therefore clear that the first verse belongs to the poet's jointure and the second to the original folk tale narrative.

With regard to the jointure in the prologue, the evidence is not as conclusive, but it is highly suggestive, nonetheless. It is noteworthy that the original continuation of the tale, "And *all his brothers and sisters and all his former friends came* and ate bread with him in his home and *commiserated with him and consoled him* for all the trouble the Lord brought upon him" (42:11), bears a striking resemblance both in theme and language to the first link inserted by the poet, "And Job's friends heard of the trouble that had come upon him and they came each man from his place, Eliphaz the Temanite, Bildad the Shuhite, and Zophar the Naamathite, and *they met together to come and commiserate with him and to console him* (2:11).

The closing jointure being completed, there follows the conclusion of the original framework tale. His kinsfolk and friends help to re-establish him by giving him gifts. The Lord grants Job double the number of cattle, camels, and asses he had originally owned, as a compensation for his suffering. In lieu of the seven sons Job lost, he is given fourteen.[48] In characteristic Semitic fashion, however, the narrative does not double the number of his daughters! What is added is that the three daughters now born to him are outstanding in beauty, a trait to which few men have ever been indifferent. After his trial Job lives one hundred and forty years, double the usual life span of three score and ten. He lives long enough to behold not two but four generations of his descendants, dying old and satisfied with life.

Thus an ancient and familiar tale, retold by a great literary craftsman and profound thinker, provides a superb framework for a poem that passionately protests against human suffering and boldly seeks to grapple with the mystery of evil.

VII

Job and His Friends:
The First Two Rounds

WITH THE ARRIVAL of the Friends—Eliphaz, Bildad, and Zophar—the stage is set for the great debate. But not quite yet. The tragic transformation of their respected friend, now seated on the ash heap, wasted by disease and bereft of family and wealth, robs them of speech. For seven days and nights they sit with him like mourners on the ground and utter no word.

Then Job begins a lament, cursing the day of his birth. It is not addressed to the Friends, of whose presence he is scarcely conscious. Job delivers a soliloquy, an apostrophe to a cruel fate that has ordained that he must live. Why had he been conceived in his mother's womb and come forth into the world? How much better for him had he died at birth and slept with the princes of the earth. Even the lot of a stillborn baby who received no formal burial would be preferable to his misery, for in the world of the dead the wicked cease from troubling and the victims of injustice are at peace. Death levels all, the great and the small, free man and slave alike. Job has thus far uttered no complaint against his Maker, limiting himself to a description of the peace that would have waited for him in the grave (chap. 3).

As Job subsides into silence the Friends begin to speak. Readers have different impressions of the personalities of the three friends and their approaches to the issue at hand. Thus, Sir Arthur Quiller-Couch declares, "I find Eliphaz more of a personage than the other two; grander in the volume of the mind, securer in wisdom; as I find Zophar rather noticeably a mean-minded greybeard, and Bildad a man of the stand-no-nonsense kind."[1] H. Wheeler Robinson, on the other hand, sees in Eliphaz a mystical temperament[2]—a view that is unconvincing. It is true that Eliphaz describes at length a direct communication from on high.[3] Yet the content of his revelation—that all men are imperfect vis-à-vis God—does not transcend the canons of reason or contradict the evidence of experience. It is authentic Wisdom teaching.

The poet makes no effort to delineate the individual personality traits of the three friends. Undoubtedly Eliphaz, the most dignified and urbane of the Friends, is the profoundest spirit among them; his intense religious convictions have not robbed him of sympathy for the distraught and suffering Job. Bildad is a traditionalist who contributes little more to the discussion than a restatement of accepted views. Zophar, probably the youngest, possesses the brashness and dogmatism associated with youth. He is not deterred from drawing the most extreme conclusions about Job's real character if they seem to him to be called for by his theological attitudes. He never lets facts interfere with his theories.

Eliphaz, presumably the oldest and most respected of the three, is the first to respond (chaps. 4, 5). His sole purpose is to bring a measure of comfort to his sorely afflicted friend. It develops into the first cycle of the dialogue only because Job responds. Each of the other friends then feels called upon to speak; as a result, Job is goaded into replying again and again.

At the outset Eliphaz tactfully reminds Job how often he himself has sought to console men in their suffering by reminding them of the truth—universally accepted by all good men—that justice prevails in God's world, that therefore no innocent man is ever destroyed, and that those who sow iniquity inevitably reap its fruit. It is noteworthy that the author, whose sympathies are clearly on Job's side,[4] nevertheless gives the fullest and fairest presentation of the conventional theology to be found anywhere, in the Bible or without it.

Because the doctrine of reward and punishment seems to run counter to much of human experience, Eliphaz does not content himself with setting it forth in bald form but makes a few highly significant additions to its content. There may be some delay in the law of retribution, he says, but those who plough evil and sow iniquity are sure to reap a baneful harvest. Often the sinner's just penalty is visited upon his children. This argument, frequently repeated during the debate, was felt to be decisive, because it was highly congenial to the ancient concept of the solidarity of the family. Eliphaz then describes a vision from on high which has disclosed to him the basic truth that all men are imperfect, so that not even the righteous may justly complain if he suffers. Moreover, God is not responsible for sin and the suffering it brings in its wake, for it is a human creation (5:6, 7).

Eliphaz now intones two elaborate hymns. In the first he extols the goodness of God as manifested in the life-giving blessing of rain and in His power to destroy the cunning and to succor the distressed. Eliphaz then briefly notes that suffering often serves as a discipline— and hence it, too, is a mark of God's love (5:17). In the second hymn, Eliphaz describes the multitudinous calamities that can come upon men and declares that the righteous man is ultimately saved from them all, attaining peace and contentment at last. It therefore behooves Job to be patient and wait for his restoration.

Still weighed down by his misery, Job has scarcely heard Eliphaz' arguments. For all its urbanity, the address of Eliphaz contains the clear implication that Job must be a sinner, since suffering is the result of sin. Job lashes out in the bitterness of his soul, describing the misery which has befallen him and insisting that his lament is not without cause. He makes only one request of God—that He destroy him utterly —and ironically declares that he, who has never denied the words of the Holy One, deserves this consideration at the hands of his Maker (6:10). He then turns in fury upon his friends, who have failed him and betrayed him when he needed them most. He compares them to a *wadi*, a river bed in the East, which is weighed down by snow in the winter but evaporates in the summer heat, precisely when its life-giving waters are desperately needed by thirsty caravan travelers in the desert. He offers a pathetic picture of the brevity of human life and the misery that awaits man upon the earth, from which there is no refuge even in sleep, because of the nightmares which affright him. He pleads with God:

> I loathe my life; I shall not live forever.
> Let me alone, for my days are but a breath.
>
> [Job 7:16]

The psalmist had gloried in the paradox that man, who is physically insignificant, is yet worthy of God's care:

> When I consider Your heavens, the work of Your fingers,
> The moon and the stars, which You have ordained;
> What is man, that You are mindful of him?
> And the son of man, that You visit him?
> For You have made him little lower than the angels,
> And have crowned him with glory and honour.
>
> [Ps. 8:3–5]

The divine concern for man, which calls forth the psalmist's gratitude, elicits a bitter parody from Job:

> What is man that You exalt him
> And You give him Your attention,
> That you visit him each morning,
> And You test him every moment?
>
> [Job 7:17, 18]

Thus Job raises a question that is never answered, "Why is man important to God?" Indeed, the question is unanswerable—except by the faith that it is the will of God, whose desire it was to fashion at least one creature in His image, endowed with intelligence, freedom, and responsibility. Job does not claim to be perfect; he insists only that he is not a willful sinner and should not have been tormented for his failings. He asks to be forgiven, and as the sign of that forgiveness pleads for his total annihilation (chaps. 6, 7).

Job's attack upon his friends, his vivid description of his physical pain and mental anguish, and his indignant rejection of the accepted religious teaching expounded by the Friends serve to convince them all the more that he is a sinner. For is it not the height of impiety for a man arrogantly to proclaim his innocence before God, and thus assume, at least by implication, his right and capacity to pass judgment on his Maker?

Bildad now enters the discussion by restating some of the ideas of conventional theology, with a few modifications designed to meet some of the objections raised against it. God is just—that is fundamental—and therefore the trials of Job will surely prove temporary. He adds that the retribution of the wicked may require more than one generation to work itself out. As for the fact that Job's children have perished, they must surely have been guilty of wrongdoing. Job has only to beg for God's mercy and all will be well with him. Bildad paints a vivid picture of the destruction of the wicked and the ultimate restoration of the righteous. The house of the sinner is like a spider's web, while the righteous man is like a hardy plant that can even break through rocks to reach the sun, or if need be can be transplanted to better surroundings (8:14–18). It is crystal-clear to Bildad that "God does not despise the upright nor does He uphold the hands of the sinners." Job has only to be patient and joy will return to his heart (chap. 8).

Job now takes up the argument in earnest (chaps. 9–10). He does not deny God's power—it is His justice that he calls into question. Job proceeds to imitate Eliphaz' earlier hymn of praise to the might of God, but with a significant difference which is nonetheless powerful for being implicit. Job declares that it is God who moves mountains, causes the earth to tremble, commands the sun to cease from shining, and seals up the stars—all, be it noted, negative manifestations of the divine power. Weak as Job is, he insists upon confronting his divine opponent, although he knows full well that God can twist the very words in his mouth, so that even if he wash himself in snow he will be dipped into the blackest pit. Having lost everything, Job has nothing more to lose, and so he charges God with cosmic injustice:

> It is all one—I say—
> The blameless and the wicked He destroys alike.
> When disaster brings sudden death
> He mocks the plea of the innocent.
> The land is given over to the hand of the evildoer
> Who is able to bribe the judges.
> If not He, who then is guilty?
>
> [9:22–24]

Then comes one of the lightning changes of mood in which the passionate and pathetic nature of Job reveals itself. Increasingly, he has become convinced that his friends have not only maligned him but have traduced the true God, who must surely love righteousness. Job therefore expresses the desire for some impartial arbiter to decide between him and the heartless power that has tormented him (9:32–35).[5] Job's rebelliousness now turns to entreaty. Cannot God, eternal and

ll-knowing, judge more wisely than man? God knows him thorough-
y, having created him. Surely He can have pity on the work of His
own hands.

Zophar, least discreet of the Friends, has been goaded into indigna-
ion by Job's protest. He denounces Job's boasting and urges him to
repent his secret sins. That he must be a secret sinner is clear to Zophar,
not only from Job's recalcitrance, but on deeper grounds. Zophar is
acutely conscious that the world itself is a mystery beyond man's ken
and equally certain that God's justice is unassailable. He too promises
that if Job repents and avoids sinning in the future he will be restored to
well-being.

Job's closing response is the longest and most moving of his speeches
in the first cycle (chaps. 12–14). The opening section of his response
(chap. 12) has long been misunderstood because of the failure to
recognize several stylistic traits characteristic of Wisdom literature
generally and of Job in particular. As a result, many commentators
have excised substantial sections of the chapter, some leaving intact
only three or four verses out of the twenty-five in the present text.
This extensive deletion not only destroys the integrity of the text, but
robs the book of a great deal of its color and strength.

The key to the chapter lies in a recognition of Job's penchant for
irony and his varied use of quotations. He begins by mocking the
Friends' claim to a monopoly on truth (12:2, 3). In their security and
ease they can afford to indulge in artificial arguments far removed
from the painful realities of life: no wonder they look with contempt
on the sufferings of their fellow men (vss. 4, 5). Then follows Job's
recapitulation of the Friends' position as he sees it. They have to admit
the prosperity of the wicked (vs. 6) and therefore seek, in effect, to
deflect Job's attention elsewhere by calling on him to admire God's
perfection as reflected in the natural order (vss. 7, 8; cf. 5:9 ff.;
11:7 ff.).

In these verses (7 and 8) Job uses the second person singular instead
of the plural form that we would have expected if he were addressing
his three hearers.[6] Actually, he is citing—and lampooning—the kinds
of speeches addressed to him by the Friends. Job meets their attempt
to sidetrack his argument by replying that there is nothing new in the
idea that God has boundless power (vss. 9, 10). He then proceeds to
quote some familiar proverbs that seem irrelevant to the argument (vss.
12, 13), but are, in fact, adduced to disprove the comfortable conten-

tion of the Friends that all truth and wisdom are with the aged. Job insists that he can portray God's might far more effectively than the Friends and proceeds to demonstrate it in a paean of his own (vss. 11–25).

This passage is frequently excised by commentators as an interpolation. Aside from the violence done the text, this procedure suggests a misunderstanding of the essential character of the section. The passage differs significantly from the conventional descriptions of the greatness of God that are found in the words of the Friends (5:9 ff.; 25:2–6; 26:6–14).[7] They stress the beneficent and creative functioning of the Almighty as revealed in the gift of rain (5:10), the discomfiture of the wicked (5:12 ff.), the glories of the heavens (26:2–3), and the process of creation (26:5 ff.).

Job's description of the power of God (12:11–25, as in 9:4 ff.) is radically different in tenor. He emphasizes the negative and destructive manifestations of the divine power: God moves the mountains, makes the earth tremble, and shuts up the sun and stars so that they give no light (9:5 ff.). God destroys beyond rebuilding and imprisons men so that they cannot escape. He withholds water to cause drought and pours it forth to cause inundations. Nations are exalted only to be destroyed (12:14, 15, 23). Judges are made fools, the power of kings is broken, and priests are stripped naked; all the mighty are brought low (vss. 16–21). It is significant that the poet treats the overthrow of the power of the upper classes as similar to calamities of nature, seeing them both as manifestations of the destructive might of God. This fact sheds important light on the social orientation of Wisdom literature.[8]

Having concluded his sardonic hymn of praise to God, Job declares that he knows all this as well as his friends, being not inferior to them in wisdom (13:1, 2). Yet he still insists on confronting the Almighty (13:3). A translation of the salient sections of this passage (12:4–13:3) will demonstrate its unity and power and clarify the progression of thought:

> I have become a mockery to God's friend
> Who calls to Him and is answered—
> A mockery to the perfect saint!
> The unfortunate deserve only contempt
> In the opinion of the safe and secure—
> A beating is proper for those who stumble!

You admit,
"The tents of robbers are at peace,
The dwellings of those who provoke God,
Of those who have deceived Him."[9]
"But," *you say,*
"Ask the cattle to teach you,
And the fowl of the sky to tell you,
Or speak to the earth that it instruct you,
And let the fish of the sea declare to you."
Who does not know in all this,
That the hand of the Lord has made it,[10]
In whose hand is the life of every living thing
And the breath of all human kind!
Surely the ear tests words
As the palate tastes food!
You say,
"With the aged is wisdom,
In length of days is understanding."
But I say,
"With God is wisdom and strength,
His are counsel and understanding."
Behold, He destroys and it cannot be rebuilt,
He imprisons a man and he is not released.
He shuts up the waters and they dry up,
Or He sends them forth and they overwhelm the earth.
With Him are strength and sound counsel;
The misled and the misleaders—all are His.
He leads counselors away stripped,
And of judges He makes fools.
He opens the belt of kings
And removes the girdle from their loins.
He leads priests away stripped
And the mighty ones He confuses.
He deprives counselors of speech
And removes the discernment of the elders.
He pours contempt on princes,
And looses the girdle of the strong.
Behold, all this my eye has seen;
My ear has heard and understood it.
What you know, I know too;
I am not inferior to you.
But I wish to speak to the Almighty;
I desire to argue my case with God.

The failure of the Friends to come to grips with the basic problem arouses Job's indignation. He feels contempt for their effort to defend God by falsehood, being convinced that their defense, dishonest and biased as it is, is not calculated to win His favor. Instead of looking to them, Job flees from God to God, believing that beyond the God of power stands the God of righteousness, and behind the painful reality of the present, the glorious ideal, which will be vindicated in the future:

> Is it for the sake of God that you speak falsehood,
> On His behalf that you utter lies?
> Will you show partiality toward Him;
> Is it for God that you are arguing?
> Will He declare you in the right,
> If you show partiality to one side?
> Will not His majesty affright you
> And His awe fall upon you?
>
> [13:7, 8, 10, 11]

With the Friends unable to understand him and God unwilling to meet him, what use is there in Job's speaking? He must, however, speak out for the sake of truth:

> Yes, He may slay me; I have no hope,
> But I will justify my ways to His face!
>
> [13:15]

From this defiance Job turns again to entreaty, pleading for God's answer and for pity, "for man who is born of woman is brief of days and filled with sorrow." He asks a little peace before he completes his brief career on earth.

The thought of death suggests to Job the hope of a resurrection, an idea already prevalent in many Jewish circles in the poet's day. A tree, he muses, when it grows old may indeed be transplanted and renew its youth. If man only possessed the same attribute, it would perhaps be worth enduring the pain of the present in the hope of a happier future. But like Koheleth, the poet finds himself unable to accept this nascent faith. Sorrowfully he rejects the possibility. Death comes to all, knowledge and sentience die, and man's career of agony ends in nothingness:

As waters wear away stones
And a torrent washes away the earth's soil,
So do You destroy man's hope.
You seize him, and he departs forever;
You change his countenance, and send him off.

[14:19, 20]

Throughout their history the Hebrews had a preoccupation—an obsession, if you will—with children, whom they saw as the indispensable instruments of immortality.[11] It is characteristic that for Job the ultimate pathos of death lies in the fact that he will no longer be able to share either the joys or the sorrows of his offspring:

His sons may grow great, but he will never know it,
Or they may be humbled, but he will be unaware of it.
Yet his flesh will be pained within him
And his spirit will be in mourning.

[14:21, 22]

Thus the cycle ends as it began, not in debate, but in mournful contemplation of man's fate: life is sad and death ends all.

The second cycle (chaps. 15–21) does not represent a genuine progression of thought,[12] but is essentially a more passionate restatement of the same points previously expressed. Efforts have often been made to rearrange the material so that a logical development of ideas will emerge (in terms of Western logic),[13] or to eliminate substantial blocks on the grounds that they are "irrelevant" to the context or out of keeping with the temper of the passage.[14] These proposals betray a lack of insight into the lyrical character of the book and the lightning-like changes of theme and mood that are characteristic of ancient Semitic poetry in general and of Hebrew literature in particular.

Eliphaz reminds Job that it is impious to attack the justice of God from the vantage point of a human life, which is brief and inconsequential. This is all the more true since Job is young—a fatal defect to the oriental mind—and thus lacks the maturity which comes with age. Eliphaz proceeds to overcome this deficiency by reminding him of the wisdom and experience of the generations gone by. He emphasizes the belief that after a temporary period of prosperity the wicked will meet their ultimate destruction, whether in their own person or in that of their offspring. Eliphaz then adds one new and significant note.

Even during the period of his ostensible prosperity the sinner lives in trepidation, never knowing when the blow will fall. His psychological punishment begins long before his physical doom (15:20–22).

Job does not dignify these contentions by trying to refute them. Instead, he pictures again his misery and calls upon the earth not to hide his suffering. He does not hesitate now to picture God as a foe, a warrior rushing out to annihilate him on the battlefield.

Communication between Job and his friends has now all but disappeared. Their concept of God is meaningless for him. He proceeds to discover a new faith—forged in the crucible of his undeserved suffering, a faith as unshakable as his knowledge of his own innocence—the conviction that behind the cruel injustice of man's suffering a just order must exist in the world. He can find no sympathy or understanding among his erstwhile friends. Somewhere there must be, there *is*, a witness on his behalf:

> O earth, cover not my blood;
> Let my cry have no resting-place.
> Behold, even now, my witness is in heaven,
> And He who vouches for me is on high.
> Are my friends my intercessors?
> No, to God my eye pours out its tears,
> That He judge between a man and God,
> As between one man and his fellow.
>
> [16:18–21]

Out of his anguish Job makes another basic contribution to high religion. He insists that, though his unjustified suffering must arouse universal pity, righteous men will not be deflected from the good life by the spectacle of his undeserved misery. Thus Job boldly cuts the nexus in utilitarian morality between virtue and prosperity, making righteousness its own justification:

> Upright men will be horrified at this,
> And the innocent will rise up against the godless.
> But the just will hold fast to his way,
> And he who has clean hands will increase his strength.
>
> [17:8, 9]

Bildad's second address (chap. 18) describes at length the destruction of the wicked, the collapse of his home, and the blotting out of his very memory among men as a result of the death of his descendants. This time he has no word of comfort or even of admonition for Job.

In his reply Job declares that his friends, far from comforting him, have added to his misery by seeking to justify the shame that has come upon him. After describing the marks of God's hostility, he declares that his kinsfolk are estranged from him, the servants in his household despise him, his wife and children are alien, and the very children on the street malign him. Alone in the world, with neither God nor man on his side, he calls once again to his friends for mercy, although he expects nothing from them:

> Have pity on me, O my friends, have pity,
> For the hand of God has struck me.
> Why do you persecute me like God
> And are not satisfied with my flesh?
>
> [19:21, 22]

Now Job undergoes a complete transformation of mood, the most striking in the book, although not the only one. This sudden and drastic change of temper, which leaves the logician helpless, is entirely credible psychologically. From the depths of despair Job soars to the height of faith. Twice before he has stood poised on the brink—ready to deny life and its Giver—but each time he recoiled from the abyss and found his way to a stronger affirmation of life's meaning. In his torrential outpouring of speech we find not a systematic development of thought but an upward-sweeping spiral of feeling. Job's soul is an ocean, surging with the flow and ebb of the tide—each wave of faith rushes in on the strand and then falls back under the impact of his loneliness and pain. Then a new and more powerful breaker roars in further upon the shore, until it too recedes with the tide.

In his first round, Job expresses a longing for an arbiter (*mōkkiaḥ*) who might judge between him and his Adversary (9:32–33). In the second outpouring of faith, that wish becomes a firm conviction that there already stands a witness (*ʿēdh*) in the heavens ready to testify on his behalf (16:19). Now Job reaches the peak of his faith. In a moment of mystical ecstasy he sees his vindication: a redeemer who will not merely speak but will act to avenge his suffering (19:25). The term he uses, *gōʾel*, means a kinsman, a blood-avenger, who in early Hebrew law was duty-bound to see that justice was done to his injured brother.[15]

Who is this redeemer to whose appearance, however delayed, Job looks forward? Some commentators have suggested that this is an independent "mysterious figure," not further identified, who has the power to summon God and Job to judgment and to vindicate Job.[16] Such an interpretation of the thought of a biblical writer is impossible; the idea that there could be a being more powerful than God would be more than blasphemy to a Hebrew thinker—it would be the ultimate absurdity.

Job cannot conceive of life in an immoral universe, and so behind the present manifestation of God's power he sees the future revelation of God's justice. In all of Job's speeches two themes have been heard setting one another off, like point counterpoint. Again and again Job has attacked the God of power,[17] but with equal frequency he has appealed to the God of justice and love.[18] Now the two themes are united in a great climax as Job appeals "from God to God."

In this connection, some interpreters who have sensed the spirit of Job's affirmation have cited Tennyson's poem "Despair":

> Ah, yet—I have had some glimmer, at times, in my gloomiest woe,
> Of a God behind all—after all—the great God, for aught that I know;
> But the God of love and of hell together—they cannot be thought,
> If there be such a God, may the Great God curse him and bring him to nought.

The parallel is not at all adequate. For the English poet, as the title and last two lines indicate, the final mood is that of despair because the two aspects of life remain distinct and irreconcilable: the Gods are two, not one. The Hebrew poet, on the contrary, voices his unshakable faith in Job's rectitude and in his ultimate vindication, because the universe is governed by a God who is one.

Far closer to Job than Tennyson is the great eleventh-century Hebrew poet, Solomon ibn Gabirol, who preserved the spirit as well as the language of Job:

> Therefore though You slay me, I will trust in You.
> For if You pursue my iniquity,
> I will flee from You to Yourself,

And I will shelter myself from Your wrath in Your shadow,
And to the skirts of Your mercies I will lay hold
Until You have mercy on me,
And I will not let You go till You bless me.[19]

There are inherent difficulties in communicating a mystic vision such as Job now experiences. These are aggravated by grave problems in the text of this famous passage.[20] I believe these verses should be rendered as follows:

Oh that my words were now written;
Oh that they were inscribed on a monument,
That with an iron pen and lead
They were hewn in the rock for ever!
For I know that my Redeemer lives,
Though He be the last to arise upon earth!
Deep in my skin this has been marked,
And in my very flesh do I see God.
I myself behold Him,
With my own eyes I see Him, not with another's—

[19:23–27a, b]

But the momentary vision of God flees; Job falls back into the tragic world of reality: "My heart is consumed with longing within me!" (19:27c).

Similarly, the modern Jewish saint, Rabbi Abraham Isaac Kuk, has sought to describe the ecstasy of the experience of "the nearness of God," which extends beyond "the walls of deed, logic, ethics and laws." But exaltation is followed by depression as the mystic sinks back "into the gray and tasteless world of conflict, contradiction and doubt."[21]

Zophar begins his second address declaring that he has been aggrieved by Job's words. He describes the calamity which awaits the sinner. At the very peak of his well-being he is plunged into disaster, so that his place knows him no more and his offspring must appease the poor and return his ill-gotten gains. The evil that he had cherished like a sweetmeat under his tongue will now poison him, and he will vomit forth all that he had swallowed. For this is the law of the universe:

The heavens will reveal his sin
And the earth will rise up against him.
This is the sinner's portion from God,
And the evildoer's inheritance from God.

[20:27, 29]

Unsympathetic and unfeeling as Zophar appears, it is worth remembering that, by their lights, he and his colleagues are performing a vital task: they are defending man's faith in a moral universe, a world governed by the principle of justice, which is not merely a deep desire of the human soul but an indispensable instrument of social control.[22]

The second cycle is concluded by Job with a powerful refutation of the Friends' arguments. As against the comfortable doctrine that the wicked are ultimately destroyed, Job paints a more realistic picture of the malefactors enjoying happiness and security during their lifetimes and dying quickly without pain. In this, the closing address of the second cycle, Job once more cites the Friends' arguments and then proceeds to refute them. The failure to recognize this stylistic trait has again led to widespread deletions and emendations of the text, all of which are unnecessary; one only needs to add the quotation marks or introductory formulas of speech to find the meaning and the connection crystal-clear.

With great vigor, Job attacks the contention that the sinner will ultimately be punished, or, if not he, that his children will pay the penalty. He himself should be brought to book—and immediately. As for the argument that God is beyond man's comprehension, Job does not dispute it, but he subtly undermines its relevance. He calls attention to the disparity between the lot of the righteous man whose days are embittered by trouble, and the destiny of the sinner, who enjoys life to the full. Awaiting them both at the end is the same silent death. As for the Friends' insistence that the house of the wicked will be suddenly destroyed, Job sarcastically invites his friends to ask any passer-by to point out the proud mansions of the evildoers. Far from coming to an ignominious end, the wealthy malefactor caps his career with an elaborate funeral! Koheleth also was revolted by the fact that at their funerals sinners are praised instead of being unmasked: even in the moment of truth, there is no truth!

Indeed, I have seen the wicked being borne to their graves
and men return from the sacred place, and they are praised
in the city where they had so acted. Indeed, this is vanity.[23]

[Eccles. 8:10]

Job's recapitulation of the Friends' position and his own refutation is
as follows:

> Their houses are safe from fear,
> And no rod of God comes upon them.
> Their bull genders, and does not fail;
> Their cow calves, and does not lose her young.
> They send forth their youngsters like a flock,
> And their children go dancing.
> They sing to the timbrel and harp
> And make merry to the sound of the pipe.
> They spend their days in well-being
> And in peace they go down to Sheol.
> Yet they say to God, "Depart from us.
> We do not wish to know Your ways.
> What is the Almighty that we should serve Him?
> And what shall we gain if we pray to Him?
> Indeed, our prosperity is not in His hands!"
> Far be from me the counsel of the wicked!
> How often do the sinners' lamps go out
> And calamity come upon them
> As He metes out punishment in His anger,
> That they become like stubble before the wind,
> Like chaff which the storm has swept away?
> *You say,*
> "God saves his punishment for his children"—
> Let Him recompense *him*, that *he* may know it!
> Let his own eyes see his destruction,
> And he himself drink of the Almighty's wrath.
> For what concern has he for his house afterwards,
> After the number of his months is cut off?
> *You ask,*
> "Shall anyone teach God knowledge,
> Seeing that He judges those on high?"[24]
> One man dies in the fullness of strength,
> Wholly at ease and secure
> With his limbs full of milk
> And the marrow of his bones being moist;

And another dies in bitterness of soul,
Never having tasted of joy.
Alike they lie down in the dust,
And the worm covers them both.
Behold, I know your thoughts
And the schemes you plot against me.
If you say, "Where is the house of the nobleman,
And where is the dwelling of the wicked?"
Why not ask the passers-by—
You cannot deny their evidence!
You declare,
"The sinner is being saved for the day of calamity;
He will be led to his doom on the day of wrath."
But who will denounce his way to his face,
And for what he has done—who will requite *him?*
But in fact, he is borne in pomp to the grave,
And men keep watch over his tomb.
The clods of the valley are sweet to him;
And all men follow his bier,
And before him marches an innumerable host.
How then do you comfort me with empty words,
While your answers are nothing but falsehood?

[21:9–34]

The Friends have sought to comfort Job and, failing that, to confute him by calling upon the inspiration of vision, the teaching of tradition, and the testimony of human experience. Far from convinced, Job has been confirmed in his position: he has his own vision of a just God and consequently no respect for a tradition trafficking in comfortable illusions. His own bitter experience has opened his eyes to the reality of man's suffering in God's world. He stands fast in his demand for vindication from on high.

VIII

The End of the Debate: The Third Cycle

JOB HAS NOT BEEN SILENCED, nor have the Friends conceded defeat. The debate accordingly moves into the third cycle. Unfortunately, this section of the dialogue is in grave disorder and some of the original material has been lost, as is obvious from even a superficial examination of the text. Probably these sheets of the original manuscript of Job, or of an early transcript from which all other copies were made, suffered a physical accident. Some of the later pages in this section were evidently disarranged or mutilated, and succeeding scribes put the material together as well as they were able. Fortunately, the damage is not irreparable.

The cycle begins, quite in order, with Eliphaz' speech (chap. 22). Job's recalcitrance has finally goaded even the urbane Eliphaz to anger. He does not hesitate to accuse Job of heinous crimes against his fellow men—depriving the poor of food and water, oppressing the widow, and crushing the orphan.

Eliphaz proceeds to reveal the psychological motivation that he believes has led Job to become a sinner. Job is evidently convinced that God is too far off to be concerned with the actions of men, being separated from the earth by darkness, thick clouds, and immense distance.

In the ancient world, for both Oriental and Greek, atheism did not mean a denial of the existence of God—only the conviction that God or the gods were unconcerned with human activity.[1] This was the standpoint of Epicurus and other Greek skeptics, as well as the attitude of the "fool" whom the psalmist castigated:

> The fool says in his heart, "there is no God."
> They corrupt and contaminate their actions,
> Doing no good.
>
> [Ps. 14:1]

Against this denial of God's concern for His creatures, biblical faith insisted that God does care, scrutinizing man's actions, rewarding good and punishing evil:

> The Lord looked down from heaven
> Upon the children of men
> To see if there were any that did understand
> And sought God.
>
> [Ps. 14:2]

Job, Eliphaz says, belongs to the circle of these non-believers:

> "Indeed God is in the lofty heavens,
> And see the topmost stars, how high they are!"
> So you said,
> "What does God know?
> Can He judge through the thick cloud?
> Clouds cover Him, so that He cannot see
> As He strolls about the circuit of heaven."
>
> [Job 22:12–14]

Nonetheless, Eliphaz does not close without a word of comfort for his erring and sinful friend. He adds an additional facet to his defense of God's justice. As an exponent of the doctrine of group solidarity, Eliphaz, like the other two friends, emphasizes the traditional belief that God visits the sins of the fathers upon the children. According to this doctrine of "vertical responsibility," all generations of men are a unit, linked through time. Eliphaz now adds the less familiar but equally traditional concept of "horizontal responsibility" in space, uniting the destinies of all men in a given generation.

This unity operates both for good and for ill. Thus Joshua and his three thousand chosen soldiers sustain a crushing defeat at the hands of the inhabitants of the city of Ai because of the secret sin of Achan, who appropriated some of the sacred booty for himself (Josh. chap. 7). In King David's day, the entire people suffer a plague because of the monarch's sin in conducting a census (II Sam. 24:1 ff., 11 ff.). On the other hand, it is this interdependence of mankind which makes it possible for the saint, by his presence, to redeem his sinful contemporaries, as when Abraham sought to save Sodom for the sake of a righteous minority in the city (Gen. 18:17 ff.). It is this doctrine which the prophet Ezekiel cites—and rejects—when he declares that even the presence of the three righteous men (Noah, Daniel, and Job) in Jerusalem could not save it from destruction (14:14 ff.). Another case in point is Job's intercession for his friends in the prose epilogue (42:8, 10).

The doctrine never disappeared from post-biblical religion. Even after the idea of individual responsibility was accepted, it continued in the idea that a saint could set aside even God's decree, as in the talmudic utterance, "Said the Holy One, blessed be He, 'I rule over man, but who rules over Me? The saint, for when I issue a decree [gōzēr gᵉzērāh], he sets it aside.' "[2] The same idea persisted in the widespread Jewish folk belief in thirty-six saints whose lives glorify God's presence and preserve the world from ruin (lamed-vav ṣaddikim).[3]

It is from the standpoint of "horizontal," corporate responsibility that Eliphaz speaks. A righteous Job will not only be restored to personal safety (22:21, 23) and prosperity (22:25), he will also regain his great influence among men and with God. His mere word will suffice to save those humbled in society, and even the guilty will escape divine punishment because of Job's transcendent righteousness. Accordingly, Eliphaz promises Job that if he repents and makes his peace with God, he will be able to intercede for sinners and save them:

> When you issue a decree it will be fulfilled for you,
> And light will shine upon your ways.
> When men are brought low you will say, "Rise up,"
> And he who has been humbled will be saved.
> Even the guilty will escape punishment,
> Escaping through the purity of your hands.[4]

[22:28–30]

Job has scarcely heard, let alone been persuaded by Eliphaz' arguments
or by the considerably more heated and less illuminating speeches of
the other friends. His energies are all but sapped; he has no more
strength for argument. He can only repeat his fruitless wish to face
God directly:

> But I go to the east and He is not there;
> To the west, and do not perceive Him;
> To the north, where He is concealed, and I do not behold Him;
> He is hidden in the south, and I cannot see Him.
>
> [23:8–9]

Job wants only to find God, so that he may set forth his case without
fear and receive an answer without favor. God must surely know of
his basic innocence:

> But He knows the way that I have taken;
> If He tested me, I would emerge pure as gold.
> In His footsteps I have followed;
> His way I have kept without swerving.
> From His commandments I have not departed;
> In my bosom I have treasured the words of His mouth.[5]
>
> [23:10–12]

Then follows a difficult chapter in which two themes alternate with
one another: (1) a description of the ceaseless oppression by evildoers
of the poor and the weak; and (2) a picture of the misery of the oppressed who, driven from their homes, must search for food like beasts
in the wilderness.[6] The chapter ends with the challenge:

> If this is not so, who will prove that I lie,
> And show that my words are worthless?
>
> [24:25]

It is at this point that the structure of the third cycle breaks down.
In our present Masoretic text, Bildad makes a short speech of only
five verses, emphasizing the greatness of God and the corresponding
imperfection of men. However appropriate its substance, the response
seems far too brief. This observation is strengthened by the fact that
Job's reply in our text is much too long, extending over five chapters.
Because of the length of this section, an editor was led to add special

superscriptions to chapters 27 and 29: "And Job continued to proclaim his parable, saying. . . ."

The length of this passage assigned to Job (chaps. 26–31) is the least of the difficulties it poses. Much of it is inappropriate for Job; part of it is contradictory; and one section, chapter 28, is radically different in structure and form from the rest of the book. The facts may be set forth briefly. Most of chapter 26 is irrelevant to Job's position. The bulk of the chapter (vss. 5–14) describes the limitless power of God as revealed in creation; even Sheol, the realm of the dead, is naked before Him, and the very shades tremble in His presence. The poet speaks of God as crushing the monsters of the deep: *Yam*, god of the deep, *Rahab*, the sea-monster, and the "straight serpent," who, together with the "crooked serpent," are now known to us from Ugaritic literature. These were the adversaries of the creative god in primordial Semitic mythology.[7] In chapter 27 the difficulties are even greater. Here we encounter ideas which are thoroughly opposed to everything Job has so passionately maintained.[8] Verse 9, for example, doubts whether God hearkens to the cry of the wicked: "Will God hear his cry when trouble comes upon him?" In verses 14 to 17 the destruction of the wicked and the suffering of their children are described entirely in terms of the conventional doctrine which the Friends have been expounding and which Job has been attacking:

> If his children be multiplied, it is for the sword,
> And his offspring will lack for bread.
> Those who survive him will be buried by the plague,
> And his widows will not mourn for him.
> If he heaps up silver like dust,
> And stores up clothing like clay,
> He may store it up, but the just will wear it,
> And his silver, the innocent will divide.
>
> [27:14–17]

The next chapter (chap. 28) poses problems of its own. Finally, there is no reply at all for Zophar in our present text.

Virtually all students of the book agree on the diagnosis. Indeed, there is substantial agreement on the remedy, though not on the specific details. Many scholars have tried their hand at a solution by an independent division of the extant material among the participants—a procedure thoroughly justified in this case, in view of the obviously disorganized state of the text.[9]

My own restoration has the virtue of requiring a minimum amount of dislocation in the Masoretic text.[10] Following Job's address (chaps. 23–24), Bildad describes the power of God (25:1–6) in a speech which is completed by chapter 26, verses 5–14, so that he emerges with a substantial and thoroughly adequate address.

Job's response is almost surely incomplete. He upbraids his opponents for having given him neither strength nor wisdom in the face of his suffering (26:1–4). He then swears by God that his lips are free from falsehood and that he has remained steadfast in his righteousness (27:2–6).

The next passage (27:7–13) has proved a problem to the interpreters. Most scholars have felt that as it stands this avowal that evil will be punished is inappropriate for Job. On the other hand, these verses are couched in the first person (vs. 7), the hearers are addressed in the plural (vss. 11, 12), and the entire section is deeply emotional in spirit. It cannot, therefore, be integrated into the speeches of the Friends. The key to an understanding of this passage lies in recognizing that we have, once again, a virtual quotation without an external sign.[11] What Job expresses here is his original state of mind before the calamities befell him, a restatement of his earlier faith in the moral government of the world. The unity and power of the entire utterance are unmistakable:

> My righteousness I have held fast, and never let it go;
> My heart harbored no blasphemy all my days.
> For I said, "Let my enemy be in the wrong
> And my opponent be the evildoer,
> For what hope has the evildoer when God cuts him off,
> When God calls for his life?
> Will God hear his cry
> When trouble comes upon him?
> Is he free to implore the Almighty—[12]
> Can he call upon God at any time?"
> Let *me* teach you, speaking on God's behalf;[13]
> What He has in mind, *I* shall not deny.
>
> .   .   .   .
> .   .   .   .
> .   .   .   .
>
> Indeed, you have all seen this—
> Why then do you spew forth emptiness?
>
> [27:6–12]

What the missing portions of Job's reply contained, we can only speculate. Perhaps he pointed out how life's tragic experiences had stripped him of his illusions, but not of his rectitude or his devotion to the truth.

Then follows Zophar's third reply, only a fragment of which has been preserved in our text (27:13–23). He describes the calamities that are inevitable for the evildoer and his family. His ill-gotten wealth will go to the righteous, and terrors will overwhelm him even before he is swept away, as with a storm. Though we must regret the loss of much of Zophar's speech, it is unlikely that new and startling ideas were expressed in the missing section.

Job does not dignify this speech of Zophar's by a reply. The Friends and their arguments fade from his consciousness. He ends as he began, with a soliloquy, his last great utterance. At the outset, Job recalls the high estate of dignity and honor he once occupied and the universal esteem he once commanded. This condition he contrasts with the contempt now visited upon him by the lowest strata of society, "striplings whose fathers I despised to put with my sheep dogs." Alienation from his God, estrangement from his fellow men—that is his present situation:

> My lyre is turned to mourning
> And my flute to the sound of lamentation.
>
> [30:31]

Job sweeps on to a magnificent climax—his "Confession of Integrity." This classic statement may be described as the "code of the Jewish gentleman." It has never been surpassed in the religious literature of the world.[14] Job recounts his standard of personal morality with regard to women, his fair dealing with slaves, whose basic human equality he affirms, and his consideration for the poor, the widow, and the orphan. With the exception of a brief reference to the worship of heavenly bodies, the code is exclusively ethical and non-ritualistic in character.

It is significant in evaluating the character of Hebraic ethics that the fourteen offenses against which Job has guarded himself include several sins of the spirit, as well as overt acts against his fellows. Thus he has kept himself free from the arrogance that comes with wealth and from the vindictiveness that rejoices in the discomfiture of foes. Above all, he has not been ashamed to confess his errors for fear of the scorn of the mob. He has been upright without self-righteousness, self-respecting without conceit, humble without weakness. The integrity of his actions toward others has been matched by the inner probity of his soul.

The impact of this "Confession of Integrity" is heightened by the form in which it is couched. A series of rhetorical questions, in which Job denies any wrongdoing on his part, alternates with passionate oaths of clearance, in which he calls down condign punishment upon himself if he has really been guilty of a moral breach.[15]

Job brings his uncompromising affirmation of innocence to a close with a final call to God to come forth and answer his accusations:

> Oh that I had someone to hear me—
> Behold, this is my desire:
> That the Almighty answer me,
> And my opponent write out his indictment.
> Upon my shoulder I would carry it,
> And like a crown bind it upon me.
> An account of my steps I would give Him;
> Like a prince would I approach Him.
> The words of Job are ended.
>
> [31:35–37, 40]

Imbedded in this section attributed to Job is chapter 28, generally called the "Hymn to Wisdom." In it the poet pays tribute to Wisdom, the primal plan which God used to create the world and which is therefore a key to its true nature. As we have seen, Hokmah is personified by other Wisdom writers in Proverbs (8:22–32) and Ben Sira (1:1–10). Here, this supernal Wisdom is called *Hahokmah*, with the definite article, to distinguish it from *Hokmah*, its more mundane and practical counterpart.

That the "Hymn to Wisdom" in Job is an independent literary unit is clear on several counts: it is lyrical and not polemical in character; there is no indication of listeners or of antagonists surrounding the speaker. Moreover, the poem is a self-contained literary unit possessing a refrain:

> But Wisdom, where may she be found [or, "whence does she come"]
> And where is the place of Understanding?
>
> [28:12, 20]

The hymn begins with a description of the great technical skill and extraordinary effort men display in order to mine silver, gold, and precious stones. To achieve this goal they carry on operations in distant lands and in the wilderness, cutting channels through the rock, binding up streams, and revealing dark places. But the ultimate Wisdom cannot be found through human exertion. The refrain is then repeated and a new theme is introduced. Divine Wisdom cannot be acquired in exchange for gold or silver, for topaz or pearls, on which men have expended such boundless energy.

It may be an extension of the poet's thought (though perhaps not unwarranted) to see here a recognition of the ironic fact, fraught with so much peril today, that man's conquest of nature outstrips his mastery of himself, his technical knowledge being far ahead of his self-understanding. In Terrien's words, *"Homo faber is always one step ahead of homo sapiens!"*[16]

The poet then declares that the deep does not know where Wisdom lies; even death has heard only its echo. God alone understands its path and knows its place. What is available to man, therefore, is not transcendent Wisdom, the key to the universe and the meaning of life, but practical Wisdom (without the definite article), which expresses itself in piety and moral behavior. The Hymn therefore concludes:

> But Wisdom, whence does she come,
> And where is the place of Understanding?[17]
> For she is hidden from the eyes of all living things,
> Concealed even from the birds of the air.
> Abaddon and Death say,
> "We have heard only her echo."
> But God understands her way
> And He knows her place,
> For He looks to the ends of the earth
> And sees everything under the heaven.
> When He gave the wind its weight
> And meted out the waters by measure,
> When He made a law for the rain
> And a way for the thunderbolt,
> Then He saw Wisdom, and described her;
> He established her and searched her out.
> But to man He said,
> "To be in awe of the Lord—that is wisdom,
> And to avoid evil—that is understanding."

[28:20–28]

It is patent that the "Hymn to Wisdom," which in our present text is placed in the mouth of Job, is totally irrelevant to his concern. Nor is it to be assigned to Zophar.[18] It is true that Zophar in an earlier speech had stressed the thought that there are "secrets to wisdom" (11:6) and that God is beyond human understanding (11:7), but his purpose was neither subtle nor profound—he wished only to insist that Job was guilty of secret sins that were not hidden from God. The broad serene spirit of the "Hymn to Wisdom," quite aside from its lyrical form, is entirely inappropriate to the impetuous, hot-headed Zophar.

The theme of the poem, the overarching mystery of existence, of which the suffering of man is only one aspect, is essentially, as we shall see, the conclusion which emerges from the God speeches and constitutes the basic message of the book as a whole. Retaining it in the text at this point makes the rest of the book an anticlimax, while its form makes it impossible to insert it elsewhere in the text. Nevertheless, in the profundity of its thought, in the wide knowledge of human activities it displays, and in the beauty of its form, the "Hymn to Wisdom" is eminently worthy of the genius of the author of Job.[19]

Its position in our present text is therefore best explained by the assumption that it represents an early treatment in lyrical form of the basic theme with which the author was to be concerned throughout his life, and to which he was later to devote his masterpiece—the mystery of the universe and of man's suffering in it.

As we shall see in the next chapter, this preliminary and probably youthful effort, which preceded the composition of Job, has its parallel in his later writing on the same theme, which followed the completion of the book. This later material, which probably emanated from the poet's old age, was integrated into the book with substantial success. In the case of the "Hymn to Wisdom," its inappropriateness in the structure suggests that the author, whose architectonic gifts were of the highest order, did not himself include it in the book. As a product of the same poet's pen, the Hymn remained among the sheets containing the text of the Book of Job. When, by some scribal accident, the third cycle became gravely disarranged and a good part of the text lost, the sheet containing the "Hymn to Wisdom" was fortunately preserved and was placed by some scribe in the concluding cycle.

This lifelong preoccupation with a great theme has its parallels elsewhere. Goethe became interested in the Faust theme in early youth.

He wrote various Faust fragments, some of which he later incorporated into his great drama.[20] So, too, Wagner's music-drama, *Tristan and Isolde*, was preceded by the "Liebestod" and several independent *Gedichte*, published later. The creation of Job was the lifework of a great poet. The "Hymn to Wisdom," a minor gem in its own right, emanated from the poet's earlier period. Preserved for us by a fortunate accident, it was a harbinger of the greater masterpiece to come.

With the conclusion of the "third cycle," the Friends subside into silence and the words of Job are ended.

IX

Elihu the Intruder

IN HIS CONCLUDING WORDS at the end of the third cycle
Job calls on God to answer him. Reply comes from a totally unexpected quarter. A young man named Elihu, son of Barakhel, inter-
venes. In a long introduction he tries to justify his interruption. His
wrath has been kindled against Job for daring to assume a righteousness greater than God's. He is equally indignant with the Friends for
their failure to answer Job adequately. Elihu is conscious of his youth
and has therefore waited for the aged, who presumably possess the
wisdom needed for a reply, to finish their discourse; but he has come
to the conclusion that the mere passing of days is no guarantee of
insight:

> I thought, "Age should speak,
> And the years should teach wisdom,"
> But it is the spirit in a man,
> And the breath of the Almighty that gives understanding.
> Not always are old men wise;
> Or do the aged understand the truth.
>
> [Job 32:7–9]

Elihu's long brash apology may strike the modern reader as prolix.
It can only be understood against the background of ancient civilization, and Semitic society in particular, where age and wisdom were

quated and the young were expected to be respectful—and silent.[1]

In the next four chapters (33–36 inclusive) Elihu proceeds to unburden himself. He cites Job's three major contentions in order to refute them: (1) that he is innocent (33:8, 9); (2) that God's persecution is therefore an act of wanton power and injustice (33:10–11); and (3) that God has ignored his suffering by refusing to answer him (33:12–13).

In accordance with Semitic usage, Elihu proceeds to answer these arguments in reverse order.[2] In chapter 33, Elihu denies that God has a lack of concern for His creatures. Job has failed to note that God actually speaks to man in many ways. Through visions and dreams in the night God often seeks to turn man from evil and from the arrogance that all too commonly flows from the consciousness of virtue (33:14–18). If this mode of communication proves ineffective, God may use illness and pain as His instruments. When man is brought to the very threshold of death, his virtues redeem him. Once restored to youthful vigor and health he recognizes that he was indeed sinful and that the suffering he has undergone has chastened his spirit—that the discipline has saved him from perdition (33:19–28).

This is the heart of Elihu's position. He then proceeds to refute Job's other contentions. It is wrong, he avers, to deny God's justice. Actually God plays no favorites, for He is the Creator of all and is beholden to no one. God destroys the mighty in their wickedness (chap. 34). Man has only to observe the glories of nature in order to see evidence of the creative power of God. God is so exalted over man that it is laughable to imagine that man's actions affect Him for good or ill. Only men suffer from man's inhumanity and sin (chap. 35).

Elihu then proceeds to recapitulate his views (chap. 36). Through suffering, men are warned against sin. If they take the message to heart they are restored to well-being. If not, destruction, the inevitable consequence of sin, comes upon them. As Elihu speaks, the signs of a gathering storm are seen in the sky (36:27–33).[3] Elihu begins to describe the majesty of God as revealed in the tempest, and His power to use the rainstorm either as a rod of chastisement or an instrument of mercy (37:13). The squall passes and the sky is revealed in its golden glory. Although God's might cannot fully be grasped by man, it is certain that He will not afflict the just: the man who is righteous and wise will ultimately emerge out of the storms of adversity and pass into the light of God's favor (chap. 37).

The authenticity and relevance of the Elihu speeches have long

been subjects of contention in the study of the Book of Job. Th
Church Father, Gregory the Great (died c.e. 604), dismissed the Elih
chapters as being of little value. This view has been widely accepte
today with regard to both the content and the literary quality of th
speeches. It is fair to say that today most critical scholars regard ther
as a more or less clumsy effort at interpolation by a defender,[4] or b
several defenders,[5] of the orthodox religion of the time. Relativel
few scholars have defended the authenticity of the Elihu speeches,
and these often on contradictory or unconvincing grounds.

Before embarking on a detailed investigation of the evidence, w
may note the growing disfavor in which the atomization of ancien
literary documents is viewed by contemporary scholarship. Increas
ingly, the study of ancient literatures, like that of the Homeric epics
has been focusing attention on the unity and meaning of the whol
work rather than upon the disparity of the constituent elements. Tha
the indiscriminate (and even accidental) lumping together of scat
tered literary fragments by an obtuse redactor, who often did no
understand the material he was working with, could produce a mas
terpiece—that naïve faith of nineteenth-century literary critics is n
longer widely shared today.[7]

It is self-evident that this change of intellectual climate will, of it
self, not suffice to reverse the view of the inauthenticity of the Elih
chapters, still widely held among scholars. The impressive argument
in favor of this position need to be analyzed and evaluated.

Those who eliminate the Elihu chapters maintain that there are im
portant differences in language between them and the rest of the poeti
dialogue.[8] Thus a marked variation is noted in the use of divine names
Elihu uses the name *El* far more frequently than the other names
Eloah and *Shaddai*, while in the rest of the book they are used witl
almost equal frequency.[9] To a more marked degree than is the case
in the earlier portions of the poetic dialogue, Elihu prefers the shorter
form ɔ*anī* to ɔ*anōkhī* as the first person singular pronoun.[10] Elihu use
less frequently the longer, archaic forms of the prepositions[11] and
avoids the archaic forms of the enclitic particles ending in *mō*.[12] It has
also been claimed that Elihu's vocabulary differs, since he uses terms
like *dēʿa*, "opinion," *tāmīm*, "perfect," instead of *tām*, and *nōʿar*,
"youthfulness," instead of *neʿūrīm*.[13]

The style, too, offers several divergent features. Particularly noticeable is the higher concentration of Aramaisms in Elihu's speech.[14]

There are also a large number of highly obscure verses that give the impression of a very labored style.

The structure of the book has also been adduced to deny the authenticity of these chapters. There is no reference to Elihu in the prologue or the epilogue. While he refers to the Friends and cites their statements, they do not return the courtesy. He appears without warning and disappears without a trace. Moreover, Job in his last speech (31:35 ff.) appealed for God's answer. If Elihu were eliminated, such an answer would come directly in God's speech in chapter 38. Finally, and most crucially, it has been said that Elihu adds nothing significant to the argument and is therefore entirely superfluous.[15]

These contentions cannot be dismissed out of hand, but they are by no means conclusive. With regard to the argument concerning language, it should be noted that the alleged variations are relative rather than absolute. It is principally the proportions that have shifted, not the usage. This is true of the divine names, the pronouns, and the prepositional forms, all of which occur throughout the book. Any literary composition, particularly a short one, may turn up words lacking in another composition by the same author. The fact that Elihu cites arguments from the preceding speeches, far from being an argument against his authenticity,[16] is a point in his favor. Elsewhere we have called attention to the use of quotations as a basic element of biblical and Semitic rhetoric, particularly common in Wisdom literature and especially characteristic of Job's style. It is noteworthy that in each of Job's concluding addresses—at the end of the first cycle (chap. 12), at the end of the second cycle (chap. 21), and in his brief rejoinder after God's second speech (42:2–6)—he employs this same literary device. That Elihu does the same strengthens the view that his speeches come from the same author.[17]

Budde's original contention that Elihu's style is identical with that of the earlier dialogue is untenable, as he himself came to recognize later. It is important not to exaggerate either the variations or the similarities, both of which are genuine. The differences are not significant enough to justify the assumption of a different author (a view which is ruled out by other considerations as well). It should be added that the Elihu speeches seem to have suffered a higher degree of textual corruption than other sections of the book. This occurs in literary documents where part of the text has been more poorly preserved than the rest.[18] From the present state of the text it is clear that the middle portions of the book (now chaps. 24–37) sustained some major accidents in transmission, suffering far greater damage than either the opening or the closing sections. In the third cycle the material was gravely disarranged and an unknown number of verses was lost altogether. In the Elihu speeches, not a few lines became indistinct and unclear and then further corrupted by copyists.

Moreover, judgments as to the quality of style are notoriously subjective. S. R. Driver characterizes the style of the Elihu speeches as "prolix, laboured, and sometimes tautologous," and Buttenwieser calls the style "pompous and diffuse, with much empty repetition." Marshall, on the other hand, pronounces the Elihu speeches to be "on an immeasurably higher plane than the Dialogue," while Cornill declares, "In the entire range of Holy Writ there are few passages which in profundity of thought and loftiness of feeling can compare with the Elihu-speeches: in content they form the summit and crown of the Book of Job."[19] The latter judgments are probably too flattering, but they serve to counterbalance the all too prevalent view which denigrates the Elihu speeches.

The arguments concerning structure are also far from decisive. Elihu's absence in the prologue is not at all strange. That the dignified elders have taken no notice of him is entirely understandable from the Semitic viewpoint, since he is confessedly an interloper and a stripling to boot. The author obviously wishes us to conceive of Elihu as one of the anonymous group of interested bystanders, who might conceivably be permitted to listen to the deliberations of their elders but were certainly not expected to participate in the argument, let alone contradict those wiser than themselves. Elihu's absence from the epilogue, as will be indicated below, is also explicable in terms of the content of the book and the history of its composition.

It is true that if the Elihu speeches are eliminated the Lord appears immediately after Job's plea for His presence. However, from the very first cycle, Job has repeatedly asked God to enter into fair and open debate with him, thus offering him an opportunity for self-vindication (9:3, 14 ff., 32–35; 13:3, 15–23; 16:18–22; 19:24–27)—to no avail. On the contrary, the debate of the human protagonists continues for two more cycles with no intervention from God. There is therefore no reason to expect that Job's demand for God's reply in chapter 31 must be answered at once. Moreover, it should be noted that the closing portion of Elihu's speech (37:21–24), which describes the advent of a storm and its aftermath, provides an excellent prelude to the Lord's appearance out of the whirlwind.

The heart of the argument against the authenticity of the Elihu speeches lies in the content, in the contention that Elihu contributes nothing new or significant to the discussion. But this argument, if it were true, would be self-defeating, for it would raise the unanswerable question of why an interpolator took the trouble to compose the speeches at all.

Here again, Budde, seeking to defend the authenticity of the section, overstates the case. He argues that Elihu gives the author's main answer to the problem of suffering—that suffering is God's disciplinary measure designed to prevent men from sinning—an idea expressed by no one else.[20] The fact is, however, that suffering as a divine chastisement, the mark of God's love, has already been adumbrated by Eliphaz, though in only one verse (5:17). What is even more important, if this idea were the principal conclusion of the author, it is incomprehensible that he would have followed it by another section (the God speeches) which then necessarily becomes an anticlimax. As a matter of fact, everything points to the God speeches as the climax of the author's insight into life and its meaning. It is unlikely that the supremely gifted poet and thinker who wrote Job could seriously regard the disciplinary role of human suffering as an adequate explanation of the mystery of pain. He was surely too sensitive to the complexity of life and the depth of human misery to regard this as a sufficient answer. Budde's defense must be regarded as unconvincing.

Pfeiffer, on the other hand, explains the Elihu interpolations as the work of an orthodox reader who "was so shocked, after reading that Book of Job in its original form, that he felt the urge to write a refutation which he placed in the mouth of a character which he invented, Elihu. It is significant that Elihu's polemic is addressed not only against Job, whose position was decidedly heretical, but also against the friends and even, in a more subtle manner, against the speeches of Jehovah."[21]

It is true that Elihu attacks both the Friends and Job bluntly and aggressively. There is, however, no evidence whatsoever that he challenges the conclusion of the God speeches, either subtly or openly. Their standpoint is summarized by Pfeiffer, albeit too summarily, as maintaining that "God's ways are incomprehensible to man." Nowhere is this idea refuted by Elihu, who, on the contrary, emphasizes the fact that God is too exalted to be affected by human actions

(35:4–7) or to be understood by man (30:24 ff.; 37:14–20). It may also be pointed out that if the Elihu chapters were a refutation of the God speeches, they should have followed, not preceded them.

Finally, Pfeiffer begins with the critical assumption, frequently made in the past, that heterodox ideas were subjected to extensive interpolation to make them palatable to the orthodox. This once-popular assumption is highly questionable. As we have demonstrated elsewhere, this hypothesis is both unnecessary and erroneous with regard to the Book of Ecclesiastes.[22] In ancient times, a far more effective device was available for countering unorthodox doctrine: since manuscripts of any given work were few, it was easy to suppress the material completely. If copies of the book in question were consigned to the *Genizah*, the storehouse of abandoned documents, the work would be withdrawn from circulation and thus condemned to oblivion.

Virtually all the apocryphal and pseudepigraphical works of the Second Temple period, which were originally written in Hebrew or Aramaic, emanated from groups which differed in greater or lesser degree with normative or pharisaic Judaism in doctrine, practice, or both. The leaders of the dominant group in Judaism subjected these books, not to critical interpolation, but to total neglect. As a result the originals were lost and only translations into Greek, Latin, Syriac, Ethiopic, and other languages have survived. These versions were safeguarded, not by the Synagogue, but by the Church, which found them congenial to its outlook and useful in its work.

That ancient readers would employ large-scale interpolations to counter the main thrust of literary works to which they were opposed is a theory of doubtful validity and should be invoked only as a last resort. There is no proof whatever of any such intent in the Elihu speeches.

We are now in position to draw the conclusion to which all the evidence points. The style of the Elihu chapters is by no means totally different from the rest of the book, but it does exhibit variations. These are entirely explicable by the assumption that the Elihu section emanates from the same author writing at a later period in his life. Many readers have been struck by the greater difficulty and complexity of many passages in these chapters. More than one verse seems crabbed and overly concentrated in form, sometimes to the point of unintelligibility. This fact can also be explained by the theory that these chapters were written by the poet in his later years. The history of literature can point to many instances in which a writer's style grows increasingly complex and difficult with his advancing years. A classic example is afforded by Shakespeare's *Tempest* and by other plays of his last period. The later poems of William Butler Yeats, and James Joyce's last novel, *Finnegans Wake*, on which the novelist worked twenty years, reveal the same trait.

An even more instructive parallel is Goethe's *Faust*. The *Urfaust* goes back to the poet's *Sturm und Drang* period, the third decade of his life; the first part of *Faust* did not appear until more than thirty years later, in 1808; and the second part was completed shortly before his death in 1832. In the sixty-year gestation period of the work, Goethe's conception of his theme and of the characters, as well as his poetic style and vocabulary, underwent a profound transformation. Every reader notices at once the change from the epigrammatic style of Part I to the involved, complicated mode of expression characteristic of Part II. The radical differences in subject matter are summarized by J. G. Robertson in these words: "The Second Part is far removed from the impressive realism of the *Urfaust* or even the classicism of the First Part. It is a phantasmagory; a drama, the actors in which are not creatures of flesh and blood but shadows in an unreal world of allegory. The lover of Gretchen had, as far as poetic continuity is concerned, disappeared with the close of the first part. In the second part, it is virtually a new Faust who, accompanied by a new Mephistopheles, goes out into a world that is not ours. Yet behind the elusive allegories . . . there lies a philosophy of life, a ripe wisdom born of experience, such as no other modern European poet has given us."[23]

Equally worthy of a great poet's entire lifetime would be a masterpiece like the Book of Job, which, though less extensive in compass than *Faust*, is no less profound in theme, moving in spirit, or eloquent in form. In the case of Job, the new insights drawn from the poet's experience found expression in the Elihu chapters, which the poet inserted before the great climax of "the Words of the Lord."

The problems of structure are also solved by this theory that the Elihu speeches were added years after the bulk of the book had been written. As the framework for the great debate the poet utilized and retold the traditional folk tale of the righteous sufferer, Job, adding only the jointures between the prose and the poetry, in the prologue (2:11–13) and in the epilogue (42:7–10). The traditional folk tale was so familiar to its readers in every detail that any deviation would at once have been recognized and almost surely resented. Having written the prose framework in an earlier period, when the dialogue was composed, the poet would feel no need in later years (at the time of his maturity or in old age) to recast the text by inserting a reference to Elihu. Moreover, Elihu is not the object of the Lord's condemnation, as are the Friends, since his ideas are regarded by the poet as having a substantial measure of validity. Finally, and most important of all, Semitic writers were not concerned with a complete congruence of details when combining various traditions into one consecutive whole.[24]

As for the substance of the Elihu chapters, it is noteworthy that Elihu is at least as antagonistic to the Friends as he is to Job. Actually, he denies the truth of both positions—though only in part. The Friends have maintained that God is just and that therefore suffering is both the penalty and the proof of sin. Job has denied both contentions. He insists that his suffering is not the result of sin, and therefore he charges God with injustice. Elihu denies the conclusions of both Job and the Friends, declaring that although suffering may not be the penalty of sin, yet God's justice remains unassailable.

This distinctly "intermediate" position injected a virtually new idea which had been advanced in another form by Deutero-Isaiah, the anonymous prophet of the Exile. In his day, the people of Judah were in ignominious exile under the Babylonian Empire. This posed an agonizing problem: how was the misery and degradation of Israel to be explained? It could not be justified in terms of Israel's sin, for at its worst Israel was better than its pagan conqueror. Unless these tormenting doubts were met, the people would be plunged into a despair that would be the prelude to dissolution. A message of hope and courage was needed—for Israel's sake and for God's cause—for the members of this people, weak and imperfect as they were, remained "God's witnesses" (Isa. 43:10). A rabbinic comment spells out the implications of the Deutero-Isaianic metaphor: "Ye are My witnesses, saith the Lord. If ye are My witnesses, I am the Lord, but if ye are not My witnesses, I am not the Lord."[25] The prophet accordingly evolved the doctrine of the Suffering Servant of the Lord. Israel is not merely God's witness, but man's teacher, whose suffering at the hands of other nations is evidence of their moral immaturity. Her tribulations are destined to end when Israel's true greatness is recognized:

> Behold, My servant shall prosper,
> He shall be exalted and lifted up and shall be very high.
> Surely our diseases he did bear, and our pains he carried;
> Whereas we did esteem him stricken,

> Smitten of God, and afflicted.
> But he was wounded because of our transgressions,
> He was crushed because of our iniquities;
> The chastisement of our welfare was upon him,
> And with his stripes we were healed.
> Therefore will I divide him a portion among the great,
> And he shall divide the spoil with the mighty;
> Because he bared his soul unto death,
> And was numbered with the transgressors;
> Yet he bore the sin of many,
> And made intercession for the transgressors.

> [Isa. 52:13; 53:4, 5, 12]

Thus, for the first time, the prophet affirmed the possibility of national suffering that was not the consequence of national sin, but, on the contrary, an integral element in the process of the moral education of the human race. This insight of Deutero-Isaiah was not lost on the author of Job, who applies the doctrine of suffering as a discipline to the life of the individual. This is expressed by Eliphaz in one verse:

> Behold, happy is the man whom God reproves;
> Do not then despise the chastisement of the Almighty.

> [Job 5:17]

But the entire tenor of Eliphaz' address makes it clear that he is referring to suffering as a discipline for sins *already committed*.[26] His position was a familiar one in the conventional Wisdom literature, as, for example:

> The corrections of the Lord, my son, do not despise,
> And do not scorn His chastisement.
> For he whom the Lord loves He chastises
> And speaks with him,[27] as a father with his son.

> [Prov. 3:11, 12]

In any event, the theme is dismissed with this one verse in Eliphaz' discourse—proof-positive that at the time the passage was being written, the still young author was not particularly impressed with the idea as a key to the problem of evil.

Elihu goes substantially further—he sees suffering as a discipline and warning to the righteous, not only against sins both actual and patent, but against offenses potential and latent (33:16–30; 36:9–12). Above all, he calls attention to the sin of pride, the complacency of the virtuous, the *hybris* or arrogance of those conscious of their own rectitude, which are so often the prelude to wrongdoing. One may recall the comment of a modern Hasidic teacher, "Far better a sinner who knows he is a sinner than a saint who knows he is a saint." It was against this insidious threat to spiritual nobility, which Budde calls "the pet sin of the righteous," that Job in his prosperity had tried to guard, by offering sacrifices of atonement for his children, who might have "cursed God in their hearts" (1:5).

Suffering as a discipline is certainly not the whole answer to the problem of evil in God's world. But how could the idea be given its proper weight? Obviously the doctrine could not be placed in the speeches of the Friends, with whom the author is manifestly out of sympathy.[28] Nor could it be expressed by Job, who denies that there is any justification for the suffering of the righteous. Nor could it be included in the God speeches, where it would weaken the force of the main answer. By creating Elihu, who opposes the attitude of the Friends as well as that of Job, the author is able to express this secondary idea, giving it due place in his world view.

Job has contended that God avoids contact with man. On the contrary, Elihu insists, God does communicate with man through dreams and visions, and when these fail, through illness and suffering. This recognition of the uses of pain is the kind of mature insight that would come to a man through years of experience. For life teaches at every hand how insufferable are those who have never suffered. It is frustration and sorrow that are man's passports to fellowship and sympathy with his brothers.

A full treatment of the principal insight of the author of Job with regard to the mystery of suffering will be presented later.[29] A brief indication is, however, needed here, especially since it is implied rather than explicated.[30] The God speeches, by virtue of their vivid and joyous descriptions of nature, declare that the world is more than a mystery: it is a cosmos, a thing of beauty. Just as there are order and harmony in the natural world, so there are order and meaning in the moral sphere. Man cannot fathom the meaning of the natural order, yet he is aware of its beauty and harmony. Similarly, though he cannot expect to comprehend the moral order, he must believe that there are rationality and justice within it.

The author of Job is not merely a great artist. He is a profound thinker, too deep to believe that any neatly articulated system of man can encompass the beauty and the tragedy of existence. Yet he is too great an intellect to abdicate the use of reason and reflection in grappling with the mystery of evil and in seeking to comprehend as much of it as we can. He would endorse the unemotional words of the third-century sage, Jannai: "It is not in our power to understand the suffering of the righteous or the well-being of the wicked" (*Aboth* 4:15). But he goes further. There is a residuum of the unknown in the world, but we have good grounds for holding fast to the faith that harmony and beauty pervade God's world. The mystery is also a miracle.

This is the major theme, and in the superb architecture of the book it properly comes at the end. But the minor theme, that suffering frequently serves as a source of moral discipline and is thus a spur to ethical perfection, is far from unimportant, and it is placed in the mouth of Elihu as a prelude to the God speeches.

One more consideration, not hitherto noted, may be advanced in favor of the authenticity of the Elihu speeches. The protagonist of these chapters is given as "Elihu, the son of Barakhel, the Buzite, of the family of Ram." The significance attached to names in the ancient world, among the Semites in particular, is documented on every page of the Bible. Unlike the names of the three friends, which have Edomite or South Semitic sources or analogues, most of Elihu's elaborate name is Hebrew in origin. Ram is known as one of the ancestors of David, of Judean or Jerahmeelite stock (Ruth 4:19; I Chron. 2:9, 25). Buz is the brother of Uz, a nephew of Abraham (Gen. 22:21). Barakhel occurs in the business documents of the Murashu family as the name of several Jews in the reign of Artaxerxes I.[31]

But the meaning of the names is even more important than their provenance. *Barakhel* means "bless God," or "God has blessed"; *rām* means "exalted, high"; and *būz* means "scorn, contempt." To one familiar with the tendency of biblical and rabbinic thought to etymologize names, these would be an excellent description of the young intruder, scornful of his elders and conscious of his high role as a defender of God.

But it is the young man's own name which is of the greatest significance. "Elihu," which is likewise of Hebrew origin, represents a variant spelling of *Elijahu*, the name of the prophet Elijah. The difference in punctuation goes back only to the Masoretes, who changed the vocalization.[32] The name, meaning "Yah is my God," is highly appropriate for its bearer.

Nor is it accidental that in selecting a name for the protagonist who is to precede God in the book, the author chose a name identical with that of the great prophet Elijah. In history, the prophet plays precisely the role of the "defender of God" (I Kings, chaps. 17–21). In Malachi, the last of the prophets, he is "the forerunner of the Day of the Lord":

> Behold, I will send you Elijah the prophet
> Before the coming of the great and dreadful day of the Lord:
> And he shall turn the hearts of the fathers to the children,
> And the hearts of the children to their fathers,
> Lest I come and smite the earth with a curse.
>
> [Mal. 4:5, 6]

In later literature, the Apocrypha, the Pseudepigrapha, the New Testament, the Talmud, and the Midrash, Elijah becomes the precursor of the "Messiah." In later Jewish folklore he is the reconciler of all unsolved contradictions.[33] We may also recall that in the Bible Elijah is transferred heavenward in a storm, which is described by the identical term (se‹ārāh) that appears in Job (38.1): "And it came to pass, when the Lord was about to take up Elijah into heaven by a whirlwind, that Elijah went with Elisha from Gilgal" (II Kings 2:1).

In sum, Elihu's address supplements the major theme of the God speeches with a secondary but important idea. His name suggests to the Hebrew reader, who was thoroughly at home in his Bible and religious tradition, that he is fulfilling the function of his great namesake, the prophet Elijah, as "the forerunner of the Lord" who will appear out of the whirlwind. The relative variations in style between the Elihu chapters and the rest of the book suggest the normal changes which an author undergoes with the passing of time, while Elihu's basic idea represents the fruit of years of observing the educative and disciplinary role of suffering. This is not the whole truth with regard to the mystery which lies at the heart of existence. But, as the author of Job has stated with unequaled clarity and power, the whole truth is not with man, but with God.

X

The Lord out of
the Whirlwind

AS ELIHU'S WORDS END, a storm is seen rising in the east.
The Lord himself appears in the whirlwind and addresses Job
in two speeches, after each of which Job offers a brief reply.[1] These
chapters are among the greatest nature poetry in world literature.
Their purpose, however, is not the glorificaton of nature, but the
vindication of nature's God.

The contention of the Friends that Job must be a sinner because
he is a sufferer is treated with the silence it deserves. Nowhere does
God refer to the misdeeds of which he had been accused by the
Lord's "defenders." This silence is richly significant on several counts.
It speaks eloquently of God's rejection of the conventional theology
expounded by the Friends, which begins in untruth and ends in cruelty. (Eliphaz, who begins the dialogue with courtliness and consideration [chaps. 4, 5], ends by wildly accusing Job of every conceivable
crime [chap. 22].) Later, when God and Job are reconciled, the Lord
passes severe judgment upon the Friends: "The Lord said to Eliphaz
the Temanite, 'My anger is kindled against you and against your two
friends, for you have not spoken the truth about Me as has My
servant Job'" (42:7); but at the present juncture, silence is the most
effective refutation of their position.

The Lord consciously refrains from referring to Job's suffering, not from callous indifference but, on the contrary, from exquisite tact and sensibility. Job's agony cannot be justified by the platitudes of conventional religion, nor can it be explained away as imaginary. If man is to bear his suffering at all, the entire problem must be raised to another dimension. This is the burden of the words of the Lord spoken out of the whirlwind.

Can Job comprehend, let alone govern, the universe that he weighs and now finds wanting? Earth and sea, cloud and darkness and dawn, sleet and hail, rain and thunder, snow and ice, and the stars above—all these wonders are beyond Job. Nor do they exhaust God's power. With a vividness born of deep love and careful observation, the poet pictures the beasts, remote from man, yet precious to their Maker. The lion and the mountain goat, the wild ass and the buffalo, the ostrich, the wild horse, and the hawk, all testify to the glory of God (chaps. 38, 39).

The creatures glorified by the poet are not chosen at random. For all their variety they have one element in common—they are not under the sway of man, nor are they intended for his use. The implication is clear—the universe and its Creator cannot be judged solely from the vantage point of man, and surely not from the limited perspective of one human being. This call to rise above the anthropocentric view will be emphasized even more strikingly in the Lord's second speech. Job is overwhelmed and confesses his weakness:

> Job answered the Lord, saying,
> Behold, I am of small account; how can I answer You?
> I lay my hand to my mouth.
> I have spoken once, and I will not reply again;
> Twice, but I will proceed no further.
>
> [Job 40:3–5]

God, however, ignores Job's surrender and with torrential force launches into His second speech. He begins by asking whether Job is ready to subvert the entire order of the universe so that he may be vindicated:

> Will you deny My justice,
> Put Me in the wrong, so that you may be in the right?
>
> [40:8]

The climax of this divine irony, infinitely keen yet infinitely kind, is now reached: God invites Job to assume His throne and take the reins of majesty and power into his own hands. If he is able to humble the arrogant and crush the evildoers, God himself is prepared to do obeisance to him!

> Have you an arm like God;
> Can you thunder with a voice like His?
> Deck yourself in majesty and dignity,
> Clothe yourself with glory and splendor.
> Scatter abroad your mighty wrath,
> And as you see each proud sinner—abase him!
> As you look on each arrogant one—bring him low,
> And tread down the wicked in their place.
> Bury them all in the dust,
> Press their faces into the grave—
> Then I, too, will render thee homage,
> When your right hand will have brought you victory.
>
> [40:9–14]

Here on the one hand is God's moving acknowledgment that the world order is not perfect, and on the other, an affirmation of the complexity of the universe and of the conflicting interests which divine concern must encompass and reconcile.[2] All these elements man must reckon with before he presumes to pass judgment on the universe and its Governor.

Thus God has conceded that there are flaws in His creation, and evils which He has not conquered. Yet the world is not evil merely because there is evil in it. Evil is not dismissed as illusory or unimportant, but neither is it permitted to usurp a position of dominance in the universe.

Then follow exultant descriptions of two massive beasts—*Behemot*, the hippopotamus (40:15–24), and *Leviathan*, the crocodile (40:25–41:26). These are not literal, exact delineations, but poetic pictures rich in hyperbole. It is possible that, carried along by his enthusiasm and exultation, the poet borrowed images from ancient oriental myths which tell of the creative god who fights and conquers primordial beasts of terrifying dimensions.[3] But he is not interested in imaginary creatures from the dim mythological past[4]—he is concerned with the actual present, with the vast universe as it is governed by its Maker.

The hippopotamus and the crocodile are real beasts and their choice for inclusion in these paeans of praise is by no means accidental. The first speech of the Lord has glorified creatures like the mountain goat, the ostrich, the horse, and the hawk. To be sure, they were not created for man's use, yet they do possess a beauty and grace that man can appreciate. The poet now goes a step further. The hippopotamus and the crocodile can lay no claim to beauty, but on the contrary, are physically repulsive. When the poet glorifies these beasts he is calling upon us to rise completely above the anthropocentric point of view which, however natural for man, distorts his comprehension of the world. Precisely because they are unbeautiful by human standards, these monstrosities, fashioned by God's hand, are a revelation of the limitless range of God's creative thought. Since His ways are not man's ways, how can man's thoughts grasp God's thoughts—and what is more, pass judgment upon Him?

Job replies briefly and for the last time (42:1–6). It is noteworthy that exactly as in his closing responses in the first and second cycles of the dialogue, he employs the device of quoting his opponent's words, using them as a basis for his own reply:

> Then Job answered the Lord,
> I know that You can do all things
> And that no purpose of Yours can be thwarted.
> You have said,
> "Who is this that hides My plan without knowledge?"
> Indeed, I have spoken without understanding,
> Of things too wonderful for me which I did not grasp.
> You have said,
> "Hear, and I will speak;
> I will ask you, and do you inform Me."
> I have heard of You by hearsay,
> But now my own eyes have seen You.
> Therefore I abase myself
> And repent in dust and ashes.
>
> [42:1–6]

With these words of submission, the dialogue ends.

No reader can fail to be stirred by the power and beauty of these magnificent poems in praise of the wonders of nature and of nature's God. Herder undoubtedly had these chapters in mind, along with other biblical passages, when he wrote in his famous *Vom Geist der Ebräischen Poesie:*

> I have been particularly struck by its (the Jewish people's) perfect sympathy with brutes and the whole animate creation and was delighted even in childhood to find that it treated the brute animals (so called because they are dumb) as the brothers of man who want nothing but the power of speech. The wild beasts that the Hebrew language calls 'living creatures' *are* the living, because domestic animals are in comparison, as it were, still and dead. I was delighted when I found the voice and language of brutes so forcefully expressed in the language; when the prophet coos with the crane and the turtle dove, and mourns with the ostrich in the wilderness. I rejoiced at finding the form of the stag, the lion and the ox, sometimes their strength, stateliness, and velocity, at others, the acuteness of their senses, their habits of life and their character described and painted in appropriate terms. I wished that in place of some of the sacred songs we had more of its fables, parables and riddles respecting the brute creation, in short, more of the poetry of nature; for this seems to me to be among this people the most happy and the most perfect simplicity.

Granted the magnificence of the God speeches, several important questions arise. Most readers have been struck by the fact that these chapters make no reference whatsoever to the theme of man's suffering, with which the rest of Job is concerned. This has led some critics to assume that the work was left unfinished and that another poet added these chapters which, however beautiful in themselves, are irrelevant. Some of these scholars assume that the book originally was confined to a discussion of Job's misfortunes and that it grew to its present size via successive editions.[5]

This view, rightly stigmatized by Pfeiffer as "gratuitous," is generally rejected on several grounds. One argument is based on the literary greatness of these chapters. Driver, after paying high tribute to the literary quality of the God speeches, makes the wise comment, "It is difficult to believe that there could be found a second poet of equal scope (as the author of the Dialogue) to retouch the work of the first."[6] Another argument is based on the fact that throughout the dialogue Job has demanded that God answer him; the book would be highly unsatisfactory without some reply from the Lord. Most scholars, therefore, accept the view that the God speeches are authentic, although many critics have deleted one or more sections: the passage on the ostrich (39:13–18) in the first speech of the Lord, or the descriptions of the hippopotamus and the crocodile which constitute the bulk of God's second speech.

The section on the ostrich has been rejected principally because it does not appear in the Septuagint.[7] The fact is, however, that the Greek translation of Job represents a very drastic abridgment of the text, being fully one-sixth shorter.[8] This is undoubtedly due to the manifold difficulties of the Hebrew text, which frequently proved too great for the Greek translator, and for that matter, for all interpreters to the present day. Moreover, the long poetic passages which employ the Semitic device of parallelism would seem repetitious and hence uncongenial to a Greek reader. Since the description of the ostrich is particularly difficult, there would be every inducement for the translator to eliminate it from his version even if it existed in the original. Moreover, it should be noted that the ostrich passage leads directly into the description of the horse (39:19 ff.), the authenticity of which is not doubted.

Many critics have sought to delete the sections on *Behemot* and *Leviathan*.[9] Several arguments concerning style have been adduced in this connection, some readers maintaining that the second speech is inferior to the first as literature. This is a highly subjective point of view which I do not share. Only a great poet could paint the vivid picture of the hippopotamus, lying at his ease in the Nile among the lotus leaves, swallowing an entire river in one mouthful (40:24)! There is undeniable power, too, in the portrait of the mighty crocodile, encased in his coat of mail and impervious to the harpoon as he swims through the waters, stirring them up and leaving behind him a trail of white foam like an old man's beard (41:24).

Some critics have pointed out that the passages on the hippopotamus and the crocodile are not couched in the question form which is characteristic of the descriptions in the first speech.[10] There is, however, no reason for assuming that the poet would monotonously employ a single rhetorical form throughout four long chapters (chaps. 38–41). On the contrary, as a gifted poet he would be far more likely to vary his style.[11] Moreover, an analysis of the text discloses a regular pattern—each God speech consists of sections alternating between the question form and the direct statement, thus retaining both the force of repetition and the interest of variety.[12]

Considerations of content have probably been most influential in leading critics to delete these sections. It has been argued that God's second speech adds nothing to the discussion and that Job's second recantation is also an unnecessary duplication. If these paragraphs are deleted (and the remaining material transposed) we are left with only one speech for God, and Job's two responses can be combined into one.[13]

If we penetrate to the full meaning of the poet it becomes clear, I believe, that the proposed solutions are unnecessary and have served only to create new problems. As has already been indicated, the second speech is far from being a repetition of the first: it represents a higher level in the argument, an ascent from God's creative power as manifested in creatures that are independent of man, to God's creative joy in creatures that are positively dangerous and repugnant to man.

Job's responses are not redundant either, nor can they easily be combined. The final verse in Job's first reply ends with the words, "I will proceed no further" (literally, "I shall not continue to speak"). This is entirely appropriate if Job now subsides into silence, but not if we append another passage, as some critics would have us do. Moreover, each of the two responses is informed by a different spirit, with a crescendo of emotion in each corresponding to the progression of thought in the two God speeches.[14] Job's first answer strikes the note of submission and silence; it is only in the second that he attains a measure of repentance and acceptance. Job is convinced by God's words, but not easily: two stages are required for the argument.

It is, of course, impossible to "prove" that none of the passages in these chapters was interpolated by a later hand and that the sections are all in their proper sequence. What is clear is that if we fully understand the meaning of the received text and take into account the architecture of the book as a whole, we find the entire section highly relevant in content and thoroughly appropriate in form.

The question of the authenticity of the various passages in these chapters, though interesting, is far less important than another basic issue: What are the meaning and relevance of the God speeches? Unless we solve this problem, Job has eluded us. In all the magnificent nature description of the God speeches there is no concern with the problem of suffering and sin. Are we then to assume that the author of Job, after giving ample testimony of his intellectual powers, threw up his hands and permitted his masterpiece to end in a total collapse of thought? Obviously we should not "impose the strait-jacket of Aristotelian logic and consistency on an Oriental poet of great imagination and insight,"[15] for the Hebrew genius had its own canons of thought and concept of beauty; but we have a right to expect that the tragic theme of the book not be totally abandoned.

A modern philosophical writer raises the issue clearly when he asks, "What did God reveal to him that suddenly rent asunder the cover of darkness over Job's soul and made divine truth shine forth before him in all its splendor?" He then answers, "The poor logic and weakness of God's arguments and speeches against Job are truly astonishing. Actually, He does not reply at all. He explains nothing. He only makes sport of the little worm Job; He only unfolds before him gigantic images of creation as seen in nature and taunts him: Canst thou do this? Dost thou at least understand how this is done?"[16]

That an author of transcendent genius should be guilty of a total abdication of logic and reason, particularly when dealing with the theme of his lifework, is not merely astonishing—it is unbelievable. To adopt such a view of the poet is a confession of failure.

This effort to impugn the author's intellectual powers is at times associated with an attack on his moral character. Thus a twentieth-century biblical scholar comes to the conclusion that "the author's wonder before the magnificence of nature, which conveys but a faint idea of the power and wisdom of the Creator, contrasts with *his contempt for miserable human beings, in whom God is no more interested than in wild animals*" (my italics).[17]

Now the Book of Job is incontrovertible proof that the tragic fate of one human being preoccupied the poet for years. Is this compatible with the notion that he, or his God, would exhibit nothing but "contempt for miserable human beings"? There is not the slightest warrant in the text for attributing to God such an attitude, either toward man or toward the other animals. The entire section expresses God's deep joy in the wild creatures of the field, crag, and desert, and His care for them and their young.[18] Even if God's concern for man were no greater than for the wild animals, that would be interest indeed!

A subtler but even more far-reaching attack on the integrity of the poet is inherent in another approach to the God speeches.[19] According to this view, the heart of the book is to be sought in Job's passionate protest against God's cruelty and injustice, which is the burden of the first two cycles of the dialogue (chaps. 3–19). As for the remainder of the book, nearly all of it is unauthentic: the third cycle is not only disorganized, but critically suspect of having been tampered with by orthodox apologists; the Elihu chapters are obviously interpolated; chapters 38–41, the second God speech and Job's second reply, are also to be deleted. In this view, only the first God speech (38:1–40:2) and the first confession of Job (40:3–5) are genuine. Coming immediately after chapters 3–19 they form the original conclusion of the book.

What is significant, according to this theory, is that these authentic sections in the God speeches were deliberately written by the poet ambiguously, with tongue in cheek. They were intended by the author for two totally different classes of readers, the traditionalists and the skeptics. The pious believer would find a conventional religious answer in God's reaffirmation of His power and in Job's submission, while the critical thinker would derive from the same lines the heterodox conclusion that the world as a whole and man's suffering in it constitute a riddle to which there is no solution. The motive for adding these God speeches with their *double entendre* was to get a hearing for the dialogue in circles that it would not otherwise have reached.

This ingenious theory rests upon no objective evidence in the text, either for the extensive interpolations or for the conscious deception. It should be noted, too, that by this theory the Book of Job would not be a case in which an author is misunderstood by his readers, but one in which he consciously seeks to mislead them. Moreover, several basic questions remain unanswered: What could the author of Job hope to accomplish if he disguised his true meaning so effectively that conventional readers would find only conventional answers? How does this kind of deception comport with the poet's preoccupation with Job's integrity and love of truth throughout the book? What need is there for the long and passionate dialogue by Job and his friends if no reference is made to the theme of their discussion thereafter and no solution to the problem is offered except the cold and impersonal conclusion that life is a meaningless riddle?

Another striking interpretation of the intent of the God speeches, and by that token of the book as a whole, has recently been advanced by E. M. Good, who interprets the book as exhibiting "the irony of reconciliation."[20] Good finds that after the God speeches Job "repents for a sin he now knows perfectly well and it has nothing to do with external suffering." His sin has consisted of "his being satisfied to know all about God at second hand and for elevating himself to Deity's rank."[21] In conclusion, "God finds man guilty and acquits him. That is the fundamental irony of the Book of Job and of biblical faith."[22]

Unfortunately, this interpretation, acute as it is, does not carry conviction. Neither element of the irony that Good finds in the God speeches appears in the text either explicitly or by implication. Nowhere does God declare Job to be guilty and nowhere does He acquit him of his "guilt." Not only is no sin imputed by God to Job but, on the contrary, he is explicitly vindicated in the jointure following the poetic dialogue when the Lord informs the Friends, "You have not spoken the truth about Me as has My servant Job" (42:7, 8).

Whatever may have been the case with the Greeks, it was no act of *hybris*, of insolence or arrogance, for a Hebrew to demand justice of his God: the patriarch Abraham, whose faith was exemplary, voiced the challenge, "Shall not the Judge of all the earth do right?" (Gen. 18:25.)[23]

Differing in spirit but not in substance is the view of the God speeches that seems to be presented by the American poet, Robert Frost. When a modern writer uses a biblical or classical theme we cannot be certain whether he is setting forth his understanding of the original source or is simply utilizing the familiar material as a framework for his own independent vision. A case in point is afforded by Frost's "A Masque of Reason." In an ironic passage God thanks Job for "liberating" Him from ethical enslavement to the human race by denying His righteousness. Job has thus freed his Maker from the obligation of observing the moral law that men have imposed upon Him when they demand that the good must prosper and the wicked suffer. In governing the world, God is now free to disregard the moral imperative.

Frost seems here to go beyond the contention that man's reason cannot demonstrate a universal and inevitable correspondence between his actions and his destiny. It is not merely that the moral standards of God are beyond man's comprehension but that morality is man's own invention, one he has sought to foist upon God. Actually, God is "beyond good and evil," free to rule His world untrammeled by the necessity of seeing justice done.

Intriguing as this view may be to some modern minds, it does not represent the thought of the ancient Hebrew poet, whose God could not so easily abrogate the law of justice in the world. Throughout the dialogue, as we have seen, Job has steadfastly insisted upon an arbiter, a witness to speak for him (9:33; 16:19). He has expressed his passionate conviction that a Redeemer exists who will vindicate him. He has demanded that his cause be engraved on a monument to last into the future. In spite of all provocations and temptations, Job has held fast to two convictions—that his agony is unjustified and that there must be justice in the world.

In the brief passage (42:7–10) by which the poet links his dialogue to the traditional epilogue, the Lord twice declares to the Friends, "You have not spoken the truth about Me as has My servant Job" (42:7, 8). Far from denying Job's insistence that justice must somehow inhere in the universe, the Lord vigorously confirms it. Job has spoken the truth not only about his unmerited suffering but "about Me," the nature of God. Thus the Book of Job demonstrates what could have been inferred a priori—a God without justice is no God to an ancient Hebrew.

To be sure, reconciling Job's two basic convictions is a difficult task. Therein lies the major problem in understanding the book as a whole and the God speeches in particular. But it does not help matters to attribute to the author of Job an incapacity for rational thought, a devious mentality, or a callous indifference to human suffering. A convincing explanation of the meaning of the God speeches must disclose their relevance to the themes of human suffering and God's justice, and, by that token, to the other sections of the book. Most students of Job have therefore attempted, in a variety of ways, to relate the God speeches to the earlier dialogue.

One widespread view maintains that God wins Job over by picturing His limitless might as seen in Creation. But this answer does not hold water. Job has frequently conceded God's might himself during the earlier debate with the Friends. If this be the point of the God speeches they are entirely unnecessary; Job himself has given more than one description of God's power as reflected in the world of nature.[24] It is not God's might but His righteousness that Job calls into question:

> However wise and stouthearted a man might be,
> Has he ever argued with God and emerged unscathed?
> If it be a matter of power, here He is!
> But if of justice, who will arraign Him?
> Who would remove God's rod from me,
> So that my dread of Him would not terrify me.
> Then I would speak, and not fear Him,
> For He is far from just to me!
>
> [Job 9:4, 19, 34, 35]

Who does not know in all this,
That the hand of the Lord has made it?
With God are wisdom and strength,
His are counsel and understanding.

[12:9, 13]

Remove Your hand from me,
And let not the dread of You terrify me;
Then You may call and I shall respond,
Or I shall speak, and You answer me.

[13:21–22]

Oh that I knew where to find Him,
That I could come to His dwelling!
I would lay my case before Him,
And my mouth would not lack for arguments.
Would He contend with me merely through His great power?
No, He would surely pay heed to me.

[23:3, 4, 6]

If Job suddenly surrendered before the spectacle of power which he had so passionately challenged in his cry for justice, it would be a stultifying conclusion to a brilliant debate. Were this the intent of the God speeches one would be driven to Cornill's view that they are of "unparalleled brutality, which is usually palliated and styled divine irony, but which, under such circumstances and conditions, should much rather be termed devilish scorn."[25]

This conclusion is so thoroughly contradictory to the theme of the book and the entire tenor of biblical thought that scholars have been driven to the opposite extreme: it has been suggested that the message of the God speeches is that God remains near to man in his suffering. Throughout the dialogue, Job has contended that his Maker oppresses him while remaining indifferent to his misfortune. This unconcern is disproved by the mere fact that God appears to Job in the whirlwind and speaks to him. Job has won because he has succeeded in compelling God to answer him, and his vindication is marked by his experiencing the nearness of God.[26] Thus one writer movingly declares, "It is as though a child who, lost and alone at night in a dense forest, scratched by thorns, terrified by the ghosts he sees in every tree, in every bush, were suddenly to hear the steps and the voice of his father, were to feel himself lifted up in the paternal arms and carried home. Who listens then to the scolding words of the father, and what difference does it make what happened! He is safe, close in the paternal embrace. . . . This was certainly also the psychology of Job, 'Formerly I merely heard about Thee, now mine eye beholds Thee!'—and an end to all questions."[27] Another, more theologically oriented scholar finds in the God speeches the voice of a suffering God and sees in the Book of Job a foreshadowing of the need for a Christ.[28]

To be sure, the idea that God shares in the suffering of His creatures does find expression in biblical thought. It is an extension of the doctrine of the covenant between God and man which unites their destiny in an indissoluble bond: "I shall be your God, and you shall be My people" (Lev. 26:12, and often). On the one hand, this common link between God and Israel becomes the basis for the prophets' castigation of the wayward people who violated the covenant at Sinai. On the other hand, the notion of the bond is used by the prophets in their intercessions on behalf of sinful Israel, since the destruction of the nation would represent a profanation of the divine name.[29]

From the concept that God and man are linked together by mutual responsibilities under the covenant, religious faith makes the bold leap to the conviction that God Himself suffers when man is in agony. This theme is articulated in both the Prophets and the Psalms:

> In all their affliction He was afflicted,
> And the angel of His presence saved them;
> In His love and in His pity He redeemed them;
> And He bore them, and carried them all the days of old.
>
> [Isa. 63:9]

> He shall call upon Me, and I will answer him;
> I will be with him in trouble;
> I will rescue him, and bring him to honor.
>
> [Ps. 91:15]

> The Lord is nigh unto all them that call upon Him,
> To all that call upon Him in truth.
>
> [Ps. 145:18]

In post-biblical thought this theme was further broadened to include the conviction that God shares in the exile and suffering of Israel, as well as in its redemption. To cite one rabbinic utterance,

"When Israel went into exile, the Divine Presence went with them."[30] In Christianity, the doctrine of the suffering God assumed a central role which needs no elaboration here.

The biblical doctrine of God is, however, characterized by polarity. Side by side with this emphasis on the nearness of God is the frequent stress on the vast gulf between God and man in creative power, in wisdom, and in moral quality. It is God's perfection and man's imperfection that lie at the root of the differences in their natures: man is changeable and perverse, but God is trustworthy and constant in His purpose; man is capable of falsehood and cruelty, while God is merciful and just.[31] The divine transcendence and the consequent mystery of God's being are expressed in Moses' encounter with the Unseen God and his fruitless request to "see His face" (Exod. 33:12–23). They underlie the prohibition in the Decalogue against making an image of the Deity (Exod. 20:3; Deut. 5:8). They are basic to the vision of Isaiah, whose God cannot be seen by human eyes because of man's sinfulness (6:5), though He is exalted through man's righteousness:

> Man is bowed down,
> Man is brought low,
> And the eyes of the lofty are humbled;
> But the Lord of Hosts is exalted through justice,
> And God the Holy One is sanctified through righteousness.
>
> [Isa. 5:15, 16]

Biblical religion is the result of the creative tension between God's covenant and His transcendence, the sense of man's intimacy with God and the recognition of the vast difference between them. Both elements of this polarity find matchless expression in the Eighth Psalm. Here the pettiness and the grandeur of man are both related to the greatness of God; it is not God descending to man, but man ascending to God!

> When I behold Your heavens, the work of Your fingers,
> The moon and the stars that You have made,
> What is man that You are mindful of him,
> And the son of man, that You have regard for him?
> Yet You have made him little lower than divine
> And crowned him with glory and honor.
>
> [Ps. 8:4–6]

The tension between these two themes was expressed by the Hasidic
teacher Rabbi Bunam: "A man should carry two stones in his pocket.
On one should be inscribed, 'I am but dust and ashes.' On the other,
'For my sake was the world created.' And he should use each stone as
he needs it."

This sage counsel to draw upon each element of the polarity of God
and man as needed was anticipated and followed by the author of Job.
The conviction that God is near was deeply imbedded in Job's spirit
during his days of well-being. In his final pathetic soliloquy he recalls
with longing his previous intense intimacy with God:

> Oh, that I were as in the months of old,
> As in the days when God watched over me,
> When His lamp shone upon my head
> And by His light I walked through darkness;
> As I was in my days of vigor
> When God was an intimate in my tent,
> When the Almighty was still with me,
> And my children were all about me.
>
> [Job 29:2–5]

In an earlier plea as well, he recalled this loving fellowship:

> Your hands fashioned and made me
> Altogether—yet now You destroy me!
> Remember that You made me of clay
> And will return me to the dust.
> In Your love You granted me life;
> Your command kept me alive.
>
> [10:8, 9, 12]

More than once he passionately pleads for a restoration of this relationship, which had expressed God's erstwhile love, now unaccountably turned to cruelty:

> If a man die, can he live again?
> All the days of my service I would wait,
> Till my hour of release should come.
> You would call and I would answer You;
> You would be longing for the work of Your hands.
>
> [14:14, 15]

We may gain an insight into man's yearning for fellowship with God in a significant observation by Gershom Scholem. In his classic work on Jewish mysticism[32] he points out that there are three main stages in monotheistic religion: (1) the *primitive*, when the communion between God and the worshiper is immediate and no abyss exists between them; (2) the *creative*, when consciousness of the transcendence of God develops, so that the distance between God and man is acutely felt as absolute; and (3) the *mystical*, which Scholem calls the "romantic" period, when the attempt is made to bridge the abyss by evolving new means of communion and by re-establishing unity between man and his Maker. The observation may be made that the third stage thus reverts to the first or mythical level, but with significant differences. At all events, the first and third periods are mutually illuminating.

Whether or not this suggestive thesis is accepted, it is clear that nowhere in the God speeches in Job is it indicated, even by implication, that God is near to man and his suffering. On the contrary, it is the transcendental aspect of the Deity which finds expression here. With all the power at his command the poet underscores the tremendous chasm between Job and his Maker.

To be sure, Job is comforted by God's speaking to him, by the knowledge that he is not ignored. That sin separates man from God is clear from the very beginning of the Bible, when Adam, after his sin, is thrust out of the Garden of Eden.[33] Hence, if suffering is the result of sin, at least part of the penalty lies in the sense of alienation from God. It is this estrangement from God which Job feels so keenly, and it is in the re-establishment of their relationship that he finds evidence of his vindication.

But if it were merely a matter of God's manifesting His fellowship with Job, His appearance itself, perhaps augmented by a few words of sympathy, would have sufficed. Actually, the God speeches express no sympathy for Job's suffering, which, as we have previously indicated, is nowhere referred to. Nor is the length of God's rejoinder to be ignored: not merely that God speaks, but what He says, is crucial. The content of God's words must therefore have a bearing upon the basic issue of evil in a world created by a good God.

The beauty of these chapters is not their sole excuse for being: they are distinctly germane to the issue at hand. What is needed is a recognition of the extensive role which allusiveness (the use of indirection and implication rather than categorical assertion) plays in the Hebrew literature of all periods.[34] The ancient reader could be counted upon to understand a hint and, what is more, to revel in the intellectual pleasure of gathering the meaning from an indirect presentation of the theme under discussion. This rhetorical usage by the poet is particularly effective here, where he is concerned with issues that transcend the mundane and the experiential, so that a hint is far more eloquent than an outright statement. Not denotation, but connotation, is the heart of poetry in general, and of the God speeches in particular.

All of man's explanations of human suffering, varied and imperfect, have been set forth by the Friends and Elihu and have been countered by Job. The human protagonists are now silent. Any deeper word must be spoken by God, who makes His point by implication, but nonetheless effectively on that account. The vivid and joyous description of nature is not an end in itself: it underscores the insight that nature is not merely a mystery, but is also a miracle, a cosmos, a thing of beauty. From this flows the basic conclusion at which the poet has arrived: *just as there is order and harmony in the natural world, though imperfectly grasped by man, so there is order and meaning in the moral sphere, though often incomprehensible to man.*

The analogy is compelling, not only on the logical and psychological level, but aesthetically. For the poet, the harmony of the universe is important as an idea and as an experience. When man steeps himself in the beauty of the world his troubles grow petty, not because they are unreal, but because they dissolve within the larger plan, like the tiny dabs and scales of oil in a painting. The beauty of the world becomes an anodyne to man's suffering—and the key to truth. In Robert Louis Stevenson's words, "The true realism, always and everywhere, is that of the poets: to find out where joy resides, and give it a voice far beyond singing. For to miss the joy is to miss all. In the joy of the actors lies the sense of any action. That is the explanation, that the excuse."[35]

The force of the analogy and its implications are not lost upon Job, and it is before this truth that he yields. He repents his attack upon God, in which he failed to reckon with the limitations in his own understanding. Thus he is able to submit to God's will in a spirit of genuine acceptance.

In the author of Job we have a superb example of the creative artist at work, as Havelock Ellis describes him:

> Instead of imitating these philosophers who with analysis and syntheses worry over the goal of life and the justification of the world, and the meaning of the strange and painful phenomenon

called Existence, the artist takes up some fragment of that existence, transfigures it, shows it: There! And therewith the spectator is filled with enthusiastic joy, and the transcendent Adventure of Existence is justified. All the pain and the madness, even the ugliness and commonplace of the world, he converts into shining jewels. By revealing the spectacular character of reality he restores the serenity of his innocence. We see the face of the world as of a lovely woman smiling through her tears.[36]

The poet's ultimate message is clear: Not only *Ignoramus*, "we do not know," but *Ignorabimus*, "we may never know." But the poet goes further. He calls upon us *Gaudeamus*, "let us rejoice," in the beauty of the world, though its pattern is only partially revealed to us. It is enough to know that the dark mystery encloses and in part discloses a bright and shining miracle.

XI

Job and the Mystery
of Suffering

THE ANCIENT HEBREWS had little gift—or perhaps little
taste—for abstract speculation. Unlike the logical Greeks, who
questioned and analyzed every proposition placed before them, the
biblical prophets, historians, and sages never debated their belief in the
existence of God and of the moral imperative. Even when they
enunciated new and specifically Hebrew ideas, such as the prophetic
philosophy of history, the inevitable advent of God's Kingdom on
earth, the unity of mankind, and the election of Israel and its role in
the world, they felt them intuitively and asserted them with unshakable certitude.

The one great issue which agitated the spirit of biblical religion beyond all others was the mystery of suffering or, more precisely, the
mystery of unjust suffering. The axis on which all Hebrew religion
turns has as its two poles faith in God as the just Ruler of the universe
and the fact of widespread human suffering. This basic tension finds
classic expression in the words of Jeremiah, for whom it constituted
an agonizing personal experience:

> You are in the right, O Lord,
> Whenever I argue with You,

Yet I must set forth my charges against You:
Why is the way of the wicked successful,
All who are treacherous secure?
You plant them and they take root,
They grow and bring forth fruit.
You are near in their mouths,
But far from their hearts.

[Jer. 12:1, 2]

The problem was expressed even more tersely by the rabbis: "Why do the wicked prosper and the righteous suffer?"[1] The profoundest spirits in Israel labored to resolve the tragic paradox of evil in God's world. In the process, an imposing body of thought grew up as the lawgiver, the prophet, the historian, and the sage tried to reconcile the contradiction.

It is therefore clear that Job's tragedy goes far deeper than one man's undeserved suffering. The author of Job is challenging not minor or peripheral ideas, but the very heart and essence of biblical faith. The full dimensions of the problem for him, and by that token the extent of his contribution, cannot be understood without a survey, however brief, of biblical teaching on the subject.[2]

The groundwork of the problem was laid at the first confrontation of God and Israel at Sinai. The Decalogue rests on faith in the justice of God as an effective force in the universe. As the medieval philosopher Judah Halevi noted in another connection,[3] God had introduced Himself not as the Creator of heaven and earth, but as the Redeemer of the oppressed: "I am the Lord, Thy God, who brought thee forth out of the land of Egypt, out of the house of bondage" (Exod. 20:2). The implications of this first commandment, though surely not evident to all of Moses' contemporaries or successors, are far-reaching—the God of Israel holds sway even in Egypt; His power is not limited to His own territorial domain, like the gods of the Canaanites, the Ammonites, and the Moabites. Even more significant is the fact that the God of Israel had delivered the weak from slavery in a foreign land and had executed judgment upon their oppressors. Thus Mosaic religion rested upon the conviction that God was both all powerful and all just.

From this basic conviction, the Pentateuchal doctrine of retribution follows naturally: righteousness will be rewarded and wickedness punished. This doctrine is expressed in the famous passage in Deuteronomy (11:13–17) which was later incorporated into one of the basic prayers of post-biblical Judaism, the *Shema:*

> It shall come to pass, if you hearken diligently unto My commandments which I command you this day, to love the Lord your God and to serve Him with all your heart and with all your soul, that I will give the rain of your land in its season, the former rain and the latter rain, that you may gather in your corn, wine, and oil. And I will give grass in your fields for your cattle, and you shall eat and be satisfied. Take heed lest your heart be deceived, and you turn aside and serve other gods and worship them; and the anger of the Lord be kindled against you, and He shut up the heaven so that there shall be no rain and the ground shall not yield her fruit; and you perish quickly from the good land which the Lord is giving you.

The same principle was elaborated with graphic power in the two great "comminations" or warnings which appear at the conclusion of Leviticus (chap. 26) and of Deuteronomy (chap. 28). Here the Lawgiver sets forth for the nation the reward of righteousness and the penalty of sin. Although the first passage is couched in the plural, "If ye do not hearken to Me" (Lev. 26:14), and the second in the singular, "If thou dost not hearken to the voice of the Lord, thy God" (Deut. 28:15), it is the people as a whole being addressed; both the sin and the retribution are collective.

The doctrine of retribution could be held with total conviction because in the early periods of Hebrew history group consciousness was all powerful and the individual was conceived of as little more than a cell in the larger organism. From the standpoint of religion, a man's personal destiny had no existence apart from the family, the clan, and later, the nation, to which he belonged. Faith in the collective reward of virtue and the collective punishment of vice rests upon a doctrine of corporate solidarity which did not originate with the Hebrews. Quite the contrary, it was universally accepted throughout the ancient Near East, from the Nile to the Euphrates. The concept of family solidarity was joined to that of *lex talionis* ("measure for measure") and became a cardinal principle in the legal system of the ancient Babylonians, Assyrians, and Hittites.[4]

To cite one instance, the Code of Hammurabi (secs. 229–30) ordains that if a house collapses as a result of the builder's negligence and kills the owner, the builder is to be put to death. If the owner's son loses his life, the builder's son is to be executed.[5] This provision of the Babylonian Code explains a formerly enigmatic passage in the biblical "Book of the Covenant." Hebrew law ordains that if a man or woman is killed by a goring ox because of the owner's negligence, he must forfeit his life, or a fine is to be assessed. Then follows the verse: "If the ox kill a son or a daughter, the same procedure [as the one already set forth] shall be done to him [i.e., to the owner]" (Exod. 21:31). In other words, it is forbidden to hurt the owner's child for injuries caused to another child.

That children may not be punished for their fathers' offenses, and vice versa, was generalized as a juridical principle in Deuteronomy:

> Fathers shall not be put to death for their children, nor shall children be put to death for their fathers. Every man shall be put to death for his own sin.
>
> [Deut. 24:16]

Although visiting the sins of the fathers upon the children was forbidden to a human agency, it was recognized as an ineluctable fact of life and therefore regarded as the will of God:

> . . . For I the Lord thy God am a jealous God, visiting the iniquity of the fathers upon the children unto the third and fourth generation of them that hate Me; and showing mercy unto the thousandth generation of them that love Me and keep My commandments.
>
> [Exod. 20:5, 6]

This conception of family responsibility eventually became embodied in a folk proverb: "The fathers have eaten sour grapes, and the children's teeth are set on edge" (Jer. 31:29; Ezek. 18:2).

It must be remembered in this connection that collective solidarity is not merely "vertical," linking men together in time through the generations of a family; it is also "horizontal," uniting men in a single generation across space. The Book of Deuteronomy, the great repository of the doctrine of group responsibility, gives this idea graphic form in the law of "the heifer in the valley" (21:1–9). If a murder is committed in the open countryside by an unknown hand, a special sacrifice must be brought by the elders of the nearest city. This is accompanied by a rite of expiation in which the elders are commanded to wash their hands ceremonially as a symbolic affirmation of the innocence of all their fellow-inhabitants. They must then declare: "Our hands have not shed this blood, neither have our eyes seen it. Forgive, O Lord, Your people Israel, whom You have redeemed, and do not permit innocent blood to remain in the midst of Your people Israel."

Both "temporal" and "spatial" solidarity are commingled in the narrative of Achan's stealing some of the booty consecrated to God, the *ḥērem*, in the days of Joshua. His act is described as the sin of the entire people: "But the children of Israel committed a trespass concerning the devoted thing; for Achan, the son of Carmi, the son of Zabdi, the son of Zerah, of the tribe of Judah, took of the devoted thing; and the anger of the Lord was kindled against the children of Israel" (Josh. chap. 7). As a result, the entire nation suffers defeat in battle at Ai, and when the offender is discovered, he is stoned and burnt, together with his sons and daughters and all his possessions (7:24, 25), in disregard of the Deuteronomic law but in conformity with far older and more compelling patterns of behavior. When, a few centuries later, David violates a primitive folk belief and takes a census, he is given a choice of punishments—seven years of famine, three months of defeat in battle, or three days of plague—all, be it noted, to be visited upon the people who were his contemporaries (II Sam. 24:11 ff.).

The doctrine of collective solidarity could also be positive, operating as a principle of reward. The virtue of the fathers, as well as their sin, affects the destiny of their descendants. Thus Isaac is promised the blessing of God "because Abraham obeyed My voice and kept My precepts and commandments" (Gen. 26:5). The life stories of the patriarchs and David are detailed, not because of any interest in mere history or even solely for edification; the merits of the fathers are invoked time and again for the benefit of the children. Similarly, David's virtue is used to buttress the faith that his dynasty will endure forever (e.g., Ps. 132:10 ff.).

The positive aspect of the doctrine of family solidarity is not limited to the saintly or the famous. In the words of the psalmist:

> Happy is the man who fears the Lord,
> And delights greatly in His commandments.
> His offspring shall be mighty upon earth;
> The generation of the upright shall be blessed.
>
> [Ps. 112:1, 2]

In rabbinic literature the idea received elaborate development in the doctrine of *zekhut 'abot*, "the merit of the fathers," and it occupies a significant position in the traditional ritual as well.[6]

It is, however, clearly foreshadowed in biblical thought, and like its

negative counterpart it operates both "vertically" in time and "hori
zontally" in space. In the great colloquy of God and Abraham, i
which the patriarch bargains for the deliverance of the sinful city o
Sodom, it is clear that the presence of fifty, forty, thirty, twenty, o
even ten righteous men in the city would have availed to spare th
entire population (Gen. 18:23–33). The prayers of Abraham fo
Abimelech (Gen. 20:7), like all the intercessions of the saints for thei
contemporaries, are instances of this collective responsibility in spac
linking all men together in a common destiny. It is because of the ex
treme sinfulness of his generation, which is beyond remedy, that th
prophet Jeremiah is commanded by the Lord: "Therefore do not pra
for this people, neither offer any prayer for them or intercession to Me
for I will not hear you" (Jer. 9:16). The same hopeless state of affair
impels his younger contemporary Ezekiel to declare that even if hi
generation included such great saints as Noah, Daniel, and Job, i
would be of no avail (Ezek. 14:20–21).

Eliphaz, however, in his final speech, promises Job that if he repent
he will be able to intercede for sinners and by his own purity sav
them from punishment (Job 22:28–30).[7] There is therefore ironi
justice in the epilogue, where it is Job who must plead with God fo
Eliphaz and his friends. Thus it is the much maligned hero who is vin
dicated, rather than his unsympathetic and condescending friends wh
have set themselves up as the defenders of God.

Until the destruction of the First Temple, biblical thought neve
attempted to deny the doctrine of family or tribal solidarity. To b
sure, biblical law sought to restrict the concept of clan responsibilit
by limiting the powers of the $g\bar{o}'\bar{e}l$ or "blood avenger," establishin
"the cities of refuge" for an accidental killer. But this change was du
not to any weakening of the doctrine of collective responsibility an
group retribution, but to the growth of a broader concept of grou
solidarity. Instead of the narrow primordial loyalties, with a code o
in-group morality (Binnenmoral) limited to family, clan, and tribe
the Torah and the Prophets sought to place the nation, and ultimatel
the human race, in the center of each man's concern. It hardly needs t
be pointed out that the goal has yet to be achieved in our day, nearl
thirty centuries later.

This doctrine of collective retribution applied to the nation serves a
the cornerstone of the philosophy of the biblical historians, the author
of Joshua, Judges, Samuel, and Kings. Especially in Judges and Kings
the ebb and flow of national prosperity and disaster is explained i

erms of the people's fluctuating obedience or resistance to the word
f God. When a "righteous" king suffers defeat, as in the case of
osiah, it is attributed to the sins of his father, the wicked king Ma-
asseh (II Kings 23:25, 26), striking evidence of the potency of the
rinciple of vertical responsibility.

The principle of moral retribution, which the historians invoke in
heir judgments on all the kings of Judah and Israel, is equally funda-
ental in the prophets, as they pass judgment on the nation. Hosea
mphasizes that the law of consequence is rooted in the universe and
xpresses it in a metaphor drawn from nature:

> For they sow the wind, and they shall reap the whirlwind. . . .
> Sow to yourselves in righteousness, reap in mercy,
> Break up the fallow ground,
> For it is time to seek the Lord,
> Till he come and teach you righteousness.
> You have plowed wickedness, you have reaped iniquity,
> You have eaten the fruit of lies.
>
> [Hos. 8:7; 10:12, 13]

he same principle, that the justice of God is the law of history, is
pplied by Amos, Hosea's older contemporary, to world affairs. He
nds in it the measuring rod for judging the destinies of all neighboring
ations as well as those of Judah and Israel (Amos, chaps. 1, 2).

The doctrine of retribution is a direct and unavoidable consequence
f faith in a God whose attributes include both power and righteous-
ess. Yet even in its collective form as applied to the nation, the belief
aced immense difficulties. These grew ever graver as the well-being
f the nation declined and was ultimately destroyed by the Assyrian
dvance and later by the Babylonian conqueror. For the theory was
ow contradicted by two facts of experience: the actual character
nd condition of Israel, on the one hand, and the nature and position
f its enemies, on the other. Both facts challenged Israel's faith in her
God.

In the earlier period, when the lot of the Hebrew nation seemed
olerably hopeful, the first issue was paramount. Later, when the
ingdoms of Israel and Judah decayed and fell before mighty em-
ires, the second became increasingly prominent. In their effort to
esolve the basic conflict between faith and experience, the prophets
eepened the content of Hebrew religion.

The first difficulty had already been felt by the eighth-century prophets. If God is all righteous, it follows that a sinful people, even if it be Israel, deserves to perish. Loving their people as well as their God, the Hebrew prophets could not accept this logical but devastating conclusion. Thus, Amos, confronted by the prosperous and corrupt kingdom of Israel, sought first to win the Northern Israelites to repentance. But when Amaziah, the priest at the sanctuary of Beth-el, eager to defend law and order and to protect "God and country," expelled the prophet, Amos no longer had any expectation that Israel might reorder its national existence. He then had no alternative but to foretell the annihilation of the northern state.

The total disappearance of his people was, however, an intolerable prospect. Therefore, because he was convinced that God needed a spokesman in an idolatrous world, even after his expulsion from the Northern Kingdom, Amos did not abandon either his hope or his activity. Instead, he transferred his hope for the future to the smaller and weaker kingdom of Judah:

> Behold, the eyes of the Lord God are upon this sinful kingdom [of Israel], and I will destroy it from the face of the earth. But I will not completely destroy the house of Jacob, says the Lord, For behold, I will command, and I will shake the house of Israel among all the nations, like corn being sifted in a sieve, but no pebble shall fall upon the earth. All the sinners of My people shall die by the sword, who say, "Evil shall not overtake or meet us." In that day will I raise up the fallen tabernacle of David and repair its breaches and raise up its ruins and rebuild it as in the days of old.[8]
>
> [Amos 9:8–11]

A generation later, Amos' spiritual descendant, Isaiah of Jerusalem, faced the same heart-rending challenge of a righteous God judging His sinful people, now reduced to the boundaries of Judah. Isaiah refined still further Amos' faith that part of the Hebrew people would survive, enunciating his great doctrine of the "Saving Remnant"—not all of Judah, but a part, would be saved.[9] For Isaiah, the greatest intellect among the prophets, history was a process of the survival of the morally fittest, directed by God who would thus preserve those capable of regeneration.

This profound concept, with its polarity of destruction and salvation, is central to the prophetic message of Isaiah in his Inaugural Vision (chap. 6):

Then I said, "How long, O Lord?"
And He answered:
"Until cities lie waste without inhabitants,
And houses without men,
And the land becomes utterly desolate,
And the Lord removes men far away,
And the forsaken places are many in the midst of the land.
While there is yet a tenth remaining, it will be burnt again,
Like a terebinth or an oak in the autumn,[10] whose trunk remains.
The holy seed is its trunk."

[Isa. 6:11, 12, 13]

The prophet reverts to this theme time and again. "A remnant shall return, even the remnant of Jacob, to the mighty God. For though your people, O Israel, be as the sand of the sea, only a remnant of them shall return. Destruction is decreed, overflowing with righteousness" (Isa. 12:21, 22). In fact, he names one of his sons *She'ār Yāšūbh*, "A remnant shall return," and thus gives living and dramatic form to his basic faith.

Not quite explicit, and yet clearly implied in this idea of the Saving Remnant, is the insight that suffering is integral to the sifting process and that purification cannot be achieved without pain. Thus Isaiah, who followed in Amos' footsteps, was able to reconcile God's justice with the survival of an unrighteous people through the dynamic concept of the Saving Remnant.

Yet another challenge confronted Isaiah as the destinies of the Hebrew state moved toward catastrophe. The Assyrian conqueror was infinitely crueler and more arrogant than Israel had ever been, yet he was treading all other nations under foot. How could this spectacle of evil triumphant be reconciled with a just and almighty God? Isaiah resolved the contradiction through another profound insight—his concept of "the rod of God's anger." Assyria, pitiful in its conceit, was merely an unconscious instrument in God's hand for rooting out the evil and ushering in the good. When its function was accomplished it would pay the penalty for its crimes against God and man.

O, Assyria, the rod of My anger,
The staff in the hand[11] of My wrath.
Against a godless nation, I send him,
And against the people of My wrath I command him.
But he can not imagine this,
His mind does not think so,

For his intention is to destroy
And to cut off nations not a few.
It shall come to pass,
When the Lord has finished all His work
On Mount Zion and in Jerusalem,
I shall visit punishment on the arrogant boasting of the king
    of Assyria,
And on his haughty pride.
Can the axe vaunt itself over him who hews with it,
Can the saw magnify itself over him who lifts it?

[Isa. 10:5–7, 12, 13, 15]

This doctrine of "the rod of God's anger" also became basic to the prophetic world view, Habakkuk applying it to the Babylonian con querors of his day.[12] It is notable that centuries later the books o. Isaiah and Habakkuk were avidly studied and profoundly revered by the Dead Sea sectarians, who found in them a prophecy of the ulti mate doom of the hated oppressors of their own day.[13]

God's justice thus continued to be challenged on the basis of two adverse historical trends—the triumph of arrogant pagan conqueror and the exile and degradation of Israel. A century and a half later the challenges confronted the Unknown Prophet of the Babylonian Exile in far more acute form. How should one explain the misery and homelessness of Israel? It could not be justified in terms of Israel's sin for at its worst Israel was better than the heathen Babylonians. Unless these tormenting doubts were met the people would be plunged into a despair that would lead to national dissolution. A message of hope and courage was needed, not only for Israel's sake, but for God's cause, for it was this people, weak and imperfect, that remained "God's witness" in a pagan world (Isa. 43:10). A rabbinic comment aptly spells out the implications of the Deutero-Isaianic metaphor: " 'Ye are My witnesses,' saith the Lord. 'If ye are My witnesses, I am the Lord but if ye are not My witnesses, I am not the Lord.' "[14]

Deutero-Isaiah accordingly evolved the doctrine of the Suffering Servant of the Lord. Israel is not merely God's witness, but man' teacher. As she proclaims the light of God's law to the world, she suffers indignities at the hands of the nations because of their mora immaturity. While they regard Israel's misery as proof of her un worthiness, it is actually the mark of her greatness, of her cosmic role in history. Indeed, the suffering of the Jewish people is an inevitable

onsequence of the interdependence of humanity, for whom Israel is
o serve as "a covenant people, a light to the nations."

The doctrine of the Suffering Servant of the Lord explicates what
vas implicit in the earlier concept of the Saving Remnant—that all
1en are involved in one another and bear each other's burdens,
vhether they will it or not. The prophet declared that Israel was
uffering because of the sins of the nations. The day would come, he
aid, when this truth would be recognized by the world; Israel's trib-
lations were destined to end, and the servant of the Lord would attain
lory and honor:

> Behold, My servant shall prosper,
> He shall be exalted and lifted up, and shall be very high. . . .
> The nations will say,
> "He was despised and rejected by men,
> A man of pains and acquainted with sickness,
> A man from whom men hide,
> We despised him and esteemed him not.
> Surely he has borne our sicknesses
> And carried our pains.
> Yet we esteemed him stricken,
> Smitten by God, and afflicted.
> But he was wounded because of our transgressions,
> He was crushed because of our iniquities;
> Upon him was the chastisement that made us whole
> And with his stripes we were healed."
> Therefore will I divide him a portion with the great,
> And he shall divide the spoil with the mighty;
> Because he laid bare his soul to death,
> And was numbered among the transgressors,
> Yet he bore the sin of many,
> And made intercession for the transgressors.

> [Isa. 52:13; 55:3, 4, 5, 12]

Thus, for the first time, the prophet affirmed the possibility of na-
ional suffering that was not the consequence of national sin, but on
he contrary, a tragic, yet indispensable element in the process of the
noral education of the race.[15] For the first time the nexus between
uffering and sin is severed. This insight of Deutero-Isaiah was destined
o be deepened by the author of Job.

The tension between the faith in God's justice and the visible evi-
lence of wickedness was also met in another way by the prophets,

who utilized an older folk belief in "the Day of the Lord." The Hebrews had long believed that the day would come when the God of Israel would give His people victory over its foes and establish its hegemony over its neighbors. This doctrine was by no means limited to Israel. The comfortable conviction that God will naturally protect His people and advance its cause under all circumstances has its parallels in ancient and in modern times among all nations—and is all too evident today. The Hebrew prophets did not attack or denounce the doctrine—they reinterpreted it in moral terms and thus completely transformed it. They agreed emphatically with the masses that the day would come when the Lord God of Israel would arise and bring victory to His cause. However—and this was crucial—that did not mean the inevitable triumph of Israel as it was, but rather the emergence of a vastly better, truly righteous Israel. This Day of the Lord was therefore more likely to prove a calamity than a blessing to the sinful people: "Why do you want the Day of the Lord? It will be darkness and not light."[16]

Yet the prophets, and most notably Isaiah, did not see this day exclusively or even principally in negative terms. On the contrary, it represented the consummation of history, toward which human events were inevitably moving, guided by the will of God. On that day justice and brotherhood would be established for all nations, with peace and plenty for all men and dignity and freedom for a regenerated Israel.

As Isaiah and the prophets pondered the tragic conditions of their own day this goal seemed further and further away, at "the end of days," at the furthest period conceivable to man. They therefore envisioned the establishment of the Kingdom of God (as later thought called it) as coming in the "End-Time."[17] For several of the prophets, notably Isaiah, Jeremiah, and Zechariah, the instrument of God's purpose in the world was to be the anointed scion of the house of David.[18] The messianic age represented the triumph of the righteousness of God in an imperfect world. Justice would prevail—what was needed was patience in the present and faith in the future.

In sum, the major issue in biblical religion was the problem of evil. From the need to resolve the tension between faith in God's retribution and the spectacle of injustice triumphant in the world came most of the deepest insights of biblical faith.

In essence, the contradiction was resolved by imbuing human experience with a sense of time and endowing history with the dynamism of process. The universe is not static, it is on the march to the future. The evils of the present world order will be overcome in the messianic age when the sovereignty of God is recognized by all men and nations.

Now to wait patiently for the triumph of God's justice was relatively easy so long as the nation was the unit under consideration, for God has eternity at His command and nations are long-lived. This is particularly true of Israel. In Ben Sira's words:

> The life of man is but a few days,
> But the life of Jeshurun, days without number.

[37:25]

Yet the role of the collective consciousness must not be exaggerated. From the very beginning the individual played a significant part in the religious thought of Israel. His hopes and desires, his fears and frustrations, could not be wholly submerged in the destiny of the nation. The people might prosper and a man might be miserable; the status of society might be critical, yet the individual could still find his personal life tolerable. Even in its oldest formulations, the Law demanded obedience from the individual.[19] Was it unfair to expect that righteousness and sinfulness would receive their due reward and punishment in the life of the individual as well? Thus the problem of divine justice emerged in the days of the First Temple. Isaiah took the simplest course by reaffirming the traditional doctrine of collective retribution and applying it to the individual:

> Say of the righteous, that it shall be well with them;
> For they shall eat the fruit of their doings.
> Woe unto the wicked! It shall be ill with him;
> For the work of his hands shall be done to him.

[Isa. 3:10–11]

This conviction that justice would prevail in the life of every man was the foundation stone of faith for the psalmists, the fervent exponents of traditional religion:

> Who is the man that fears the Lord?
> He will instruct him in the way to be chosen.
> He himself shall abide in prosperity;
> And his children shall possess the land.

[Ps. 25:12, 13]

With sublime disregard for the evidence of reality, one psalmist could go so far as to declare: "I have been young, and now am old; yet have I not seen a righteous man forsaken, or his children begging bread" (Ps. 37:25).[20] What was needed was faith, which would flower into patience:

> Sing praises to the Lord, O you His saints,
> And give thanks to His holy name.
> For His anger is but for a moment,
> And His favor is for a lifetime.
> Weeping may tarry for the night,
> But joy comes with the morning.
>
> [Ps. 30:4, 5]

The destruction of the larger and more prosperous Northern Kingdom proved to be only the prelude to the destruction of the Kingdom of Judah. As inexorable doom descended on the nation, and the small Judean state saw its lifeblood ebbing away, the mere reiteration of conventional ideas became more and more unsatisfactory. Now there was little comfort and no compensation in the doctrine of collective retribution. Moreover, since the individual was now the center of concern, a counsel of long-range patience was sadly irrelevant, for man flowers but an instant.

The prophets Jeremiah and Ezekiel, whose tragic destiny it was to foretell and to witness the destruction of the Temple and the Babylonian Exile, agonized over the prosperity of the wicked and the suffering of the righteous. Ezekiel, in particular, emphasized the doctrine of individual responsibility and retribution. Concerned with the teaching of ethical living, he stressed the idea that each man determines his own destiny (chap. 18); yet he never succeeded in formulating a complete theodicy, a comprehensive view of God's justice operating in the world. Other men of faith, psalmists and poets, continued to urge obedience to God's will, buttressed by the traditional faith that righteousness would soon triumph in the life of the individual:

> The Lord is good unto them that wait for Him,
> To the soul that seeks Him.
> It is good that a man should quietly wait
> For the salvation of the Lord.
>
> [Lam. 3:25, 26]

This shift in emphasis from the destiny of the group to the welfare of the individual became dominant after the return from the Babylonian Exile. The tiny Jewish commonwealth, subservient to a succession of foreign masters, beset by hostile neighbors, and torn by dissension within, offered a limited theater of activity for the operation of God's law of righteous retribution applied to the nation. It could not satisfy the deeply human desire to see justice established in the world. But when the law of consequence was transferred to the lives of individual men and women, it was crystal clear that experience contradicted it at every turn.

Tradition in general, and Jewish tradition in particular, finds it much easier to supplement, modify, and reinterpret older beliefs and attitudes than to discard them when they prove inadequate. As Israel Abrahams wrote, "This is the virtue of a historical religion, that the traces of history are never obliterated. . . . The lower did not perish in the birth of the higher, but persisted."[21] We have only to substitute "earlier" and "later" for "lower" and "higher" to have a fair description of the process of religious growth and reinterpretation. Not altogether irrelevantly it may be added that in science, too, this is generally the procedure—hypotheses are rarely scrapped, but generally undergo modification as new phenomena are discovered that must be reckoned with.

This characteristic is strikingly exemplified in the history of the doctrine of reward and punishment in normative Judaism, from the biblical epoch down to the modern age. Layer upon layer was added to older ideas, while little was surrendered. The traditional Hebrew emphasis upon the group and collective responsibility was never abandoned. When the individual, with his personal hopes and fears, swam into the religious consciousness the doctrine was applied to him as well: sin was still the cause of punishment and virtue the source of well-being.

The Book of Job concerns itself with single-minded devotion to this theme—the operation of the divine law of justice in the life of the individual. In the course of the discussion the author necessarily restates the conventional views of biblical religion on the subject. While his sympathies are obviously with Job in his affliction, he sets forth the accepted beliefs with unmatched eloquence and fairness, notably in the speeches of Eliphaz, Bildad, and Zophar. At the very outset Eliphaz presents this outlook succinctly and clearly:

Think now, what innocent man was ever destroyed;
Where was the upright cut off?
Whenever I have seen those who plow iniquity
And sow trouble—they reap it!

[Job 4:7, 8]

The only important addition to the doctrine came from the older view of group responsibility: children personally guiltless may be expiating the sin of their fathers. Eliphaz pictures the fate of the fearsome lion whose offspring must wander about in search of food:

The lion roars, the fierce beast cries—
But the teeth of the whelps are shattered.
The mighty lion wanders about without prey,
And the young of the lioness are scattered.

[4:10, 11]

Bildad expresses the same thought in his description of the wicked (18:6, 12).

The light grows dark in his tent,
And his lamp above him is put out.
His child will go hungry;
And disaster awaits his wife.[22]

Even in this form, the doctrine of divine justice faced obvious difficulties. Various qualifications were therefore introduced to explain "exceptions" to the law of retribution. The most obvious answer, repeated time and again, is that the prosperity of the wicked and the suffering of the righteous alike are only temporary; ultimately, justice is done and the balance redressed. Eliphaz adds a subtler psychological nuance (15:20 ff.): even during the period of his good fortune the wicked man is not free to enjoy his prosperity, because, like the sword of Damocles, the threat of punishment is always hanging over him. In effect, he is being punished throughout the period of his ostensible prosperity; long before doom descends upon him he is expiating his crimes. In at least one important passage which occurs earlier (5:6 ff.), the theme that man, not God, is the source of sin is stressed. Man, by his very nature, is imperfect; how then can he expect to avoid sin or its consequences? Therefore, even the most righteous of men must expect a measure of retribution for his actions.

In spite of the contradictions afforded by experience, the Friends continue to hold fast to the conviction that evil is the invariable consequence of sin and that suffering can therefore be avoided by the practice of justice. This insistence upon the traditional doctrine derives from the fear that to weaken faith in divine retribution is to open the floodgates of violence and immorality. To reverse a later rabbinic apothegm, "If there be no Judge, there will be no justice."

These ideas form the overt, positive content of the dialogue. Yet scarcely less important than the affirmations in Job are the negations. What is rejected or passed over in silence is as significant as what is accepted. The doctrines taught by traditional religion could not assuage the passion and the pain aroused by the common spectacle of "the suffering of the righteous and the prosperity of the wicked." To meet this imperious cry for justice in men's hearts, post-Exilic Judaism elaborated the concept of a life after death, with a judgment beyond the grave—a doctrine which became basic to normative Judaism and to Christianity. It is not easy to pinpoint the emergence of a belief in an afterlife. One passage in Psalms and several verses in the Book of Isaiah seem to express this faith, but they are unclear and impossible to date with any assurance. The first clear-cut affirmation of the doctrine of a judgment after death occurs in Daniel, which emanates from the first quarter of the second century B.C.E., the period of the Antiochian persecutions which preceded the Maccabean revolt.[23]

It is obvious that the doctrine did not appear full-blown, nor did it win universal assent. Centuries later the upper-class Sadducees continued to deny it even after it had become widely accepted by the masses. The Sadducees could point to the absence in the Bible of any clear-cut warrant for the idea.[24] There were, however, deeper psychological and social factors that predisposed them to view it with skepticism.[25] The upper classes found their present position in society thoroughly tolerable and, what is more, eminently justified by their virtues! They therefore felt no need to compensate for the inequities of this world by adopting a belief in a judgment in the world to come.

Biblical Wisdom literature, which flowered in an earlier period, emanated from the same social strata and may therefore fairly be described as proto-Sadducean. Accordingly the Wisdom writers find themselves unable to accept the idea of an afterlife.[26] It is noteworthy that the Friends, for whom this faith should have proved a godsend, make no reference to the idea. In a deeply moving passage, Job himself does refer to this new faith springing up in his day, but sorrowfully

finds himself unable to accept it.²⁷ Koheleth, too, considered the possibility but rejected it as unproved, with little overt regret.²⁸

In sum, the conventional doctrines on reward and punishment as
maintained by biblical religion as late as the third century B.C.E. are
re-stated effectively by the Friends. However, the original contribution of Job to religious thought lies not in the speeches made by the
Friends but in the words of the other participants. In the past, Job had
always accepted this body of religious teaching as the truth. Then
came the crisis in his life, catastrophe following catastrophe, leaving the
temple of his existence a mass of rubble. We who have read the tale of
the wager between God and Satan in the prologue know that Job's
degradation and misery constitute a cosmic experiment to discover
whether man is capable of serving the ideal for its own sake, without
the hope of reward. But Job has no inkling of the wager. For him, the
accepted religious convictions of a lifetime are now shaken to the
foundations by his personal experience. His faith is contradicted by his
knowledge that he is not a sinner, certainly not sinful enough to de-
serve the succession of blows that fall upon his defenseless head.

It is characteristic of Hebrew thought that in spite of all his calamities Job does not yield to atheism. He cannot deny the clear evidence
of his senses—his bitter suffering is a challenge to the justice of God.
But neither can he surrender the prompting of his heart. In his darkest
hour he retains the faith that behind the cruel God who is afflicting
him stands the righteous God who will ultimately vindicate him. Indeed, as the chasm between him and his friends widens, and he finds
in them less and less sympathy and understanding, Job experiences a
crescendo of faith that God is on his side. At first he wishes only for
an arbiter to judge fairly between him and the God of violence at
whose hand he has suffered so cruelly:

> If only there were an arbiter between us
> Who would lay his hand upon us both,
> Who would remove God's rod from me
> So that my dread of Him would not terrify me.
> Then I would speak, and not fear Him,
> For He is far from just to me!²⁹
>
> [9:33–35]

As the debate grows warmer, Job knows that in God he possesses
a witness—far more dependable than his fickle friends—ready to testify
on his behalf.

> Behold, even now, my witness is in heaven,
> And He who vouches for me is on high.
> Are my friends my intercessors?
> No, to God my eye pours out its tears,
> That He judge between a man and God,
> As between one man and his fellow.
>
> [16:19–21]

The peak of Job's faith is reached, though it lasts only an instant: God is more than an impartial arbiter, more than a witness ready to speak out for him—He is his *Goʾel*, a redeemer ready to avenge injustice to a kinsman:

> For I know that my Redeemer lives,
> Though He be the last to arise upon earth![30]
>
> [19:25]

Thus Job stands poised on the threshold of dualism. But the uncompromising Hebrew faith in the Divine Unity prevents him from postulating a dichotomy between a God of might and a God of justice, or even from conceiving of the possibility of a cleavage between the two.

The pathos of Job's protest is heightened by the belief, which he himself had originally shared, that the religious ideas he now opposes are indispensable to morality. His adversaries can, therefore, in all sincerity accuse him of undermining the foundations of society. In Bildad's words:

> O you who tear yourself to shreds in your anger,
> Shall the earth be forsaken on your account,
> Or the rock be removed from its place?
>
> [18:4]

For the conventional believer, faith in divine retribution is basic to ethical behavior—deny the first and the second will crumble.

It is here that Job, refuting the accepted pattern of religious thought, makes his major positive contribution. Faced with the tragic dilemma of a righteous man's suffering in an immoral world created by a righteous God, Job is nevertheless unwilling to surrender his ideal of rectitude. To be sure, good men will be struck with horror at his plight, and virtue has certainly brought him no reward!

But the just will hold fast to his way,
And he who has clean hands will increase his strength.

[17:9]

The Mishnah is therefore correct in concluding that Job served God not out of fear but out of love.[31] Job has surrendered the idea of a utilitarian morality—an insight never again lost in high religion. The truly ethical life is motivated not by the desire for extraneous reward but by its own inherent satisfaction.

Nevertheless, the role of Job is essentially that of the critic who negates the inadequate views of the conventional religion of his day. The poet's own positive views on suffering are reserved for the two final sections of the book. Since they have already been discussed in the analysis of the poem, they may be summarized briefly here. The young brash intruder Elihu stresses the idea that suffering frequently serves as a source of moral discipline. When other communications from God, like visions and dreams, fail, sickness and other forms of pain serve as potent warnings against sin before it is committed. Above all, they are a defense against the perils of pride and complacency. Thus suffering, even when it is not punishment, is to be justified as a spur to higher ethical attainment.[32]

The poet regards this recognition of the educative function of suffering as valid, but hardly as sufficient for the principal answer. This is reserved for the climax, the words spoken by "the Lord out of the whirlwind." As we have emphasized, the substance of God's response is expressed by indirection and is to be sought in the silences as well as in the speeches. It is noteworthy that God nowhere attempts to justify Job's suffering by charging him with sin. Nor does he attempt to assuage that suffering by voicing His sympathy. Thus the Lord concedes the truth that the suffering of the innocent is a reality. The prophet Deutero-Isaiah had utilized this insight to explain the suffering of his exiled people. The author of Job now transfers it from the collective to the individual.

Perhaps, the poet muses, there are imperfections in the divine plan which appear in the cosmic pattern in quarters where God's power has not penetrated. The Lord offers to defer to Job if he can set right the inequities of the world. But this is a task more difficult than Job has imagined:

As you look on each arrogant one—bring him low,
And tread down the wicked in their place.
[40:12]

And these irregularities, however painful to the sufferers, are minor. They are insufficient to negate the pervasive harmony of the universe. Man's suffering represents an infinitesimal part of the cosmos. When the world is viewed from a perspective broader than man's, the evil in it is not enough to call God's rule into question:

Will you deny My justice,
Put Me in the wrong, so that you may be in the right?
[40:8]

But how can a man retain his faith in the goodness as well as the power of God? God knows that for man his suffering bulks exceedingly large. As the modern Hebrew poet Bialik once observed, when a man catches his thumb in a door, his entire personality seems concentrated and enters into the injured finger. It is man who suffers; how can men believe? It is to this question that the God speeches are directed. The answer the poet gives is not merely agnostic. He is not satisfied with the argument that since man cannot fathom the mystery of nature he cannot hope to penetrate the secrets of man's fate. The poet has a more positive basis for holding fast to the righteousness of God.

As we have seen, this faith is to be sought in the vivid and joyous descriptions of nature in the God speeches. Through them the poet voices his faith that nature is not merely a mystery, but a miracle. Man cannot fully fathom the pattern and order of the natural world, yet he is conscious at every turn of its beauty and harmony. Similarly, though he cannot expect to comprehend all elements in the moral order, he must believe that there are rationality and justice within it. As Immanuel Kant pointed out, if it is arrogant to defend God, it is even more arrogant to assail Him.

Yet after all partial explanations of suffering, like those proposed by the Friends or Elihu, are taken into account, a mystery still remains. Hundreds of years later, the third-century sage, Jannai, expressed in abstract and unemotional form the truth which the author of Job had discovered through bitter experience: "It is not in our power to understand either the suffering of the righteous or the prosperity of the wicked."[33]

Any view of the universe that pretends to explain it fully is, by that very token, untrue. Yet the analogy of the natural order gives the believer in God grounds for facing the mystery with a courage born of faith in the essential rightness of things. What cannot be comprehended through reason must be embraced in love. For the author of Job, God is one and indivisible, the moral order is rooted in the natural world.

The author of Job is too deeply religious to believe that any system of thought neatly articulated by man can fully explain the beauty of the universe and the tragedy of existence. Yet he is too great an intellect to abdicate the use of reason and reflection in pondering the mystery of evil and in seeking to comprehend it. There is a stubborn residue of the unknown in the world, but it is more than whistling in the dark to believe that beauty and order pervade God's world. The author is too clear-sighted to ignore the fact that all too often men find the world "a land whose light is blackness, gloom and disorder, where the light is as darkness,"[34] a dark forest where they stumble into briars and cut themselves on the rocks. Yet it is no self-deception to hold fast to the faith expressed in the Creation narrative in Genesis: "God saw all that He had made, and behold it was very good."

Strictly speaking, the author of Job offers no justification for suffering from man's point of view. But he has done far more. He has demonstrated that it is possible for men to bear the shafts of evil that threaten their existence if they cultivate a sense of reverence for the mystery and miracle of life, seek to experience joy in the world, and strive to discover intimations of meaning in its beauty. Hence the Book of Job will be read, pondered, and loved as long as men possess moral and intellectual integrity and refuse to yield either to self-deception or to despair.

XII

The Language and Style of Job

EVERY WRITER OF CONSEQUENCE wishes to be more than a writer—he aspires to be a thinker, even a philosopher. For the author of Job this desire was abundantly gratified, if we interpret "philosopher" in its original sense as a lover and practitioner of wisdom. The rich content of the book, the range and the depth of its thought, bear witness to the extraordinary intellectual gifts of the author.

The profundity of Job is matched by its literary greatness. The author is generally included among the half-dozen transcendent literary geniuses of all time, along with Homer, the Greek dramatists, Dante, Shakespeare, and Goethe.

The artistry of Job is revealed in its superb structure. We have seen how the traditional prose tale of the pious suffering Job is utilized by the poet in masterly fashion as a framework for the dialogue. Both parts, the prologue and the epilogue, are linked to the poetry by brief jointures written by the author. The prose tale itself has been retold with consummate artistry. In terse moving style the five scenes of the drama unfold, alternating between earth and heaven. The four disasters that befall Job come in a climactic series—the first two through human agencies, robbing him of his possessions; the last two of divine origin, destroying his family, and all but destroying him.

Then follow the three cycles of speeches by Job and his friends. The progression they reveal lies not in the logical development of ideas, such as we meet in a Platonic dialogue, but in the crescendo of emotion. The Friends who have come to comfort Job by reminding him of the eternal verities grow more and more helpless and angry as the chasm between them widens. As the dialogue continues, Job is driven both to greater bitterness and to a new and deeper faith. As he sees himself thoroughly misunderstood by even the wisest and best of men, his conviction grows that he will be vindicated by God, the great arbiter—nay more—his eternal witness, indeed, his ultimate redeemer.

But before God appears there is another word to be spoken by man. The poet introduces Elihu, who opposes Job for attacking God's justice, and the Friends, for defending it so poorly. He himself proceeds to set forth his own solution, which is the secondary answer to the problem of evil. Elihu's words serve as a foil and a prelude to the great speeches of the Lord, which contain the primary answer. Here the poet sets forth his basic insight: the universe, miracle as well as mystery, is the background against which the dark burden of suffering is to be borne even when it cannot be understood. Before this truth, which neither belittles nor justifies Job's tragic experience, the sufferer submits and is reconciled.

The last word has now been spoken. It remains only to take up the strands of the familiar tale. In the highly significant jointure which links the poetry to the prose narrative it is made clear that Job has been vindicated. It is he who must intercede for the Friends who, in spite of their role as God's defenders, have not spoken the truth about Him. The story is now resumed in all its naïve simplicity. Job is restored to prosperity, the number of his sons is doubled, his newborn daughters are beautiful, and he lives twice the normal life span, dying an old man, "satisfied with life."

The beauty of Job is revealed not only in its over-all structure, but in many specific details as well. Again and again, the author reveals a keen observation of all the phenomena of nature, whether it be the streams in the desert, the river flowing into the sea, the wild beasts in search of prey, the sturdy plant cleaving its way through rocks, the transplanted tree coming back to life, the mountain goats crouching to give birth, or the eternal constellations of the heavens. He looks at life with the fresh and unclouded eyes of the poet who sees the world being created anew each day, with the morning stars singing together and all the sons of God shouting for joy. And like the God whom he worships, he exults equally in the swift grace of the horse and the sluggish might of the crocodile.

Thomas Carlyle's enthusiastic panegyric is in no way extravagant:

> There is the seeing eye, the mildly understanding heart. So true everyway; true eyesight and vision for all things; material things no less than spiritual: the Horse,—'hast thou clothed his neck with thunder?'—he 'laughs at the shaking of the spear!' Such living likenesses were never since drawn. Sublime sorrow, sublime reconciliation; oldest choral melody as of the heart of mankind;—so soft, and great; as the summer midnight, as the world with its seas and stars! There is nothing written, I think, in the Bible or out of it, of equal literary merit.[1]

Equally acute is the poet's eye for the human parade. The limitless ills of human existence, the ravages of disease, the miracle of human birth, the clash of wills in the law court, the rise and fall of classes and nations, the attack of the warrior upon his adversary, the thief plotting his evil schemes, the poverty-stricken harvest worker shivering in the cold of night, the rich malefactor living in luxury and ease—all these are transfixed through a telling phrase, a striking image. Nowhere else has the existential tragedy of man, whether in the brief hour of his contentment and joy or in the moment of his death and nothingness, been caught more poignantly or unforgettably.

Each reading discloses new beauties in Job, even if the book is read in a language other than Hebrew. The wonder is that so much has been successfully captured in translation, particularly in the magnificent King James Version. The reasons for its success are several. The Committee of Translators of 1611 possessed native literary gifts of the highest order and an ear for the cadence and sound of words second to none. Moreover, it was their good fortune to live at the flood tide of the Elizabethan era, when English possessed a richness and plasticity never attained before or since. Finally, the translators made themselves willing captives of the Hebrew original, even when it meant creating new English idioms out of Semitic turns of phrases. These ultimately became integral to the English language because of the sway held by the Authorized Version over the English-speaking peoples.

It does not derogate from the achievement of the translators to point out that their work was facilitated by the character of biblical poetry. Unlike classical Greek and Latin poetry, biblical meter does not depend on a pattern of long and short syllables arranged in a given form. Nor does biblical poetry depend on rhyme and the fixed succession of stressed and unstressed syllables, as most modern verse does—features generally impossible to capture in translation. Rhyme is practically non-existent in biblical verse.

Biblical poetry is characterized by two features that are bound up with its content rather than its form. First, the patterns of biblical rhythm are generally based on the principle of one beat or accent for each word or thought-unit, irrespective of the number of syllables. The second feature is that of parallelism: the impact of an idea or emotion is heightened by having one poetic line or stich followed by another line which echoes, contrasts, or completes the content of the first.[2] Both these features, the non-syllabic meter based on thought-units and the *parallelismus membrorum,* pose a substantial challenge to any translator, but they are not totally beyond the scope of a gifted writer.

As is to be expected, the poetic qualities of the book are fully revealed only in the original. Our understanding of the rich texture of Job's style has been tremendously advanced by the last three hundred years of research in Semitic linguistics and prosody and by the discovery of significant remains of ancient Near Eastern literature.

Job has more words of unique occurrence and a richer vocabulary than any other biblical book.[3] For example, the author uses four nouns for "lion," six terms for "trap,"[4] and four synonyms for "darkness."[5] He knows the names of the constellations,[6] of metals, and of many precious stones.[7] He is familiar with the detailed anatomy of great beasts,[8] the technical language of the law courts,[9] and the occupations of mining[10] and hunting.[11]

The richness of his vocabulary stands the poet in excellent stead. Because of the variety of language at his disposal he is able to sustain the reader's interest through forty chapters of poetry written in parallelistic style. His skillful use of synonyms prevents the repetition of the same idea in adjoining stichs from becoming monotonous.

At the same time, he is master of the rules, not their captive. In spite of his extraordinary command of the resources of Hebrew, he does not hesitate to break with the pattern. At times he will use the root twice in the same verse. Thus in 13:7 the same verb (*dibber,* "speak") occurs in both stichs:

Is it for the sake of God that you speak falsehood,
On His behalf that you utter lies?

This repetition is, moreover, too frequent in Job to be a scribal error.[12] We may be sure that the poet's command of the language was at least equal to that of his modern readers.[13] The usage is due either to the desire for emphasis or to some psychological reason that now eludes us.

In order to elucidate the rich vocabulary of Job, the modern scholar has recourse to other Semitic languages such as Akkadian, Ethiopic, and Ugaritic, but most especially to Arabic, Aramaic, and post-biblical Hebrew. The varied rationale for this technique is not always clearly understood even among students. When we turn to a cognate language for help in elucidating a Hebrew text, there is, to be sure, the possibility that the particular term was borrowed from a neighboring people together with the object which it represents.[14] This is, however, a comparatively rare phenomenon. The basic assumption in invoking cognate roots is that Hebrew and its sister languages are all descended from a proto-Semitic tongue. Hence a word that has come down to us in the relatively limited vocabulary of the Hebrew Bible may be explained by its use in another Semitic language where it occurs more frequently and its meaning is more certain.

It has long been noted that Job has a large number of Arabisms, that is to say, words that are best explained by reference to the rich vocabulary of classical and dialectical Arabic.[15] It does not follow that the poet knew Arabic, although this assumption is not completely ruled out by any evidence at our disposal. There is, however, no basis whatever for assuming that our book is a translation of a non-existent Arabic original.[16] These so-called Arabisms are generally not borrowings but authentic Hebrew words fortunately attested by their provenance in the far richer Arabic lexicon.

Even more frequent are the so-called Aramaisms in Job.[17] Here the situation is more complex because of the close relationship of the two languages and the extensive contacts of the Hebrews with Aramaic at several periods of history. This has often been overlooked or misunderstood. Not only are Hebrew and Aramaic both Semitic languages, but they also belong to the same sub-group of North-West Semitic, so that the resemblances are closer than between any other two languages in the Semitic family. The relationship between the Hebrews and the Aramaic-speaking peoples of Mesopotamia and Syria existed throughout the history of the Hebrew nation. According to the Bible, Jacob's father-in-law Laban, with whom he lived for twenty years, spoke Aramaic (Gen. 31:47). Throughout the First Temple period, the Aramean kingdoms and Israel shared a common border and stood in close contact, friendly or hostile, with one another.[18] During the Babylonian Exile and in the post-Exilic period, Aramaic became the *lingua franca*, universally used for government and business throughout the Middle East.

The decrees from the Persian government archives cited in the Book of Ezra are written in Aramaic. So are the letters sent to the Persian governor Bagoas in Jerusalem by the Jewish military colony at Elephantine on the upper Nile, as indeed are all the extant remains of that fascinating outpost of Jewish life. These documents and other inscriptions testify to the extensive use of Aramaic throughout the Middle East during the fifth century B.C.E., if not earlier.[19] Ultimately, Aramaic pre-empted the position of Hebrew in the Jewish community of the Second Temple, becoming the language of law, literary composition, and ordinary conversation.[20]

It is therefore methodologically unsound to lump all Aramaisms together, and on that basis to assign a later date to the literary documents in which they occur.[21] Actually, the Aramaisms in biblical Hebrew are to be subsumed under four distinct categories: (1) examples of the North-West Semitic vocabulary and usage indigenous to both Aramaic and Hebrew, at times frequent in Aramaic but remaining rare (or poetic) in Hebrew (such forms are generally early and cannot be invoked for a late date);[22] (2) earlier Hebrew borrowings from nearby Aramaic during the pre-Exilic period, especially in the heyday of the Syrian kingdom;[23] (3) later Hebrew borrowings during the Babylonian Exile and the post-Exilic period;[24] (4) idioms and morphological forms introduced into Hebrew and patterned after Aramaic usage, with which the Hebrew writer or speaker was familiar.[25]

It follows that the occurrence of a few Aramaisms in a Hebrew text is insufficient to determine its age or origin. Only when we encounter a heavy concentration of words, idioms, or grammatical forms patterned on Aramaic, is it a fair presumption that the author was accustomed to thinking in Aramaic and used it freely in his daily speech.[26] This last situation obtains in Job, where Aramaisms are plentiful both in vocabulary and in morphology.[27]

Another source for the understanding of biblical Hebrew in general, and the language of Job in particular, is to be found in the extensive

orks of post-biblical literature. In the past, the significance of rab-
nic Hebrew was all too often ignored or minimized on the ground
ıat it was a "degenerate" or "artificial" form of the language. Today
is generally recognized that the Hebrew of the Mishnah, the Tal-
ud, and the Midrashim, and even of the medieval era, represents
ter stages in the evolution of the same language. By every canon of
ientific method, parallels from later Hebrew should be recognized
, being at least as significant as cognates from other languages and
ien culture-spheres, with which the Hebrews may have had only
ight and superficial contacts, or perhaps none. This is not intended
) deny the value of the "horizontal" aspect, through space, of com-
arative Hebrew philology, but to underscore the importance of the
vertical" aspect, through time.[28]

In Job, as in other biblical books, there are usages best explained by
ıbbinic Hebrew.[29] This, in spite of the fact that Job uses poetic
iction, while most of the extant rabbinic sources are in prose, much
f it being technical to boot. The frequency of Aramaisms in Job
ıpports the conclusion, to which other criteria also point, that Job
ʾas written in a period when Aramaic was widely used for conver-
ıtion and that the author was thoroughly familiar with the language.[30]
ʾo be sure, there are relatively fewer Aramaisms and late Hebrew
)cutions than in other biblical books that emanate from the same era.
ʾhe reason inheres in the important distinctions in style between po-
try and prose. In poetry, the author has a tendency to use exalted
ɔeech and therefore to archaize and to retain the vocabulary and
orms of the classical language. Thus, even the latest of the Psalms are
ır freer of Aramaisms than the prose works of the post-Exilic period,
ke Ecclesiastes, Esther, and Chronicles. The Dead Sea Scrolls exhibit
ıe same feature. The prose writings of these sectarians, like the
Manual of Discipline (*Serekh Hayaḥad*), approximate proto-mishnaic
Iebrew, while the poetic *Hymns of Thanksgiving* (*Hodayot*) betray
ıte Hebrew influences much more rarely, being modeled after the
iblical Psalms.[31] The dialogue of Job may therefore be described as
he supreme example of late biblical poetry in both style and vocab-
ılary.

The prose tale in the prologue and epilogue is written in exquisite
ıiblical Hebrew, on a par with the classic narratives in Genesis and
ɔamuel. This has suggested to some scholars a very early date for the
ɔrose tale, but as we have seen, there are irrefutable considerations of
ɔontent that preclude a pre-Exilic date for the story in its present form.

What we have here is a superb example of literary archaizing, a striking *tour de force* by the author, who wished to place his protagonists in the patriarchal past. Moreover, the readers knew the tale as one of hoary antiquity. Hence in retelling it, the author uses perfect classical Hebrew with practically no trace of a later style.[32] There are other examples of such skillful archaizing by gifted writers who give few telltale signs of their own age. The Book of Ruth, likewise post-Exilic, is written in a style reminiscent of the Book of Judges. In modern literature, Thackeray's *Henry Esmond* follows the style and structure of the eighteenth-century English novels, while Thomas Love Beddoes, a Victorian poet, wrote in Elizabethan and Jacobean style.

As has been noted earlier in this chapter, the poetic sections of Job are naturally marked by the two basic traits of biblical poetry, *parallelism* and *meter*. Scholars have disagreed on the question of the basic meter employed in the book. While most regard the 3:3 pattern as basic, Pfeiffer has argued strongly for 4:4 as the meter.[33] Many commentators have insisted that the book consists exclusively of distichs. Hence, whenever a verse in the present text contains a third stich, they have proceeded to eliminate it as spurious. Since the problem is gratuitous, the proposed solution is uncalled for. In a work as long as Job, any single rhythm pattern would have become unbearable. Indeed, other biblical poems which are far shorter than Job, like "The Song of the Sea" (Exod. chap. 15), "The Song of Deborah" (Judg. chap. 5), Isaiah's "Great Arraignment" (Isa. chap. 1), and Koheleth's "Allegory of Old Age" (Eccles. 11:7–12:8), all exhibit a variety of meters, since monotony is the cardinal sin of literature.[34] To be sure, redoubtable surgeons did not hesitate to subject these texts as well to amputation in order to make the meter conform to their preconceived theories. But the discovery of a variety of meters in the Ugaritic poems[35] has demonstrated what should have been clear all along—that while a poem is written in a basic meter, the author will often introduce variations in the pattern in order to express different emotions and to stimulate the reader's interest.

The facts are clear and beyond dispute. There is, however, room for differences in interpretation. Thus, Gordon believes that "the poetry of the ancient Near East, Akkadian, Ugaritic, Hebrew, Egyptian, did not know of exact meter."[36] In view of the variety, complexity, and technical skill exhibited by biblical and oriental poets, this view does not commend itself. Their conception of meter differed from hat of classical or Western poetry. Their meter patterns, however, ιre much too regular to be dismissed as non-existent. In view of our gnorance of the musical modes in which ancient oriental verse was ιntoned, we can only assume the general principle of one stress for ιach word or thought-unit, modified in rare cases by metric consid-ιrations. As for variations in meter, they are thoroughly explicable ιs part of the poet's craft.

In Job the basic pattern is a verse consisting of two stichs, each containing three beats. But this meter (which is, incidentally, the most frequently used in biblical poetry) undergoes every conceivable variation, in the number of stichs in the verse and the number of stresses per stich.[37] In addition to the balanced rhythm pattern, where each stich has the same number of beats, we also meet with the haunting meter called the *Kinah* rhythm, where the second stich is shorter than the first.[38] Special power inheres in the rarer use of a staccato rhythm.[39] As is true of other biblical poets, the author will at times follow the natural tendency to conclude a speech in a literary crescendo, bringing it to an end with an increase in either the number of stresses or stichs in the closing line.[40] The general principle is exhibited everywhere: while one meter predominates, variety is nearly always present.[41]

It should therefore be clear that it is a methodological error to delete words or stichs merely for metrical reasons. Metrics can play a legitimate role in textual criticism only when re-enforced by other textual and exegetical considerations.[42]

In biblical poetry it is usual for the stichs to be in *consecutive parallelism* to each other; that is to say, stich *a* is parallel to *b*, and stich *c* to *d*.[43] This pattern (*a* | *b*; *c* | *d*) occurs in the vast majority of poetic lines, as, e.g., in Job 4:4, 5:

a) Your words have upheld the stumbling,
b) and you have strengthened the weak-kneed.
c) But now that it has come to you, you cannot bear it;
d) it touches you, and you are dismayed.

Much rarer is the pattern of *alternate parallelism*, where the first stich is parallel to the third, and the second stich to the fourth (*a*, *b* | *a*¹, *b*¹).[44] A good example occurs in Hos. 5:3:

a) I have known Ephraim,
b) and Israel is not hidden from me.
*a*¹) For now you have committed harlotry, O Ephraim,
*b*¹) and Israel has defiled itself.

Of the greatest interest is the pattern of *chiastic parallelism*, whe the first stich is parallel to the fourth and the second stich to the thi (a, b | b^1, a^1).[45] This less obvious form often proves a valuable clue the connection and meaning of difficult verses and of entire passage An instance occurs at the end of Psalm 1, where it establishes the lir between verses 5 and 6 and obviates the need for the emendatio proposed by some scholars:

a) Therefore the wicked shall not stand in judgment,
b) nor sinners in the community of the righteous,
b^1) for the Lord loves the righteous,
a^1) but the way of the wicked must perish.

Another striking example of chiastic parallelism is found in Job 20:2,:

a) Indeed, my thoughts force me to answer
b) because of the feelings within me.
b^1) I hear words of censure which insult me,
a^1) And my spirit of understanding impels me to reply.

Chapter 8 is so difficult that commentators have been unable t decide whether the closing section (vss. 16–19) refers to the wicke or to the righteous! Chiasmus supplies the key. When this rhetoric form is recognized it becomes clear that verses 12–15 describe tl destruction of the wicked (a), and verses 16–19, the survival of tl righteous (b). Then comes the conclusion of the chiasmus in 8:20:

b^1) Indeed, God will not spurn the blameless man,
a^1) nor will He uphold the evildoers.

We have noted the author's freedom from slavish adherence to tl usual canons of meter and parallelism. This applies also to his use c rhetorical figures. Alliteration is common, but he does not carry it t mechanical extremes. A case in point is afforded by 5:8:

As for me, I would seek after God [*El*]
And to God [*Elohim*] entrust my cause. . . .

In the Hebrew text, consonantal *Aleph* begins every word except tl last (*dibhrāthī*). It is easy enough to substitute a synonym beginnin with *Aleph*, such as ʾ*imrāthī*, "my word," as some textual critics hav proposed. The poet is less hidebound and departs from the alliteratio at will.

Even more common than alliteration is his remarkable use of asso nance. In 12:2, Job addresses a sarcastic utterance to his friends:

No doubt you are the people that count,
And with you all wisdom will die!

ere every one of the seven words in the Hebrew contains the hum-
ing sound, "m," which suggests Job's mocking sarcasm.

The book is characterized by various rhetorical figures which are
pounded by the Greek and Latin grammarians as well as the Arab
etoricians. Similes and metaphors are both common and self-explan-
ory.[46] We also encounter other rhetorical usages which help our
iderstanding of the book, such as *zeugma, hendiadys,* and *hysteron
oteron,* all familiar from classical literature.[47]

One of the most familiar figures of speech in the Bible is *paronoma-
1,* in which the author uses one word because of its similarity in
und to another.[48] For example, Isa. 5:7:

He hoped for justice (*mišpāṭ*),
   but behold bloodshed (*mispāḥ*).
For righteousness (*ṣedāqāh*),
   but behold, a cry (*ṣᵉāqāh*).

ere the prophet selects these two pairs of nouns, rather than any of
teir synonyms, because he wishes to point up a contrast which is
eightened by the similarity of sound. Plays on words are extremely
ommon in all languages and literatures. In our day they tend to be
ooked down upon as a low form of humor, but they were far more
ighly regarded in the past, as the Bible, Homer, and Shakespeare
oundantly attest.[49]

One more literary device of greater subtlety, which has not been
ifficiently noticed heretofore, should be indicated. The Arab rhetori-
ians in their study of Arabic poetry called it *talḥin.*[50] No other biblical
riter uses it as frequently or as effectively as the author of Job.[51]
his usage is to be distinguished from paronomasia, the pun or the
lay on words. In *talḥin,* the effect derives not from the sound but
rom the meaning. The poet uses a word which has two distinct de-
otations, one primary to the context and the other secondary but
lso appropriate. His choice of the particular word, rather than a
ynonym, is dictated by the desire to bring both meanings simultane-
usly to the consciousness of the reader, who derives a delicate aes-
tetic pleasure from the instantaneous recognition of both meanings.

Thus in Lam. 2:13 we have an example which can fortunately be

imitated in English: "For your break is great as the sea." Here th
poet uses the Hebrew word *šebher*, "break," rather than any of it
countless synonyms, because of his simile "like the sea." *Šebher* sug
gests the related word *mišbār*, "breaker, wave," and is thus doubl
appropriate to the context.

A very moving instance occurs in Job 7:6, which cannot be dupli
cated in translation. The Hebrew text reads:

> My days are swifter than the weaver's shuttle;
> They end in the absence of hope.

The word for "hope" used here is the common *tiqwāh*. This noun
however, has a homonym, identical in form, which means "thread"
(as in Josh. 2:18). The poet has spoken of man's days as fleeing swiftly
and lacking in hope. The figure of the weaver suggests the secondary
meaning of the shuttle of life running out of thread. Both senses o
the word *tiqwāh* enter the reader's consciousness together and are ex
perienced simultaneously.

These attributes of style suggest but do not exhaust the boundles
artistry of the poet. In the magnificent architecture of the whole an
in the perfection of each detail a master stands revealed.

XIII

The Use of Quotations in Job

ONE OF THE MOST COMMON PROBLEMS confronting readers of the Bible is the occurrence of passages that appear out of place in the context, either in mood or in thought. The ideas expounded may seem irrelevant and even contradictory to the theme of the passage in which they are imbedded; or the emotion expressed may seem radically different from the spirit of the surrounding verses. To meet this difficulty scholars have adopted three basic procedures. In some instances they have rearranged the text, placing the offending passages in what they regard as a more "logical order." In other cases they have analyzed or atomized the literary document, on the theory that the present text is a collection of originally independent writings put together none too skillfully by one or more editors. Finally, and most frequently, they delete stichs, verses, and even entire sections of the received text on the ground that they are later, unauthentic additions. Often the additional assumption is made that these alleged interpolations were added by readers and scribes opposed to the views of the original writers, which they sought to counteract by these insertions into the text.

During the heyday of biblical hypercriticism, and even today, scholars rarely stopped to note that these radical solutions were almo completely subjective and arbitrary and therefore methodologica unsound. Underlying them all was a basic error—the failure to reco nize the wide disparity in time, space, and culture pattern between t modern Western mind and that of an ancient oriental poet. T canons of logic and aesthetics congenial to a modern Western writ cannot be mechanically applied to a literary composition of the ancie East.

In the West, material is organized on the basis of presumed logic coherence. In the Semitic world, the structure tends to be based the association of ideas, often on the similarity of an opening phra in two passages. Such diverse works as the prophetic oracles in t Bible, the Mishnah, the Talmud, and the Koran offer countless illu trations of the truth of this observation.[1]

So, too, with regard to the expression of emotion. The relati restraint and gradual shifting of mood characteristic of Weste writers, to which we are accustomed, are poles away from the violen and lightning changes in feeling poured out by the Hebrew poet. F him, faith and rebellion, love and hate, hope and despair, bitterness ar serenity, misery and joy, alternate rapidly and disconcertingly. T Psalms and Job particularly are replete with illustrations of this trut

To force the biblical writer into the Procrustean bed of Westei logic and aesthetics is to maim him beyond recognition. To "reco struct" the text to suit alien conceptions of proper logical sequence ar seemly emotional expression is to distort the work beyond recover Humility is more than a moral virtue; it is indispensable to the genui scientific spirit. The exegete must seek to follow the lead of the autho to penetrate to his spirit and do justice to the text before him, not t revise and improve upon it.

These a priori objections to the widespread use of transpositio divisions, or deletions of the accepted text are supported by the fac that there is no objective evidence in favor of these drastic manipula tions of the text. The extant Hebrew manuscripts and the Ancier Versions, including the Septuagint, the oldest witness, nearly alway reproduce the contents and order of our received text, including th allegedly interpolated passages.[2]

Equally unsatisfactory is the proposed explanation that later reade were opposed to the contents of the original text and therefore adde their contradictory views in rebuttal. The question of why reade should have taken the trouble to add so much additional material, whe a far easier procedure was available to them, was not raised, let alone answered. All that was necessary was to destroy the manuscript or consign it to some *Genizah* or storage room of discarded texts, and thus effectively remove it from circulation. A striking case in point is afforded by the entire corpus of apocryphal literature, which was not admitted to the canon of Hebrew scriptures because of legal, doctrinal, or other divergences from normative Judaism. As a result, the Hebrew originals of books like Jubilees, the Maccabees, Judith, Tobit, and many other works of quality and importance, disappeared. Only translations of these books were preserved, and then only because of the interest manifested by the early Church. Even Ben Sira, a book which the rabbis knew, admired, and quoted, suffered the same fate. Its historical references clearly dated it after the end of "the period of divine inspiration."[3] It was excluded from the canon and as a result was eventually lost. Only some stray manuscripts survived in later copies that were found by Solomon Schechter nearly two millennia later in the *Genizah* of the Cairo synagogue. When total suppression was so much easier and more effective, why should orthodox readers of heterodox books undertake the arduous task of interpolating their own views?

Moreover, the sheer extent of these alleged "additions" should have raised serious doubts about their deletion. Thus in the case of Ecclesiastes, Jastrow finds over 120 interpolations in a book of 222 verses. Barton, less extreme, claims that a pious glossator is responsible for 15 important additions and that a "Wisdom" interpolator is the author of 30 more (in addition to many other, lesser changes). Volz eliminates an equal number of passages, which do not, however, coincide with Barton's. The "analysis of sources" was applied by Siegfried to Ecclesiastes. He finds nine distinct major sources for this small book and assigns each verse, with enviable omniscience, to its author. Eissfeldt protests vigorously against this assumption of composite authorship and assumes only nine pious additions in the body of the book. However, he saves the authenticity of the text only by assuming that Koheleth contains no clear-cut, integrated philosophy, but consists merely of a series of rambling reflections that often contradict one another.[4]

In wielding the scalpel with such confidence, scholars did not always stop to notice the fragments left behind after the surgical process was completed. Thus in Job, chapter 12, which contains 25 verses, Grill and Siegfried eliminate 22 verses, Driver and Gray delete nine, Jastrow omits 12, in whole or in part, while Volz retains only five verses of the total.[5] In Job, chapter 21, widespread excision and emendation have been resorted to in order to make verses 19–34 relevant and intelligible, the net result often being the creation of impossible Hebrew.[6] Moreover, the testimony of the Ancient Versions supports the integrity of the present text of chapters 12 and 21. This is true even of the Septuagint, which often contracts the poetic sections of Job because of the difficulty of the text and the redundancy of Hebrew parallelism to Greek ears.[7]

Over two decades ago, my researches in Wisdom literature, and Ecclesiastes in particular, led me to reject this procedure of wholesale deletion, not only because it does violence to the integrity of the biblical text, but also because it destroys the content and timbre of the book. It is gratifying to note that the formerly widespread theory of interpolation by uncomprehending or hostile readers is losing ground increasingly among contemporary scholars.[8] Thus Aage Bentzen observes: "The separation of sources is sometimes driven to a caricature, as in *Ecclesiastes* and *Job*. The British pun 'Is the Pentateuch Mosaic or a mosaic?' is not only characteristic for the sentiment among opponents of literary criticism, but also among the younger generation of scholars as a whole."[9]

Recognizing the inadequacies of the hypercritical procedures is, however, not enough. It is at least as important to propose a new approach to solving the problems with which these earlier methods grappled unsuccessfully. Basically, the key lies in a deeper insight into the spirit and form of the literature being studied—two aspects of a single whole.[10] For the spirit of the author, the unique aspects of his personality as well as the elements derived from his background, are all revealed in his style. When an effort is made to penetrate to the inner spirit of biblical Wisdom with sympathy and insight, several significant stylistic phenomena, hitherto overlooked, come to light.

Two such elements, I believe, are fundamental for an understanding of Wisdom literature. One, particularly characteristic of the style of the author of Ecclesiastes, is the use of a traditional religious vocabulary to express an unconventional world view.[11] Of more general application, and more directly relevant to Job, is another stylistic trait to which I have called attention—the varied use of quotations without any external sign to indicate their character.[12] Evidence for this usage in all branches of oriental literature—Sumerian, Akkadian, Egyptian, and Ugaritic—though previously unrecognized, grows increasingly abundant.[13] It serves as a key to the understanding of many passages in the

Prophets, the Psalms, and above all, in the biblical Wisdom books. The usage is also amply illustrated in rabbinic literature.[14]

What is significant is that these quotations are not indicated by any outward sign. Not only are they not marked by a system of punctuation (which naturally did not exist in ancient times), but they are not introduced by a *verbum dicendi* or *cogitandi*, a verb of speaking or thinking (as, for example, "I thought"; "you said"). That the passage in question is nevertheless a quotation must be understood by the reader, who, in Semitic literature, is called upon to supply not only the punctuation but the vocalization as well.[15] In the absence of any external sign of a quotation, the decision must obviously depend upon the insight of the interpreter. There is therefore room for difference of opinion over any given passage. This merely underscores the truth, applicable everywhere, that there is no substitute for exegetical tact in penetrating to the meaning of a literary text.[16]

It should be understood that the quotation may be the original work of the author, or a citation from another individual, or it may be drawn from the wells of folk wisdom and hence is to be regarded as collective in origin. As Archer Taylor points out in his learned and stimulating study of *The Proverb:*

> We shall never know, for example, which of the Exeter Gnomes in old English poetry are proverbial and which are the collector's moralizing in the same pattern. . . . In a dead language the means which are available are various, but not always effective or easily applied. A passage, when it varies grammatically or syntactically from ordinary usage or from the usage of the context, can be safely declared to be proverbial.

Taylor also cites countless examples of the difficulty in distinguishing folk sayings and the work of individuals and remarks:

> Of course, an individual creates a proverb and sets it in circulation. The inventor's title to his property may be recognized by all who use it or his title may be so obscured by the passage of time that only investigation will determine the source of the saying.

In his discussion of biblical proverbs he observes:

> Biblical proverbs, and among them perhaps even those which we have discussed, may have been proverbs before their incorporation into Holy Writ.[17]

It should also be noted that the tendency to omit the verb of speaking or thinking is particularly common where several quotations occur in succession. Here the verb may be used in one passage and omitted in the next.[18]

In sum, the term "quotations" refers to words which do not reflect the present sentiments or situation of the speaker, but have been introduced by the author to convey the standpoint either of another person or of another situation. Hence the term includes quotations in the usual sense, that is to say, citations from previously existing literature, whether written or oral. It is, however, not limited to them. It also embraces passages that cite the speaker's words or thoughts whether actual or hypothetical, past or present, which are distinct from the present context.

It will be evident that the various types of quotations do not represent distinct categories, but closely related developments of the same basic technique. While a full discussion of this usage in biblical and oriental literature is available elsewhere, it will be useful to list the ten principal categories of quotations to be found in the Bible:

1. Citations from the current folk wisdom, generally couched in the form of an apothegm or a rhetorical question. This is characteristic of Wisdom literature, but not limited to it. It constitutes a valuable key to the understanding of Ecclesiastes.[19]

2. The speaker's direct quotation of the words of others, such as his foes,[20] his friends,[21] his God,[22] or the people.[23] This usage is frequent in the Psalms and the Prophets.

3. The development of an elaborate dialogue where the identity of the particular speaker must be inferred by the reader.[24] This stylistic trait is particularly noticeable in the prophets Hosea and Jeremiah, between whom a marked affinity of spirit exists. The recognition of the use of dialogue in the Song of Songs, though long noted, is important for the interpretation of many passages.[25]

4. Presentations of the unspoken thought of the speaker,[26] a usage often employed in passages describing the naming of children.[27]

5. The citation of prayers offered on earlier occasions[28] or promised for the future when deliverance comes.[29]

6. The presentation of ideas previously held by the speaker or writer.[30]

7. A hypothetical idea that might or should have occurred to the subject.[31]

8. The citation of a proverb, either without comment[32] or expanded by an additional observation by the author, supporting or opposing the sentiment embodied in the quotation.[33]
9. The use of contrasting proverbs to negate one view and affirm another.[34]
10. The citation of the arguments of one's opponents in debate. This is almost never literal and generally contains a greater or lesser degree of exaggeration and even of distortion. This type of quotation is highly significant in Job.
11. Indirect quotations with or without a *verbum dicendi.*

Our concern here is naturally limited to those categories of quotations that occur in Job. The types of quotations numbered above as 2, 3, 5, and 7 are not found in the book.

1. Brief citations from folk wisdom are to be met frequently in Job. This usage is particularly congenial to Wisdom writers, who invoked the accumulated observation and experience of the past for the edification and guidance of the present. As we have seen, the basic literary form of Wisdom is the *māšāl*, literally, a "comparison" or "analogy." The term also developed the meaning "apothegm" or "proverb" (usually limited to one or two verses). Later it was applied to longer literary units, and then meant "parable, fable," and "Wisdom discourse."[35] Most frequently, however, *māšāl* refers to a generalization about life couched in a brief statement.

Folk sayings, because of their wide currency, often become clipped in form and are not always easily comprehensible. An instance occurs in the prologue:

> Then Satan answered the Lord saying,
> "Skin for skin!
> All a man has
> He will give for his life!"

> [Job 2:4]

The first half of Satan's speech bears all the earmarks of a folk proverb. Witness the parallelism of structure, the realistic character of the generalization, and above all the idiomatic brevity of the first stich (*'ōr bᵉ 'ad 'ōr*), which creates difficulties for the modern exegete.[36]

Other apothegms, whether the author is quoting from the extant literature, or, as is more probable, is writing in its spirit, are:

Anger surely kills the fool,
And impatience slays the simpleton.
Indeed, misfortune does not come forth from the ground,
Nor does evil sprout from the earth.
It is man who gives birth to evil,
As surely as sparks fly upward.[37]

[5:2, 6, 7]

But a stupid man will get understanding,
As soon as a wild ass's colt is born a man.

[11:12]

The poet expresses the fact that human life fades and vanishes without
a trace by the metaphor of the drying up of a river. The sentiment
gains in power because so much is left to the imagination and insight of
the reader:

As water vanishes from a lake,
And a river is parched and dries up,
So man lies down and rises not again;
Till the heavens are no more he will not awake,
Nor will he be roused from his sleep.

[14:11–12]

This figure the author of Job borrowed from the prophet Isaiah,
who used it to describe the imminent destruction of Egypt, which is
frequently pictured as "the River" because of the importance of the
Nile for its existence:

The waters of the Nile will be dried up,
And the River will be parched and dry.

[Isa. 19:5]

The poet has, however, given the figure a broader, universal meaning.
In another passage, Job insists that his friends are dispensing wisdom
to him very generously, when their own stock of the commodity is all
too slender. He uses a proverbial utterance to make his point by an
analogy which is again left to the reader's understanding:

"He invites his friends to share his bounty,
While the eyes of his own children grow faint from hunger!"[38]

[Job 17:5]

Do you not know this from of old,
Ever since man was placed upon earth,
That the exultation of the wicked is short-lived,
The joy of the godless but for a moment?

[20:4, 5]

This practical Wisdom may be expressed in two forms, declaratively and interrogatively. The rhetorical question has the advantage of being more exciting, since it actively involves the listener or the reader, who is called upon to answer with a resounding "No!" Thus we may compare the familiar cry of dissension which re-echoed during the early days of the Hebrew Kingdom and which occurs in both forms in our sources. The declarative formulation reads:

We have no portion in David,
No inheritance in the son of Jesse;
Every man to his tents, O Israel!

[II Sam. 20:1]

The interrogative form is more vigorous:

What portion have we in David?
No inheritance in the son of Jesse,
To your tents, O Israel!

[I Kings 12:16]

Because of the greater vitality of the rhetorical question, the Wisdom writer will frequently summarize the fruits of practical experiences in interrogative form. The writer expects that the analogy, which is generally left to be inferred, will not be lost upon the reader.

The superiority of the rhetorical question over the declarative maxim may also be illustrated by comparing an Akkadian saying with its Sumerian original, each of which indicates that something is an utter impossibility. The Akkadian proverb says:

Without copulation she conceived,
Without eating she became plump!

The Sumerian original is:

Without his cohabiting with you,
Can you be pregnant?
Without his feeding you,
Can you be fat?[39]

This use of the question form is highly characteristic of the prophet Amos:

> Do two walk together
> Unless they have made an appointment?
> Does a lion roar in the forest
> When he has no prey?
> Does a young lion cry out from his den
> If he has taken nothing?
> Does a bird fall in a snare on the earth
> When there is no trap for it?
> Does a snare spring up from the ground
> When it has taken nothing?
> Is a trumpet blown in a city
> And the people are not afraid?
> Does evil befall a city
> Unless the Lord has done it?
>
> [Amos 3:3-6]

> Do horses run upon rocks?
> Does one plow the sea with oxen?
> But you have turned justice into poison
> And the fruit of righteousness into wormwood.
>
> [Amos 6:12]

In the first instance the analogy is explicated; in the second, it is only implied.

This usage is equally popular with the author of Job. The passage 6:5-6 is particularly interesting. Job wishes to emphasize that his impatient outcry is not without cause, and that, conversely, his friends who are not suffering themselves find it easy to retain their composure. He makes both these points effectively in one interrogative apothegm:

> Does the wild ass bray when he has grass,
> Or the ox low over his fodder?

He then wants to say that their words of comfort addressed to him are tasteless and senseless. (It should be noted that the Hebrew noun *ta'am* means both "taste" and "sense.") He conveys this idea, again by implication, through a folk proverb, once more in the form of a rhetorical question:

> Can tasteless food be eaten without salt,
> Or is there any savor in the juice of mallows?
>
> [Job 6:6]

Later in the dialogue, Bildad wishes to stress the fact that Job's suffering must be the result of sin, because all effects have causes. He cites the wisdom of the elders in the form of a question:

> Indeed, they will teach and inform you
> And out of their understanding utter these words:
> "Can papyrus grow where there is no marsh?
> Can reeds flourish without water?"
>
> [8:10,11]

It is entirely appropriate that the Lord, whose wisdom (unlike that of men) is not derived from experience and observation, does not make use of proverbs. However, in the deepest sense, His entire speech is a transcendental *māšāl*, a cosmic comparison or analogy between the natural world and the moral order, both of which we are called upon to see as possessing pattern and meaning.

4. Direct quotations of the thoughts of the subject, where a verb of thinking must be supplied in order to express a present thought or motive, also appear in the book.

Job 7:4 is rendered by RSV:

> When I lie down, I say:
> "When shall I arise?"
> But the night is long,
> And I am full of tossing to and fro
> Until the dawning of the day.

Here the parallelism indicates that the closing clause is a quotation. The verse is to be rendered:

> When I lie down, I ask, "When shall I arise?"
> But the night is long, *and I say,*
> "I have had my fill of tossing till daybreak."

In Job, chapter 15, Bildad describes the lot of the wicked. Verse 21 is translated by RSV:

> A sound of terrors is in his ears;
> In prosperity the destroyer shall come upon him.

However, as the context makes clear, the second clause is not a picture of his actual doom, but a description of the sinner's psychological terror during his apparent prosperity. Hence a verb of thinking needs to be supplied if the meaning is to be properly understood. The second verse following (vs. 23) also requires a *verbum dicendi* ("asking"). The entire passage is to be rendered as follows:

> All his days, the wicked is atremble
> Throughout the few years stored up for the oppressor.
> The sound of terror is always in his ears;
> Even while at peace *he fears* the despoiler coming upon him.
> He does not hope to escape from the darkness,
> But can look forward only to the sword.
> He wanders about for bread, *asking*, "Where is it?"
> Knowing that the day of darkness awaits him.[40]

Job, chapter 22, offers two more illustrations of this usage. In verses 5–9 Eliphaz charges Job with heinous crimes against his fellow men. Verse 8 seems to be a generalization, which is deleted by many commentators as being irrelevant to the context.[41] To ease the problem, the verse is rendered in the past tense by others and then taken as an oblique reference to Job.[42] Thus RSV translates:

> The man with power owned the land,
> And the favored man dwelt in it.

This procedure is unnecessary, for what we have here is the rationale for Job's alleged misdeeds. The passage is accordingly to be rendered:

> In fact, your wickedness is immense,
> There is no end to your iniquities.
> For you have taken pledges even from your kinsmen for no
>   reason,
> And stripped the naked of their clothing.
> No water have you given to the weary,
> And from the hungry you have withheld bread.
> *For you believe,*
> "The man of violence owns the land,
> And he who is powerful lives upon it."

The second instance in this chapter occurs in verses 12–14. Because verse 12 seems irrelevant, some scholars rearrange the verse order or delete it completely as a gloss. This is unnecessary. We need only recognize that verse 12 is a statement of the thoughts attributed to Job:[43]

You thought,
"Indeed God is in the lofty heavens,[44]
And see the topmost stars, how high they are!"
So you said,
"What does God know?
Can He judge through the thick cloud?
Clouds cover Him, so that He cannot see
As He strolls about the circuit of heaven."

6. Quotations embodying a previous point of view or thought of the speaker, which he has now surrendered, are found in Job. These passages need to be introduced by a formula in the past tense, such as "I thought."

The great "Confession of Integrity" in Job, chapter 31, illustrates this usage. Job describes his lifelong standard of integrity and moral behavior toward all human beings, which derives from his vivid sense of the presence of God. Throughout the years of his prosperity he had maintained a deep faith that justice governs the world and that evil is punished. What is needed here is a recognition that verses 2 and 14 are virtual quotations, setting forth his earlier faith in God's retribution.[45] The same theme is stated directly in verse 23:

For I always feared a calamity coming from God,
And I could not have borne His destroying me.[46]

The various deletions and transpositions proposed by the commentators for the chapter are thus unnecessary—indeed they do violence to the deeper dimensions of Job's "Confession."[47] The salient portions of the passage are to be rendered:

I made a covenant with my eyes;
How then could I look lustfully upon a maid?
For I thought, "If I sinned,
What would be my portion from God above
And my lot from the Almighty on high?
Surely calamity waits for the unrighteous
And disaster for the workers of iniquity!
God will certainly see my ways
And count all my steps!"
Have I despised the cause of my manservant,
Or of my maidservant, when they contended with me?

For I always remembered,
"What shall I do when God rises up,
And when He examines me, how shall I answer Him?
Did not He make him in the womb, as He made me,
And fashion us both alike in the womb?"[48]

[31:1–4, 13–15]

This use of quotations is the key to the understanding of Job, chapter 27, which is crucial to the restoration of the third cycle (chaps. 25–31).[49] In our received text, chapter 27 is assigned to Job. Nonetheless, it is evident that it is not homogeneous, but falls into three sections which must be considered separately (vss. 2–6, 7–12, 13–23).

It is clear that the first section (vss. 2–6), in which Job's innocence is passionately averred, is appropriate to him and constitutes an authentic portion of his speech. On the other hand, the third section (vss. 13–23), which describes the doom of the wicked in thoroughly conventional fashion, cannot belong to Job. It is best assigned to Zophar, who otherwise would not appear in the third cycle at all.[50]

It is the central section (vss. 7–12) which has proved a major stumbling block to the interpreter. These lines express the conviction that the sinner is punished by being excluded from the favor of God. This is surely not Job's standpoint as expressed in the dialogue. Hence the passage is usually assigned either to Bildad or to Zophar.[51] But this procedure does not commend itself for several reasons.[52] In the first instance, verse 8 is linked by the conjunction "for" (*kī*) to verse 7, which can only emanate from Job, as is clear from the first person singular suffixes, "my enemy, my foe" (*'ōyebhī, mithkōm⁶mī*). Second, the use in verses 11–12 of the second person plural in direct address (*'ethkhem, kullekhem, tehbālū*) indicates that these verses must also belong to Job and are being addressed to his friends. Indeed, they probably mark the conclusion of Job's speech, such attacks being characteristic of several of his earlier perorations (6:26–29; 21:34). We thus find ourselves in a difficult position: the section is contradictory to Job's position, but it is obviously addressed by him to the Friends!

The solution to the problem lies in recognizing that the entire passage (vss. 7–12) belongs to Job and is a unit with the preceding section (vss. 2–6). It contains a description of Job's earlier outlook during his previous state of happy innocence and prosperity.[53] The substance of this passage resembles Job's "Confession of Integrity" in chapter 31 (vss. 2–4, 14–15, 23). The unity and the power of the entire section become clear in the translation of chapter 27 to be found in Part Two of this book.

8. A proverb may be cited as a text, which is then elaborated on, modified, or contravened by the writer. While this usage is particularly characteristic of Ecclesiastes, it occurs in Job as well. Thus the youthful Elihu rejects the universal assumption of his day that wisdom is limited to the aged. He does so by citing a conventional proverb and then commenting on it:

> I am young, and you are old,
> Therefore I was afraid, and dared not
> Voice my opinion in your presence.
> *I thought,*
> "Age should speak,
> And the years should teach wisdom,"
> But it is the spirit in a man,
> And the breath of the Almighty that gives understanding.
> Not always are old men wise;
> Nor do the aged understand the truth.
>
> [32:6–9]

9. Another instance of quotation in Job comes in the use of contrasting proverbs. Since proverbs generally embody practical though partial observations of life, they often contradict each other. One has only to recall such English sayings as "Absence makes the heart grow fonder" and "Out of sight, out of mind," or "Fools rush in where angels fear to tread" and "He who hesitates is lost." In the Book of Proverbs, which is a Wisdom anthology, two such contradictory proverbs are juxtaposed: "Answer not a fool according to his folly, lest you become like him" and "Answer a fool according to his folly, lest he be wise in his own eyes" (Prov. 26:4, 5).

The unconventional Wisdom writers utilize this device of contrasting proverbs for their own purpose. In order to refute a widely held view they will cite a proverb and then follow it with another of opposite intent, the second representing their own viewpoint. Thus Koheleth, wishing to refute the respectable doctrine that hard work is praiseworthy, quotes one proverb extolling diligence and juxtaposes another in praise of indolence. For the modern Western reader, but not for the ancient Hebrew, introductory formulas are needed:

Some men say,
"The fool folds his hands and thus destroys himself."
But I declare,
"Better a handful acquired with ease,
    Than two hands full, gained through toil and chasing of
        wind."⁵⁴

[Eccles. 4:5, 6]

The recognition of this device helps to explain an otherwise abrupt transition in Job 12:12, 13. Throughout the dialogue, Job's friends, in true Semitic fashion, regard it as self-evident that the truth is with them because they are older than he and because they are expounding the wisdom of the ages:⁵⁵

Were you born the first among men,
And brought forth before the hills?

For inquire, I pray you, of an earlier generation,
And heed the insight of their fathers—
(For we ourselves are mere yesterdays and know nothing;
Our days, only a shadow upon earth)—
Indeed, they will teach and inform you
And out of their understanding utter these words.

[Job 15:7; 8:8–10]

What do you know that we do not;
What do you understand that is beyond us?
Both the graybeard and the aged are among us,
Older in years than your father.⁵⁶

[15:9, 10]

Job denies this universally held principle by citing it in one proverb and refuting it in another. Here, too, the use of quotation marks and an introductory formula makes the connection clear:

You say, "With the aged is wisdom,
    In length of days is understanding."
But I say, "With God are wisdom and strength,
    His are counsel and understanding."

[12:12, 13]⁵⁷

It should be noted that strictly speaking the two proverbs do *not* contradict each other directly, since the first praises the sagacity of the aged and the second asserts the wisdom of God. It is only because they are placed in juxtaposition to one another that the second subtly serves to undermine the first. Since both sayings are true, it is to be expected that neither will directly negate the other.

An Akkadian proverb collection offers another instructive example of contrasting but not contradictory proverbs. Here, too, the writer's (or anthologist's) sympathies seem to be with the second apothegm, which has "the last word":

> *You say,* From before the gate of the city whose armament
> is not powerful
> The enemy cannot be repulsed.
> *I answer,* You go and take the field of the enemy;
> The enemy comes and takes your field.

As Pfeiffer points out, the first is the perennial argument for preparedness; the second, in contrast, is the argument of the pacifist.[58]

To revert to our passage in Job, the authenticity of both proverbs—and the contrast between them—emerges from the terms employed in the two verses. "Wisdom" and "understanding" are attributed to the aged (vs. 12), but to God more is given: "wisdom and might" and "counsel and understanding" (vs. 13).[59]

10. The most characteristic use of quotations in the book lies in their use in argumentation. Again and again Job quotes the utterances of his opponents, even distorting them in some degree, and then proceeds to refute them.

Job's closing speech in the second cycle (21:19–34) affords a superb illustration. Here commentators have resorted to wholesale excisions and emendations in order to make the passage intelligible. These expedients are not needed if we recognize that Job is here restating no less than four arguments of the Friends and rebutting each in turn. Since the passage has already been discussed above, it suffices to summarize these four points:

1. The Friends have argued repeatedly that the sins of the father will be visited upon the children (e.g., Job 5:4; 18:12; 20:10, 26). In 21:19a, Job quotes this view; in 21:19b–21, he rejects it.
2. Another argument of the Friends is that God is too exalted for hu-

man comprehension, and hence His wisdom is legitimately beyond man's criticism. This is a favorite theme of Eliphaz (4:17; 15:8, 14) and Zophar (11:6 ff.). This view Job cites in 21:22:

> "Shall anyone teach God knowledge,
> Seeing that He judges those on high?"

His rejoinder is in verses 23–26.

3. The Friends have frequently pointed out that while the sinner may seem to be well intrenched in his prosperity, calamity will suddenly come upon him, destroying his habitation and leaving nothing to mark the site of his former glory. This position has been emphasized by Eliphaz (5:3 ff.; 15:32 ff.), Bildad (8:22; 18:5–21), and Zophar (11:20; 20:26).

Job quotes this favorite doctrine of the Friends in the form of a rhetorical question addressed to him (21:28):

> "Where is the house of the nobleman,
> And where is the dwelling of the wicked?"

Job's sarcastic reply that any passer-by can point out the mansion of the oppressor standing unharmed in all its glory is in verse 29.

4. The Friends have insisted all along that punishment ultimately overtakes the sinner, no matter how long the delay. Koheleth points out that it is this delay in punishment that encourages men to commit crime (Eccles. 8:11 ff.).[60] Job, however, is concerned with the fundamental injustice involved. He quotes the opinion of the Friends (vs. 30), but he insists that justice demands an immediate punishment of the sinner. Instead, Job says, the transgressor lives a life of ease, and to cap it all, is buried with pomp and ceremony at the end (vss. 30–34).

The entire passage (21:19–34), translated above in chapter vii, is a striking example of effective argument, marked by passion, irony, and logic.[61]

It is noteworthy that three times there is no *verbum dicendi* (vss. 19, 22, 30), while once (vs. 28) a verb does occur, a variation in usage we have noted elsewhere.

Another form of quotation used in the argumentation by Job may be described as "oblique restatement." At times Job cites the opinion of the Friends not literally but ironically, in a form bordering on parody.

Failure to recognize this fact has vitiated many attempts to interpret chapter 12, one of Job's most striking utterances, which we have already discussed.

In brief, chapter 12 illustrates several categories of the use of quotations. In verses 7–8 the use of the singular verb and suffixes ("ask thou," "will teach thee," "to thee," "speak thou") makes it clear that Job cannot be speaking to his friends, whom he always addresses in the plural (6:21–29).[62] The passage is, therefore, a restatement by Job of the Friends' admonition to him. Verses 12–13 are a pair of contrasting quotations, designed to refute the notion that wisdom is the private preserve of the aged. Finally, verses 14–25 contain a paean of praise to God, couched in negative terms, a parody of similar descriptions by the Friends of God's beneficent power.

It is noteworthy that this oblique restatement by Job of the position of the Friends occurs in his closing speech in the first cycle, exactly as his detailed refutation of the Friends' standpoint is found in chapter 21, Job's concluding speech of the second cycle.

No such recapitulation by Job occurs at the end of the third cycle. This may be merely the result of the disarrangement and loss of material which the third cycle has sustained in our present text. It is, however, more likely that the absence of this usage is due to the fact that the third cycle ends in a soliloquy (chaps. 29–31) which parallels Job's original lament. In the soliloquy, all argument has ended and Job is no longer conscious of the presence of the Friends.

Job uses the device of quotations once more, after the other side has spoken.[63] In his final reconciliation with God he repeats His words, but this time with no distortion or exaggeration. The Lord speaking out of the whirlwind, begins:

> Who is this that darkens My plan
> By words without knowledge?
> Gird up your loins like a man;
> I will question you, and you may inform Me.
>
> [38:2–3]

After God has spoken, Job is overcome. He is overwhelmed by the disclosure of the vast miracle and mystery of the world, of which man's existence and suffering constitute only a minor facet. In voicing his submission, Job repeats the Lord's opening challenge to him, but again without any external sign of a quotation. After each citation he adds his humble comment. In his humility there is a note of triumph that God has deigned to meet and argue with him:

> I know that You can do all things
> And that no purpose of Yours can be thwarted.
> *You have said,*
> "Who is this that hides My plan without knowledge?"
> Indeed, I have spoken without understanding,
> Of things too wonderful for me, which I did not grasp.
> *You have said,*
> "Hear, and I will speak;
> I will ask you, and do you inform Me."
> I have heard of You by hearsay,
> But now my own eyes have seen You.
> Therefore I abase myself
> And repent in dust and ashes.

> [42:2–6]

That this use of quotations occurs not once but three times in the book, and in each case in Job's final reply, is scarcely a coincidence. On the contrary, it helps to demonstrate that this rhetorical use is a device favored by the poet. This similarity of usage also strengthens the view that the dialogue with the Friends and the God speeches emanate from the same pen.

11. Indirect quotations with or without a *verbum dicendi* constitute another category of quotations hitherto unrecognized because of its infrequency. Nonetheless, it is to be met in both biblical[64] and extra-biblical literature.[65] This usage occurs a few times in Job. Naturally it is rare, since the book consists largely of direct confrontations by the antagonists.

In 19:28, Job cites his friends both directly and indirectly:

> When you say, "How shall we persecute him,[66]
> Since the root of the matter must be found in me?"
> I answer, "Be afraid of the sword."

> [19:28–29a]

In Elihu's address to Job (35:2–3) we have a direct quotation, then an indirect one, followed by a direct quotation once more:

> Do you consider this to be right,
> To say, "I am more righteous than God!"
> Or to ask, "What advantage is it for you [i.e., for Job],
> What good, if I avoid sin?"[67]

A far more important and difficult passage, one which has long baffled the commentators, occurs in 13:14. The plethora of radical emendations and deletions which have been proposed is, I believe, unnecessary. We need only to recognize the presence here of an indirect quotation without a *verbum dicendi*. The verse is to be rendered:

> *You ask* why I place my flesh in my teeth
> And take my life in my hand [i.e., endanger my life
>   by my protests]?
> Yes, He may slay me; I have no hope,
> But I will justify my ways to His face!
>
> [13:14, 15]

It is clear that the use of quotation in Job (as elsewhere in biblical and oriental literature) is a highly important element in the author's style, and by that token, a significant key to the meaning of the book.

XIV

The Rhetoric of Allusion and Analogy

THE GREATNESS OF JOB resides not merely in the passion of its speeches but in the power of its silences. When Keats said, "Heard melodies are sweet, but those unheard are sweeter," he was concerned with beauty, but his insight applies to truth as well. What our poet hints at or leaves unsaid is at times more significant for his basic theme than what he sets forth explicitly.

As we have seen, the God speeches contain no direct confrontation with Job on the fundamental issues of evil, sin, and suffering. The Lord makes only the briefest reference to the moral government of the universe (40:7–14), and then only to concede obliquely that evil does exist in the world and has not been fully conquered. The Lord's reticence on this basic issue is Job's vindication. The sufferer's innocence is affirmed by implication; it is spelled out only in the epilogue, when the Lord informs the Friends that it is not they who have spoken the truth about Him, but Job, and when He adds—supreme irony—that Job must intercede for them (42:7–8)!

Job has been right in insisting that his suffering is no proof of his sin, but wrong in seeing the entire universe refracted through the prism of his personal agony. It is to this basic theme that the bulk of the God speeches is directed. But, as has been maintained above, their intent is not explicated but implied, not stated but suggested, not demonstrated but left to be inferred from analogy.

Instead of dealing directly with man and his problems, the God speeches depict the glories of nature as a manifestation of God's creative power—indeed, of His deep concern for all His creatures. In his conceit and self-centeredness, man may dismiss the lower animals as brutes, useless for his purposes, often ugly in appearance, and even dangerous to his life. But their Maker revels in them and sees in them beauty, strength, and the joy of creation.

Yet the God speeches do bear directly on the fundamental question to which the book is devoted. The author makes an analogy between the world of nature and the world of man, which the reader is expected to understand. With infectious enthusiasm and joy, the poet makes it clear that the natural world, though incomprehensible to man and in part irrelevant to his concerns, possesses order and beauty. So, too, the moral universe, the area of man's action and experience, though largely beyond man's understanding and indeed not determined solely by his standards, possesses order and meaning.

Support for this approach to the basic theme of Job is to be sought in many areas. The evidence, drawn from several different intellectual disciplines, can be set forth only partially and imperfectly here. That an author should express his basic theme by indirection and depend upon the sensitivity and insight of the reader to grasp it fully may seem rather strange to modern readers. We are accustomed to having our intellectual tasks lightened for us by every conceivable means. Today we take for granted such time-honored devices as punctuation, paragraphing, and the use of illustrations and diagrams. Actually, they are all relatively recent innovations in the history of culture. Moreover, ours is the age of audio-visual aids, of the motion picture, the tabloid newspaper, and the television screen. It is no wonder that reading is fast becoming a lost art. Many of our contemporary youth have never learned, or have been weaned away from, the arduous task of transforming the symbols we call words into ideas. As a result, contemporary educators are wrestling anew with the problem of evolving techniques for teaching the art of reading.

In the ancient Semitic world far greater demands were made upon the reader than upon his modern counterpart. At their inception, most Semitic languages possessed only a consonantal alphabet, the vowels remaining without any representation for centuries.[1] The lack of vowel letters meant that in order to understand the meaning of a text, the reader himself had to supply the proper vowels upon which meaning depended. Thus, for example, the three Hebrew consonants *k-d-š*, which bear the root meaning of "set apart, holy," can be vocalized as seven different words,[2] and this variety is in no sense exceptional. To decide which word belongs in a given context constitutes an intellectual challenge of no mean order and one that confronted the reader on every line. Slowly vowel letters were added by scribes in setting down inscriptions and other texts. Even then the vowel signs were inserted principally at the ends of words, where the possibility of error and variation in reading was greatest.

When a sacred scripture came into being among some of the Semitic peoples—the Jews, later the Syrian Christians, and much later, the Arabs—the custodians of the text were confronted by two seemingly contradictory objectives. On the one hand, there was the desire to make the book accessible and intelligible to many readers. On the other, there was the need to prevent divergences and possible errors from entering the sacred text. Nor could each scribe and copyist be permitted to add vowel letters to the sacred text as he pleased, in accordance with his knowledge or ignorance. In order to achieve both purposes—to ease the difficulties of reading and yet safeguard the received text from changes—a technique of vowel signs was slowly evolved after considerable experimentation. Various systems of vocalization came into being for use in reading the Hebrew Bible, the Syriac *Pešita*, and the Arabic *Qoran*.[3] Even in Hebrew, Syriac, and Arabic, however, all other texts continued to be written and read without vowel signs and with a minimum of vowel letters. Moreover, in the case of the scriptures, most manuscripts were left unvocalized since the insertion of vowel signs was a tedious and difficult process. Indeed, in Judaism the rabbis made it mandatory that the scrolls of the Law, the Prophets, and the Five Megillot used for public reading in the synagogue be left unvocalized, as they are to the present day.

An additional problem for the Hebrew reader was the absence of any system of punctuation and paragraphing. For example, as every student of the Talmud knows full well, each reader has to decide for himself whether a given passage is a continuation of the previous section or a new one and whether it is to be understood as a statement or as a question, as an objection or as a refutation. By and large, however, the talmudic student regards these difficulties as a stimulus and a source of satisfaction when the hurdles are overcome.

The active intellectual effort to which ancient readers were accustomed explains the widespread use in Semitic literature of quotations without any external mark to indicate their character.[4] As we have seen, such "virtual quotations" are to be found in all branches of oriental literature, but are particularly frequent in Wisdom writings.

We have thus far concerned ourselves with the problems confronting the art of reading in the Semitic world. These difficulties, like the absence of reading aids, such as vocalization and punctuation, were basically practical. They were due to the fact that Semitic texts were written relatively early in the history of literature, when the techniques were primitive and still largely undeveloped. As new devices were discovered and perfected, the reader encountered less and less difficulty in understanding a given text.

Of an altogether different order are the abiding and complex problems inherent in the process of communication per se, to which philosophers, psychologists, and creative artists are giving ever greater attention.[5] Today we are more conscious than ever before that all true communication, in literature, art, music, or speech, is a mutually creative activity of both participants: the artist and the one to whom he directs his efforts—the reader, the listener, the viewer.

This insight derives from the growing recognition that symbolism plays a fundamental role in virtually every human activity and relationship. Today the central position of symbols in literature, art, philosophy, and religion is being intensively explored. With no pretense to completeness on so complex a subject, we may set down some basic observations on symbolism.

Every symbol is an effort to express some aspect of reality through the medium of an analogy resting upon a similarity, whether of word, sound, image, or act. The affinity between the object and the symbol may be inherent in their substance, as in a Passover ritual that dramatizes the historical event of the Exodus, or in a pagan fertility rite that re-enacts the natural process of procreation. Or the resemblance between the symbol and its object may be accidental and external, as in a rhetorical figure like paronomasia, where two words chance to sound alike. Or the analogy may be purely arbitrary and conventional, as when a flag possessing certain colors becomes the accepted symbol of a nation.

In every case, the symbol, be it a word, an image, or a ritual, constitutes only half the correspondence between reality and its representation. The second half, the reality to which the symbol points, must be inferred by the reader of the poem, the viewer of the image, or the participant in the ritual. In other words, a symbol operates not merely through the power of analogy inherent in its similarity to the external world, but also through the technique of allusiveness which the human agent must recognize.

It therefore follows that the role of the so-called passive partner in all these forms of communication is of fundamental importance. His function is almost as active and creative as that of the initiator of the symbolization. Indeed, if the former is unable or unwilling to play his part, the latter has failed.

The creation and acceptance of symbols is not so much a logical demonstration as it is a psychological enterprise. A symbol does not argue, it persuades, and this primarily through its emotional and aesthetic appeal. Freud has taught us that symbols may seem utterly remote and unconvincing to a detached observer and yet may exert a powerful hold upon the active participant. Modern psychoanalysts frequently propose interpretations of dreams, petty mistakes, acts of forgetting, and slips of the tongue which seem "far-fetched" to common sense. The proposed relationships depend upon analogies they discover between the unpleasant reality that the patient seeks to suppress and the harmless expression that he gives to it through some minor abnormal action. The various manifestations of the psychopathology of everyday life as well as major neuroses and psychoses are all instances of the symbol-making proclivity of human nature, which is one of its most fundamental traits.

Because of its frequently arbitrary or conventional character, a symbol is subject to many "legitimate" interpretations. The history of religions demonstrates that a given ritual will often remain unchanged, while the explanation advanced for its observance will be modified with advancing views or changed circumstances. It is this feature which makes possible both continuity and change in religion, as in all other areas of social experience. In general, however, the greater the genuine similarity between the object and its symbol, the more easily it wins general acceptance and carries conviction.

Our concern here is to recognize the basic role of analogy and allusiveness in the communication of ideas and attitudes and the active and creative function of the so-called passive partner in the process. It is the recognition of the importance of these factors that has prompted the widespread concern in contemporary philosophy with linguistic analysis and semantics, an area into which we cannot enter here. In the field of religious philosophy Martin Buber has made communication the cornerstone of his thought. For him, the "I-Thou" relationship is the essence of man's humanity. He sees the confrontation of man and God as the highest form of this relationship, as the very essence of the religious experience.

Revelation, which lies at the heart of religion, has accordingly been described by many religious thinkers as a two-way process of communication between God and man. Hence, the Bible, the deposit of revelation, is the product of both participants and partakes of the nature of the divine, unchanging Initiator—God, and the human, fluctuating, and imperfect recipient—man. In this "cosmic symbiosis," God depends upon man as truly as man depends upon God.[6]

The active role of the viewer is particularly obvious in the visual arts, especially in the dominant contemporary schools. Modern visual art, be it painting or sculpture, is largely non-representational. To a greater degree than in traditional forms, modern abstract art calls upon the viewer to play a creative role in the process of artistic experience—the vision of the artist is not consummated until his work has been interpreted by the consciousness of the spectator.

The co-operative character of the creative process has always been clear in the least concrete of the arts—music. Here communication becomes a triple partnership. The listener may legitimately find meanings and nuances not intended by either the composer or the performer. This truth is expressed in somewhat exaggerated form in Walter Kaufmann's statement, "Art is created not by the artist, but by posterity."[7]

Poetry, which represents both the poet's communion with his experience and his endeavor to communicate it to others, makes the greatest demands upon the reader. Since the magic of poetry lies in its power to evoke images, ideas, and moods beyond its explicit content, its nuances are more potent than its declarations. Hence, figures of speech are no mere embroideries upon the fabric, but the very essence of the pattern. By their vividness they recapture an experience, revive a presence, or conjure up an object that would otherwise have no real existence for the reader. Because of their power to suggest more than they state, they are the very substance of poetry.

These rhetorical figures are a source of keen aesthetic and intellectual pleasure as well. By invoking an analogy, they reveal to the reader, as in a lightning flash, a relationship between two objects of which he was not hitherto aware. The delight the reader experiences derives from the suddenness of his perception and his active role in recognizing the similarity. The psychological process has been described as "the astonishment that the poet has caused the reader to feel and the opportunity that he has given him to think, to solve and to find."[8] It does not matter whether the comparison rests upon a similarity of substance as in the case of metaphor or simile, or upon a resemblance or identity in sound, as in paronomasia and *talḥin*.

Robert Frost has gone so far as to identify poetry with metaphor. "Poetry is simply made of metaphor, saying one thing and meaning another, saying one thing in terms of another, the pleasure of ulteriority." Edgar Allan Poe spoke of the mystic expression of a sentiment as having "the vast force of an accompaniment in music." Poe's use of this phrase and his notion of "a suggestive indefiniteness" demonstrate according to a modern critic, that "Poe has hit on the essential nature of modern poetry—the suggestive overtones or undertones of implication which lie parallel with the surface meaning." Walt Whitman used the same concept of "suggestiveness" to express the essence of poetic expression.[9]

Thus, the very nature of poetry resides in the quality of allusiveness its penchant for implications that are left to be felt and understood— above all, to be shared and participated in—by the reader. In poetry, words are significant not merely for their *denotations*, the specific meanings which may be found catalogued in the dictionary, but above all, for their *connotations*, the nimbus which envelops them, the nuances which cluster about them, the associations which they arouse with other words, either because of the similarity or the contrast in sound between them.

A contemporary critic in assessing the greatness of Shakespeare underscores this truth:

> The great majority of men use language in an essentially unreflective, utilitarian way; they take words to have a fixed, single meaning. They regard speech as if its potential could be set down in a primer, in a pocket dictionary of basic usage. With education and the complication of our emotional needs through literature, we are made aware of the polyphonic structure of language, of the multiplicity of intents and implications, at times contradictory, latent in individual terms, in their placing and stress. We grow alert to the fact that none but the most formal or rudimentary of linguistic propositions has a single equivalence.

In Shakespeare, this alertness, this mastering response to the sum of all potential meanings and values, reached an intensity far beyond the norm. When using a word, or set of words, Shakespeare brings into controlled activity not only the range of definitions and current modes noted in the dictionary; he seems to hear around the core of every word the totality of its overtones and undertones; of its connotations and echoes. The analogy would be certain extreme subtleties and acuities of the musical ear. To Shakespeare, more than to any other poet, the individual word was a nucleus surrounded by a field of complex energies.[10]

This exclusive judgment needs to be broadened to include the author of Job, Goethe, and a handful of other supreme poets.

It therefore follows that form in poetry is no external cloak for content, to be doffed or replaced at will.[11] In Goethe's words, "The content determines the form and the form has no existence without content." The French poet Mallarmé went even further. When a painter friend complained that he was unsuccessful in writing poetry in spite of the wealth of his ideas, Mallarmé replied, "My dear Diego, poems are written not in ideas but in words."[12]

Form in poetry is naturally not limited to the individual word.[13] Its full significance is revealed only within the context of the sentence, the passage, the work as a whole. In the words of a contemporary interpreter of biblical literary structure:

> Poetry lives only to the degree that it is shaped in form. Its content has no existence except insofar as it is revealed in form. In the case of a historical source, a philosophic essay, if you ask for their meaning, they will answer you directly, in clear words, in explicit phrases; they will transmit ideas to you and teach you facts. Not so poetry. Poetry does not seek to express ideas, to tell facts, to teach a lesson, or even to express an emotion—but to fashion it, to give it shape. It follows that poetry reaches its full meaning only in the particular form in which it is embodied, in its vocabulary, in the order of its sentences, in its syntactic phenomena, in the totality of its motifs, in its rhythm and meter, in its structure as a whole.[14]

This emphasis upon the importance of form in literary analysis is, of course, not new. But it has gained momentum in our day, particularly through the exponents of the school called *Werkinterpretation* or the New Criticism. As is almost universal in the history of literary musical, and artistic movements, the New Criticism has vigorously attacked the earlier schools of literary interpretation. We do not, however, have to deny the validity of these older views to appreciate the contribution of the new. There is abiding value in the approach of the historical school, which seeks to relate a given literary work to its cultural background and sees in the history of literature a record of the history of ideas and institutions. By and large, the earlier schools of interpretation tended to emphasize the points of similarity between any given work and other documents of the same or related backgrounds. The New Criticism, on the other hand, has emphasized the specificity of each literary and artistic work, which it analyzes as the product of a unique, non-repetitive experience undergone by an individual. It thus serves as a welcome corrective to the widespread tendency to treat literary works mechanically, cataloguing parallels in language and similarities in pattern with other writings, and regarding these similarities as holding the key to their interpretation.

The New Criticism, building upon the discoveries of modern psychology, has also highlighted the role of the unconscious in literary creativity. It has insisted that it is not enough to discover the conscious intentions of the author or even to elucidate how his contemporaries understood this work. The New Critics have sought to reveal the unconscious motifs underlying the creative process. As a result, some of them have reached the paradoxical conclusion that the function of the interpreter is "to understand the creation better than did its creator."[15]

Stripped of its exaggerations, this formulation underscores the existence of a far more intimate relationship between a literary work and its interpreters than has generally been admitted heretofore. It has defined literary interpretation as a partnership between the creation and its elucidators, whose role partakes "less of recognition and more of self-identification with the poetry."[16]

Thus, contemporary criticism buttresses the two principal theses of this chapter: that the reader is a creative partner with the poet in the process of communication; and that central to the poet's communication of his experience is the connotation, the allusion, the analogy, which he does not spell out, but leaves to the reader to grasp, understand, and share.

We are now in position to appreciate more fully the central role of figures of speech like metaphor and simile in poetic composition. Suzanne K. Langer has defined symbolization as "a constructive response o experience." It therefore follows that "a metaphor is the very essence of poetic creation, the poet's unique expression of his personal vision, expressing what could not be expressed without it."[17] It is this private world with which the poet wishes to commune in private and which, paradoxically, he also feels a need to communicate to his readers. From this tension there arises the "obscurity" which is frequently charged against modern verse, though it is actually much older, being rooted in the nature of poetry itself.[18]

This truth lies at the basis of the figurative use of language in classic religious texts, both within the Bible and without. Anthropomorphic descriptions of the Deity are not to be dismissed out of hand as being the mark of the intellectual limitations of men's reason. They are to be recognized as expressions of the outward reach of human speech, which seeks to convey through its connotations what cannot be explicated through the denotations.[19] When this is lost sight of, the vision of the prophet and the song of the poet congeal and harden into the formulas of dogma.

In sum, analogy and allusiveness are the very warp and woof of all poetry. In biblical Wisdom the role of analogy is even more basic. This is true not only because Hebrew Hokmah historically includes the arts of poetry and music. In its literature, Wisdom seeks to transmit its ideas about man's duty and destiny to readers and pupils. To achieve this objective, one of its principal methods is to call attention to the similarity existing between two objects, activities, situations, or types of character, thus revealing a relationship which the reader had not previously suspected.

It is this recognition of the incongruity between appearance and reality which constitutes the essence of irony, though not its only characteristic.[20] Good, who finds irony a pervasive trait in the Hebrew Scriptures, speaks of "the burden of recognition which is imposed by irony upon hearers and readers."[21] Like the exponents of the New Criticism he emphasizes the fact that once it is produced, a work is independent of its creator. He declares, "The author's intentions do not mark off the limits within which we read him. . . . What he says may have an ironic effect on us whether or not he worked for that effect. . . . The work stands before us . . . as a living voice whose actions we hear and with which we enter conversation. . . . What happens is a new relationship between reader and writer, a conversation in which each acts upon the other."[22]

The techniques of analogy and allusiveness are the basis of the two literary genres characteristic of Wisdom, and indeed, give them their names: the *ḥīdāh*, "riddle," and the *māšāl*, literally "comparison," which is extended to include the proverb, the parable, the fable, and the allegory. There are two other, less frequent, terms: *šīr*, "song," and *mᵉlīṣāh*, "figure, satire, taunt-song." Three of the four terms occur in the proem of the Book of Proverbs, where the goals of Wisdom are set forth:

> To know wisdom and instruction,
> To comprehend the words of understanding,
> To receive the discipline of wisdom,
> Justice and right, and equity;
> To understand a proverb, and a figure (*māšāl umᵉlīṣāh*)
> The words of the wise, and their riddles (*ḥīdōtam*).[23]
>
> [Prov. 1:2, 3, 6]

The principal categories, however, are the *māšāl* and the *ḥīdāh*. It is noteworthy that both literary genres are attested for the earliest period of Israelite history. The speech of Jotham, which is a fable of telling force, and the riddle of Samson, which is less impressive, both go back to the age of the Judges (Judg. 9:7–15; 12:14), but are undoubtedly older in origin.[24]

A hundred years later, all the genres of Wisdom literature are explicitly associated with King Solomon. His wisdom is expressed in his proverbs, parables, and songs:

> For he was wiser than all men:
> Than Ethan the Ezrahite, and Heman, and Calcol, and Darda,
> the sons of Mahol;
> And his fame was in all the nations round about.
> And he spoke three thousand proverbs;
> And his songs were a thousand and five.
> And he spoke of trees,
> From the cedar that is in Lebanon, even unto the hyssop that
> springs out of the wall;
> He spoke also of beasts, and of fowl, and of creeping things,
> and of fishes.
>
> [I Kings 5:11–13]

Solomon is also a master of riddles, whether in life situations, as in the case of the harlots and the infants (I Kings 3:16 ff.), or in the conundrums posed by the Queen of Sheba (I Kings 10:1).[25]

Centuries later both terms, "parable" and "riddle," were used synonymously by the prophet Ezekiel in reference to an allegory (Ezek. 17:2), and by the psalmist for his profound reflections on the mystery of life and death (Ps. 49:5).

An organic relationship links these two forms together. A riddle is an unrecognized comparison; a proverb is a riddle that has been answered. Thus, the passage in Proverbs 30:15–16 is a proverb because it is in the declarative:

> The leech has two daughters,
> Crying, "Give, give."
> Three things are never satisfied,
> Four never say "Enough":
> Sheol; the barren womb;
> The earth ever thirsty for water;
> And the fire which never says "Enough."

If the proverb were re-phrased interrogatively it would become a riddle:

> Who are the leech's daughters,
> Always crying, "Give, give"?

The intimate relationship existing between a poem and a riddle is highlighted in an observation of Aldous Huxley: "One of the pleasures we derive from poetry is precisely the crossword-puzzler's delight in working out a problem. For certain people the pleasure is peculiarly intense."[26]

Today, riddles, like puns, are not highly regarded in the Western world, but in ancient Semitic culture they were accorded great respect. The tribute which the great biblical scholar N. H. Tur-Sinai has paid to the riddle, far from being excessive, is eminently justified:

> The riddle ceased to be for the ancients a matter of cleverness and entertainment. The solving of a riddle became an understanding of wisdom and high knowledge, concerned with matters between man and his God, the search for the way by which a creature of flesh and blood could penetrate the mysterious counsel of the Godhead.[27]

Both literary genres, the *māšāl* and the *ḥīdāh*, are ideal instruments for suggesting the analogy which one life situation bears to another, and for shedding light on the mystery of the unknown and the unknowable, within which men live and move and have their being.

The parable and the allegory, which are also expressed by the Hebrew term *māšāl*, are longer literary forms than the proverb. Like the latter they belong to the genre of the riddle as long as their meaning is not disclosed. When it is revealed, they become *mĕšālîm*, analogies which give an insight into human life and destiny. The meaning of the great "Song (*šîr*) of the Vineyard" in Isaiah (5:1–7) is left unexplained until the shattering climax in the last verse. So, too, Ezekiel's "Vision of the Valley of Dry Bones" (37:1–14) is not interpreted until the close. On the other hand, in each of the three allegories in Ezekiel explicitly identified by the prophet as a *māšāl* (17:2; 24:3; 21:5), the technique differs. In the first, each detail is specifically interpreted; in the second, the meaning is given in general terms; in the third, it is left unexplained and remains unclear to the very end.

Perhaps the most moving allegory in the Bible is the poignant description of old age which constitutes the climax of the Book of Ecclesiastes (11:9–12:8). It is noteworthy that no word for "old age" occurs in the poem, only the haunting allusion: "Before the evil days come of which you will say, 'I have no delight in them.' " The reader is expected to recognize the meaning himself. As we shall see, the same poetic reticence is employed by the author of Job. The details of the picture painted by Koheleth are not easily identifiable and have, in fact, been variously explained by different interpreters.[28] Indeed, it seems probable that the author has utilized more than one metaphor to depict the dissolution which comes with age. Yet in spite of the absence of total explicitness—perhaps because of it—the allegory speaks powerfully to the reader, whose emotions become deeply involved in its somewhat mysterious content and melancholy spirit.

Here again, aesthetic fashions change with the times. Combined and even mixed metaphors were not regarded in the past with the distaste voiced by modern critics. Thus, Psalm 23 pictures God as both a shepherd and a host. In Psalm 48, the trembling of the foreign kings before the majesty of Jerusalem is compared to a woman in travail and to a mighty east wind.[29] Many centuries later, Shakespeare frequently mixed metaphors. The most famous example, "take arms against a sea of troubles," appears in Hamlet's soliloquy, "to be, or not to be." Editors in the Age of Reason simply could not believe Shakespeare capable of this and tried to emend the text.[30] Other British poets guilty of mixed metaphors include William Blake, Matthew Arnold, and Dylan Thomas.

As Robert Gorham Davis sagely observes:

> In one sense every metaphor is mixed. That is its interest. When we call a man a pig, or a girl a flower, we mix the bestial and botanical with the human. When Donne compared lovers to a pair of compasses, he mixed Eros and geometry. . . . Who is to set rules? There are no metaphors in external nature. All verbal figures are products of the mind and imagination, working toward different ends under varying conditions of intensity and freedom. Tact, taste, feeling for words, experience, vision, all are needed.[31]

We need only add that these gifts of the poet are needed almost equally by the reader if he is to fulfill his creative role in communication.

The use of allusion rather than explicit statement as a basic literary device became even more prominent in *piyyut,* medieval Hebrew poetry.[32] Here biblical men and events were almost never mentioned by name. The poet displayed his ingenuity by oblique and cryptic references to them through citations of biblical and rabbinic passages. The reader found an absorbing intellectual pastime and a prime source of aesthetic gratification in identifying these allusions. In the words of Shalom Spiegel, the outstanding authority on medieval Hebrew poetry in our day, "The poet counted on his listeners (or on some of them at least) to be familiar with Rabbinic comments in their usual form. He therefore sought to entertain them with something new and astonishing . . . by interchanging the revealed and the hidden in his language."[33]

A few instances out of hundreds must suffice. The early medieval poet Eleazar Kalir is the author of two acrostic poems that are now part of the Seder liturgy on Passover Eve. The first ("It came to pass at midnight") describes a long series of biblical events that took place at night, from Abraham's victory over the four kings (Gen. chap. 14) to the death of Belshazzar, the salvation of Daniel, and the plot of Haman. Yet all these happenings are only alluded to. Thus, the strophe referring to these last three events reads:

> He who became drunk with the sacred vessels was killed at night,
> He was saved from the den of lions, who interpreted the terrors
> of the night,
> The Aggagite nursed his hatred and wrote missives at night—
> It came to pass at midnight.

The reader is expected to recognize the references here to Belshazzar, Daniel, and Haman.

A similar situation obtains with regard to the companion *piyyut*
chanted on the second night of Passover, which deals with a long series
of events that rabbinic tradition ascribed to Passover.³⁴ So, too, the
Prayer for Dew, traditionally recited on the first day of Passover, and
the *Prayer for Rain* in the liturgy of the Shemini Atzeret Festival in
the fall invoke the merits of Abraham, Isaac, Jacob, Moses, Aaron,
and David, without mentioning any by name, referring to them
obliquely by incidents in their careers.³⁵ Additional examples of this
widespread rhetorical usage can be cited from almost every page of
medieval Hebrew poetry.

This preference for allusiveness is, moreover, far older than the
Middle Ages. Apocalyptic literature abounds in instances in which the
author avoids an explicit identification of men, events, and places, thus
adding an aura of mystery to his pronouncements. This technique is
obviously useful when a writer seeks to delineate the shape of things
to come, concerning which he himself has no sure knowledge! He
is able to safeguard the oracular character of his prophecies by veiling
them in cryptic phrases, clear only to the initiated. However, even
when the writer is referring to past and present events on which he
is well informed, he may follow the same practice. Here the psychological and aesthetic impulses that underlie the rhetorical usage play
their part. But whatever the motives involved, the reader is expected
to participate actively in discovering the author's meaning.

The apocryphal Wisdom book, the Wisdom of Solomon, is, generally speaking, not esoteric in character. Yet in the closing part (11:2–
19:22), which contains a historical retrospect of Israel in Egypt, the
name of the oppressor is practically not mentioned. Allusiveness, not
explicitness, marks the entire section.³⁶

To cite another instance from the same period, the Dead Sea Scroll
are deeply concerned with the men and events of their day, yet they
practically never use actual proper names.³⁷ Contemporary scholars
therefore find themselves deeply divided on the identification of the
Man of Lies, the Teacher of Righteousness, the Kittim, the Wicked
Priest, the Preacher of Lies, to cite only the references occurring in
one book, the Qumranite *Commentary on Habakkuk*.³⁸

In surveying the role of analogy and allusion in human thought and
speech, we have had occasion to wander far afield, ranging over wide
areas of human activity. We have noted the important role of symbols

n the process of reading itself, particularly in Hebrew and Semitic literature. Symbolization, as expressed through figures of speech like metaphor and simile, which are the very essence of poetry, calls upon the creative participation of the reader at every turn. This function becomes, if possible, even more basic in Wisdom literature. Its characteristic literary genres, the *māšāl* and the *ḥīdāh*, become complete only when communication is established between the speaker and the listener, between the writer and the reader.

It is therefore not astonishing that Job, the high-water mark of Hebrew Hokmah, should offer many illustrations of this use of allusion and analogy which is basic to the *māšāl* in all its forms—proverb, parable, and allegory. We have already had occasion to analyze the varied use of proverbs in Job, those composed by the poet himself and those drawn from the traditional lore of Wisdom.[39] Our concern here is only to highlight the allusive use of proverbs.

When Job wishes to express the idea that his bitter lament is not without cause but is rather the result of his boundless pain, he does so by indirection. In characteristic proverbial language he asks whether a well-fed animal is likely to emit sounds of dissatisfaction:

> Does the wild ass bray when he has grass,
> Or the ox low over his fodder?
>
> [6:5]

When Job wishes to stigmatize the sentiments of his friends as conventional platitudes, he asks whether tasteless food can be expected to please the palate:

> Can tasteless food be eaten without salt,
> Or is there any savor in the juice of mallows?
>
> [6:6]

The difficult verse 17:5 has been rendered:

> "He invites his friends to share his bounty,
> While the eyes of his own children grow faint from hunger!"

The most plausible view of the verse is that it is intended to suggest that the Friends can ill afford to dispense their wisdom so liberally to Job, in view of their own limitations.[40]

Bildad wishes to observe that cause and effect operate universally in the moral sphere in order to imply that Job's suffering is the result of his sin. This point he makes obliquely, but nonetheless effectively, by a proverbial analogy drawn from the world of nature:

> "Can papyrus grow where there is no marsh?
> Can reeds flourish without water?"
>
> [8:11]

This apothegm serves as the preface to an interesting and somewhat enigmatic passage which describes the contrasting fate of two plants (8:12–20). The reader is expected to recognize that the prematurely withered first plant refers to the sinner, while the other, making its way among rocks, alludes to the upright man triumphing over his obstacles. What is more, the shift from sinner to righteous man is made suddenly, without any transition (in vs. 16), the poet again counting upon his reader to understand his meaning. Not until the closing verse is the theme made fully explicit.[41] The passage is to be rendered:

> While yet in flower—not ready to be cut down—
> Before any other plant, it withers.
> Such is the fate of all who forget God:
> The hope of the godless must perish.
> His self-confidence is mere gossamer thread,
> His trust but a spider's web.
> He leans upon his house, but it will not stand;
> He takes hold of it, but it will not endure.
>
> It is fresh even under the hot sun,
> As its shoots spread beyond its garden.
> Even over a stone heap the roots are entwined,
> As it cleaves its way among rocks.
> If its place should destroy it
> And deny it, saying, "I have never seen you,"
> Behold, it goes forth on its way,
> And from the earth elsewhere it will sprout again.
>
> Indeed, God will not spurn the blameless man,
> Nor will He uphold the evildoers.[42]
>
> [8:12–20]

One of the most difficult passages in the book is chapter 24, which contains great and possibly insoluble problems with regard to both its detailed interpretation and to the meaning and relevance of the passage as a whole. The closing section (vss. 18–24) seems, as many interpreters have noted, to be more appropriate to the Friends than to Job. Some scholars, therefore, transfer the passage to Zophar's third speech. I believe, however, that it is correctly placed and that it is Job's citation of the conventional standpoint of the Friends.[43]

Scarcely less difficult is the interpretation of the opening section of chapter 24 (vss. 1–17). I suggest that the key to this enigmatic passage lies in recognizing the use of allusion. This entire section seems to alternate between a description of the crimes of the wrongdoers and the suffering of their victims. Yet, at no time are the groups identified or are the transitions indicated. The reader must recognize that in verses 2–4 the wicked are described, in verses 5–8, the homeless and the weak; verse 9 reverts again to the despoilers of the poor, verses 10–12 to the sufferers; verses 13–17 once more picture the evildoers, whose major crimes are committed at night.[44]

It is in the God speeches that the use of analogy and allusion reaches its highest point. The poet's basic message is expressed here through both analogy and silence, by what is said and by what is left unsaid. Nowhere does God attack Job's rectitude or undertake to defend His own perfect justice. Instead, He describes the manifold aspects of nature, which is not only mysterious but beautiful, bringing joy to its Creator. The *māšāl*, or analogy, is clear. Just as the natural world possesses an order and pattern, though not completely comprehensible to man, so man may believe that the moral order, which he cannot wholly fathom, nevertheless has a pattern and meaning of its own.

The author of Job expresses this insight into the nature of reality, not through a process of painful ratiocination, but through the medium of imperishable poetry. The Book of Job is perhaps the finest illustration of the truth of Lawrence Durrell's observation: "A good poem is a congerie of symbols which transfers an enigmatic knowledge to the reader. At its lowest power you can find the faculty in the nickname or the nursery rhyme: at its highest it reflects a metaphysical reality about ourselves and the world."[45]

The God speeches, which reveal the panorama of nature and exult in its beauty, communicate a truth that can be taught only by suggestion, by "the strategy of indirect approach," to use John Press's fine phrase. For, as De Quincey remarked, poetry "can teach only as nature teaches, as forests teach, as the sea teaches, as infancy teaches,— viz. by deep impulse, by hieroglyphic suggestion."[46]

Like the Book of Ecclesiastes, the Book of Job expresses a joyous acceptance of life in spite of all its limitations. But because the author sees man's life within the larger framework of the cosmos, he attains a level of faith which Koheleth does not reach. This is no mere victory of the will over the intellect, no easy triumph of belief silencing the voice of reason. In Job the will and the intellect are united in a great synthesis. The poet's mind and heart have won their way to a deep and enduring harmony which rests upon the analogy between the world of nature and the realm of human experience, both of which have their origin in God.

In striving to see himself against the background of a greater universe, a man may discover an anodyne for his suffering. If he succeeds in the struggle, as the author of Job did, he may learn to accept even what he cannot understand, and thus find life, in spite of its dark hours, a never-failing fountain of light and joy.

XV

The Author:
His Provenance and Date

THE UNIQUE LITERARY GENRE of Job, the wide range of its subject matter, the unparalleled profundity of its thought, and the absence of historical allusions have rendered it difficult to identify the background and period of the author. An added complication is to be found in its extraordinarily rich vocabulary, which far exceeds that of other biblical writing and which abounds in Aramaisms[1] and Arabic parallels.[2]

These Arabic and Aramaic cognates have suggested different conclusions with regard to the provenance and date of the book. Thus, as long ago as the twelfth century, the medieval Hebrew commentator and grammarian Abraham ibn Ezra declared, "It seems likely to me that *Job* is a translated book and therefore is difficult to interpret, like every translated book."[3]

That the work is a translation from the Arabic was independently suggested by Thomas Carlyle centuries later, when he declared: "Biblical critics seem agreed that our own book of Job was written in that [i.e., Arab] region of the world. One feels indeed as if it were not Hebrew; such a noble universality different from noble patriotism or sectarianism reigns in it."[4] Renan found "nothing particularly Hebraic" in the essential ideas of the book.[5] Carlyle and Renan are by no means the only writers in whom a high appreciation of Hebrew literature is united with a penchant for denigrating its creators. The same ambivalence led Voltaire to a similar theory in his article on Job in the *Dictionnaire Philosophique*.

The argument for an Arabic origin for Job, also advanced by one modern scholar,[6] is, however, entirely unconvincing. Nothing in the limited remains of pre-Islamic Arabic literature remotely suggests a masterpiece of the dimensions of Job. Moreover, the primitive cultural and religious conditions of the Arab-speaking world, in which polytheism was prevalent, cannot possibly have furnished the background for the spiritual and intellectual concerns which created Job. Finally, the argument based on Arabisms in Job falls short of the mark. The poet is drawing upon the full resources of Hebrew, which were far more extensive than the vocabulary that has survived in the pages of the Bible. From the linguistic point of view, the Bible is a limited collection of fragments or selections from ancient Hebrew literature. It is no wonder that nearly every literary document and inscription that is brought to light by archaeological discovery adds new words to our Hebrew dictionaries. The author of Job undoubtedly possessed an unrivaled command of Hebrew. He had occasion to use many rare words which Hebrew shared with the other Semitic languages, notably with the rich Arabic vocabulary.

Recently, Tur-Sinai has argued vigorously that Job is a translation from a lost Aramaic original.[7] The prevalence of Aramaisms in several later biblical books has led a few scholars to suggest an Aramaic "translation theory" for Daniel,[8] Esther,[9] and Ecclesiastes.[10] The proponents of the theory of an Aramaic original for these books rest their case on two assumptions. The first contention is that the present Hebrew text gives evidence of "mistranslation" of the non-existent Aramaic original, which can be "recovered" by "retroversion." In spite of the ingenuity expended upon discovering examples of these alleged mistranslations and the warmth with which the thesis is at times defended, a careful analysis of the evidence in each case proves it to be unconvincing.

The problems of text and interpretation are solved more easily and convincingly in other ways, without postulating the whole series of assumptions needed by the translation theory. These include an original composition in Aramaic, the attainment by this Aramaic text of canonical status or at least of sufficient sanctity to warrant its being translated into Hebrew, the disappearance of the Aramaic original without a trace, and the acceptance of the Hebrew version as authentic and sacred. Moreover, the processes of composition, diffusion, translation, and canonization must all have taken place within a relatively brief period. Only with regard to Daniel does the translation theory seem plausible, since more than half of the biblical book (2:4–7:28) is actually extant in Aramaic. It is, however, not impossible that the crabbed and cryptic style in Daniel may be a characteristic of apocalyptic writing. Because the author is picturing the future, which is necessarily unknown to him, he takes refuge in obscurity.[11]

The second argument offered to support the translation theory is more general. As we have observed, Ibn Ezra advanced the theory that a difficult text is to be explained as a translation of an original in another language. While this idea is often repeated, analysis makes it clear that the opposite is true: a difficult text is prima facie evidence of its original character.

A translator faced by a difficult original may misread it because he lacks an adequate knowledge of the vocabulary and misconstrues the grammar; he may tacitly emend the text, read irrelevant matters into it, and generally fail to penetrate its meaning; but ultimately he must decide upon some view of the passage which he then expresses in his idiom. His version may be incorrect, but it will normally be clear and intelligible—more so than the original—for all the difficulties and alternatives will have been ignored or obscured in the process. One has only to compare a difficult verse in the Hebrew of Hosea, Ezekiel, or Job with any English version to see how the manifold difficulties of the Hebrew "disappear" in the smooth English renderings.

Other things being equal, it may therefore be maintained that a difficult text is probably the original rather than a translation. The difficulties of the Hebrew text of Job bear witness to its being the original.

A few other scholars have suggested other locales for the authorship of Job. Pfeiffer maintains that Job is a work of Edomite Wisdom, insisting that it is "thoroughly Edomitic."[12] This is in line with his highly personal recasting of the Documentary Hypothesis of the Pentateuch. According to Pfeiffer the documents J, E, D, H, and P, which are traditional in the Higher Criticism, are to be augmented by an Edomite source, which he called S for Seir, the mountain of Edom.[13]

Whatever the validity of this addition to the Documentary Hypothesis—and it has won little support among scholars—the evidence for an Edomitic provenance for Job is extremely tenuous. That the names and locales mentioned in Job are to be found to the south and east of Palestine in the proximity of Edom is, of course, true. But this fact testifies only to the Near Eastern character of the original Job tale utilized by the author. The subsequent development of the narrative and the poetic dialogue, which is the heart of the book, are thoroughly Hebraic in content and spirit. Even more tenuous is the contention that the statement in Jeremiah's oracle against Edom (Jer. 49:17) that "wisdom is no longer to be found in Teman" proves that important centers of Wisdom literature existed in Edom. We know virtually nothing regarding Edomite culture or religion, and what little is known of Edomite history would scarcely suggest that the spiritual level was calculated to produce a masterpiece like Job. Pfeiffer's theory of an Edomite provenance for Job may therefore be dismissed as wholly unwarranted.

These theories do not exhaust the search for a foreign background for Job. Humbert has argued that the book is of Egyptian origin.[14] He calls attention to the extensive development of Wisdom literature in Egypt. He notes the detailed and knowledgeable descriptions of *Behemot*, the hippopotamus, and *Leviathan*, the crocodile, and the reference to ships of papyrus plying the waters (9:26). Undoubtedly, Wisdom was extensively developed in ancient Egypt; nevertheless, there is no ground for assuming any direct dependency of Job on Egyptian Wisdom, as is the case, for example, with the biblical Book of Proverbs and the *Maxims of Amenemope*.[15] Moreover, nothing in Egyptian Wisdom literature begins to approach the profundity or the scope of Job. As for details in the book relating to Egyptian flora and fauna, they are easily explained in terms of an author both learned and widely traveled.

In sum, the only tenable conclusion is the most obvious and natural —the Book of Job was written by a highly learned Hebrew in his native tongue. He seems to have had firsthand experience of such foreign countries as Egypt, and of such varied areas as the desert, the mountains, and the sea. Such opportunities for travel, incidentally, would be open only to members of the upper classes, thus adding supporting testimony to the upper-class orientation of Wisdom literature.

Gifted with a strong sense of curiosity, keen powers of observation and a vivid intelligence, the author reveals a high degree of familiarity with the arts and sciences of his day. His unforgettable pictures of the wild beasts and birds and of the great land and sea monsters in the God speeches[16] are impressive proof of his intellectual gifts as well as of his poetic powers. He is familiar with the sea and the clouds, snow and hail, rain and ice.[17] He has observed the refraction of light.[18] The stars in their constellations are known to him,[19] as are the paths and streams of the desert and the mountain.[20] He is familiar with the wonders of birth for man and beast, his description of the fashioning of the human embryo being unparalleled in poetry.[21] He knows the art of horticulture, including the transplantation of trees,[22] and is at home with the craft of the hunter, using no less than six terms to describe various kinds of traps.[23]

In choosing an Oriental as the protagonist of his great poem, the author has followed the outlines of a familiar Semitic tale, widely diffused through the ancient Near East, like the legend of Dan'el[24] or the story of Ahiqar.[25] But he has done far more. He reveals his genius by raising the action above the limitations of national loyalties and ethnic religion. The problem of man's place in the universe and the mystery of his suffering in God's world can be dealt with without involving the questions of ritual, piety, and purity that would arise if Job were pictured as a Hebrew.

The poet is an exemplar of the universalism of spirit which existed in Second Temple Judaism side by side with more particularistic views. This attitude finds expression in the idyllic Book of Ruth, with its gentle insistence that nobility of character and faith in God are to be found among all human beings, Jew and Gentile alike. It reaches its apogee in the Book of Jonah. Here the pagan sailors are pictured more favorably than the Hebrew prophet. With matchless irony the truth is underscored that the God of Israel is the God of mankind, whose love embraces all His creatures—including even the inhabitants of Nineveh, the capital of Assyria, arch-enemy and destroyer of Israel.

The assumption that the broadly human background in Job is incompatible with its Hebrew origin is frequently made, but is no less mistaken on that account. It rests upon a basic failure to reckon with the innate balance between particularism and universalism which characterizes Judaism especially in the biblical age, but which survives in the rabbinic era and later periods as well. This inability to recognize the creative tension between polarities in the Jewish tradition has distorted the understanding of biblical and post-biblical Judaism to the present day.[26]

When this prejudice is laid aside it is clear that the patent universalism in Job is authentically Hebrew, going hand in hand with the poet's deep roots in the tradition of Israel. The evidence for his Hebraic background is most impressive since it is incidental and unconscious. That he generally uses the generic names for God, *Eloah, Shaddai, El,* and *Elohim,* is to be expected in a Wisdom book.[27] The appearance of the national name for God, *JHVH* (12:9), is a welcome slip of the pen testifying to his reminiscence of a familiar passage in Deutero Isaiah (41:20), whose influence on the poet went far beyond the language. Another unconscious sign of the poet's Palestinian origin is his use of the proper name "Jordan" when he wishes to refer generically to a river. In describing the hippopotamus swallowing vast amounts of water as he placidly lies in the stream, the poet says: "Behold he empties an entire river without haste; he lies at ease as he draws a Jordan into his mouth" (40:23).[28]

Undoubtedly, the search for parallels and borrowings from other biblical books has been carried too far, many of them being insignificant or accidental.[29] Thus, there is no proof that the descriptions (in 12:17–25) of national catastrophes and the migrations of peoples are to be referred to the exile of Israel or of Judah, though the author may well have thought of these calamities as familiar events illustrating his point. Many scholars believe that Job's moving lament on his birth (chap. 3) is an elaboration of Jeremiah's plaintive cry on the same theme (20:14 ff.). Yet there is no real evidence of priorities or of any dependency whatever. The theme would arise whenever men contemplated their sorry lot. It is, however, quite otherwise with the passage:

> What is man that You exalt him
> And You give him Your attention,
> That You visit him each morning,
> And You test him every moment?
>
> [Job 7:17–18]

Here is a bitter and heart-rending parody of the joyous affirmation by the psalmist of God's loving concern for His creatures:

> What is man, that You are mindful of him?
> And the son of man, that You think of him?
> Yet You have made him but little lower than the angels,
> And have crowned him with glory and honor.
>
> [Ps. 8:5, 6]

To be sure, the date of the Eighth Psalm cannot be established with assurance, but the dependence of Job on the Hebrew psalm is certain.

Another striking case of dependency occurs in Job 15:7–8. Eliphaz is mocking Job's claim to wisdom:

> Were you born the first among men,
> And brought forth before the hills?

The full significance of the second stich becomes clear when one recalls that it is virtually identical with a line in the Hymn of Praise to Wisdom in Proverbs (8:21–32). Here Wisdom boasts of being the first and best beloved of God's creations:

> The Lord created me at the beginning of His work,
> The first of His acts of old. . . .
> Before the mountains had been shaped,
> Before the hills, I was brought forth.
>
> [Prov. 8:22, 25]

Unfortunately, the date of the passage in Proverbs cannot be fixed exactly, but that it was familiar to the author of Job cannot be doubted.

It is also noteworthy that the ethical code in Job's "Confession of Integrity" (chap. 31) reflects at every turn the ideals of justice, equality, reverence, and consideration for the weak, enjoined by the Torah and the Prophets. The most natural sources for many other references in Job would be the Pentateuchal legislation. The illegal removal of landmarks (Job 24:2) recalls the law in Deuteronomy 19:14; 27:17. The three basic sins of murder, theft, and adultery (Job 24:14–16) are mentioned together as they appear in the Decalogue, and in the same sequence as in Hosea's catalogue of major crimes (Hosea 4:2). Job may (in 22:6; 24:3, 9) be referring to the retention of pledges taken from the widow and the orphan. This would recall the ancient law (in Exod. 22:25; Deut. 24:12–13) commanding the return of the pledged garment at nightfall, the violation of which aroused the condemnation of the prophets Amos (2:8) and Ezekiel (18:12).

Finally, the sophistication of the religious outlook in Job is most naturally explained as the culmination of a long development of religious thought which we have sought to trace above in some detail. That the author of Job was "greater than his brothers" may readily be granted, but that he was one among them, nurtured by the same Hebraic inheritance, is clear.

With regard to the dating of the book, opinions have varied wide-ly.[30] Because of the patriarchal setting of the prose tale, the Talmud ascribes it to Moses. This view was apparently shared by the Dead Sea sectarians. The documents found in Qumran cave number eleven in January, 1956, include the text of the Book of Job in Hebrew and in an Aramaic Targum. It is striking that the Qumranite Hebrew texts of Job, like the Pentateuch, are sometimes written in a paleo-Hebrew script, thus testifying to the belief in the Mosaic authorship of these books.[31] It is undoubtedly for the same reason that the *Pešita*, the Syriac version, places Job immediately after the Pentateuch.

Other rabbinic sources suggest a variety of periods in which Job may have lived, ranging from the time of Isaac and Joseph to that of Cyrus and Ahasuerus.[32] Virtually all modern scholars date Job some-where between 700 and 200 B.C.E. One group believes that the author lived in the closing decades of the First Temple period and so was a contemporary of Jeremiah and a predecessor of Deutero-Isaiah.[33] Others date the book in the period of the Babylonian Exile.[34]

Most scholars today would agree that the weight of evidence favors an early post-Exilic date, after Deutero-Isaiah.[35] I would assign the period between 500 and 300 B.C.E. As is generally the case in ques-tions of this kind, the evidence is cumulative. The most natural time of composition for Job would be that of the early days of the Second Temple, which marked the heyday of Wisdom literature, when the concern with the individual became paramount in religious thought.

Two considerations strongly support the view that Job is later than Deutero-Isaiah. The prophet of the Exile developed the insight that suffering was not necessarily the consequence and the proof of sin and applied it to the destiny of the nation. The poet, who knew the writings of Deutero-Isaiah, transfers this idea to the lot of the individ-ual. Moreover, while Deutero-Isaiah must still debate a faith in one God against the polytheism rampant in Babylonia, Job takes mono-theism for granted. We have already noted the use in Job (12:9) of a phrase from Deutero-Isaiah (41:20).

On the other hand, a date later than the fourth century is unlikely. The book echoes none of the turbulence which seized the Near East after Alexander. Satan, who figures in the prologue, is probably a borrowing from Zoroastrianism, which saw the world as a battle-ground between Ahura Mazda, the god of light and righteousness, and Ormuzd, the god of darkness and evil. But Satan has not yet become a quasi-independent figure, as happened in the post-Christian period.

What is more, he is not yet a fully distinct personality, but is merely one of "the sons of God," a member of the entourage in the heavenly court. In the Hebrew text of Job he is called *ha-satan*, "the Adversary." The first reference to Satan as a proper noun, without the definite article, occurs in the Book of Chronicles, which emanates from the third century.[36] In the Wisdom of Solomon, dated 100 B.C.E., Satan is already pictured as a fallen angel, through whose envy death came into the world.[37] In the Book of Job, Satan possesses neither a proper name nor a cosmic function. Job would therefore precede both Chronicles and the Wisdom of Solomon.

Also pointing to the early Second Commonwealth as the period of composition is the fact that Job is familiar with the idea of an afterlife, but like Koheleth and the other Wisdom writers finds himself unable to accept it (14:7–22). That he is able to dismiss it with no argument suggests the earlier period of the Second Temple, when the idea was beginning to make headway but had not yet won general acceptance. The linguistic pattern, and notably the Aramaisms already discussed, indicate the same period. More general in character is the poet's familiarity with the Eighth Psalm and the "Wisdom Hymn" in Proverbs.

External criteria are helpful in fixing the terminus *non post quem*, the latest possible date for Job. The Wisdom writer Ben Sira, who flourished about 190 B.C.E., seems to have a reference to Job in his "Hymnus Patrum," a long poem in praise of the worthies of Hebrew history. However, the text (49:9) is doubtful and he may be referring to Job the saint, who is mentioned in Ezekiel (14:14), rather than to the Book of Job and its hero.[38] On the other hand, there would be no reason for Ben Sira to praise Ezekiel for a brief incidental reference to an obscure figure. All in all, the balance of probability favors the view that Ben Sira was referring to the Book of Job, although we cannot assume that it had already won its place in the canon.[39]

However, the existence of references to translations of Job, which can be dated with some exactness, constitutes tangible evidence that the book was recognized as Scripture. From the Greek encyclopedist Alexander Polyhistor we know that the Book of Job was extant in Alexandria in a Greek translation by the first century B.C.E., or earlier. This reference also makes it clear that the Elihu chapters were included in the text.[40]

In Palestine, Aramaic had largely displaced Hebrew as the spoken language of the masses of the people by the beginning of the Christian

Era. As a result the practice had developed of having a *Meturgeman* or "public translator" in the synagogue to offer an oral translation into Aramaic of the scriptural reading. The teachers of normative Judaism were greatly concerned lest the Hebrew original be displaced. They therefore insisted—as long as they were able—that these Aramaic translations remain oral and not be consigned to writing.[41] Ultimately, necessity triumphed over other considerations and the various written Targums came into being.[42]

This early opposition to written translations makes all the more impressive the reference to a Targum of Job in the first century C.E., before the destruction of the Temple. According to the report, the patriarch Rabban Gamaliel the Elder was shown a copy of a Targum on Job on the slopes of the Temple hill in Jerusalem, whereupon he ordered the builder to bury it in the masonry of the Temple. Two generations later, at the beginning of the second century C.E., his grandson and namesake, the patriarch Rabban Gamaliel of Jamnia, was upbraided, on the basis of the earlier incident, for reading a written Targum on Job.[43]

In sum, Job was regarded as canonical by the beginning of the Christian Era, not only in normative Judaism but also in sectarian circles. This is clear from the Dead Sea scroll containing the Hebrew text of Job as well as a written Aramaic Targum referred to above. The Greek reference carries us further back, a century or more before that.

A minimum of two hundred years must be allowed as the time required for a book to achieve recognition, attain a position of sanctity, and be accepted into the canon of Scripture, so that its translation into the Greek and Aramaic vernaculars would be called for. Thus we arrive at 300 B.C.E. as the very latest possible date for the composition of Job. Since the book postdates Deutero-Isaiah, its composition cannot be earlier than 500 B.C.E.

All in all, we may assign Job to the period between 500 and 300 B.C.E., with the probabilities favoring the fifth rather than the fourth century. Greater exactness is ruled out by the universal, lyrical character of the book. It was during this obscure but highly creative era in the history of Israel that its greatest masterpiece was produced.

XVI

The Later Fortunes of Job: In the Canon, the Versions, and Legend

L ONG BEFORE THE BOOK took shape, the tale of the right- eous and afflicted Job had cast a powerful spell upon men. In the centuries since the book was written, its hero has won an even greater hold upon the human spirit. But there are two radically different Jobs in the biblical masterpiece. One is the hero of the prose tale, whose righteousness is matched by his piety and who retains his faith and patience under the gravest of provocations. The other is the Job of the dialogue, a passionate rebel against the injustice of undeserved suffer- ing, who challenges God Himself.

We cannot understand the influence of this powerful and disturbing book on the Western world unless we remember that most of the twenty-five centuries that have elapsed since its composition have been ages of faith. During this long expanse of time it was, by and large, the long-suffering Job of the prologue, and not the passionate and pain-wracked Job of the dialogue, who occupied men's thoughts. The vast majority of readers saw Job epitomized in his declaration of resignation, "The Lord gave, and the Lord has taken away. Blessed be the name of the Lord" (1:21). Few and far between were the readers whose image of Job was molded by the rebellious outbursts in the dialogue, such as his outcry, "It is all one, I say, the blameless and the wicked He destroys alike" (9:22). This fact undoubtedly explains the relative ease with which the book was accepted by all groups in Judaism. With little or no opposition it was canonized as Holy Scripture, was speedily translated into the languages spoken in Palestine and the Diaspora, and was elaborated upon in post-biblical literature.

We must now turn our attention to the later fortunes of the book as reflected in its canonization, in the Ancient Versions, and in the elaborate treatment the theme received in post-biblical legend and in the apocryphal literature.

We have already discussed the translations of Job into Greek and Aramaic, the two vernaculars spoken by the Jews during the centuries before and after the Christian Era. These versions appeared relatively soon after its completion, in spite of the extraordinary difficulties of the text. In ancient times translations were no mere literary exercise; that they were undertaken at all bears witness to the fact that the book was early accepted as Holy Writ.

The canonization of the books of the Hebrew Bible is a complex problem, concerning which little is certain. Particularly with regard to the Hagiographa or Sacred Writings, the third section of Scripture, details are scanty.[1] In 132 B.C.E. the Wisdom of Ben Sira was translated into Greek by his grandson living in Alexandria. In the preface the translator informs us that his grandfather had read deeply in "the Law and Prophets and the other books of our fathers." This last phrase undoubtedly refers to the Hagiographa, but the full extent of the third section of Scripture in his day cannot be determined.

By the beginning of the Christian Era, however, all the books now included in the Hagiographa were fixed,[2] though their order varied for centuries thereafter.[3] Several books in this section continued to arouse opposition or at least to evoke discussion with regard to their sacred character. These books included the Song of Songs and Ecclesiastes, and probably Proverbs, Esther, and Ruth, as well as Ben Sira or Ecclesiasticus.

To dispose of the question, a rabbinic synod was convened in the year 90 C.E. at Jamnia. Scholars are generally agreed that the Hebrew canon was fixed even before this historic session. At this gathering, referred to in talmudic literature as *bō bayōm* ("that very day"), the canonical status of various biblical books was discussed, but purely as an academic question.[4] At this Council, the canonicity of all these books was officially reaffirmed.[5] Only the Wisdom of Ben Sira, though highly esteemed by the rabbis, was declared outside the sacred corpus, primarily because its contents clearly indicated its late date, after divine inspiration was believed to have ceased.[6]

Though changes in the canon were no longer possible after the Council of Jamnia, many of the arguments continued to reverberate for centuries, if only for theoretical purposes. The sacred character of Ecclesiastes in particular was subjected to challenge on many grounds. It was pointed out that it bristled with contradictions;[7] it consisted of mere "sayings" and was not to be regarded as Scripture;[8] it contained the wisdom of Solomon and was not divine.[9] Most fundamental of all, it contained ideas which might lead to skepticism and heresy.[10]

The incisiveness of these criticisms of Ecclesiastes is particularly striking in view of the total absence of such attacks upon Job, either before, after, or during the Council of Jamnia. It would surely have been easy to point to passages in Job's speeches that incline to skepticism and heresy. The doctrine of the resurrection of the dead was explicitly denied in 14:12:

> So man lies down and rises not again;
> Till the heavens are no more he will not awake,
> Nor will he be roused from his sleep.

The faith in God's just government of the world was vigorously negated time and again, as in 9:23–24:

> When disaster brings sudden death
> He mocks the plea of the innocent.
> The land is given over to the hand of the evildoer,
> Who is able to bribe the judges.
> If not He, who then is guilty?

Nevertheless, the canonicity of Job, independently attested by the Greek and Aramaic version, is nowhere questioned. The only issue that seems to have arisen at Jamnia concerned the underlying spirit of Job's piety. An ancient Mishnah reads as follows:

> That very day[11] R. Joshua b. Hyrcanus expounded: Job served the Holy One, blessed be He, only from love, as it is written. *Though he slay me yet will I wait for him* (13:15).

Thus far the matter rests in doubt [whether it means] 'I will wait for him' [*lō* = 'for him'] or 'I will not wait' [*lō* = 'not'].¹² Finally, Scripture says, *Till I die I will not surrender mine integrity* (27:5), teaching that he acted from love. R. Joshua said, 'Who will remove the dust from your eyes, O Rabban Johanan ben Zakkai! For all your days you expounded that Job served the Holy One, blessed be He, only from fear, for it is written, *The man was perfect and upright, fearing God and avoiding evil.* Now Joshua, your disciple's disciple, has taught us that he acted out of love!'¹³

The ready acceptance of the Book of Job into the canon of Scripture is to be explained by the fact that only the Job of the prose tale impinged on the consciousness of ancient readers. The disturbing ideas in the debate were, after all, couched in difficult poetry and their import would not be easily understood by the average reader in many cases. In other instances, traditional views could be read into the text homiletically, thus softening the impact of heterodox ideas.¹⁴ The fact that Job is explicitly justified by God in the epilogue (42:7–8) made the process of orthodox reinterpretation all the easier. Finally, Job differed from Ecclesiastes and other similarly disputed books, such as the Song of Songs, Ruth, and Esther, in one salient respect—it alone contained the words of the Lord himself, speaking out of the whirlwind (38:1 ff.). Here was no merely human voice, prone to error, but God himself speaking to man.¹⁵

The overriding interest of the age of faith in the Job of the prose tale is clearly reflected in the Ancient Versions, of which the Septuagint is the oldest and most important.¹⁶ Our present Greek text is largely co-extensive with the Hebrew, but it is clear that the original Septuagint on Job was between one-fourth and one-sixth shorter. While our present Hebrew text contains about 2,200 poetic stichs, the original Greek contained only 1,850 stichs, or, according to some sources, as few as 1,600.¹⁷ The briefer Septuagint text was filled out by renderings borrowed from the later Greek versions, Aquila, Symmachus, and principally, Theodotion. Virtually all scholars are agreed that the Hebrew text is the original and the Greek a contraction.¹⁸

As we have already noted, the Greek translator was undoubtedly led to omit many stichs because of the difficulty of the Hebrew, which he often did not understand. Another motive he might have had for abbreviating the Hebrew was the fact that the Greek reader was unaccustomed to Semitic parallelism and would therefore find the Hebrew redundant. The truth of these contentions is borne out by the observation that all the excisions made occur in the poetic sections. The prose narrative is actually amplified by two passages which may be of later origin.[19] At the end of the book, the Greek version identifies Job with the Edomite king Jobab, who is mentioned in Genesis 37:33–34.[20] The other addition is an extended speech made by Job's wife when the calamities fell upon him:

> When much time had passed, his wife said to him, "How long will you hold out, saying, 'Behold I wait yet a little while, expecting the hope of my deliverance?' For, behold, your memory is abolished from the earth, your sons and daughters, the pangs and pains of my womb, which I bore in vain with sorrows; and you yourself are seated among the corruption of worms, spending the night in the open air, and I am a servant and a wanderer from place to place and house to house, waiting for the setting of the sun, that I may rest from my labors and my pangs which now beset me; but say some word against the Lord, and die."

This moving adjuration possesses both elegance and eloquence, rhetorical qualities that a Greek reader would find highly congenial. But it lacks the sinewy strength of the six Hebrew words to which it corresponds: ʿŌdekhā maḥazīk bethummatekhā, bārēkh ʾelōhīm vāmūth, "You still are holding fast to your piety—curse God and die!"

Like all the Ancient Versions, the Septuagint was prepared for the uneducated masses. It therefore sought to transmit acceptable religious ideas to its readers and to exclude heretical notions.[21] Thus Job voices skepticism about the doctrine of man's resurrection, which had already been accepted by many Jewish circles, but not by the Wisdom schools. The Hebrew Job asks, "If a man die, can he live again?" (14:14). The Greek Job eliminates the doubt by the simple device of changing the interrogative into a declarative: "If a man dies, he will live again!" The theme is stated again in the Greek addition to the closing verse of the book (42:17): "And Job died, an old man and full of days; and it is written that he will rise again with those whom the Lord raises up." In sum, the Greek version of Job is a welcome witness to the text, but its contractions and difficulties make it less useful for textual and exegetical purposes than we could have wished.

The Syriac version, though based on the Hebrew, has been corrected by the Greek so that it is not an independent witness.[22] As for the Aramaic translation in our hands today, there is no proof that it is identical either with the Targum shown to Rabban Gamaliel the Elder before the destruction of the Temple, or the one which his grandson, Rabban Gamaliel of Jamnia, was seen reading two generations later.[23] It, too, seeks to reinterpret the heretical sentiments of the book along orthodox lines. Thus, Job's doubt about resurrection is restricted to sinners: "If a *wicked* man die, is it possible that he will live again?" "The gates of Sheol" (38:17) are equated with Gehenna and "the breadth of the earth" (38:18) with Paradise.[24] The Latin Vulgate partakes of the same general character as the other translations.

The Ancient Versions all testify to the enduring and widespread interest in Job the man, rather than in the book. Nevertheless, when properly used, the Versions disclose some variant readings worthy of consideration by the modern exegete. Generally, however, the interpreter of Job must fall back upon other resources for understanding the book.

The interest in the pious Job of the traditional tale is also reflected in the vast expanse of rabbinic literature. Since the book was not read officially at synagogue services like the Torah or the Five Scrolls, few special Midrashim or homiletic commentaries on Job were compiled. Instead, homiletic and ethical comments on the book are scattered throughout the Babylonian and Palestinian Talmuds and the various Midrashic collections.[25]

The three basic traits of the rabbinic Aggadah, or religio-ethical literature, are clearly in evidence here.[26] First is the universal mythopoetic faculty which is to be found in all legends and folk tales, the desire to fill out lacunae in the lives of past heroes by additional incidents. Second is the desire to inculcate proper religious and ethical sentiments based on the lives of these worthies. These two traits are widespread in all legend and folklore. The third, a specific characteristic of rabbinic literature (and of its Christian counterparts), is the technique of deriving these incidents and ideas from the biblical text. The exegesis that is employed may be ingenious or far-fetched, but in any case it frequently has its own independent value and attractiveness.

In the mass of rabbinic comment on Job, one striking critical opinion is quoted. An anonymous scholar once told Samuel ben Nahmani, "Job never existed and was never created, but was a parable."[27] Virtually the same words are attributed to the fourth-century Palestinian Amora, Simon ben Lakish.[28] So critical a view could not be permitted to stand unmodified, and therefore his utterance was interpreted to mean, "Job was not exposed to the sufferings described, but he could have endured them if they had come upon him!"[29] Another reading changes the text slightly and reads, "Job was created . . . only to serve as a parable."[30]

This individual opinion aside, it was generally taken for granted that the prose narrative was historical. Falling back upon the slightest of verbal resemblances between passages in Job and other parts of Scripture, the rabbis assigned the hero to varying periods. Because of the patriarchal setting in the prologue he was associated by some with Abraham. Others considered him a contemporary of Jacob or of Jacob's sons, while one legend said that he married Dinah, Jacob's only daughter.[31] Still other views made Job a contemporary of Moses and Pharaoh.[32] Others assigned him to much later ages, including that of the Persian king Ahasuerus and the period of the return from the Babylonian captivity.[33] The general consensus, however, tended to place him in an earlier age.

Rabbinic legend amplifies with many details the account of Job's stupendous wealth, which is described in circumstantial, and at times statistical, detail. So, too, with regard to his restoration after his trials. The period of his trial lasted twelve months, according to the Mishnah. When he was restored to prosperity, all his blessings, including the number of his sons, were doubled. Only the number of his daughters remained the same, but their beauty was increased. He lived one hundred and forty years longer (twice the normal life span of seventy), for a total of two hundred and ten years.

More significant are the two opposing religious motives underlying the rabbinic treatment of Job. On the one hand, the rabbis wished to justify the biblical description of Job as pious and God-fearing. Many details are accordingly given of his scrupulous piety and multifarious acts of charity. Job is described as one of "the saints among the Gentiles."[34] On the other hand, one notes a tendency to place limits on his virtue. One reason was the fear lest his righteousness place the patriarch Abraham and the other Jewish saints in the shade.[35] More important was the need felt to justify the suffering that God brought upon him. Quite properly, the wager with Satan was not regarded as a sufficient explanation.

A moving legend accordingly declares that Pharaoh had three advisers whom he consulted with regard to his plan to drown all the male children of the Israelite slaves. One counselor, Jethro, opposed the plan forthrightly and fled to the wilderness. He was rewarded by becoming the father-in-law of Moses. Another, Balaam, later the false prophet of ill fame, urged Pharaoh to exterminate the male infants at birth. The third was Job, who remained silent in the face of the plan and was therefore punished by suffering. A later form of the same legend declares that at first Job had encouraged Pharaoh in his plan, but later turned evasive, suggesting that "the king may do as he pleases." Because he gave tacit approval to injustice and cruelty, the calamities described in the narrative came upon him.[36]

In another passage the rabbis disagree as to whether Job's complaints were directed against God and therefore constituted blasphemy or were directed against Satan and were therefore justified.[37] Finally, the statement is offered that Job denied the resurrection of the dead, which is a clear inference from the moving passage in chapter 14.[38] In general, Job is charged with being a rebel against God, but the substance of his complaints is usually passed over in silence.[39]

Job is also the subject of a remarkable apocryphal work, the *Testament of Job*,[40] which has been long neglected. As in the addition to the Greek translation, Job is called Jobab here. Just as later legend supplied the name "Zuleika" for Potiphar's wife in the tale of Joseph, so the *Testament of Job* gives the name of Job's wife as Sitis or Sitidos.[41] Along with many details of Job's charity, which can be paralleled in rabbinic sources, the *Testament of Job* adds a few poignant notes to the relationship of Job and his wife. When destitution overtakes him, she sells her hair in order to secure three loaves of bread for her ill and starving husband. Later, she pleads with the Friends to help her bury her children, who lie crushed under the ruins of their home.

In the same work we encounter a strikingly negative attitude toward Elihu which, to be sure, is not altogether without parallel in rabbinic sources.[42] Undoubtedly basing itself on the text of the epilogue, which declares that Job won forgiveness for Eliphaz and his two companions (42:7–9), but makes no mention of Elihu, the *Testament of Job* explicitly states that Elihu was not pardoned. Indeed, he is described as "the evil one," "the son of darkness, the lover of the Serpent, the Northern one,[43] the hater of the saints, who is cast down to Sheol."

Thus, such varied phenomena as the canonization of Job and the characteristics of the Ancient Versions, as well as rabbinic legend and

)ocryphal literature, all bear witness to the fact that throughout the
;es of faith it was "the patience of Job" which was at the center of
en's interest.[44]
Only a rare medieval philosopher like Maimonides or Gersonides
ould turn to Job for ideas bearing on God and the problem of evil.[45]
ot until the modern period does Job the rebel, the hero of the dia-
gue, become the prime focus of attention. A philosopher as uncom-
·omisingly rationalist as Immanuel Kant found in the book a spring-
)ard for his own reflections on theodicy.[46]
Though the resemblance is slight, modern writers have often com-
ired Job to the Greek Prometheus, who challenged the reign of the
)ds. The rise of literary appreciation of the Bible toward the end of
·e eighteenth century, through Herder and Lowth, stimulated a
cognition of the poetic greatness of the book. Throughout the nine-
enth century it was the artist and the writer who were drawn to this
·eat work. Goethe used the prologue of Job as a prototype for his
'rologue" to *Faust*, elevating Mephistopheles to a unique position in
s drama, and incidentally forging a link between two of the world's
anscendent masterpieces. William Blake, enthralled by the panorama
creation described in the God speeches, produced his magnificent
)rawings for the Book of Job."
Today, Job the passionate rebel has come into his own again, as men
ve been confronted by the monstrous evils of the twentieth century
d have been forced to face ultimate issues of human existence and
·stiny. With the problems of faith looming ever larger for modern
en they have been stirred to a deeper interest in and admiration for
·e courage and integrity of Job, who dared to challenge the right-
·usness of God. After World War I, H. G. Wells utilized the scheme
the dialogue of Job and his friends as the framework for his treat-
ent of the tragic mystery of the senseless death of the young in war.
his novel, *The Undying Fire*, a country estate serves as the setting
·r a debate between the host, whose son has been killed in battle, and
·e friends who have come to console him.
Following the devastation of World War II and the widespread
llapse of faith in man's capacity to build his world, the American
·et and dramatist, Archibald MacLeish, turned to Job and used the
·mework of the biblical book for his drama, *J.B.* Indeed, he used
·ny of the lines of the biblical text in his play, which sought to deal
th the agonizing problem of man's undeserved suffering in a world

in which he is victim more often than sinner. For all their talents, nor of those who have borrowed from Job have equalled, much less sui passed, the original.

As our age of doubt perseveres in its quest for a vital faith, men ma be led to recognize that both the prose and the poetry of Job are esser tial elements in the architecture of the book and that the whole greater than the sum of its parts. In its passion and power, its pro fundity, insight, and integrity, Job remains man's supreme expressio of the mystery and the miracle of existence, the matchless embodimer of man's unconquerable faith that despite all its frustration and pai life has beauty and meaning.

Part Two

THE BOOK OF JOB

Structure and Contents

The Hymn to Wisdom (28)

Job's Soliloquy
In Remembrance of Happier Days (29)
The Misery of the Present Condition (30)
The Code of a Man of Honor (31)

The Words of Elihu
The First Speech (32–33)
The Second Speech (34)
The Third Speech (35)
The Fourth Speech (36–37)

The Lord out of the Whirlwind
The Lord's First Speech (38–40:2)
Job's Response (40:3–5)
The Lord's Second Speech (40:6–41:26)
Job's Response (42:1–6)

THE EPILOGUE
The Jointure (42:7–10)
Job's Restoration (42:11–17)

TO PRESENT HIS IDEAS on the eternal problem of man's suffering in God's world, the poet utilizes a traditional tale as a framework. Several stages of this familiar story, which was well known in
the ancient Middle East, can be reconstructed.

The first half of the tale, which describes Job's original prosperity
and his succeeding trials, serves as the prologue (1:1–2:10). Then follows the elaborate poetic dialogue which is the heart of the book (3:1–
42:6). The concluding part of the traditional narrative is used as an
epilogue (42:11–17) to describe Job's eventual restoration to well-
being.

The prologue and the epilogue are linked to the intervening dialogue
by two brief passages (2:11–17 and 42:7–10) written by the poet,
which connect the conventional prose tale with the profundities of the
poetic debate.

THE PROLOGUE

THE TALE OF THE RIGHTEOUS JOB (Chapters 1–2)

The story of Job is told in five scenes, alternating between earth and
heaven. In the land of Uz there lived a righteous and prosperous man
named Job, surrounded by his large and united family. When the Lord
in heaven boasts of Job's piety, Satan, the prosecuting angel in the
heavenly court, cynically insists that Job has served God only because
he has been well rewarded. Stung by this challenge, the Lord permits
Satan to subject Job to a series of trials in order to test his virtue. In
rapid succession four disasters, alternately natural calamities and man-
made troubles, destroy Job's possessions and annihilate his children.
Even this accumulation of catastrophes is unable to destroy Job's faith.
He utters no word of complaint against his Maker but accepts these
blows as the will of God.

233

Satan is only slightly disconcerted by his apparent failure. He insists
that if Job be struck in his own person his piety will crumble. The Lord
extends the wager to permit Satan to attack Job himself. The sufferer
is stricken with a loathsome skin disease. He takes his place among the
lepers on an ash-heap outside the city which had been the scene of his
former prosperity. Unable to witness his agony, Job's wife urges him
to curse God and die. Job, however, sternly reminds her that he who
has accepted God's blessings must be prepared to accept God's burdens,
and he remains silent in his affliction.

In a brief connecting passage the scene is set for the poetic dialogue
Three of Job's friends, men of repute and position in their communities,
Eliphaz the Temanite, Bildad the Shuhite, and Zophar the Naamathite,
hear of the calamities that have befallen him. They come together from
afar to comfort Job, but when they see the tragic change in him they
are struck silent, and for seven days and nights no word is spoken.

1 There lived a man in the land of Uz whose name was Job. And
2 that man was blameless and upright, fearing God and avoiding evil.
3 There were born to him seven sons and three daughters. His property
 was seven thousand sheep, three thousand camels, five hundred yoke of
 oxen, five hundred she-asses, and a very large household of slaves, so
4 that this man was the greatest among all the people of the East.
 His sons used to hold a feast in the house of each one in his turn, and
5 they would send and invite their three sisters to eat and drink with
 them. When the days of feasting had run their course, Job would send
 for them and sanctify them, rising early and offering burnt offerings
 according to the number of them all. For Job thought,
  "Perhaps my children have sinned
   by blaspheming God in their hearts."
 Thus Job was wont to do continually.

6 Now one day, the sons of God came to stand in the presence of the
7 Lord, and Satan, too, came among them. And the Lord said to Satan,
  "Whence have you come?"
 And Satan answered the Lord and said,
  "From roaming the earth and walking to and fro on it."
8 Then the Lord said to Satan,
  "Have you noticed My servant Job?
  For there is no one on the earth like him:
  a man blameless and upright,
  fearing God and avoiding evil."

9 But Satan answered the Lord saying,
10   "Is it for nothing that Job has been fearing God?
   Have You not safely hedged him in,
   and his house, and all he owns on every side?
   You have blessed the work of his hands
   and his possessions have increased in the land.
11   But put forth Your hand and touch whatever he owns
   and he will surely curse You to Your face!"
12 So the Lord said to Satan,
   "Behold, all he has is in your power.
   Only upon the man himself, do not lay your hand."
So Satan went forth from the Lord's presence.

13   Now the day came when his sons and daughters were eating and
14 drinking wine in the home of their oldest brother. And a messenger
came to Job saying,
   "The oxen were plowing
   and the she-asses grazing nearby.
15   Then the Sabeans fell upon them and took them captive.
   The slave boys they put to the sword;
   and I alone have escaped to tell you."
16 While he was still speaking, another came and said,
   "A great fire fell from heaven
   and burned the sheep and the slaves and consumed them;
   and I alone have escaped to tell you."
17 While he was still speaking, another came and said,
   "The Chaldeans formed three companies
   and swooped down upon the camels and took them captive.
   The slaves they put to the sword;
   and I alone have escaped to tell you."
18 While he was speaking, another came and said,
   "Your sons and daughters were eating and drinking wine
   in the home of their oldest brother.
19   Suddenly, a mighty wind came across the desert,
   and it struck the four corners of the house;
   it fell upon the young people, and they died.
   And I alone have escaped to tell you."

20   Then Job arose and rent his robe and shaved his head, and fell upon
21 the earth and worshiped. And he said,
   "Naked I came from my mother's womb,
   naked shall I return.
   The Lord gave, and the Lord has taken away.
   Blessed be the name of the Lord."
22 Yet in all this, Job did not sin or charge anything unseemly to God.

2   Again there was a day when the sons of God came to stand in the
Lord's presence, and Satan also came among them to stand in the Lord's
2   presence. And the Lord said to Satan,
      "Whence have you come?"
And Satan answered the Lord saying,
      "From roaming the earth and walking to and fro on it."
3   Then the Lord said to Satan,
      "Have you noticed My servant Job?
      For there is no one like him on the earth,
      a man blameless and upright,
      fearing God and avoiding evil.
      He still holds fast to his integrity
      though you incited Me against him
      to destroy him without cause."
4   Then Satan answered the Lord saying,
      "Skin for skin!
      All a man has
      he will give for his life!
5   But put forth Your hand
      and touch his own flesh and bones
      and he will surely curse You to Your face."
6   Then the Lord said to Satan,
      "He is in your power,
      but preserve his life."

7   So Satan went forth from the presence of God and he struck Job
with loathsome sores from the sole of his foot to the crown of his head
8   so that he took a potsherd with which to scrape himself as he sat in the
9   midst of the ash-heap. Then his wife said to him,
      "Are you still holding fast to your piety?
      Curse God and die."
10   Then he said to her,
      "You talk like an impious, foolish woman.
      Shall we accept good from God
      and not accept evil?"
Yet even in all this, Job committed no sin with his lips.

11   Then Job's three friends heard of all the trouble that had come upon
him. And they came, each from his place—Eliphaz the Temanite,
Bildad the Shuhite, and Zophar the Naamathite—having arranged to-
12   gether to come to condole with him and comfort him. Now when they
caught sight of him from afar, they could not recognize him. So they
raised their voices and wept and rent their robes and threw dust over
13   their heads toward the heavens. They sat with him on the ground for
seven days and for seven nights, no one saying a word, for they saw
that his agony was very great.

THE DIALOGUE

Job's Lament (Chapter 3)

Job breaks the silence with a lament on his cruel fate. His words are addressed neither to his friends, of whose presence he is only dimly aware, nor to God, whom he does not yet directly charge with his calamities.

Job curses the day of his birth, which marked his entrance into the land of the living. How much better it would have been if he had never been conceived or, failing that, had died in his mother's womb, or had perished at the moment of birth. Even to be an untimely birth and thus be deprived of a proper burial would have been preferable to his present lot.

Were he dead he would be in Sheol, the land of shadows, where kings and princes fare no better than slaves, and where the oppressor and his victim are equally at rest. Why is life given to men who suffer and would rejoice if death came? So he, too, wishes to escape from his life which is an unending succession of terrors.

3	Afterwards, Job began to speak and cursed the day of his birth. Job
2	spoke, saying,
3	Perish the day when I was born,
	and the night which said:
	"A man-child is conceived."
4	That day—may it be utter darkness!
	Let God not seek it from above
	and let no light shine upon it.
5	Let blackness and gloom reclaim it;
	may clouds rest upon it
	and the demons of the day terrify it.
6	That night—may deep darkness capture it!
	Let it not be counted in the days of the year
	or enter in the number of months.
7	May that night be lonely as a crag
	and no joyful sounds penetrate it.
8	Let them curse it who curse their day,
	who are skilled in stirring up Leviathan.
9	Let the stars of its dawn be dark;
	may it hope for light, but have none,
	nor see the eyelids of the morning,
10	because it did not shut the doors of my mother's womb
	or hide misery from my eyes.

11   Why did I not die in the womb?
        Or perish as I came forth from it?
12   Why were there knees to receive me?
        And why breasts for me to suck?
13   For then I should have lain down and been quiet,
        I should have slept and been at peace
14   with kings and counselors of the earth
        who rebuild ruined cities for themselves,
15   or with princes rich in gold
        who fill their houses with silver.

16   Or even if I had been an aborted birth,
        like the stillborn infants who never see the light!

17   There the wicked cease their raging.
        There their victims are at rest.
18   All the prisoners are at ease,
        they hear the taskmaster's shouts no more.
19   There the small and the great are equal
        and the slave is free from his master.

20   Why is light given to the sufferer
        and life to embittered souls
21   who long for death—but it comes not—
        and dig for it more than for buried treasure,
22   who would exult in great joy
        and be happy to find a grave?
23   Why is life given to the man whose way is hidden,
        whom God has fenced in?

24   Indeed, my sighing comes like my daily bread,
        my groans are poured out like water.
25   For the fear I had has come upon me,
        and what I dreaded has overtaken me.
26   I have no ease, no peace, no rest.
        What has come is agony.

THE FIRST CYCLE (Chapters 4–14)

The Speech of Eliphaz (Chapters 4–5)

Eliphaz, the oldest and most urbane of the Friends, is the first to answer. He begins by asking for permission to speak. He reminds his afflicted friend how often he himself has consoled sufferers in the past by recalling the great truth of religion—that the righteous are never destroyed, but that the wicked are sure to be punished either in their own persons or through their children.

Eliphaz then describes a revelation from on high that has brought him new insight: all men are imperfect in the eyes of God; therefore, even the suffering of the righteous has its justification. In view of these two great truths it is foolish for Job to lose patience and surrender his faith in the divine government of the world.

After picturing the punishment which ultimately overtakes sinners, Eliphaz delivers himself of a third doctrine: neither God nor His universe can fairly be charged with the creation of sin and suffering, because evil is a human invention. Since man is the source of sin, he must be prepared to suffer.

Rather than speak of man's limitations, however, Eliphaz prefers to extol God's great wisdom. He makes a fleeting reference to a fourth basic idea: suffering serves at times to discipline and instruct the righteous, and thus guards them against evildoing.

Eliphaz concludes with a triumphant hymn of praise to God, the savior of the just. He describes the various calamities to which man is exposed, from which God saves the righteous. Since Job has always been upright, he may expect to attain harmony with the world of nature and man and to end his life at a ripe old age in serenity and peace.

In the proud consciousness that he has effectively presented the basic doctrines taught by religion—as is indeed the case—Eliphaz calls upon Job to recognize and accept the truth he has proclaimed.

4   Eliphaz the Temanite then answered, and said,

2   If one tried a word with you, would you be offended?
           Yet who can refrain from speaking?

3   Behold, you have encouraged many
           and strengthened weak hands.

4   Your words have upheld the stumbling,
           and you have strengthened the weak-kneed.

5   But now that it has come to you, you cannot bear it;
           it touches you, and you are dismayed.

6   Indeed, your fear of God should be your confidence
           and your hope—the uprightness of your ways!

7   Think now, what innocent man was ever destroyed;
           where was the upright cut off?

8   Whenever I have seen those who plow iniquity
           and sow trouble—they reap it!

9   By the breath of God they are destroyed,
        and by the blast of His wrath they are consumed.
10   The lion roars, the fierce beast cries—
        but the teeth of the whelps are shattered.
11   The mighty lion wanders about without prey,
        and the young of the lioness are scattered.

12   Now to me a word came stealthily,
        and my ear caught an echo of it
13   amid thoughts and visions of the night,
        when deep sleep falls upon men.
14   Terror came upon me, and trembling,
        and all my limbs it frightened.
15   A wind passed before my face;
        a storm made my skin bristle.
16   It stood still,
        but I could not tell its appearance;
     a form stood before my eyes;
        silence—then I heard a voice:
17   "Can a human being be righteous before God?
        Can a mortal be pure before his Maker?
18   Even in His servants God puts no trust;
        Even His angels He charges with folly.
19   How much more so those who dwell in clay houses,
        whose foundation is in the dust,
     who are crushed like a bird's nest!
20   Between morning and evening they are crushed;
        with none to pay heed, they are destroyed forever.
21   Indeed, their tent cord is plucked up within them;
        they die, with no one the wiser."

5   Call out—who is there to answer you?
        To whom can you turn rather than to God?
2   Anger surely kills the fool,
        and impatience slays the simpleton.
3   I myself have seen a fool striking root,
        but I declared that folly's dwelling must be cursed.
4   His sons will be far from safety;
        they will be crushed in the judgment gate
     with none to deliver them.
5   His harvest the hungry will devour;
        his substance the starving will carry off,
     and the famished will snatch away his wealth.

6   Indeed, misfortune does not come forth from the ground,
        nor does evil sprout from the earth.

7   It is man who gives birth to evil,
        as surely as the sparks fly upward.

8   As for me, I would seek after God
        and to God entrust my cause,

9   who does great things without end,
        wonders without number.

10   He gives rain to the earth
        and sends water upon the open places.

11   He sets the lowly on high,
        and the afflicted are raised to safety.

12   He confounds the plans of the crafty
        so that their hands achieve no success.

13   He traps the wise in their own cunning,
        and the schemes of the perverse come to a speedy end.

14   In daylight they encounter darkness
        and at noon they grope as in the night.

15   But from their sharp tongue and mighty hand
        He saves the needy,

16   so that the poor have hope,
        and injustice shuts her mouth.

17   Behold, happy is the man whom God reproves;
        do not then despise the chastisement of the Almighty.

18   For He wounds, but binds up;
        He smites, but His hands bring healing.

19   From six troubles He will save you,
        and in seven, no evil will touch you.

20   In hunger He will redeem you from death,
        and in battle, from the power of the sword.

21   When the tongue of fire moves about, you will be hidden;
        nor need you fear the onrushing flood.

22   At the devastation of famine you will laugh,
        and the beasts of the earth you will not fear.

23   For with the stones in the field you will be leagued,
        and the beasts of the field will be at peace with you.

24   You will know that your tent is at peace;
        when you visit your home, you will find no one missing.

25   You will know that your children are many
        and your offspring like the grass of the earth.

26   You will come to your grave in ripe old age,
        like a shock of grain to the threshing floor in its season.

27   Behold, this we have searched out—it is true—
        We have heard it, now you take it to heart.

Job's Reply to Eliphaz (Chapters 6–7)

Job seems not to have heard Eliphaz' elaborate argumentation. Weighted down with his own misery, he indulges in a painful reverie. Life is a burden that he cannot bear. He wishes to die and end his agony. Perhaps he has been unrestrained in his grief, but it is only the measure of his agony. If all were well with him he would have no cause for complaint, any more than an animal at a well-filled trough.

The truth is that he has heard Eliphaz all too well but has found his words tasteless and meaningless. In the face of these finespun explanations Job knows only that he has not violated the commands of God. Bitterly he calls upon God to reward him—by a speedy death—for he can bear his torture no longer.

Job then turns in fury upon his friends, who have proved unreliable when he needed them most. In a powerful figure he compares them to a desert stream which the footsore and thirsty traveler struggles to reach, only to find it frozen over in the winter and dried up in the summer.

In repeating the threadbare argument that justice always prevails, Eliphaz has implied that Job is sinful. Pathetically Job protests his innocence and asks for sympathy. He paints a moving picture of his physical pain and mental anguish, which is all the more difficult to bear because life is fleeting, with little time or hope for improvement.

Job's only relief lies in speaking out against the injustice he suffers at the hands of the God whom he has worshiped and served. In a bitter parody of the Eighth Psalm he asks why man is worthy of God's jealous and vengeful attention. Granted that he has sinned, why does God torment him? Why not kill him at once and thus end his agony?

Job raises two fundamental issues here that are never even remotely approached by the Friends, who can only restate the conventional theology of the day. The first is the question: Why is man important to God and why are his sins and weaknesses the subject of divine concern? The answer of biblical religion is implicit in its view of the nature of man. The concept that man is created in the image of God is expressed in the opening chapter of Genesis, and its major implications are spelled out in the Eighth Psalm, which Job parodies. It follows that man and God are intimately and indissolubly linked together, for man's deeds have a direct bearing upon God's purposes in the world. Stated less theologically, man is endowed with extraordinary capacities which place upon him extraordinary responsibilities.

The second problem posed by Job is equally searching: Why should a man, even a sinner, be made to suffer, seeing that he is not master of his destiny? As is characteristic of biblical thought, which did not operate in syllogistic form, Job raises here the problem of God's omnipotence and man's responsibility. The dilemma of free will versus determinism was never resolved in the tradition and remains a challenge to our own day. Rabbinic Judaism seized hold of both horns of the dilemma, as in Rabbi Akiba's classic formulation, "All is foreseen, yet free-will is given to man." A millennium and a half later, Doctor Samuel Johnson declared equally succinctly, "With regard to free-will, all philosophy is against it and all experience is for it." In spite of all the logical difficulties involved, the Judeo-Christian world view, with few exceptions, has held fast to man's freedom as the indispensable foundation for man's moral responsibility.

To rearrange the material in these chapters in accordance with Western canons of logic and relevance, as some scholars have proposed, is to violate the passion and sweep of the poetry. Job's basic theme is his unbearable agony, to which he reverts time and again when challenging God's justice, or pleading for his death, when berating his friends for their lack of sympathy, or demanding to know why he is the object of God's baleful concern. It is emotion, not logic, that constitutes the underlying unity in Job's moving outburst.

6   Then Job replied, saying,
2   If indeed my anguish were weighed
            and all my calamity placed in the scales,
3   it would be heavier than the sand of the sea—
            therefore I may have spoken rashly.
4   For the arrows of the Almighty are in me;
            my spirit drinks in their poison;
            God's terrors are arrayed against me.
5   Does the wild ass bray when he has grass,
            or the ox low over his fodder?
6   Can tasteless food be eaten without salt,
            or is there any savor in the juice of mallows?
7   My mouth refuses to touch it;
            it loathes it like diseased food.

8   Oh, that I might have my petition
            and God would grant my hope—

9   that it would please God to crush me,
      to loose His hand and cut me off!
10   For this would be my consolation
      as I trembled in pitiless agony—
      that I never have denied the words of the Holy One.

11   What is my strength, that I should wait,
      and what my end, that I should be patient?
12   Is my strength the strength of stones,
      or is my flesh made of bronze?
13   Indeed, there is no help for me,
      and effective aid has been driven from me.

14   He who pleads for kindness from his fellow man
      has forsaken the reverence due the Almighty.
15   My brothers betray me like a desert stream,
      like freshets that pass away.
16   They grow dark with ice
      upon them the snow is heaped up.
17   But in the time of heat, they disappear;
      when it is hot, they vanish from their place.
18   Their paths wind away,
      they go up into nothingness and disappear.
19   The caravans of Tema had looked to them;
      the travelers of Sheba had hoped for them.
20   But they are disappointed because they had counted on them;
      When they reach them, they are put to shame.
21   Now you have become like that stream;
      you see my disaster and are seized with fear.
22   Have I ever said, "Give something on my behalf,
      and from your wealth offer a bribe for me;
23   deliver me from the enemy's hand
      and ransom me from the hand of the oppressors"?

24   Teach me, and I shall be silent,
      and where I have erred, make me understand.
25   How forceful are true words!
      But what can your argument demonstrate?
26   Do you regard empty words as proof
      and a despairing man's speeches as mere wind?
27   You would cast lots even over an orphan
      and drive a bargain over your friend.
28   And now, pray, give me heed,
      you may turn away, if I should lie.
29   Please stay, there is no wrong in me,
      stay with me, my integrity is still intact.
30   Is there any wrong upon my tongue?
      Cannot my taste discern wrongdoing?

7 A term of hard service awaits man upon earth;
  his life is like a hireling's days.
2 Like a slave, he yearns for the shadow;
  like a hireling, he waits for his wage.
3 Indeed, I have been allotted months of emptiness,
  and nights of misery have been meted out to me.
4 When I lie down, I ask, "When shall I arise?"
  but the night is long, and I say,
  "I have had my fill of tossing till daybreak."
5 My flesh is clothed in worms and clods of dirt;
  my skin hardens and then breaks out again.
6 My days are swifter than the weaver's shuttle;
  they end in the absence of hope.
7 Remember that my life is but a breath—
  my eye will never again see good.
8 The eye of the beholder will see me no more;
  while your eyes are upon me, I am gone.
9 As a cloud fades and disappears,
  so he who goes down to Sheol rises no more.
10 He will not return to his home,
  and his place will know him no longer.

11 Therefore I will not restrain my speech;
  I will speak out in the agony of my spirit;
  I will complain in the bitterness of my soul.
12 Am I the sea, or a monster of the deep,
  that You place a guard about me?
13 When I think, "My couch will comfort me,
  my bed will share the burden of my complaint,"
14 then You terrify me with dreams
  and frighten me with visions,
15 so that I prefer strangling—
  death rather than this existence.
16 I loathe my life; I shall not live forever.
  Let me alone, for my days are but a breath.
17 What is man that You exalt him
  and You give him Your attention,
18 that You visit him each morning,
  and You test him every moment?
19 How long till You turn aside from me
  and release me for an instant?
20 If I have sinned, how have I harmed You,
  O Guardian of man?
  Why have You made me Your target
  and have I become a burden to You?
21 Why not carry off my sin,
  and remove my transgression,
  so that in the dust I can lie,
  and when You seek me, I shall be no more.

The Speech of Bildad (Chapter 8)

With none of the courtliness characteristic of Eliphaz, Bildad leaps into the fray. He has been driven into a fury by Job's denial of God's justice. Bildad has not the slightest doubt that the law of retribution prevails. Since Job's children have been killed, they must surely have sinned. If, on the other hand, Job makes his peace with God, he will again attain to prosperity and well-being. To be sure, the process of retribution needs more than the life span of a single generation to become manifest. Bildad therefore calls upon the wisdom of the ancients to bear witness to the truth of his position. As surely as effect follows cause in the natural world, suffering is the result of sin in the life of man.

Bildad now dramatizes his faith in God's justice through the use of a well-known technique in Wisdom literature. In the name of the sages of the past, whom he has invoked, he presents a parable of two plants. One is apparently verdant and fresh but doomed to shrivel quickly. The other preserves its moisture even under the hot sun, making its way through stony ground and, if need be, taking root in a new soil. In accordance with Semitic usage, the two plants are not identified, nor is there a transitional phrase between the two descriptive passages. For the modern reader I have introduced the phrases, "Here is one plant" (vs. 12), "And here is the other plant" (vs. 16).

Only at the conclusion of his speech does Bildad reveal what the reader is expected to recognize at the beginning—that the two plants being described symbolize the short-lived prosperity of the wicked and the ultimate triumph of the righteous.

8   Then Bildad the Shuhite answered, saying,
2   How long will you mouth such notions
            and the words of your mouth be a mighty wind?
3   Does God pervert justice?
            Does the Almighty pervert the right?
4   Your children must surely have sinned against Him,
            and He has dispatched them for their transgression.
5   But will you seek God
            and make supplication to the Almighty?
6   If you are pure and upright,
            He will surely watch over you
            and safeguard your righteous dwelling.
7   Your beginning may be small,
            but your future will be greatly exalted.

8	For inquire, I pray you, of an earlier generation,
	and heed the insight of their fathers—
9	(for we ourselves are mere yesterdays and know nothing;
	our days, only a shadow upon earth)—
10	Indeed, they will teach and inform you
	and out of their understanding utter these words:
11	"Can papyrus grow where there is no marsh?
	Can reeds flourish without water?
12	Here is one plant:
	while yet in flower—not ready to be cut down—
	before any other plant, it withers.
13	Such is the fate of all who forget God:
	the hope of the godless must perish.
14	His self-confidence is mere gossamer thread,
	his trust but a spider's web.
15	He leans upon his house, but it will not stand;
	he takes hold of it, but it will not endure.
16	And here is the other plant:
	it is fresh even under the hot sun,
	as its shoots spread beyond its garden.
17	Even over a stone heap the roots are entwined,
	as it cleaves its way among rocks.
18	If its place should destroy it
	and deny it, saying, 'I have never seen you,'
19	behold, it goes forth on its way,
	and from the earth elsewhere it will sprout again.
20	Indeed, God will not spurn the blameless man,
	nor will He uphold the evildoers."
21	God will yet fill your mouth with laughter
	and your lips with shouts of joy.
22	Your enemies will be clothed with shame,
	and the tent of the wicked will be no more.

Job's Reply to Bildad (Chapters 9–10)

Job now launches a vigorous attack upon the moral government of the world. He recognizes that God is mighty and man too feeble to argue with Him. Eliphaz has painted a graphic picture of God's power. Job proceeds to demonstrate that he can do as well. But his paean of praise stresses the negative and destructive aspects of God's might and thus becomes a searing attack upon God's irresponsible and unjust power. Although Job's mouth can be perverted against him, he is resolved to call God to justice, for might does not make right.

He now reaches the apex of his bitterness. The world is given over to unrighteous men, while God mocks the suffering of the innocent. No wonder Job's suffering is without limit. He relapses into a pathetic realization that since God and he are not coequal in power, he cannot prove himself upright.

Job now appeals from the God of power to the God of justice, who must exist somewhere in the universe. If only there were an arbiter, a higher power who could judge equally between Job and the God of might, he could speak out freely without fear.

Job next turns to entreaty and asks why his Maker torments him. Does God get any pleasure out of mistreating him? Is God's vision limited, that He judges Job wrongly? Is God short-lived, that He hastens to ferret out Job's sin? Surely no one knows Job better than his Maker, for every step in the process of his creation, from his conception to his birth, has been an expression of the divine will. It is clear that God's decision to punish him bears no relationship to his innocence or guilt. From his boundless suffering Job cries out once more for the peace of death.

9   Then Job answered and said,
2   I surely know that it is so,
            when you say, "How can a man be just before God?"
3   If one wished to contend with Him,
            He would not answer once in a thousand times.
4   However wise and stouthearted a man might be,
            has he ever argued with God and emerged unscathed?
5   He removes mountains and they know it not,
            overturning them in His wrath.
6   He shakes the earth from its place
            and its pillars tremble.
7   He commands the sun, and it does not rise,
            and He seals up the stars.
8   He alone stretches out the heavens
            and treads upon the crest of the sea.
9   He has made the Bear and Orion,
            the Pleiades and the constellations of the South.
10   Yes, He does great things beyond understanding,
            and wonders without number.
11   Lo, He passes by me, and I do not see Him,
            He moves on, and I do not perceive Him.
12   Behold, when He robs, who can make Him return it?
            Who can say to Him, "What are You doing?"
13   God will not restrain His wrath,
            before which Rahab's helpers were brought low.

14 How then can I answer Him,
   choosing my words with Him?

15 For even if I am right, I cannot respond,
   but must make supplication to my opponent.

16 If I called Him, would He answer me?
   I cannot believe that He would hear my voice.

17 For He crushes me for a trifle,
   and increases my wounds without cause.

18 He does not let me catch my breath,
   but fills me with bitterness.

19 If it be a matter of power, here He is!
   But if of justice, who will arraign Him?

20 Though I am in the right, my mouth would condemn me;
   though I am blameless, it would prove me perverse.

21 I am blameless—
   I am beside myself—I loathe my life.

22 It is all one—I say—
   the blameless and the wicked He destroys alike.

23 When disaster brings sudden death
   He mocks the plea of the innocent.

24 The land is given over to the hand of the evildoer
   who is able to bribe the judges.
   If not He, who then is guilty?

25 My days are swifter than a runner;
   they have fled without seeing any joy.

26 They speed by like skiffs of reed,
   like a vulture swooping upon its prey.

27 If I say, "I shall forget my complaint,
   set aside my sadness, and be of good cheer,"

28 then I am frightened by all my pains,
   and I realize You will not set me free.

29 I shall surely be condemned—
   why then labor in vain?

30 Were I to wash myself in nitre
   and cleanse my hands with lye,

31 You would plunge me into the pit
   and my own clothes would refuse to touch me.

32 For God is not a man like me, whom I could answer
   when we came to trial together.

33 If only there were an arbiter between us
   who would lay his hand upon us both,

34 who would remove God's rod from me
   so that my dread of Him would not terrify me.

35 Then I would speak, and not fear Him,
   for He is far from just to me!

10   I loathe my life—
        I will give free rein to my complaint;
        I will speak out in the bitterness of my soul.

2   I say to God: Do not condemn me.
        Let me know why You contend against me.

3   Does it do You good to practice oppression,
        to despise the work of Your hands
        and show favor to the plans of the wicked?

4   Have You eyes of flesh;
        do You see as does a mere man?

5   Are Your days short like those of a mortal,
        or Your years brief as those of a man,

6   that You search after my iniquity
        and ferret out my sin?

7   Though You know that I am not guilty,
        no one can deliver me from Your hand.

8   Your hands fashioned and made me
        altogether—yet now You destroy me!

9   Remember that You made me of clay
        and will return me to the dust.

10   It was You who poured me out like milk,
        and like cheese You curdled me.

11   You clothed me in skin and flesh
        and knitted me together with bones and sinews.

12   In Your love You granted me life;
        Your command kept me alive.

13   Yet all this You have buried in Your heart;
        I know that this was in Your mind.

14   If I sin, You stand guard over me;
        You do not let me escape my guilt.

15   If I sin, woe betide me,
        yet if I am righteous, I cannot raise my head,
        being filled with shame and sated with misery.

16   For You take pride in hunting me like a lion,
        time and again You show Your wonders against me.

17   You constantly send new witnesses against me
        and increase Your hostility toward me;
        wave after wave of foes assails me.

18   Why did You take me out of the womb?
        Would I had died and no eye had seen me!

19   Would I were as though I had never been
        and had been carried from the womb to the grave.

20   Indeed, few are the days of my life;
        turn away from me so that I may see a little light

21   before I go—never to return—
        to a land of darkness and gloom,

22   a land whose light is blackness,
        gloom and disorder,
        where the light is as darkness.

The Speech of Zophar (Chapter 11)

Zophar, who is probably the youngest of the Friends and surely the least urbane, now joins the debate. In spite of his tactlessness, Zophar is by no means negligible as a thinker.

He declares that Job's insistence upon his uprightness is both false and arrogant. Far from punishing Job unjustly, God has reduced the extent of his penalty, for there are secret sins known only to God. This is not astonishing in a mysterious universe that is beyond man's power to grasp. God's wisdom and power are limitless, and man's folly is almost equally great. If Job wishes to be restored to peace and well-being, he should repent his sins and thus become worthy of God's forgiveness and favor.

11	Zophar the Naamathite answered, saying,
2	Shall a multitude of words go unanswered and a man full of talk appear in the right?
3	Your rantings force men to silence; you mock the truth, with no one to shut you up,
4	as you say, "My doctrine is pure, and I am pure in Your eyes."
5	But Oh, if God would speak and open His lips to you,
6	and tell you the secrets of wisdom— for there are mysteries in understanding. Then you would know that God is exacting less from you than your guilt demands.
7	Can you penetrate the essence of God? Can you discover the nature of the Almighty?
8	It is higher than heaven—what can you do? and deeper than Sheol—what can you know?
9	It is longer than the earth in measure, and wider than the sea.
10	If God seizes hold and imprisons and arraigns, who can hinder Him?
11	For He is well acquainted with worthless men; He sees their sin, though He pretends not to notice.
12	But a stupid man will get understanding, as soon as a wild ass's colt is born a man.
13	If you direct your heart aright and spread out your hands to Him—
14	if there be iniquity in your hand, put it away; let no wickedness dwell in your tent—

252 / THE BOOK OF JOB

you will be able to lift your face free from blemish;
you will be firmly set, with nothing to fear;
16 all your misery you will forget,
recalling it only as waters that have passed away.
17 Brighter than the noonday will be your world;
its darkness will shine like the morning.
18 You will lie down, knowing there is hope;
you will make your couch and lie down in safety.
19 You will lie down, and none will make you afraid—
indeed, many will entreat your favor.
20 But the eyes of the wicked will fail with longing,
all escape will be cut off from them
and their hope will turn into despair.

Job's Reply to Zophar (Chapters 12–14)

Job's closing speech in the first cycle is his most extensive rejoinder. These chapters have been widely misunderstood and consequently have been subjected to a plethora of emendations and deletions. The key to their meaning and power lies in recognizing the use of quotations. At times Job cites—and inevitably distorts—the words of the Friends in order to refute them. Or he quotes maxims drawn from Wisdom literature in order to buttress his own position. This is indicated in the translation by quotation marks and brief introductory phrases.

The speech begins with a sarcastic reference to the Friends' claim that they possess superior wisdom and a more intimate knowledge of God. Were he in their place, Job, too, would find it easy to bear the calamities of the unfortunate! He parodies the speeches of the Friends, who have sought to avoid any straightforward discussion of God's justice by extolling the wonders of nature. Job then refers to the Friends' claim to greater wisdom because of their greater age by citing a traditional apothegm. This argument he undermines obliquely by citing another proverb which declares that all wisdom and might are with God.

Job now proceeds to describe God's power in a speech which differs significantly from the hymns previously intoned by the Friends. While they have praised God's creative goodness, Job pictures God's power negatively, as manifested in the destruction of the order of nature, in the overthrow of the upper classes in society, and in the changing destinies of nations.

Job then insists that the Friends' defense of God is worthless, because

God wants no partiality or false pleading on His behalf. At least God knows that Job is no flatterer and speaks the truth in his heart. Finding neither compassion nor truth in the Friends, Job flees from God to God, seeking refuge from His wrath in His mercy. He asks God that his sins be clearly set forth and his torment be brought to an end.

What is man—short-lived, impure, and frail! All Job asks is a brief respite from his misery before he dies and disappears forever. An aging tree, Job muses, may come back to life through transplanting. If man only possessed the same power of self-renewal! Job toys longingly with the idea of man's immortality, but then sorrowfully rejects it. He finds it impossible to accept this new idea of life after death, a belief which was beginning to penetrate many circles. Job concludes that death is universal and final. After a man is gone he cannot share the joys and sorrows of his children, for with death all knowledge and sentience end.

12	Then Job answered, saying,
2	No doubt you are the people that count,
	and with you all wisdom will die!
3	Yet I have a mind as well as you;
	I am not inferior to you.
	Who does not know such things as these?
4	I have become a mockery to God's friend
	who calls to Him and is answered—
	a mockery to the perfect saint!
5	The unfortunate deserve only contempt
	in the opinion of the safe and secure—
	a beating is proper for those who stumble!
6	You admit, "The tents of robbers are at peace,
	the dwellings of those who provoke God,
	of those who have deceived Him."
7	"But," you say, "ask the cattle to teach you,
	and the fowl of the sky to tell you,
8	or speak to the earth that it instruct you,
	and let the fish of the sea declare to you."
9	Who does not know in all this,
	that the hand of the Lord has made it,
10	in whose hand is the life of every living thing
	and the breath of all human kind!
11	Surely the ear tests words
	as the palate tastes food!
12	You say, "With the aged is wisdom,
	in length of days is understanding."
13	But I say, "With God are wisdom and strength,
	His are counsel and understanding."

14 Behold, He destroys and it cannot be rebuilt,
    He imprisons a man and he is not released.
15 He shuts up the waters and they dry up,
    or He sends them forth and they overwhelm the earth.
16 With Him are strength and sound counsel;
    The misled and the misleaders—all are His.
17 He leads counselors away stripped,
    and of judges He makes fools.
18 He opens the belt of kings
    and removes the girdle from their loins.
19 He leads priests away stripped
    and the mighty ones He confuses.
20 He deprives counselors of speech
    and removes the discernment of the elders.
21 He pours contempt on princes,
    and looses the girdle of the strong.
22 He reveals deep secrets from the darkness,
    and brings the blackest gloom to light.
23 He makes nations great, and then destroys them.
    He enlarges nations, and forsakes them.
24 He removes understanding from the people's leaders
    and leads them in a pathless waste astray.
25 They grope in the dark without light,
    and He makes them stagger like a drunkard.

13 Behold, all this my eye has seen;
    my ear has heard and understood it.
2 What you know, I know too;
    I am not inferior to you.
3 But I wish to speak to the Almighty;
    I desire to argue my case with God.
4 But you are plasterers of lies;
    worthless physicians are you all.
5 If only you would keep silent,
    this would count as a mark of your wisdom.
6 And now hear my argument;
    listen to the pleadings of my lips.
7 Is it for the sake of God that you speak falsehood,
    on His behalf that you utter lies?
8 Will you show partiality toward Him;
    is it for God that you are arguing?
9 Will it be well with you when He searches you out?
    Can you deceive Him as one deceives a man?
10 Will He declare you in the right,
    if you show partiality to one side?

11 Will not His majesty affright you
and His awe fall upon you?

12 Your arguments are maxims of ashes;
Your rejoinders, rejoinders of clay.

13 Be silent before me and I shall speak,
and let there befall me what may.

14 You ask why I place my flesh in my teeth
and take my life in my hand?

15 Yes, He may slay me; I have no hope,
but I will justify my ways to His face!

16 Indeed, He will surely be my salvation,
for it is no flatterer coming before Him.

17 Listen attentively to my words,
and let my declaration be in Your ears.

18 Now, if I could prepare my case,
I know that I would be vindicated.

19 But if God says, "Who dares to argue with Me?"
then I must perish in silence.

20 Spare me two things only
and I shall not need to hide from Your face:

21 remove Your hand from me,
and let not the dread of You terrify me;

22 Then You may call and I shall respond,
or I shall speak, and You answer me.

23 How many are my iniquities and sins?
Let me know my transgression and my sin.

24 Why do You hide Your face
and consider me Your enemy?

25 Will You harass a driven leaf
and pursue dry chaff,

26 that You charge my past actions against me
and make me inherit the sins of my youth?

27 You put my feet in the stocks;
You stand guard over all my paths
and mark out limits for my footprints.

28 Wasting away like a wine-skin,
like a garment devoured by the moth—

14 man, who is born of woman,
is few in days and sated with turmoil.

2 Like a flower he comes forth, and withers;
he flees like a shadow, and does not endure.

3 Is it upon such a one that You open Your eyes
and summon to judgment with You?

4 Who can tell the pure and the impure apart—
No one!

5 Indeed, man's days are determined,
his few months are fixed by You;
You have set his limits that he cannot pass.

6 Turn away from him—let him alone
until he complete, like a hireling, his day.

7 For there is hope for a tree—
if it be cut down, it can sprout again
and its shoots will not fail.

8 If its roots grow old in the earth
and its stump dies in the ground,

9 at the mere scent of water it will bud anew
and put forth branches like a young plant.

10 But man grows faint and dies;
man breathes his last, and where is he?

11 As water vanishes from a lake,
and a river is parched and dries up,

12 So man lies down and rises not again;
till the heavens are no more he will not awake,
nor will he be roused from his sleep.

13 Oh, if You would hide me in Sheol,
conceal me until Your wrath is spent;
set a fixed time for me, and then remember me!

14 If a man die, can he live again?
all the days of my service I would wait,
till my hour of release should come.

15 You would call and I would answer You;
You would be longing for the work of Your hands.

16 For then You would number my steps;
You would not keep watch over my sin.

17 You would seal up my transgression in a bag,
and You would cover over my iniquity.

18 But as a mountain falls and crumbles
and a rock is moved from its place,

19 as waters wear away stones
and a torrent washes away the earth's soil,
so do You destroy man's hope.

20 You seize him, and he departs forever;
You change his countenance, and send him off.

21 His sons may grow great, but he will never know it,
or they may be humbled, but he will be unaware of it.

22 Yet his flesh will be pained within him
and his spirit will be in mourning.

THE SECOND CYCLE (Chapters 15–21)

The Speech of Eliphaz (Chapter 15)

Eliphaz' patience is wearing thin in the face of Job's obstinacy and folly and his refusal to learn from those who are older and wiser than he. He reminds Job that all men are imperfect and therefore have no cause to complain about their suffering. Eliphaz pictures in detail the destiny of the wicked man: his prosperity is temporary; he is doomed to end in exile and suffering.

The new note added here is Eliphaz' emphasis upon the fact that even while the sinner is ostensibly at peace he lives in constant trepidation, never knowing when the sword of doom will descend upon him. Thus, in effect, he is being punished during the time of his prosperity. The ultimate punishment of the wicked is the annihilation of his offspring.

15	Eliphaz the Temanite answered, saying,
2	Should a wise man answer empty opinions
	and fill his stomach with wind?
3	Should he argue in useless talk,
	in words that do no good?
4	You are undermining the sense of reverence
	and diminishing communion with God.
5	It is your guilt that teaches your mouth
	and makes you choose crafty speech.
6	Your mouth condemns you, not I:
	your own lips testify against you.
7	Were you born the first among men,
	and brought forth before the hills?
8	Did you eavesdrop in the council of God
	and garner all wisdom for yourself?
9	What do you know that we do not;
	what do you understand that is beyond us?
10	Both the graybeard and the aged are among us,
	older in years than your father.
11	Are God's consolations too slight for you,
	or the words gently spoken to you?
12	Why does your passion inflame you,
	why do your eyes flash with ire,
13	that you let loose your anger against God,
	and let such words issue from your mouth?

14 What is man? Can he be pure?
   Can one born of woman be righteous?
15 Behold, God puts no trust even in His holy ones;
   the heavens themselves are not pure in His sight.
16 How much less one who is abominable and corrupt,
   a man who drinks in iniquity like water!

17 I will tell you—listen to me:
   what I have seen I will declare,
18 What wise men have told,
   and their fathers did not deny—
19 to whom alone the land was given,
   with no stranger passing among them—
20 All his days, the wicked is atremble
   throughout the few years stored up for the oppressor.
21 The sound of terror is always in his ears;
   even while at peace he fears the despoiler coming upon him.
22 He does not hope to escape from the darkness,
   but can look forward only to the sword.
23 He wanders about for bread, asking, "Where is it?"
   knowing that the day of darkness awaits him.
24 Anguish and agony terrify him:
   they seize him like a king ready for the attack,
25 because he stretched out his hand against God
   and played the hero against the Almighty—
26 running against Him stubbornly
   with the thick bosses of his shields,
27 his face covered with fat,
   and thick flesh gathered upon his loins.
28 He will live in devastated cities
   in houses no one inhabits,
   that are destined to be heaps of ruins.
29 He will not be rich; his substance will not endure,
   nor will his wealth remain long upon the earth.
30 He will not escape from the darkness;
   his shoots will shrivel up in the flame,
   and his branch in the breath of God's mouth.

31 Let no man believe in empty deceit,
   for emptiness will be his reward!
32 Before his time he will be cut off,
   while his branch is not yet green.
33 He will shake off his unripe grape like the vine
   and shed his blossom like the olive tree.
34 For the assembly of the godless is left desolate,
   and fire devours the tents of the corrupt,
35 who conceive evil and beget sin,
   and whose womb prepares deceit.

Job's Reply to Eliphaz (Chapters 16–17)

Job has heard the Friends reiterate the conventional doctrine that justice prevails and that suffering is the result of sin. They have not hesitated to brand Job a sinner, mitigating their attack only slightly by urging him to repent of his iniquities. Yes, Job muses, if their positions were reversed, he too could offer these easy but meaningless words of comfort. But how remote their platitudes are from the harsh reality of his situation!

Job describes his alienation from all who once loved and respected him. God is his adversary on the battlefield of life. Yet in spite of his agony, Job reaffirms his righteousness; beneath his rebellion he has an unconquerable faith that there must be justice in the world. He calls upon the earth not to hide his blood—not only from bitterness but also from faith: he knows that there is a witness in heaven who will ultimately vindicate him. Job's faith in the God of righteousness is as strong as his protest against the God of might.

As he thinks of his brief and miserable existence, he turns to God and not to his friends for understanding. Job is certain that his unjust suffering will arouse universal pity among good men but will not deflect them from virtue. Thus he introduces the idea that the righteous life is to be lived for its own sake and not for the desire of reward. Once again his misery breaks in upon him. He sees all his hopes going down to the grave with him.

16   Job answered, saying,
2   I have heard many such things;
           worthless comforters are you all!
3   Is there no end to words of wind,
           and what compels you to answer?
4   I, too, would speak as you do,
           were you in my place,
        I would string words together against you
           and shake my head at you,
5   I would encourage you with my mouth,
           and sympathy would hold my words in check.
6   If I speak, my pain is not assuaged,
           and if I forbear, what relief have I?

7   Now He has left me helpless;
           He has laid waste my whole company.
8   He has shriveled me up—
           this has been the testimony against me!

My leanness has risen up against me—
   this has been the evidence against me!
9   In His wrath He has torn me apart, for He hates me;
   He has gnashed his teeth at me;
   my foe sharpens his eyes against me.
10 Men gape at me with open mouths;
   in contempt they strike my cheeks;
   they mass together against me.
11 God hands me over to the evildoer,
   and through the hands of the wicked He wrings me out.
12 I was at ease, and He smashed me;
   He seized me by the neck, and crushed me;
   He set me up as His target.
13 His archers surround me,
   He pierces my kidneys without mercy,
   He pours out my gall to the ground.
14 He cracks me with breach upon breach;
   He rushes upon me like a warrior.
15 I have sewn sackcloth upon my skin;
   I have buried my dignity in the dust.
16 My face is red with weeping,
   and on my eyelids is deepest gloom,
17 though there is no violence in my hands
   and my prayer is pure.

18 O earth, cover not my blood;
   let my cry have no resting-place.
19 Behold, even now, my witness is in heaven,
   and he who vouches for me is on high.
20 Are my friends my intercessors?
   No, to God my eye pours out its tears,
21 that He judge between a man and God,
   as between one man and his fellow.
22 For only a few years are yet to come
   and I go the way I shall not return.

17 My spirit is broken,
   my days are burnt out;
   only the grave awaits me.
2   Indeed there are mockers all about me,
   and my eye must abide their provocations.
3   God, pray take my pledge with You;
   Who else would accept a surety from my hands?
4   Since You have closed their minds to understanding,
   You will win no glory from them.
5   As men say,
   "He invites his friends to share his bounty,
   while the eyes of his own children grow faint from hunger!"

6	God has set me up as a byword among people;
	I am one in whose face men spit.
7	My eye has grown dim from grief,
	and all my limbs are like a shadow.
8	Upright men will be horrified at this,
	and the innocent will rise up against the godless.
9	But the just will hold fast to his way,
	and he who has clean hands will increase his strength.
10	But as for you all, come back now;
	not one wise man can I find among you.
11	My days have outlasted my hopes;
	cut off are the desires of my heart,
12	which could turn night into day
	and darkness into blessed light.
13	Indeed, I have marked out my home in Sheol
	and spread out my couch in the darkness.
14	To the pit I call, "You are my father,"
	and to the worm, "my mother," "my sister."
15	Where then is my hope?
	My hope, who can see it?
16	To the chambers of Sheol it descends;
	together we shall go down to the dust.

The Speech of Bildad (Chapter 18)

Job's misery evokes not one friendly word from Bildad. He feels keenly that he and his friends have been insulted. In spite of Job's unbridled attacks upon the justice of God, the laws of the universe remain unshaken, and retribution will ultimately overtake the evildoer. Bildad proceeds to describe the punishment of the sinner: his person, his family, his very name, all will be destroyed.

18	Bildad the Shuhite answered, saying,
2	How long will you go hunting for words?
	Acquire understanding and then we can speak.
3	Why are we accounted as cattle,
	considered stupid in your sight?
4	O you who tear yourself to shreds in your anger,
	shall the earth be forsaken on your account,
	or the rock be removed from its place?
5	In due course the light of the wicked is put out
	and the flame of his fire ceases to glow.

6 The light grows dark in his tent,
  and his lamp above him is put out.
7 His strong steps grow narrow,
  and his own schemes hurl him down.
8 For he is cast into a net as he walks,
  and he must tread over a snare;
9 A trap seizes him by the heels,
  a noose closes in upon him;
10 a rope is hidden for him in the ground,
  a trap upon his path.
11 Terrors frighten him on every side
  and pursue him in his tracks.
12 His child will go hungry;
  and disaster awaits his wife.
13 Each part of his body is consumed;
  the first-born of Death devours his limbs.
14 He is torn from his tent where he felt secure,
  and is marched off to the King of Terrors.
15 Demons of destruction dwell in his tent,
  brimstone is scattered on his dwelling.
16 His roots dry up below
  and his branches wither above.
17 His memory perishes from the earth,
  and he has no name abroad.
18 He is thrust from light into darkness
  and is driven out of the world.
19 He has neither kith nor kin among his people
  and no survivor in his dwelling.
20 At his day of calamity earlier ages are appalled,
  and horror seizes later generations.
21 Surely such are the dwellings of the evildoer,
  and this the place of him who knows not God.

Job's Reply to Bildad (Chapter 19)

In this, his briefest utterance, Job touches both the depths of despair and the heights of faith. Bitterly he arraigns his friends, who have scorned him and ignored his misery. God's enmity has its counterpart in his estrangement from his kinsfolk and in the contempt of slaves and young upstarts. He pleads without hope for his friends' mercy.

In a passionate outburst, Job demands that his words be permanently engraved on a monument so that he may ultimately find vindication. In an ecstatic vision he is carried to the pinnacle of faith. In his unshakable assurance that there must be justice in the world, he sees the God of righteousness rising to his defence. God is not merely an arbiter waiting to judge him fairly, or even a witness ready to testify on his behalf, but a Redeemer who will fight his cause, even at the end of time.

In this moment of mystical exaltation, Job feels his ultimate reconciliation with God engraved on his very flesh. He yearns to hold fast to the ecstatic experience, but it flees. The vision of the future fades as quickly as it has come, and there remains only the agony of the present. In wrath Job turns upon his friends and warns them of the dire punishment that awaits them for their cruelty toward him.

19   Then Job answered, saying,
2   How long will you torment me
            and crush me with your words?
3   It is now ten times that you have insulted me
            and have not been ashamed to abuse me.
4   Even if it be true that I have erred,
            the error remains with me.
5   If, indeed, you wish to quarrel with me
            and justify the humiliation I have suffered,
6   know then that God has subverted my cause
            and surrounded me with His siegeworks.
7   Behold, I cry "Violence!" but I am not answered;
            I call out, but there is no justice.

8   He has fenced in my way so that I cannot pass,
            He has set darkness upon my paths.
9   My glory He has stripped from me,
            and removed the crown of my head.
10   He has broken me down on every side, and I perish;
            my hope He has uprooted like a tree.
11   He has kindled His wrath against me,
            and treats me as His foe.
12   His troops come forth all together;
            they have paved their road against me
            and have encamped around my tent.

13   My brethren are distant from me,
            and my friends are wholly estranged.
14   My kinsfolk and intimates no longer know me;
            the guests in my own house have forgotten me.
15   My maidservants count me a stranger—
            an alien have I become in their sight.
16   I call to my servant, but he does not answer.
            In words I must plead with him.

17   I am repulsive to my wife
          and loathsome to my own children.
18   Even youngsters despise me;
          when I rise, they talk against me.
19   All my intimate friends abhor me,
          and those I loved have turned against me.
20   My bones cling to my skin and my flesh,
          and I have escaped only with the skin of my teeth.

21   Have pity on me, O my friends, have pity,
          For the hand of God has struck me.
22   Why do you persecute me like God
          and are not satisfied with my flesh?

23   Oh that my words were now written;
          Oh that they were inscribed on a monument,
24   that with an iron pen and lead
          they were hewn in the rock for ever!
25   For I know that my Redeemer lives,
          though He be the last to arise upon earth!
26   Deep in my skin this has been marked,
          and in my very flesh do I see God.
27   I myself behold Him,
          with my own eyes I see Him, not with another's—
          my heart is consumed with longing within me!

28   When you say, "How shall we persecute him,
          since the root of the matter must be found in me?"
29   I answer, "Be afraid of the sword,
          for yours are crimes deserving the sword,
          and you will learn that there is a judgment."

The Speech of Zophar (Chapter 20)

The accepted doctrine has already been set forth fully and Zophar has nothing new to add. His sensitive nature, however, has been aggrieved by Job's onslaught, which demands an answer. Zophar proceeds to describe the short-lived prosperity of the wicked and the inevitable doom that comes both upon the sinner and his progeny.

20   Zophar the Naamathite then answered, saying,
2   Indeed, my thoughts force me to answer
              because of the feelings within me.
3   I hear words of censure which insult me,
              and my spirit of understanding impels me to reply.

4	Do you not know this from of old,
	ever since man was placed upon earth,
5	that the exultation of the wicked is short-lived,
	the joy of the godless but for a moment?
6	If his greatness rises up to heaven
	and his head touches the clouds,
7	at the height of his triumph, he is destroyed forever.
	Those who have seen him will ask, "Where is he?"
8	Like a dream he will fly off and will not be found;
	he will flee like a vision of the night.
9	The eye which saw him will see him no more,
	nor will his place behold him again.
10	His sons will try to appease the poor,
	and his offspring will return his ill-gotten gains.
11	While youthful vigor still fills his bones
	it will lie down with him in the dust.

12	If wickedness grows sweet in his mouth
	and he hides it under his tongue,
13	if he loves it and does not let it go
	and keeps it in his mouth,
14	his food in his stomach is turned
	into the gall of asps within him.
15	The wealth he has swallowed he must spew forth;
	from his stomach God will drive it out.
16	He will suck the poison of asps;
	the tongue of the viper will kill him.
17	He will never see the rivers of oil,
	the streams of honey and milk.
18	He will disgorge his wealth and not swallow it;
	he will spew forth his gain and not chew it down.
19	For he has oppressed and tortured the poor
	and seized houses which he did not build.

20	Because he knew no rest within him,
	he will not save himself for all his wealth.
21	No remnant is left of all he has eaten;
	indeed, his prosperity will not endure.
22	When all his needs seem filled he will find himself in straits;
	every embittered sufferer will attack him.
23	To fill his belly to the full
	God will send His wrath against him
	and rain down upon him in His anger.
24	If he flees from an iron weapon,
	a bronze arrow will pierce him.
25	It is drawn forth and comes out of his body,
	and its glitter as it passes casts terror upon him.

26   Total darkness waits for his treasures;
          a fire not blown will devour him
          and consume what is left in his tent.
27   The heavens will reveal his sin
          and the earth will rise up against him.
28   A flood will wash away his house,
          torrents pouring down in the day of his wrath.
29   This is the sinner's portion from God,
          and the evildoer's inheritance from God.

Job's Reply to Zophar (Chapter 21)

In contrast to Zophar's mythical picture of the misery of the sinner and his offspring, Job pictures the actual ease and contentment of the malefactor, the well-being of his family, and, finally, his quick and easy death.

In this, Job's closing speech in the second cycle, he follows the practice he employed at the end of the first cycle (chapter 12), by quoting and then demolishing the arguments of the Friends. Job cites four of the arguments that have been advanced and refutes them in turn:

(1) "The sinner's descendants are punished." Since it was he who sinned, why is he himself not punished?

(2) "God is too exalted to be taught or judged by man." Job counters this contention, not directly but obliquely. He contrasts the happy lot of the wicked with the misery of the righteous. This inevitably raises questions about the divine wisdom.

(3) "Where is the house of the prosperous sinner? It is sure to be utterly destroyed!" Far from it; any passer-by can point out the mansion standing in all its glory!

(4) "God spares the wicked only until the day of doom." "Why the delay," Job asks; "why not immediate punishment for his evildoing?"

Job adds one finishing touch to his portrait of the prosperous sinner. There is a final indignity: even in death there is no moment of truth. The evildoer is given an elaborate funeral and is borne to his grave in pomp and honor.

21   Then Job answered, saying,
2   Listen carefully to my words,
           and this will count as your consolation.
3   Bear with me, that I may speak,
           and after I have spoken, you may mock me.
4   As for me, is my complaint to a mere man?
           Why, therefore, should I not be impatient?
5   Look at me and you will be horrified,
           and put your hand to your mouth.

6   When I think of it, I am appalled,
           and a shudder takes hold of my flesh—
7   why do the wicked live on,
           reach old age, and grow hale and hearty?
8   Their children are well established in their presence;
           their kin and offspring are before their very eyes.
9   Their houses are safe from fear,
           and no rod of God comes upon them.
10   Their bull genders, and does not fail;
           their cow calves, and does not lose her young.
11   They send forth their youngsters like a flock,
           and their children go dancing.
12   They sing to the timbrel and harp
           and make merry to the sound of the pipe.
13   They spend their days in well-being
           and in peace they go down to Sheol.
14   Yet they say to God, "Depart from us.
           We do not wish to know Your ways.
15   What is the Almighty that we should serve Him?
           And what shall we gain if we pray to Him?
16   Indeed, our prosperity is not in His hands!"
           Far be from me the counsel of the wicked!
17   How often do the sinners' lamps go out
           and calamity come upon them
           as He metes out punishment in His anger,
18   that they become like stubble before the wind,
           like chaff which the storm has swept away?

19   You say,
        "God saves his punishment for his children"—
           Let Him recompense *him*, that *he* may know it!
20   Let his own eyes see his destruction,
           and he himself drink of the Almighty's wrath.
21   For what concern has he for his house afterwards,
           after the number of his months is cut off?
22   You ask,
        "Shall anyone teach God knowledge,
           seeing that He judges those on high?"

23 One man dies in the fullness of strength,
   wholly at ease and secure
24 with his limbs full of milk
   and the marrow of his bones moist;
25 and another dies in bitterness of soul,
   never having tasted of joy.
26 Alike they lie down in the dust,
   and the worm covers them both.
27 Behold, I know your thoughts
   and the schemes you plot against me.
28 If you say,
   "Where is the house of the nobleman,
   and where is the dwelling of the wicked?"
29 Why not ask the passers-by—
   you cannot deny their evidence!
30 You declare,
   "The sinner is being saved for the day of calamity;
   he will be led to his doom on the day of wrath."
31 But who will denounce his way to his face,
   and for what he has done—who will requite *him?*
32 But in fact, he is borne in pomp to the grave,
   and men keep watch over his tomb.
33 The clods of the valley are sweet to him;
   all men follow his bier,
   and before him marches an innumerable host.
34 How then do you comfort me with empty words,
   while your answers are nothing but falsehood?

THE THIRD CYCLE (Chapters 22–27)

Introductory Note

Unlike the first two cycles, which have reached us intact, the third cycle has suffered obvious dislocation and loss of material. Thus, only the opening speeches of Eliphaz (chap. 22) and of Job (chaps. 23–24) are in order. Moreover, the closing section of Job's reply (chap. 24) raises grave difficulties with regard to its interpretation and relevance.

Fortunately, much of the third cycle can be restored, especially when the stylistic traits of the book are taken into account. Chapter 25 is much too short for Bildad. Most of chapter 26, on the other hand, which is assigned to Job in our received text, is inappropriate to his position but highly congenial to Bildad's. Similarly, the latter part of chapter 27 which is also attributed to Job, stands in direct antithesis to all he has maintained. It is, however, thoroughly appropriate for Zophar, to whom no speech at all is assigned in our present text.

Chapter 28 is a "Hymn to Wisdom," differing radically in its lyrical form from the dialogic structure of the debate. It is, however, significant that it has found its way into the book. It reflects in brief compass the basic outlook of the poet, which is elaborated upon in the God speeches that constitute the climax of the book. Chapter 28 is therefore best regarded as an independent poem by the author of Job or by a member of his school.

By allocating the appropriate portions of chapters 26 and 27 to Bildad and Zophar, respectively, and by recognizing the independent character of the "Hymn to Wisdom" (chap. 28), we gain an additional advantage. We are able to reduce the dimensions of Job's reply, which is much too long, occupying six chapters in the received text (chaps. 26–31).

While the evidence of injury sustained by the text is clear, all proposed restorations, of which there have been many, are necessarily tentative and uncertain. The reconstruction proposed here requires a minimal change of order in the Masoretic text.

The Speech of Eliphaz (Chapter 22)

Job's continued recalcitrance has stripped even Eliphaz of his urbanity. He is now convinced that Job is an evildoer and therefore proceeds to offer a catalogue of his misdeeds. Eliphaz is able to explain these alleged actions of Job on the ground that he expected to be safe from punishment because God is so far away from man.

Nevertheless, all is not lost. Job has only to repent sincerely of his sins and he will be restored to God's favor. Not only will he become prosperous himself but he will be able to intercede for other sinners through his virtue. Thus, to the familiar biblical doctrine of "vertical responsibility" (in time), which is expressed in the idea of God's visiting the sins of the fathers upon the children, Eliphaz adds the concept of "horizontal responsibility" (in space). This idea underlies the narrative in Genesis which tells how the patriarch Abraham pleaded with God to spare the sinful city of Sodom because of the merit of ten righteous men who might be living in it (Gen. 18:20–33).

Thus Eliphaz, the oldest and the wisest of the Friends, who began with words of comfort, is able to close on a note of hope.

22 Eliphaz the Temanite answered, saying,

2 Does a man confer a benefit on God
  when in his wisdom he benefits himself?

3 Is it a favor to the Almighty if you are righteous,
  or His gain if you keep your ways blameless?

4 Is it because of your piety that He reproves you
  and enters into judgment with you?

5 In fact, your wickedness is immense,
  there is no end to your iniquities.

6 For you have taken pledges even from your kinsmen for no
  reason,
  and stripped the naked of their clothing.

7 No water have you given to the weary,
  and from the hungry you have withheld bread.

8 For you believe,
"The man of violence owns the land,
  and he who is powerful lives upon it."

9 Widows you have sent away empty-handed,
  and the arms of the fatherless are crushed.

10 Therefore snares are round about you,
  and sudden terror dismays you.

11 Since you cannot see through darkness
  or when a flood of waters covers you,

12 you thought,
"Indeed God is in the lofty heavens,
  and see the topmost stars, how high they are!"

13 So you said,
"What does God know?
  Can He judge through the thick cloud?

14 Clouds cover Him, so that He cannot see
  as He strolls about the circuit of heaven."

15 Will you keep to the old ways
  which wicked men have trodden,

16 who were cut off before their time,
  whose foundation a river has washed away,

17 who said to God, "Turn away from us,
  for what can the Almighty do for us?"

18 Yet it was He who filled their houses with good things—
  far be from me the counsel of the wicked!

19 The righteous will see this and be glad,
  the innocent will laugh them to scorn,

20 saying, "Indeed our enemies are cut off,
  and their wealth is consumed by the fire."

21 Put yourself in harmony with Him and make peace,
  and thus you will attain to well-being.

22 Accept instruction from His mouth
  and place His words in your heart.

3   If you return to the Almighty, you will be rebuilt;
                if you remove iniquity from your tent,

4   you can safely place your gold in the dust,
                and the gold of Ophir mid the rocks of the stream,

5   because God will be your true gold,
                and your real treasure of silver.

6   Then you will be able to plead with the Almighty
                and lift your face to God.

7   When you pray to Him, He will hear you,
                and you will pay your vows in thanksgiving.

8   When you issue a decree it will be fulfilled for you,
                and light will shine upon your ways.

9   When men are brought low you will say, "Rise up,"
                and he who has been humbled will be saved.

10   Even the guilty will escape punishment,
                escaping through the purity of your hands.

Job's Reply to Eliphaz (Chapters 23–24)

Job does not dignify Eliphaz' accusations with a direct denial. Instead, he tells of his efforts to find God, hoping to be vindicated through this confrontation. Even in his extremity Job still believes that if he could meet his divine Adversary, God would recognize his essential uprightness. Job has therefore sought Him everywhere, but God has eluded him. Nevertheless, Job stoutly reaffirms his innocence in the face of the terror and darkness that envelop him (chap. 23).

Chapter 24 is extremely difficult, both with regard to the interpretation of individual verses and to the appropriateness of the chapter as a whole to Job's outlook. Some scholars have deleted the text in whole or in part as unauthentic, or have assigned some sections to Zophar's third speech. Since the meaning of many verses is highly obscure, these procedures are methodologically questionable. It would seem sounder to try to relate the chapter to the context in which it is actually found.

Basically, the chapter seems to be a complaint about the injustice of the world. It thus belongs to a literary genre amply attested in Babylonian and Egyptian Wisdom literature. The chapter contains a series of descriptions alternating between the criminal oppressors and their hapless victims. As is frequent in Wisdom literature, the subject of each section is not explicitly identified by the poet. The reader is expected to recognize the specific theme from the context.

The complaint opens with a lament by Job that God's saints do not see the promised hour of retribution coming upon the sinners. Then follow two themes in alternation: descriptions of the acts of evildoers (vss. 2–4), the suffering of the weak (vss. 5–8), the robbery perpetrated by the rich (vs. 9), the misery of the poor (vss. 10–12), and finally the crimes of the malefactors (vss. 13–17).

Then follows a passage that contends that for all their superficial success the wicked are ultimately destroyed (vss. 18–24). This comfortable doctrine is obviously not Job's own position. It is better to regard it as a quotation by him of the conventional belief of the Friends. This stylistic usage of citation and refutation has been characteristic of Job in both earlier cycles (chaps. 12 and 21). The conventional view of retribution in this chapter must therefore have been rebutted by Job in a passage that originally followed in the text but was lost when the third cycle became disarrayed. After this lacuna comes the closing verse of the chapter, in which Job challenges the Friends to disprove the truth of his contentions (vs. 25).

23	Job answered saying,
2	Though my complaint still remains defiant,
	God's hand upon me is heavier than my groaning.
3	Oh that I knew where to find Him,
	that I could come to His dwelling!
4	I would lay my case before Him,
	and my mouth would not lack for arguments.
5	I would learn what He would answer me
	and understand what He would say to me.
6	Would He contend with me merely through His great power?
	No, He would surely pay heed to me,
7	for it would be an upright man arguing with Him,
	and I would be acquitted by my Judge for all time.
8	But I go to the east and He is not there;
	to the west, and do not perceive Him;
9	to the north, where He is concealed, and I do not behold Him;
	He is hidden in the south, and I cannot see Him.
10	But He knows the way that I have taken;
	if He tested me, I would emerge pure as gold.
11	In His footsteps I have followed;
	His way I have kept without swerving.
12	From His commandments I have not departed;
	in my bosom I have treasured the words of His mouth.
13	But He is determined, and who can turn Him back?
	Whatever He desires, that He does.

4 He will surely carry out what he has decreed for me—
and He has many more such cases!
5 Therefore am I terrified at His presence;
when I consider, I am in dread of Him.
6 For God has made my heart grow faint,
the Almighty has terrified me.
7 Indeed, I am destroyed by darkness,
and before my face is all-encompassing gloom.

24 Since the times of judgment are not hidden from the Almighty,
why do those who love Him never see the days of retribution?

2 The wicked remove the ancient landmarks;
they steal flocks and pasture them as their own.
3 They drive off the ass of the fatherless
and take the widow's ox in pledge.
4 They force the needy off the road,
so that the poor of the earth all cower in hiding.

5 Behold, as wild asses in the desert
they go forth to their toil seeking food—
the wilderness must yield bread for their children.
6 They reap in a field not their own
and must glean in the vineyard of the wicked.
7 At night they lie naked without clothes—
with no covering in the cold,
8 drenched by the mountain rains
for lack of shelter, clinging to the rocks.

9 The wicked snatch the orphaned child from the breast
and take the poor man's babe in pledge.

10 The oppressed go about naked, without clothes,
and are hungry as they carry the sheaves.
11 Mid the sinner's olive trees they press out oil,
and suffer thirst as they tread the wine vats.
12 The dying groan in terror
and the wounded cry out for help—
yet in all this God sees nothing wrong!

13 The evildoers rebel against the light;
they refuse to know its ways
and do not stay in its paths.
14 At nightfall the murderer arises,
he kills the poor and the needy,
and in the night he is a thief.

15 The eye of the adulterer also waits for dusk,
saying, "No eye will see me,"
as he places a disguise on his face.
16 In the dark they dig through houses,
shutting themselves up by day,
never seeing the light;
17 For to them all, darkness is as the morning,
they are at home with the terrors of midnight.

18 You say to me,
"They perish swiftly, like water,
their estate is cursed in the land,
no treader turns to their vineyards.
19 As drought and heat carry off snow-water,
So does Sheol those who have sinned.
20 Even his mother's womb forgets him;
the worm finds him sweet to the taste
and he is remembered no longer—
thus wickedness is broken as a tree.
21 Because he crushes the barren woman,
so that she cannot give birth,
and he ill-treats the widow,
22 God seizes the mighty one despite all his power;
when God confronts him, he despairs of life.
23 He may let him feel safe and secure,
but His eyes are on men's ways.
24 Wait just a little and they are no more.
they wither and fade like a plant
and are cut off like the head of grain."

. . . .
. . . .
. . . .
. . . .

25 If this is not so, who will prove that I lie,
and show that my words are worthless?

The Speech of Bildad (Chapters 25; 26:5–14)

The reasons for adding 26:5–14 to Bildad's speech have been explained in the introductory note to the third cycle. Even with this addition, Bildad's reply remains fragmentary. Unable to refute Job's picture of injustice rampant everywhere in the life of man, Bildad takes refuge in an eloquent description of the glory and power of God as manifest in the processes of nature.

25 Bildad the Shuhite answered, saying,
2   Dominion and awe are with Him;
            He makes peace in His high heaven.
3   Is there any number to His armies?
            Upon whom does His light not arise?
4   How then can man be just before God
            and how can one born of a woman be clean?
5   Behold, he commands the moon and it does not shine,
            and the stars are not clean in His sight.
6   How much more so man, who is a maggot,
            the son of man, who is a worm!

26   The shades below tremble before Him,
            the waters and their inhabitants.
6   Sheol is naked before God,
            and Abaddon has no covering.
7   He stretches out the north over empty space
            and suspends the earth over nothingness.
8   He binds up the waters in His thick clouds,
            yet the cloud is not split by their weight.
9   He hides the sight of His throne,
            and spreads His cloud upon it.
10   He has marked out the limit of the waters
            at the boundary of light and darkness.
11   The pillars of heaven tremble
            and are astounded at His rebuke.
12   By His might He stilled the sea;
            by His understanding He smote Rahab.
13   By His wind the heavens were stretched out;
            His hand pierced the straight Serpent.
14   Lo, these are only the outskirts of His ways.
            How small an echo can we hear!
            The full thunder of His power, who can understand?

Job's Reply to Bildad (Chapters 26:1–4; 27:1–12)

As indicated in the introductory note to the third cycle, two sections of Job's reply are to be found in parts of our present chapters 26 and 27. The remainder of his speech is missing and can no longer be recovered. When our present text emerged, Job was credited with an address extending over six chapters (chaps. 26–31). The editors sought to break up this very long speech by adding a special introductory formula at the beginning of chapters 27 and 29, "Job again took up his discourse, saying. . . ." Thus the editors recognized that there was something exceptional in the condition of the text before them.

To revert to the content, Job realizes that he can expect no help from his friends, who are unable or unwilling to understand him. He takes a passionate oath, insisting that he will never concede that he is guilty and, by that token, deserving of the agony he has suffered. Knowing that he has never blasphemed, he restates the faith in God's justice that actuated him during the earlier and happier period of his life when he had no reason to doubt the triumph of the right. The extant portion of his speech ends with a call to the Friends to desist from their empty talk.

26   Job answered, saying,

2   How have you helped him that is powerless
           and saved the arm wanting in strength?

3   What have you advised him who has no wisdom;
           what sound counsel have you given the inexperienced?

4   With whose help have you uttered your words,
           and whose breath has come forth from you?

27   (Job again took up his discourse, saying,)

2   As God lives, who has robbed me of my right,
           and by the Almighty, who has embittered my soul—

3   as long as the breath of life is in me
           and God's spirit is in my nostrils,

4   my lips will speak no falsehood
           and my tongue utter no deceit.

5   Heaven forbid that I declare you in the right;
           until I die I will not be stripped of my integrity.

6   My righteousness I have held fast, and never let it go;
           my heart harbored no blasphemy all my days.

7   For I said,
           "Let my enemy be in the wrong
           and my opponent be the evildoer,

8   for what hope has the evildoer when God cuts him off,
           when God calls for his life?

9   Will God hear his cry
           when trouble comes upon him?

10   Is he free to implore the Almighty—
           can he call upon God at any time?"

11   Let *me* teach you, speaking on God's behalf;
        what He has in mind, *I* shall not deny.

         .   .   .   .
         .   .   .   .
         .   .   .   .
         .   .   .   .

12   Indeed, you have all seen this—
        Why then do you spew forth emptiness?

The Speech of Zophar (Chapter 27:13–23)

Only a small fragment of Zophar's speech has survived. It emphasizes the doom of the wicked, who gather wealth only that the righteous may ultimately inherit it, while they themselves are swept away to destruction.

         .   .   .   .
         .   .   .   .

27   This is the sinner's portion from God,
        the heritage which oppressors receive from the Almighty—
14   If his children be multiplied, it is for the sword,
        and his offspring will lack for bread.
15   Those who survive him will be buried by the plague,
        and his widows will not mourn for him.
16   If he heaps up silver like dust,
        and stores up clothing like clay,
17   he may store it up, but the just will wear it,
        and his silver, the innocent will divide.
18   The house he builds is as frail as a nest,
        like a booth set up by a watchman.
19   He goes to bed rich, but never more—
        when he opens his eyes, his wealth is gone.
20   Terrors overwhelm him like a flood;
        in the night a whirlwind carries him off.
21   The east wind lifts him up and he is gone,
        and whirls him out of his place.
22   It hurls itself upon him without pity
        as he tries to flee from its power.
23   Men will clap their hands at him in horror,
        and whistle over him from his former place.

         .   .   .   .
         .   .   .   .

THE HYMN TO WISDOM (Chapter 28)

The "Hymn to Wisdom" is clearly an independent lyrical poem with a characteristic refrain, "Wisdom, where may she be found?" (vss. 12 and 20). Unlike the preceding dialogue, it is not argumentative and reveals no echo of a passionate debate. Moreover, the presence of the Hymn at this point in the book would weaken tremendously the impact of the God speeches and, in fact, make them anticlimactic. For it expresses virtually the same fundamental theme, though set forth more briefly—the world is a mystery to man, who will never be able to penetrate the great supernal Wisdom by which God has created and governs the universe.

There are strong grounds for believing that this independent poem was written by the author of Job. In addition to the basic harmony of outlook already mentioned, the vocabulary and style of the Hymn have many affinities with those of the God speeches. Moreover, both sections reveal the same wide knowledge of the science and technology of the day. This poem is therefore best regarded as an early effort by the poet to treat the theme which he later elaborated and deepened by the added insight that the cosmos is miracle as well as mystery.

While the beautiful "Hymn to Wisdom" is not an integral part of the book of Job, it is a highly welcome product of the poet's pen. In view of the vast dislocations sustained by the third cycle of the dialogue, it is easy to understand how this poem found its way into the text here. In its present position after the conclusion of the third cycle, the "Hymn to Wisdom" is well described as "a musical interlude" between the debate and Job's final soliloquy.

The poem describes how men mine the earth and face unknown hazards in their search for precious stones in volcanic areas far from human habitation. Yet no such search will avail to find the supernal Wisdom, nor can it be purchased with all the treasures of the world. Even the deep sea does not know its place. Only God, who created the universe, knows the transcendental Wisdom. As for man, the only wisdom that is accessible to him consists of religion and morality, reverence for the Lord and avoidance of evil.

28   Surely there is a mine for silver
          and a place where gold is refined.
2   Iron is taken from the earth
          and copper is smelted from the ore.

3   Men put an end to darkness,
           and to the furthest ends they penetrate.
       The lava, dark and pitch-black,
4   cleaves a channel from the crater
       never trodden by human foot,
           bereft even of wandering men.
5   It is a land from which heat pours forth,
           while its lower regions are convulsed as by fire,
6   a place whose stones are sapphires
           and whose dust is gold.
7   The path to it no bird of prey knows,
           and the falcon's eye has never seen it.
8   The proud beasts have not trodden it,
           nor has the lion passed over it.
9   Man puts his hand to the flinty rock
           and overturns mountains by the roots.
10   He hews out channels in the rocks,
           and his eye sees every precious thing.
11   He binds up the flow of rivers,
           and what is hidden he brings to light.

12   But Wisdom, where may she be found,
           and where is the place of Understanding?
13   Man does not know her place,
           nor is she found in the land of the living.
14   The Deep says, "Not in me,"
           the Sea says, "Nor with me."
15   She cannot be acquired for gold,
           and silver cannot be weighed as her price.
16   She cannot be valued in the gold of Ophir,
           in precious onyx or sapphire.
17   Gold and glass cannot equal her,
           nor objects of fine gold be exchanged for her.
18   Coral and crystal cannot be mentioned,
           for the price of Wisdom is above pearls.
19   The topaz of Ethiopia does not compare,
           nor can she be valued in pure gold.

20   But Wisdom, whence does she come,
           and where is the place of Understanding?
21   For she is hidden from the eyes of all living things,
           concealed even from the birds of the air.
22   Abaddon and Death say,
           "We have heard only her echo."

23   But God understands her way
           and He knows her place,
24   For He looks to the ends of the earth
           and sees everything under the heaven.

25 When He gave the wind its weight
and meted out the waters by measure,
26 when He made a law for the rain
and a way for the thunderbolt,
27 then He saw Wisdom, and described her;
He established her and searched her out.
28 But to man He said,
"To be in awe of the Lord—that is wisdom,
and to avoid evil—that is understanding."

JOB'S SOLILOQUY (Chapters 29–31)

Introductory Note

The debate has ended. Job's friends, who had come to comfort him,
are now estranged from him. They have spoken in the name of established religious doctrine, and he has responded from his own bitter immediate experience; no one has been able to bridge the abyss. The confrontation ended, the Friends fade from Job's consciousness. He began
with a lament on his tragic fate (chap. 3); he now concludes with a
soliloquy which describes first his former well-being and honor (chap.
29) and then his present agony and degradation (chap. 30). The climax
of Job's soliloquy is reached in his great protestation of integrity, in
which he sets forth the code of behavior from which he has not swerved.
His closing words are a plea for God to answer, so that he may confront Him honorably and be vindicated (chap. 31).

In Remembrance of Happier Days (Chapter 29)

Job paints an unforgettable picture of his former happy estate before
calamities rained down upon him. He describes the respect in which he
was universally held by young and old. This honor he had earned by
his sense of responsibility toward the weak and the defenseless and by
the noble dignity of his dealings with his fellow men.

29 Job again took up his discourse, saying,
2 Oh, that I were as in the months of old,
as in the days when God watched over me,
3 when His lamp shone upon my head
and by His light I walked through darkness,

4 as I was in my days of vigor
    when God was an intimate in my tent,
5 when the Almighty was still with me
    and my children were all about me,
6 when my steps were washed in milk
    and the rock poured out streams of oil for me.

7 When I went out to the city gate
    and set up my seat in the square,
8 the young men saw me and withdrew,
    and the aged stood up in silence,
9 the princes refrained from talking
    and laid their hands to their mouths,
10 the voices of the nobles were hushed
    and their tongues clove to their palates.

11 Every ear that heard me called me blessed,
    and every eye that saw me encouraged me,
12 because I delivered the poor man crying out,
    and the fatherless who had none to help him.
13 The dying man's blessing came upon me,
    and I brought a song to the widow's heart.
14 I put on righteousness and it clothed me;
    justice was my robe and my turban.
15 Eyes to the blind was I
    and feet to the lame.
16 A father to the poor was I,
    and I took up the cause of the stranger.
17 I broke the fangs of the evildoer
    and snatched the prey from his teeth;
18 and I thought, "I shall die in my nest,
    and shall multiply my days as the phoenix.
19 My roots are spread out over waters,
    and the dew lies all night on my branches.
20 My glory is fresh with me,
    and my bow is ever new in my hand."

21 Men listened to me and waited
    and kept silent for my counsel.
22 Once I had spoken they did not speak again
    when my word dropped upon them.
23 They waited for me as for the rain,
    opening their mouths as for the spring freshets.
24 When I smiled on them, they could scarcely believe it;
    they did nothing to cause me displeasure.
25 I chose the way for them
    like the leader of a camel train,
I sat at their head,
    ensconced like a king with his troops.

The Misery of the Present Condition (Chapter 30)

Job's situation has been catastrophically changed: now he is confronted by the contempt of the dregs of society. The misery of his alienation is compounded by the physical agony that his body is suffering. Despised by men and attacked by God, Job is left in loneliness and despair.

30 But now they deride me, men who are younger than I,
  whose fathers I would have disdained
  to set with the dogs of my flock.

2 For I thought,
  "What can I gain from the strength of their hands,
  from men whose vigor is spent?"

3 In want and stark hunger they flee to the desert,
  the home of the storm and the hurricane.

4 They pluck mallow with wormwood,
  and the roots of the juniper for firewood.

5 From all human fellowship they are cut off,
  and men shout after them as after a thief.

6 They must dwell in the gullies of the torrents,
  in the caves of the earth, among rocks,

7 groaning among the bushes,
  huddling together under the nettles.

8 Men without sense, without status—
  they are whipped out of the land.

9 Now I have become the subject of their mockery;
  I am a byword among them.

10 They abhor me and keep aloof from me
  and hold back no spittle from my face.

11 Because God has loosed my cord and humbled me
  they have cast off all restraint before me.

12 Against the aged the young rabble rises,
  letting loose their feet,
  and casting up against me their ways of destruction.

13 They hedge my path with thorns;
  they promote my calamity
  with no one to restrain them.

14 Like a wide torrent they rush in,
  like a storm they roll on.

15 Terrors are turned loose upon me,
  driving off my honorable estate like a wind,
  my secure position passing away like a cloud.

16 And now my soul melts in grief;
   days of affliction have taken hold of me.
17 At night He stabs my bones within me
   and my veins know no rest.
18 Because of His violence my garment is disfigured;
   He holds me tight like the collar of my tunic.
19 He has hurled me into the mire
   and I have become dust and ashes.

20 If I cry out to You, You do not answer me;
   if I remain silent, You pay me no heed.
21 You have turned cruel toward me,
   with all Your might You hate me.
22 You lift me up and make me ride the wind;
   You toss me about in the roaring storm.
23 Yes, I know that You will bring me down to Death—
   to the meeting-place of all the living.
24 Yet I believed,
  "Surely, if a man pleads, one must extend one's hand,
   when he cries out under the affliction of God."
25 Did I not weep for him whose fate was harsh;
   was I not grieved for the poor?

26 Yet when I hoped for good, evil came;
   when I waited for light, there was darkness.
27 My heart is in turmoil and knows no rest;
   days of affliction come to meet me.
28 I walk about blackened, but not by the sun;
   I rise up and cry out in a loud voice.
29 A brother have I become to jackals,
   a companion to ostriches.
30 My skin has turned black upon me
   and my bones burn with the heat.
31 My lyre is turned to mourning
   and my flute to the sound of lamentation.

The Code of a Man of Honor (Chapter 31)

Job brings his soliloquy to a close, presenting the ideals of conduct by which he has lived. In a series of oaths, he calls down punishment upon himself if he has violated any of the standards of integrity that he has professed. Job lists fourteen possible transgressions from which he has kept himself free. These are not gross crimes, which are totally beyond the realm of possibility for him, but subtler sins that often prove a temptation to the respectable and respected citizen. It is noteworthy that this "Code of a Man of Honor" is almost exclusively ethical, the only ritual element being the avoidance of the worship of the moon and the stars.

Job has adhered to the principles of personal morality in his attitude toward women, who are too weak to defend themselves. His actions have been marked by fair dealing, even toward the slave, and by consideration for the poor, the widow, and the orphan, because he has been conscious of the equality of all human beings.

He has also been sensitive to the deeper and less obvious forms of unethical behavior to which even good men are liable. He has been free from the arrogance that comes with wealth. He has never rejoiced in the discomfiture of his foes. He has not feared the tyranny of the mob, nor has he been ashamed to confess his errors in public.

Conscious of his fundamental rectitude, Job calls upon God to appear and answer him. Having nothing to hide, Job is confident that in a free and fair confrontation he would be vindicated.

31	I made a covenant with my eyes;
	how then could I look lustfully upon a maid?
2	For I thought, "If I sinned,
	what would be my portion from God above
	and my lot from the Almighty on high?
3	Surely calamity waits for the unrighteous
	and disaster for the workers of iniquity!
4	God will certainly see my ways
	and count all my steps!"
5	Have I walked with falsehood,
	has my foot ever hastened to deceit?
6	Let Him weigh me in a just balance
	and God will know my integrity!
7	If my step has turned aside from the right path
	and my heart has strayed after my eyes,
	if ever a spot has cleaved to my hands—
8	let me sow and another eat,
	and may my crops be rooted out.
9	If my heart has been enticed by a woman,
	and I have lain in wait at my neighbor's door,
10	may my wife grind for a stranger,
	and let others crouch upon her.
11	For that would be a heinous crime,
	an offense worthy of punishment

12   indeed, a fire burning to Abaddon,
          consuming all my increase to the roots.

13   Have I despised the cause of my manservant,
          or of my maidservant, when they contended with me?
14   For I always remembered,
          "What shall I do when God rises up,
          and when He examines me, how shall I answer Him?
15   Did not He make him in the womb, as He made me,
          and fashion us both alike in the womb?"

16   Have I withheld what the poor desired,
          or caused the eyes of the widow to fail,
17   eating my morsel alone
          while the orphan ate none of it?
18   Indeed, from the period of my youth
          he grew up with me as with a father,
       and all my life
          I was a support to the widow.

19   When I saw a beggar without clothes
          or a poor man without a garment,
20   did not his loins bless me,
          and was he not warmed with the fleece of my sheep?

21   If I have raised my hand against the fatherless
          because I saw my help in the gate,
22   let my shoulder blade fall from my shoulder
          and my arm be broken from its socket.
23   For I always feared a calamity coming from God,
          and I could not have borne His destroying me.

24   Have I ever put my trust in gold
          or called fine gold my security?
25   Have I rejoiced because my wealth was great
          or because my hands had acquired riches?

26   Have I looked up at the sun in its brightness
          or at the moon moving in splendor,
27   so that my heart was secretly enticed
          and I kissed my hand in worship?
28   This, too, would surely be an offense worthy of punishment,
          for I should have been false to God above.

29   Have I rejoiced at my enemy's ruin
          or exulted when evil overtook him?
30   Did I permit my mouth to sin
          by calling down a curse upon his life?
31   Did my kinsmen ever say,
          "If only we had our foe's flesh,
          we could never gorge ourselves enough!"

32   No stranger ever lodged in my street;
    my doors were always open to the wayfarer.

33   Have I ever concealed my transgressions like Adam,
    hiding my sin in my bosom
34   because I stood in fear of the crowd
    and the contempt of the masses terrified me—
    so that I kept silence and did not go out of doors?

35   Oh, that I had someone to hear me—
    behold, this is my desire:
    that the Almighty answer me,
    and my opponent write out his indictment.
36   Upon my shoulder I would carry it,
    and like a crown bind it upon me.
37   An account of my steps I would give Him;
    like a prince would I approach Him.

38   If ever my land has cried out against me
    and its furrows have wept together,
39   because I ate its yield without payment
    and brought its owners to despair,
40   let thorns grow instead of wheat
    and foul weeds instead of barley.

    The words of Job are ended.

THE WORDS OF ELIHU (Chapters 32–37)

Introductory Note

Silence has descended upon the little group huddled in the ashes. Now a new loud voice is heard: it is Elihu ben Barakhel, a young brash bystander, probably one of several witnesses to the debate. He has been following the arguments with growing impatience. He is angry not only with Job for impugning God's justice but also with the Friends for defending His cause so inadequately.

In essence, Elihu occupies a middle ground between Job and the Friends. The Friends, as protagonists of the conventional theology, have argued that God is just and that suffering is therefore the conse-quence and the sign of sin. Job, from his own experience, has denied both propositions, insisting that since he is suffering without being a sinner, God is unjust. Elihu denies both the Friends' argument that suffering is always the result of sin and Job's contention that God is unjust. He offers a new and significant insight which bears all the earmarks of being the product of the poet's experience during a lifetime: suffering sometimes comes even to upright men as a discipline, as a warning to prevent them from slipping into sin. For there are some weaknesses to which decent, respectable men are particularly prone, notably the sins of complacency and pride. In the course of his speeches, Elihu restates some of the ideas that have already been expressed. It is, however, this emphasis upon suffering as a moral discipline in the life of man that constitutes his basic contribution to the discussion.

The First Speech (Chapters 32–33)

In the ancient Orient, where age is synonymous with wisdom, the young were not expected to participate in the deliberations of their elders, let alone interrupt their discussion. Being younger than Job and the Friends, Elihu is acutely conscious of his breach of etiquette in speaking out. He therefore offers a truculent apology for joining in the discussion. He insists that the spirit within a man, and not mere age, should determine his right to speak. He has waited as long as he could for the Friends to answer Job properly, but he finds that they have not done justice to God's cause. Therefore, unable to contain himself any longer, he will speak out without fear or favor.

Job has charged God with injustice, wanton power, and a lack of concern for His creatures. What Job has failed to note is that God speaks to man in many ways. One mode of divine communication is through visions and dreams in the night. When these do not avail to restrain a man from falling into sin, God warns him through the medium of physical pain and illness. A man may be brought to the very threshold of death, when his virtues prove his salvation. As he is restored to well-being and health, man recognizes that he was indeed sinful and that the discipline of pain has chastened his spirit and saved him from perdition.

32	So these three men ceased answering Job because he still considered
2	himself to be right. Then Elihu, the son of Barakhel the Buzite, of the family of Ram, became angry. He was angry with Job for considering
3	himself more righteous than God. He was also angry with his three friends because they had found no answer and thus had placed God in
4	the wrong. First Elihu waited for Job to complete his speech, for they
5	were older than he. Now, when Elihu saw that these three men had no answer, he became very angry.
6	Elihu, the son of Barakhel the Buzite, spoke out, saying,

> I am young, and you are old,
>> therefore I was afraid, and dared not
>> voice my opinion in your presence.

7 I thought,
  "Age should speak,
  and the years should teach wisdom,"
8 but it is the spirit in a man,
  and the breath of the Almighty that gives understanding.
9 Not always are old men wise;
  nor do the aged understand the truth.
10 Therefore I say, "Listen to me,
  let me also declare my opinion."
11 Behold, I waited for your words;
  I listened for your wise thoughts
  while you searched for words.
12 I paid attention to you,
  and lo, there was no one to refute Job—
  no one among you to answer his words.
13 Beware lest you say, "We have attained wisdom,
  but only God can rebut him, not man!"
14 And I thought,
  "If Job had directed his words to me
  I would not have answered him with speeches like yours.
15 Now they are beaten, they answer no more,
  they have not a word to say.
16 And I shall wait, for they have ceased speaking,
  they are silent, they answer no more."
17 Now I, too, will give my views;
  I also will declare my opinion.
18 For I am full of words;
  the spirit within me presses upon me.
19 Behold, my bosom is like wine which has no vent,
  like new wineskins, ready to burst.
20 Let me speak and find relief;
  let me open my lips and answer.
21 I will show no partiality to anyone
  or flatter any man,
22 For if I were skilled in flattery,
  my Maker would speedily carry me off.

33 But now, hear my speech, O Job,
  and listen to all my words.
2 Behold, I open my mouth;
  the tongue in my mouth now speaks.
3 My heart proclaims words of wisdom,
  my lips declare the truth.
4 It is the spirit of God that has made me,
  and the breath of the Almighty that gives me life.
5 If you can, answer me;
  prepare for the contest, take your stand.

6   Behold, I am equal with you in God's presence;
          I, too, have been molded from clay.

7   Surely, no dread of *me* will terrify you;
          my pressure will not be heavy upon you.

8   Now you have spoken in my hearing
          and I have heard the sound of your words:

9   "I am clean, without transgression;
          pure am I, without guilt.

10   Yet God invents complaints against me,
          for He counts me as His enemy.

11   He puts my feet in the stocks,
          and watches all my paths."

12   Behold, in this you are wrong—I shall answer you
          when you declare, "God is stronger than man."

13   Why do you argue against Him, saying,
          "And therefore He answers none of man's words"?

14   For God speaks through one means
          and through another, though man takes no notice.

15   In a dream, in a vision of the night
          when deep sleep falls upon men
          while they slumber upon their beds,

16   He opens the ears of men,
          and as a warning, He terrifies them,

17   to turn man aside from secret misdeeds
          and to separate him from pride.

18   Thus He saves him from the Pit
          and his soul from crossing the river of Death.

19   Or a man may be chastened by pain upon his bed,
          by a perpetual strife in his bones,

20   so that he loathes his bread,
          and his appetite abhors the daintiest food.

21   His flesh wastes away so that it cannot be seen,
          and his bones protrude and cannot be looked upon.

22   He himself draws near to the Pit
          and his life approaches the emissaries of Death.

23   But if there be one spokesman for him,
          one advocate among a thousand
          to vouch for a man's uprightness,

24   God is gracious to him, and He commands,
          "Save him from descending to the Pit;
          I have found a ransom for him.

25   Let his flesh become fresh as in youth;
          let him return to the days of his vigor."

26   He then prays to God, and finds favor,
          and joyfully enters His presence.
          He recounts to men how he was saved,

27   and sings out to men, saying,
          "I sinned and perverted the right,
          but He did not punish me.
28   He has redeemed me from going down to the Pit,
          so that I might see the light of life."

29   Behold, all these things does God do,
          twice—yes, three times—with a man,
30   to bring him back from the Pit,
          that he may bask in the light of life.

31   Give heed, O Job, listen to me.
          Be silent and let me speak.
32   Then if you have anything to say, answer me;
          speak out, for I wish to set you right.
33   But if not, you listen to me;
          be silent, let me teach you wisdom.

The Second Speech (Chapter 34)

Citing a proverb which Job himself had quoted, Elihu declares that Job has denied the justice of God only to bolster his own pretensions to innocence. Actually, God, who is the Creator of all and is beholden to no one, has no need to play favorites. He shows no partiality to rulers or rich men. If He so wills it, He can destroy them in a moment. At times He may delay their punishment, either because the misrule of tyrants itself constitutes a penalty upon sinners, or because He hopes for their repentance.

Elihu calls upon Job to submit to God and ask for His guidance. For how can Job expect that God's actions will be governed by a man's wishes? Job has demanded that God present the indictment against him. To this plea Elihu says, "Amen." He wants Job to be tested because of his many sins, such as his trust in evildoers, his heaping up of iniquity, and his rebellion against God.

34   Then Elihu said,
2   Hear my words, you wise men;
          give ear to me, O men of knowledge.
3   For the ear tests words
          as the palate tastes its food.
4   Let us seek the right together,
          let us decide among ourselves what is good.
5   For Job has said, "I am innocent,
          but God has taken away my right.

6	Though I am in the right, I am counted a liar;
	my wound has no cure, though I am without fault."
7	Where is there a man like Job,
	who drinks up blasphemy like water,
8	who is in league with evildoers
	and consorts with wicked men?
9	For he has said, "It does a man no good
	to be in favor with God."
10	Therefore, men of understanding, hear me—
	far be it from God to do evil
	and from the Almighty to do wrong.
11	For according to a man's deeds, God requites him,
	and according to his ways, He ordains his destiny.
12	In truth, God will not act wickedly;
	the Almighty will not pervert justice.
13	Who entrusted the earth to Him,
	and gave Him charge over the whole world?
14	If He should withdraw His spirit
	and gather His breath to Himself,
15	all living things would perish
	and man would return to the dust.
16	Therefore, understand and hear this:
	listen to what I say.
17	Can one who hates justice rule—
	will you condemn God who is both just and strong—
18	who says, even to a king, "You are a knave,"
	and to a nobleman, "You are a villain";
19	who shows no partiality to princes,
	nor favors the rich man over the poor,
	for they are all the work of His hands?
20	In a moment they die—at midnight—
	the rulers are shaken up and pass away,
	and the mighty are removed by no human hand.
21	For God's eyes are on a man's ways
	and He sees all his steps.
22	There is no gloom or deep darkness
	where evildoers may hide.
23	For it is not for man to appoint the hour
	when men are to appear before God in judgment.
24	He crushes mighty men without number
	and sets up others in their stead.
25	Indeed, He knows their deeds thoroughly;
	He overturns them in the night, and they are crushed.
26	He strikes the wicked down where they stand,
	in the sight of all men,
27	because they turned aside from Him
	and had no regard for His ways,

28   thus bringing to Him the cry of the poor
        and causing Him to hear the cry of the afflicted.

29   When He grants peace, who can stir up strife;
        but when He hides His face, who can see Him—
        be it a whole nation or one man?

30   When he allows a godless man to rule,
        it is because of the sins of the people.

31   Indeed, you should say this to God,
        "I have borne my just punishment; I will offend no more.

32   What I do not see, You teach me.
        If I have done wrong, I will do it no more."

33   Is it by your leave that God should make retribution,
        depending on whether *you* reject or approve—not I?
        What you really know, declare.

34   Men of understanding will say to me,
        and the wise man who hears me will declare,

35   "Job speaks without knowledge;
        his words are without insight.

36   Would that Job were tried to the end
        because of his confidence in evildoers,

37   for he adds constantly to his sins,
        he increases impiety among us
        as he multiplies his words against God."

The Third Speech (Chapter 35)

Earlier, Job argued that it does man no good to live in harmony with God's will. Elihu now insists on the converse—God is so far exalted beyond man that it is ludicrous to imagine that man's actions affect Him either for good or for ill. One has only to observe the glories of nature to see evidence of the creative power of God. It is a man's fellow human beings who are affected or injured by his deeds.

Elihu then suggests another reason for the delay sometimes observed in the working of retribution in the world. All too often the sufferers cry out merely because of the pain, rather than from a genuine desire for God's presence. Nevertheless, God's justice does operate in the world and it is folly to deny it.

35   And Elihu said,

2   Do you consider this to be right,
        to say, "I am more righteous than God!"

3   or to ask, "What advantage is it for you,
        what good if I avoid sin?"

4   I will answer you,
            and your friends along with you.
5   Look up at the heavens, and see—
            behold the clouds, far above you.
6   If you sin, how do you injure Him;
            if your offenses are many, what harm is it to Him?
7   If you are righteous, what are you giving Him;
            what benefit does He receive from your hand?
8   Your wickedness affects only a man like yourself,
            and your righteousness, a fellow human being.

9   Because they are greatly oppressed, men are driven to cry out;
            they call for help because of the power of the mighty.
10   But no one says, "Where is God, my Maker,
            who sends forth songs in the night,
11   who teaches us more than the beasts of the earth
            and makes us wiser than the birds of heaven?"
12   Then men cry out—but He does not answer—
            because of the pride of evil men.
13   But it is not true that God does not hear,
            and that the Almighty pays no heed.
14   Although you say that you do not see Him,
            judgment is before Him; wait for it.
15   Even now, when there seems to be none,
            God keeps His wrath alive;
            He surely is well aware of men's transgressions.
16   Yet Job keeps mouthing empty talk,
            and multiplies words without knowledge.

The Fourth Speech (Chapters 36–37)

In the concluding portion of his rejoinder to Job, Elihu restates his
essential ideas. God does not disregard or despise the righteous, who
ultimately attain to honor. When suffering comes upon them it is as a
warning against sin. If they take the message to heart, they are restored
to well-being. But if they remain obdurate, they suffer destruction,
which is the inevitable consequence of sin. This is what God wishes to
teach Job through the medium of his suffering.

As Elihu speaks, the signs of a gathering storm are seen in the sky,
and he breaks into a paean of praise to the greatness of the Creator
whose mysterious ways are manifest in nature.

Elihu describes the autumn season which brings the miracle of rain.
The downpour of rain produces food on earth, while the crashing
thunder which accompanies it reveals the heavenly Judge bringing retri-

bution upon evildoers. Then comes the winter with its own comple-
ment of wonders, the snow and the storm, when men and beasts seek
shelter from the elements. Finally, the winter is past and the rains are
over and gone. As the golden light of the sun cleanses the heavens of
their clouds, the summer is ushered in.

These are the ways of the Almighty, who is great not only in power
but in justice. God is therefore worthy of all reverence.

36 Elihu continued and said,
2   Bear with me a little, and I will show you
          there is something to be said for God!
3   I will marshal my knowledge from every quarter
          as I justify my Creator.
4   For indeed, my words are not false—
          a truthful man is speaking with you.
5   Behold, God is all mighty;
          yet mighty as He is,
          He does not despise the pure of heart.
6   He does not keep the wicked alive
          but gives the afflicted their right.
7   He does not avert His eyes from the righteous;
          He sets them with kings upon the throne
          forever, and they are exalted.
8   And if He binds men in fetters
          and they are caught in the cords of affliction,
9   it is to reveal to them their deeds
          and their transgressions, when they are guilty of pride.
10   He opens their ear to discipline,
          and commands them to withdraw from iniquity.
11   If they give heed and serve Him,
          they complete their days in well-being
          and their years in pleasantness.
12   But if they do not, they pass over the river of Death
          and perish for their lack of knowledge.
13   But the godless in heart remain obdurate;
          they do not cry for help even when He fetters them.
14   They die in their youth,
          and their life ends in shame.
15   He redeems the afflicted through their affliction
          and uncovers their ear by the adversity they suffer,
16   saying to them, "I had removed you from danger
          into a broad place where there was ample room
          and the food set on your table was rich.
17   But you did not judge the case of the wicked
          nor hold fast to My justice.

18   Now beware, lest you be seduced by your wealth
        and your ample means for ransom lead you astray.

19   Will your possessions keep you from trouble,
        or all your exertions to achieve riches?

20   Do not long for the shelter of night
        when peoples are cut off in their place.

21   Beware, do not turn to evil—
        for you clearly prefer sin to suffering!"

22   Behold, God is exalted in His power;
        who can lay down the law like Him?

23   Who can prescribe the way for Him;
        who can say, "You have done wrong"?

24   Remember to extol His work of creation
        which men have praised in song,

25   upon which all men have looked,
        though they can see it only from afar.

26   Behold, God is mighty, beyond our understanding,
        the number of His years is without end.

27   He draws up the drops of water,
        and rain is distilled from His mist,

28   which the clouds pour down
        and shower upon all men.

29   Can anyone fathom the spreading of the clouds,
        the thunderings from His pavilion above?

30   Behold, He spreads His light over it
        and covers the depths of the sea.

31   For by these He judges the nations
        and provides food in abundance.

32   The tent of Heaven He covers with lightning
        which He commands against His target.

33   Its thunder-clap proclaims His presence,
        and the storm, His mighty wrath.

37   At this also my heart trembles
        and leaps from its place.

2   Hearken well to His thundering voice,
        to the rumbling that comes from His mouth.

3   His power is heard everywhere beneath the sky
        and His lightning reaches the ends of the earth.

4   After it comes a roaring sound
        as He thunders with His majestic voice;
        nor does He restrain the lightning bolts when His voice is
        heard.

5   God thunders with His wondrous voice,
        doing great things we cannot grasp.

6   To the snow He says, "Fall to the earth,"
        and to the shower and the rain, "Flow down!"

7   He shuts up every man indoors,
        so that all men may know His work.

8   Then the beasts retire to their lairs
        and remain within their dens.

9   From its chamber the whirlwind comes forth
        and the cold from the scattering winds.

10   By the breath of God ice is formed
        and the wide sea is frozen fast.

11   He loads the thick cloud with moisture,
        and the clouds scatter His lightning.

12   They turn round and round under His guidance
        to fulfill all His commands
        on the face of the inhabited world.

13   Be it for chastisement—if they do not obey—
        or for love, He brings it all to pass.

14   Hear this, O Job,
        Stop and observe the wonders of God.

15   Do you know how God lays His command upon them,
        how He makes the lightning flash from His clouds?

16   Do you know the balancings of the clouds,
        the miracles wrought by the All-knowing?

17   When your garments are hot
        and the earth is still because of the southwind,

18   can you fly with Him to the heavens
        that are hard as a molten mirror?

19   Teach us what we shall say to Him.
        We cannot draw up our case because of the all-embracing
          darkness.

20   Will He be told when I speak?
        If a man talks, will He be confused?

21   And now, men cannot gaze on the sunlight,
        when it is bright in the skies
        and the wind has passed and cleared them.

22   Out of the north comes golden splendor;
        God is clothed in awesome majesty.

23   The Almighty—whom we cannot find out—
        is great both in power and in justice;
        the man abounding in goodness He does not torment.

24   Therefore do men fear Him;
        Yes, all the wise-hearted stand in awe.

THE LORD OUT OF THE WHIRLWIND (Chapters 38–42:6)

The Lord's First Speech (Chapters 38–40:2)

Job, who has demanded time and again that God appear and argue with him, now has his wish granted, but on terms vastly different from those he imagined. Speaking out of a whirlwind, the Lord challenges Job to understand, let alone share, the task of creation. In powerful lines the wonders of inanimate nature are described. Heaven and earth, stars and sea, morning and night, light and darkness, are depicted. Does Job know the treasure-houses of snow and hail, the path of the flood and the lightning? Has he ever begotten the rain, the dew, the frost, or the clouds? And these reveal only part of God's creative power.

The Lord now expresses His joy in the world of living creatures. Can Job feed the lion's whelps? Does he know the miracle of birth of the mountain goat, the wild ass, or the buffalo? Has Job ever observed the swift ostrich or the fleet horse? Does he know the hawk or the falcon? They are the beloved creatures of God, who cares for and protects them all.

This basic theme—that the universe is a mystery to man—is explicitly set forth in the God speeches. There are, in addition, two other significant ideas implicit in the Lord's words. In accordance with Semitic rhetorical usage they are not spelled out but are left to be inferred by the reader. The first is that the universe was not created exclusively for man's use, and therefore neither it nor its Creator can be judged solely by man's standards and goals. The second is even more significant. The natural world, though it is beyond man's ken, reveals to him its beauty and order. It is therefore reasonable for man to believe that the universe also exhibits a moral order with pattern and meaning, though it be beyond man's power fully to comprehend. Who, then, is Job, to reprove God and dispute with Him?

38	Then the Lord answered Job out of the whirlwind, saying,
2	Who is this that darkens My plan by words without knowledge?
3	Gird up your loins like a man; I will question you, and you may inform Me.
4	Where were you when I laid the foundations of the earth? Tell Me, if you have any understanding.
5	Who marked out its measure, if you know it, who stretched the plumb line upon it?

6 Upon what were the earth's pillars sunk;
  who laid down its cornerstone,
7 when the morning stars sang together
  and all the sons of God shouted for joy?

8 Who shut in the Sea with doors
  when it broke forth from the womb whence it came,
9 when I made the clouds its garment
  and dark clouds its swaddling clothes,
10 prescribing the limits for the Sea,
  and setting for it bolts and doors,
11 saying, "Thus far shall you come, and no farther,
  and here shall your proud waves be stayed"?

12 Have you ever commanded the morning,
  or assigned its place to the dawn,
13 so that you might take hold of the edges of the earth
  and the wicked be shaken from it?
14 For at dawn the earth takes shape like clay beneath a seal,
  and the wicked are exposed and are put to shame;
15 light is withheld from the wicked,
  and the power of the arrogant is broken.

16 Have you trodden on the bed of the Sea
  or walked in the recesses of the Deep?
17 Have the gates of Death been revealed to you;
  have you seen the gates of the netherworld?
18 Have you observed the breadth of the earth?
  Declare, if you know it all.

19 What is the way to the home of light;
  and darkness, where is its dwelling place?
20 Can you take it to its border,
  do you know the path to its home?
21 You surely know it, for you were born then,
  and the number of your days is great!

22 Have you entered the storehouses of snow,
  have you seen the storehouses of the hail,
23 which I have reserved for the time of trouble,
  for the day of battle and war?
24 In what way are the air currents scattered
  and is the east wind spread upon the earth?
25 Who has cleft a channel for the torrents of rain
  and a path for the thunderbolt,
26 to bring rain to a land uninhabited—
  to a desert where no man lives;
27 to satisfy the desolate wasteland
  and make the dry ground bring forth grass?

28 Has the rain a father,
and who has begotten the dew drops?
29 From whose womb did the ice come forth,
and the frost of heaven, who has given it birth,
30 when water is congealed like stone,
and the face of the deep is frozen over?

31 Can you bind the chains of the Pleiades
or loose the cords of Orion?
32 Can you bring forth Mazzarot in its season
or guide the Bear with its children?
33 Do you know the laws of the heavens;
can you establish My order on the earth?
34 Can you lift up your voice to the clouds
that a flood of waters may cover you?
35 Can you command the lightnings to go forth;
will they say to you, "Here we are"?
36 Who has placed wisdom in the ibis
or given understanding to the cock?
37 Who can spread out the clouds in wisdom,
and who can tilt the pitchers of heaven
38 when the dust hardens into a mass
and the clods cleave fast together?

39 Can you hunt prey for the lion
and satisfy the young whelps' appetite
40 when they crouch in their dens
or lie in wait in their covert?
41 Who provides for the raven its prey,
when its young ones cry to God
and wander about without food?

39 Do you know the time when the mountain goats give birth,
and do you watch the travail of the hinds?
2 Can you number the months they fulfill,
and do you know the time that they give birth,
3 when they crouch, bring forth their offspring,
and are delivered of their young?
4 Their young ones grow strong, they grow up in the open,
they go forth, and do not return to them.

5 Who has given the wild ass his freedom?
Who has loosed the bonds of the swift ass,
6 whose home I have made the wilderness
and whose dwelling is the salt land?

7 He scorns the noise of the city;
　　he will hear no shouts from the driver.
8 He ranges over the mountains as his pasture,
　　and he searches after every green plant.

9 Is the wild ox willing to serve you?
　　Will he spend the night at your crib?
10 Can you bind him to the furrow with ropes—
　　will he harrow the valleys after you?
11 Can you trust him, since his strength is great,
　　and leave your produce to him?
12 Can you rely on him to return,
　　and gather in your seed and your harvest?

13 The wing of the ostrich beats joyously—
　　but is her pinion like that of the stork or the vulture?
14 For she leaves her eggs on the earth
　　and lets them be warmed on the ground,
15 forgetting that a foot may crush them
　　or a wild beast trample them.
16 Her young ones grow tough without her;
　　that her labor may be in vain gives her no concern,
17 because God forgot her when He allocated wisdom,
　　and He gave her no share in understanding.
18 Now she soars aloft
　　and laughs at the horse and his rider.

19 Do you give the horse his strength;
　　Do you clothe his neck with a mighty mane?
20 Do you make him leap forward like a locust,
　　while the echo of his snorting is terrible?
21 He paws the valley in his joy
　　and bravely goes forth to face the battle.
22 He laughs at fear and is not dismayed;
　　he does not draw back from the sword.
23 Past him the arrow whistles,
　　the flashing spear, and the javelin.
24 In fierce rage he paws the ground
　　and cannot believe that the trumpet is sounding.
25 At the trumpet's blast he says, "Aha!"
　　smelling the battle from afar,
　　the noise of the captains and their shouting.

26 Is it by your wisdom that the hawk goes soaring
　　and spreads his wings toward the south?
27 Is it at your command that the eagle mounts
　　and makes his nest on high?
28 On the rock he makes his home,
　　on the steep crag and fortress.

29   Thence he searches for food,
             his eyes ranging afar.
30   His young ones suck up blood,
             and where the slain are, there is he.

40   (The Lord answered Job, saying,)
2   Can he who argues with the Almighty instruct Him?
             Can he who reproves God answer all this?

Job's Response (Chapter 40:3–5)

Job admits that he is overwhelmed by God's power and will speak
no more.

40   Job answered the Lord, saying,
4   Behold, I am of small account; how can I answer You?
             I lay my hand to my mouth.
5   I have spoken once, and I will not reply again;
             twice, but I will proceed no further.

The Lord's Second Speech (Chapters 40:6–41:26)

The Lord, brushing aside Job's submissive response, continues his
challenge. Why does Job condemn God in order that he may emerge
righteous? If Job could successfully destroy all evil in the world, God
would willingly pay tribute to him. The implication seems to be that
there are some corners of the world where God's sway is less than total, so that a few forms of wickedness escape His punishment. But this
is no reason for impugning God's justice in general.

Then follows a rhapsodic picture of two massive creatures, *Behemot*
(40:15–24) and *Leviathan* (40:25–41:26). They are poetic descriptions of the hippopotamus and the crocodile, respectively, with overtones drawn from ancient Semitic mythology. It would be a foolhardy
man indeed who would attempt to take these powerful beasts captive
and bend them to his will. Neither of these monstrous beings can be
called beautiful by man's standard. All the more vividly do they reveal
the delight that God takes in the manifold forms of creation.

There are two basic implications in the poet's choice of these animals to be glorified. First, man, who is only one of God's creatures, is *not* the measure of all things and the sole test of the worth of creation. Second, man's suffering must be seen in its proper perspective within the framework of the cosmos. Evil will then seem less pervasive in the universe than Job's anguished cries have made it appear.

Thus the conventional theology of the Friends is ignored completely by God, who later denounces it as false. Instead, emphasis is placed upon the harmony and beauty of the natural world on a scale beyond man's comprehension. This suggests that there is a similar order and meaning in the moral universe, even though man cannot always grasp it. God does not deny that there is a residuum of evil in the world which remains a mystery. But man can bear the burden of this suffering more easily if he sees it against the larger background of the cosmos, if he drinks in its beauty and revels in its joy.

40	Then the Lord answered Job out of the whirlwind, saying,
7	Gird up your loins like a man;
	I will ask you, and do you inform Me.
8	Will you deny My justice,
	put Me in the wrong, so that you may be in the right?
9	Have you an arm like God;
	can you thunder with a voice like His?
10	Deck yourself in majesty and dignity,
	clothe yourself with glory and splendor.
11	Scatter abroad your mighty wrath,
	and as you see each proud sinner—abase him!
12	As you look on each arrogant one—bring him low,
	and tread down the wicked in their place.
13	Bury them all in the dust,
	press their faces into the grave—
14	Then I too will render you homage,
	when your right hand will have brought you victory.
15	Behold, Behemoth, whom I fashioned along with you,
	eating grass like an ox.
16	See, his strength is in his loins
	and his power in the muscles of his belly.
17	He can stiffen his tail like a cedar,
	and the sinews of his thighs are knit together.
18	His bones are tubes of bronze;
	his limbs, like bars of iron.
19	He is the first of the works of God—
	only the well-trained warrior should come near him with a sword!

20 For the mountains bring him their tribute
and all the beasts of the field gambol there.
21 Under the lotus plants he lies
in the shadow of reeds, and in the marsh.
22 The lotus trees cover him with their shadow;
the willows of the brook surround him.
23 Behold, he empties an entire river without haste;
he lies at ease as he draws a Jordan into his mouth.
24 Who can capture him with rings
or pierce his nose with a snare?

25 Can you seize Leviathan with a net
or press down his tongue with a cord?
26 Can you put a rope in his nose
or pierce his jaw with a hook?
27 Will he make supplication to you
and speak to you in soft words?
28 Will he make a covenant with you
that you may take him as a servant forever?
29 Can you play with him as with a bird
or tie him up as one of your sparrows?
30 Will traders bargain over him?
Will they divide him up among merchants?
31 Can you fill his skin with harpoons
or his head with fishing spears?
32 If you dare lay your hand upon him,
not long will you remember the battle!

41 Indeed, he who attacks him loses all hope,
since at the mere sight of him, he is laid low.
2 No one is fierce enough to stir him up,
and who can stand up to him in battle?
3 Who has confronted him and emerged unscathed?
Under all the heavens there is no one!
4 I will not keep silent concerning his limbs,
or his mighty strength, or the grace of his form.
5 Who can strip off his outer garment?
Who can penetrate his double coat of mail?
6 Who can force open the doors of his face?
Round about his teeth is terror.
7 His back is made of layers of shields
shut up tight as with a seal.
8 Each scale is so close to the other
that no air can enter between them.
9 They are joined one to the other;
they are interlocked and cannot be sundered.
10 His sneezings flash forth light;
his eyes are like the eyelids of the dawn.

11   Out of his mouth go flaming torches—
        sparks of fire leap forth.

12   Out of his nostrils comes smoke
        as from a boiling pot or a marsh.

13   His breath kindles coals,
        and a flame comes forth from his mouth.

14   On his neck, strength abides,
        and on his face terror dances.

15   The folds of his flesh are joined together,
        firmly set upon him and immovable.

16   His breast is firm as a rock,
        firm as the lower millstone.

17   When he raises himself up, the gods are frightened
        and the mighty breakers make supplication to him.

18   If one reaches for him with the sword, it will fail—
        be it the spear, the dart, or the javelin.

19   He treats iron as straw,
        and bronze, as rotting wood.

20   The arrow cannot put him to flight;
        for him slingstones turn into stubble.

21   The club he treats as straw,
        and he laughs at the rattle of javelins.

22   His underparts are sharp as potsherds;
        he spreads out like a threshing-sledge on the mire.

23   He brings the deep to a boil like a pot;
        he stirs up the sea like a seething mixture.

24   He leaves behind him a shining wake—
        one would think the deep hoary-headed.

25   Nowhere on earth is there his like,
        a creature born without fear.

26   He looks down upon all that is lofty,
        for he is king over all proud creatures.

Job's Response (Chapter 42:1–6)

The Lord's second speech has taught Job to recognize both the mystery and the harmony of the world. He now quotes the words of the Lord, to which he replies contritely. Job declares that his deepest wish has been granted, for his Maker has deigned to answer him. The beauty of His world constitutes an anodyne for his pain and serves as the basis for his renewed faith in the justice of God. This is more than submission—it is reconciliation.

42   Then Job answered the Lord,
2   I know that You can do all things
           and that no purpose of Yours can be thwarted.
3   You have said,
        "Who is this that hides My plan without knowledge?"
           Indeed, I have spoken without understanding,
           of things too wonderful for me which I did not grasp.
4   You have said,
        "Hear, and I will speak;
           I will ask you, and do you inform Me."
5   I have heard of You by hearsay,
           but now my own eyes have seen You.
6   Therefore I abase myself
           and repent in dust and ashes.

THE EPILOGUE (Chapter 42:7–17)

THE JOINTURE (Chapter 42:7–10)

The poet now adds a few verses to serve as a link between the poetry and the conclusion of the traditional prose tale, which becomes the epilogue. Earlier, Eliphaz had grandly given Job the assurance that if he repented of his misdeeds he would be forgiven by God and even be able to intercede for other sinners. With poetic justice, the Lord now tells Eliphaz that it is he and his companions who have been guilty of untruth in their attempted defense of Him, and that they will be forgiven only if Job pleads for them. This Job proceeds to do on their behalf. His own fortunes are restored; in fact, all his possessions are doubled as a compensation for the losses he has sustained.

42   After the Lord had spoken these words to Job, the Lord said to Eliphaz the Temanite, "My anger is kindled against you and against your two friends, for you have not spoken the truth about Me as has My 8 servant Job. Now then, take seven bulls and seven rams, and go to My servant Job, and offer them as a burnt offering for yourselves. My servant Job must intercede for you, for only to him will I show favor and not expose you to disgrace for not speaking the truth about Me as did 9 My servant Job." So Eliphaz the Temanite, and Bildad the Shuhite, and Zophar the Naamathite did as the Lord had told them; and the Lord 10 heeded Job's plea. Then the Lord restored the fortunes of Job, when he had interceded for his friends; and the Lord doubled all of Job's possessions.

JOB'S RESTORATION (Chapter 42:11–17)

The traditional tale of Job and his trials is now resumed in the epilogue, which together with the prologue constitutes the framework of the book. Satan does not appear, nor is God vindicated in His wager. These features of the traditional tale were probably deliberately eliminated by the poet. He must have felt, quite properly, that their reintroduction at this point would be a grave anticlimax after the profundities of the dialogue and the exalted speeches of the Lord.

Job's kinsmen and friends, who ostracized him during his suffering, come to break bread with him and comfort him, now, when he no longer needs their sympathy. Each brings a gift as a symbol of his friendship. The Lord blesses Job by giving him flocks twice the size of those he had originally owned. Since male offspring were a great blessing in the ancient Orient, he is given fourteen sons instead of the seven he had at the beginning. His daughters, however, remain three in number, though they are outstanding for their beauty, and are given an inheritance along with their brothers (an act which is striking testimony to their honored status). Job lives one hundred and forty years more, twice the normal life span, and sees four generations of his descendants.

42 Then there came to him all his brothers and sisters and all his former friends, and they ate food with him in his house, commiserating with him and consoling him for all the suffering that the Lord had brought upon him. Each man also gave him a piece of money and a golden ring.

12 So the Lord blessed the end of Job's life more than his beginning. He had fourteen thousand sheep, six thousand camels, a thousand yoke of

13 oxen, and a thousand she-asses. He also had fourteen sons and three

14 daughters. And he called the first, Jemimah; the second, Keziah; and the third, Keren-happuch. In all the land there were no women as

15 fair as Job's daughters. And their father gave them an inheritance among their brothers.

16 After this, Job lived a hundred and forty years and saw his sons, and

17 his sons' sons, four generations. So Job died, an old man, satisfied with life.

Part Three

REFERENCES

Abbreviations

Dan. — Daniel
Deut. — Deuteronomy
DG — S. R. Driver and G. B. Gray, ICC on Job

E.B. — *Encyclopaedia Britannica*
Eccles. — Ecclesiastes
Ecclus. — Ecclesiasticus
Exod. — Exodus
Ezek. — Ezekiel

Gen. — Genesis
Gen. Rabbah — Midrash *Genesis Rabbah*

Hab. — Habakkuk
Hag. — Haggai
Hos. — Hosea
HThR — *Harvard Theological Review*
HUCA — *Hebrew Union College Annual*

ICC — International Critical Commentary
IOT — *Introduction to the Old Testament*
Isa. — Isaiah

J. — Jerusalem (Palestinian) Talmud
JAOS — *Journal of the American Oriental Society*
JBL — *Journal of Biblical Literature*
JE — *Jewish Encyclopedia*
Jer. — Jeremiah
JJS — *Journal of Jewish Studies*
JNES — *Journal of Near Eastern Studies*
Josh. — Joshua
JPS — Jewish Publication Society version of the Old Testament
JQR — *Jewish Quarterly Review*
JR — *Journal of Religion*
J. *Shab.* — Jerusalem Talmud, tractate *Shabbath*
J. *Sotah* — Jerusalem Talmud, tractate *Sotah*
J. *Taan.* — Jerusalem Talmud, tractate *Taanith*
JThS — *Journal of Theological Studies*
Judg. — Judges

KMW — R. Gordis, *Koheleth—The Man and His World*
Koheleth R. — Midrash *Koheleth Rabbah*

Lam. — Lamentations
Lev. — Leviticus
Lev. Rab. — Midrash Leviticus Rabbah
"LMBH" — R. Gordis, "Lisegullot HaMelişah Bekhithebhei Haqodeš"

M. — Mishnah
Mal. —Malachi
M. Eduy. — Mishnah Eduyot
MGWJ — Monatschrift fuer die Geschichte und Wissenschaft des Judentums
"MHHH" — R. Gordis, "Al Mibneh Haširah Haivrit Haquedumah"
Mic. — Micah
Mid. — Midrash
Mid. Tehillim — Midrash Tehillim
M. Sotah — Mishnah Sotah
MT — Masoretic Text
M. Yad. — Mishnah Yadayim

Nah. — Nahum
Neh. — Nehemiah
N.T. — New Testament
Num. — Numbers

Obad. — Obadiah
O.T. — Old Testament

PAAJR — Proceedings of the American Academy of Jewish Research
Prov. — Proverbs
Ps. — Psalms

"QLU" — R. Gordis, "Quotations as a Literary Usage in Biblical, Oriental and Rabbinic Literature"

RB — Revue Biblique
RSV — Revised Standard Version

I and II Sam. — I and II Samuel
"SBWL" — R. Gordis, "The Social Background of Wisdom Literature"
Song of Sol. — Song of Solomon

Targ. — Targum
Targ. Jerusalem — Targum Jerusalem
ThLz — Theologische Literaturzeitung
Tos. — Tosefta

Tos. *Shab.* — Tosefta *Shabbath*
Tos. *Yad.* — Tosefta *Yadayim*

VSS — Versions, Ancient Versions
VT — *Vetus Testamentum*

ZATW — *Zeitschrift für die Alttestamentliche Wissenschaft*
ZDMG — *Zeitschrift der deutschen morgenländischen Gesellschaft*
Zech. — Zechariah
Zeph. — Zephaniah

Notes

I: ON READING JOB

1. Thomas Carlyle, "The Hero as Prophet," *On Heroes, Hero-Worship and he Heroic in History* (New York, 1905), p. 69.

2. J. A. Froude, *The Book of Job* (London, 1854), p. 3.

3. Carl Cornill, *Introduction to the Canonical Books of the Old Testament* (New York, 1907), p. 421.

4. See, for example, J. Neyrand in *Études Bibliques*, LIX (1922–24), 129 ff., who compares it with the Homeric poems.

5. H. M. Kallen, *The Book of Job as a Greek Tragedy Restored* (New York, 1918), regards Job as an imitation of Euripides. R. Lowth had suggested Sophocles as a prototype (*Praelectiones* [Oxford, 1753]).

6. For the Greco-Roman period, see the impressive studies of S. Lieberman, *Greek in Jewish Palestine* (New York, 1942) and *Hellenism in Jewish Palestine* (New York, 1950), and V. Tcherikover, *Hellenistic Civilization and the Jews* (Philadelphia, 1959), as well as the studies on rabbinic law and its parallels by Boaz Cohen and David Daube. On the parallels between Hebrew Hokmah and Greek Sophia in the "classical period" of Greece and the post-Exilic age in Israel, cf. Gordis, "The Social Background of Wisdom Literature," *HUCA*, XVIII (1943), 77–116, and *Koheleth—The Man and His World* (New York, 1951), pp. 29–32. The view there expressed that the parallel developments in the two cultures are independent of each other probably needs to be stated less decisively. Future research may disclose direct or indirect channels of influence between Hokmah and Sophia. For the earliest period, "the heroic age" in Aegean and Hebrew history, see C. H. Gordon, *Before the Bible* (New York,

1963), and his earlier technical studies cited in his bibliography. For a brief evaluation of his still controversial thesis and the evidence adduced, see the review by Gordis, *In Jewish Bookland* (March, 1963), p. 1.

7. For a further discussion of this important theme by the present writer see Gordis, *A Faith for Moderns* (New York, 1960), especially pp. 213–25.

8. The texts are conveniently accessible in J. B. Pritchard, ed., *ANET*, pp. 407–9, 437–40, and the literature there cited. Cf. the judicious treatment in Driver and Gray, *A Critical and Exegetical Commentary on the Book of Job* (New York, 1921), I, xxi ff. See also chapter v of this work.

9. Cf. W. G. Lambert, *Babylonian Wisdom Literature* (Oxford, 1960), p. 1, who expresses strong doubts as to the use of "Wisdom" for Babylonian literature.

II: THE ENIGMA OF JOB

1. Cf. Job 29:8 and 15:10, and see the perspicacious observation of S. L. Terrien, *Job: Poet of Existence* (New York, 1957), pp. 184–85.

2. See the Midrash quoted by R. Isaac Hakohen on Job 2:9 in *Leqet Midrashim*, ed. S. Wertheimer (Jerusalem, 1904), p. 5a; see Ibn Masnuth, *Mayan Gannim on Job*, ed. Salomon Buber (Berlin, 1889), on Job 2:10; and see also the discussion in L. Ginzberg, *Legends of the Jews* (Philadelphia, 1925), Vol. V, nn. 27, 28 (pp. 386–87).

3. One Greek text of this little-known apocryphal work was first published by Cardinal Mai in his *Scriptorum Veterum Nova Collectio* (Rome, 1833), Vol. VII, and by K. Kohler in *Semitic Studies in Memory of Dr. Alexander Kohut* (Berlin, 1897), pp. 264–338, with a translation, introduction, and notes. Another Greek MS was published with an introduction by M. R. James, in his *Apocrypha Anecdota*, 2d series (Cambridge, 1897). See K. Kohler's "Testament of Job" in *JE*, and the more recent, stimulating treatment by C. C. Torrey, *The Apocryphal Literature* (New Haven, 1945), pp. 140–45.

4. See B. *Baba Bathra* 15a: *Mōshe kāthabh siphrō uphorošath bilᶜām vesepher ᵓiyyōbh*, "Moses wrote his book (the Torah) and the section on Balaam (Numbers 22:1–25:9) and the book of Job." The Mosaic date was defended by J. D. Michaelis, G. W. Hazelton, and F. A. Lambert as late as 1919.

5. So A. C. Havernick, C. F. Keil, K. Schlottman, Franz Delitzsch, and others.

6. See chapter xv of this work, and Pfeiffer, *IOT*, pp. 676 ff.

7. See R. H. Pfeiffer, *IOT* (New York, 1941), pp. 680 ff., who attributes much of biblical Wisdom literature to Edom, a theory difficult to refute since virtually nothing is known of Edomite culture. A better illustration of *obscura per obscuriora* would be hard to find.

8. See P. Humbert, *Recherches sur les Sources égyptiennes de la Littérature sapientiale d'Israël* (Neuchâtel, 1929).

9. Abraham ibn Ezra, *Commentary on Job* (2:11): *Vehaqārōbh ᵓeilai kī hūᵓ sēpher methurgām ᶜal kēn huᵓ qāšeh kederekh kol sēpher methurgām*, "It seems

likely to me that it is a translated book and therefore is difficult, like every translated book." On the faulty reasoning which underlies the "translation theories" that postulate a non-existent original in another language to explain the difficulties of an extant text, see R. Gordis, *KMW*, pp. 60–61 and references on p. 364, n. 12.

10. F. H. Foster, "Is the Book of Job a Translation from an Arabic Original?" *AJSL*, XLIX (1932–33), 21–45, argues for an Arabic original.

11. So F. Baumgärtel and J. Lindblom; cf. H. H. Rowley, "The Book of Job and Its Meaning," *Bulletin of the John Rylands Library*, XLI (Sept., 1958), 192–93.

12. S. P. Bertie, *Le Livre de Job* (Paris, 1929); N. H. Snaith, *The Book of Job* (London, 1950), p. 15. T. H. Cheyne (in *Encyclopedia Biblica*, II, 2476) is more moderate, eliminating only chapters 20–28.

13. The catena of modern scholars deleting these chapters extends over nearly two centuries, from M. H. Stuhlmann's commentary (1804). See Pfeiffer, *IOT*, pp. 672–73; Rowley, *op. cit.*, pp. 173 ff.

14. So Helen Nichols, *AJSL*, XXVIII (1910–11), 97 ff.; M. Jastrow, *The Book of Job* (Philadelphia, 1920), pp. 77 ff.; W. A. Irwin, *JR*, XVII (1937), pp. 36 ff.

15. They include E. F. K. Rosenmüller, F. W. C. Umbreit, J. G. Stickell, C. Cornill, G. Wildeboer. K. Budde and R. H. Pfeiffer originally defended the authenticity of the Elihu chapters but subsequently changed their minds.

16. So P. Volz, E. Sellin, H. Schmidt, M. Jastrow, and F. Baumgärtel.

17. H. D. F. Kitto, *The Greeks* (Harmondsworth, Middlesex, 1951), p. 63.

18. See the author's *KMW*, *passim*, and the other recent works on Ecclesiastes cited there.

19. As, for example, in Hosea, where 2:1–3 constitutes the conclusion to the prophecy in 2:4–25 and should be transposed to the end instead of being at the beginning of the chapter. The third cycle of Job has obviously sustained damage too, as is clear from such objective criteria as the absence of a speech by Zophar, the brief rejoinder of Bildad, and the extraordinarily long speech by Job (chaps. 26–31). See chapter viii of this work.

III: THE CULTURAL BACKGROUND:
THE LAW AND THE PROPHETS

1. On these three elements of ancient Israelite culture, see M. L. Margolis, *The Hebrew Scriptures in the Making* (Philadelphia, 1922); R. Gordis, "The Bible as a Cultural Monument" in L. Finkelstein, ed., *The Jews* (2d ed.; New York, 1960), pp. 463–92; Gordis, *KMW*, pp. 8–30.

2. Reading with the *Kethib* vocalized as *ribbō*, rather than the difficult *Qere*, which is a *hapax legomenon* in the plural, *rubbei*.

3. See G. A. Cooke, *Ezekiel*, "ICC" (New York, 1937), for a recent treatment.

4. See, for example, Exod. 28:1; 40:13–15; Lev. 6:2; chaps. 13, 18; 10:13; 17:5; and especially Num. 1:51; 3:10; chaps. 16–18.

5. B. *Sanhedrin* 21b: *rā꞉uȳ hāyāh Ezrā šettināthen hatōrāh ꞉al yādō ilmālē kedāmō mōše.*

6. The classic histories of rabbinic tradition are Z. Frankel, *Darkhei Hamishnah* (Leipzig, 1859); I. H. Weiss, *Dor Dor Vedorshav* (Vilna, 1871–91); and more recently, Ch. Tchernowitz, *Toledot Hahalakhah* (New York, 1934–50); and L. Finkelstein, *The Pharisees* (2d ed.; Philadelphia, 1962). The epoch-making Hebrew essay of L. Ginzberg, "The Place of Halacha in Jewish Research," is now available in English in the volume of his essays, *On Jewish Law and Lore* (Philadelphia, 1955), pp. 77–126.

7. The literature on the prophets is enormous. For a brief conspectus, see R. Gordis in *The Jews*, pp. 475–82, and the bibliography in Pfeiffer, *IOT*, pp. 867–71. A. J. Heschel's suggestive *The Prophets* (New York, 1962) and S. H. Blank's *Jeremiah: Man and Prophet* (Cincinnati, 1961) and *Prophetic Faith in Isaiah* (New York, 1958) are more recent studies reflecting varying approaches to the prophets.

8. Cf. the contemptuous attitude of the people toward the "prophet" implied in the phrase "Is Saul also among the prophets?" (I Sam. 10:11–12; 19:24). In Hos. 9:7, "the prophet is a fool, the man of the Spirit, a lunatic," and in Isa. 28:9 ff., both of which repeat the words of the populace, and in the tragic career of Jeremiah, we have a carry-over and an intensification of this attitude applied to "the true prophets."

9. E.g., I Sam. 9:8 ff.; 10:1–13; Saul's encounter with the witch of Endor (I Sam. 28:6 ff.); and the conduct of the "prophets of Baal" toward Jezebel (I Kings 18:19 ff.); as well as various incidents in the traditions of Elijah and Elisha (I Kings, chap. 17; II Kings, chaps. 2–5, especially 3:15).

10. Cf. the entire passage in Jer. 20:7–9, which is basic for the prophetic experience.

11. I do not share the views of Yehezkel Kaufmann on the "pre-prophetic" (or unprophetic) chárácter of the biblical historians. See his monumental *Tōledōt Hā꞉emūnāh Hayisre꞉ēlīt* (8 vols.; Tel Aviv, 1937–56), *passim*, available in an English abridgment by M. Greenberg, *The Religion of Israel* (Chicago, 1960).

12. Cf. chapter xv for the evidence of his use of earlier biblical books.

IV: WISDOM AND JOB

1. Or better, read with Septuagint, "five thousand."

2. Cf. I Chron. 6:7, 16, 22; 15:19; 16:4–5.

3. See W. F. Albright, *Archaeology and the Religion of Israel* (Baltimore, 1942), pp. 125–29, who first called attention to the Canaanite origin of musical guilds. The Ugarite guilds include *šrm* and *bn šrm*, "singers" and "members of the singers' guild" (C. H. Gordon, *Ugaritic Manual* [Rome, 1955]), Glossary No. 1385. On the Ugaritic guilds in general and their possible relation-

ship to the biblical guilds associated with the Temple, see B. A. Levine, "The Netinim," *JBL*, LXXXII (June, 1963), 211–12.

4. For the noun *v'hagūt* a verb is required by the parallelism. Hence read *v'hāgāh*, or preferably revocalize *vehagāt*, the older form of 3d person fem. perf.; cf. *ᶜasāt* (Lev. 25:21), *hayāt* (II Kings 9:37 *Kethib*); Lev. 26:34; Jer. 13:19; Ezek. 24:12. On *lebh* as fem., cf. Prov. 12:25.

5. Interpreting *ᵓozni* (and perhaps revocalizing it) on the basis of *ᵓazēnekhā* (Deut. 23:14), "your implement, tool," BDB, p. 24b.

6. See the painstaking study of O. Eissfeldt, "Der Maschal im A.T.," (Beihefte, *ZATW*, XXIV [Giessen, 1913]), who makes a careful analysis of the etymology and semantics of *māšāl*. He distinguishes six meanings: (1) folk proverb; (2) taunt song; (3) proverb of individual composition; (4) didactic teaching; (5) allegory; (6) oracle. This effort to establish the genetic relationship among the six meanings he assigns to the term is not altogether successful. Thus he explains that the noun developed the meaning of "taunt song" (as e.g., Deut. 28:37; Isa. 14:4; Jer. 24:9; etc.) from "folk proverb," because "people generally prefer to mock their neighbors rather than praise them, hence *māšāl* is 'a subject of negative discussion' " (*ibid.*, p. 3). Eissfeldt's distinction between a folk proverb and an individual proverb is difficult to establish since even a folk proverb obviously has its beginning with an individual. As for the categories he calls "oracles" (Num. 23:7, 18; 24:3, 15, 20, 21, 23) and "didactic teaching" (Job 27:1; 29:1), we believe that the term *māšāl* is best regarded as synonymous with *šīr*, "song," or *ḥīdāh*, "riddle," or both, since it is couched in poetic form and deals with the mysteries of existence.

7. As, e.g., in Prov. 10:1; 25:1.

8. As, e.g., Num. 21:27; Ps. 49:5; 78:2; Job 27:1; 29:1. It occurs in parallelism with *māšāl* in Ps. 49:5; 78:2.

9. Cf. Judges 12:12 ff.; I Kings 10:1; II Chron. 9:1. See the stimulating study of N. H. Tur-Sinai, "Hidot vegilgulehen besifrut Hamiqra" ("Riddles and Their Transformations in Biblical Literature") in *Halašon Vehasepher, Kerekh Hasefer* (Jerusalem, 5711 = 1950), pp. 58–73.

10. E.g., BDB, p. 295a.

11. Cf. for these three uses Hab. 2:6; Ps. 49:5; and Ps. 78:2, respectively.

12. For the professional status of the *ḥakam*, we may note the parallel phenomenon among the Greek sophists concerning whose high fees we are specifically informed. See "SBWL," pp. 85–86, and the epilogue in Koheleth (Eccles. 12:9–10); see also Gordis, *KMW*, pp. 75, 84–85, 340.

13. See the suggestive treatment of W. F. Albright, *From the Stone Age to Christianity* (Baltimore, 1940), pp. 282–85, and his "Canaanite–Phoenician Sources of Hebrew Wisdom," *Supplement to VT*, No. III (1955), pp. 1–15, where he cites the Semitic parallels and relates them to the biblical passages. In this instance, however, I believe he does not give sufficient weight to the fundamental differences in outlook between Semitic paganism and Hebrew monotheistic thought, which was most highly developed among the Wisdom

writers. Accordingly, he fails to distinguish between mythological allusions and religious beliefs, a difference which he has repeatedly emphasized elsewhere in his discussions of Hebrew thought. B. Oppenheimer, in "Psalms 152, 153 from Qumran," in the Hebrew journal *Molad*, No. 191–92 (Aug.–Sept., 1964), pp. 328–43, goes further and argues not merely that there is divergence of outlook, but "a clear polemic intent" against paganism in the biblical writers (p. 334). The non-argumentative tone of the various Hebrew paeans to Wisdom does not support so extreme a conclusion, but his critique of Albright seems to me valid.

14. See *AJSL*, Vol. XXXVI, p. 285. While the text has several lacunae, Albright's restoration is highly convincing and the general sense is clear.

15. See chapter viii and the translation in the present work.

16. Rashi, Ibn Ezra, and many moderns, as well as Goodspeed and Moffatt ("as his foster-child"), follow AV, "as one brought up with him," in rendering the enigmatic and crucial *ʾāmōn*. RSV renders "master workman," which is supported by the reminiscence of the Proverbs passage in the Wisdom of Solomon (7:22): "For she [i.e., Wisdom], the artificer of all things, taught me Wisdom" (S. Holmes in R. H. Charles, *Apocrypha and Pseudepigrapha of the O.T.* [Oxford, 1913], I, 546). On the other hand, Wisdom of Solomon may be embodying later, post-biblical conceptions of Hokmah. (See this text.) The parallelism strongly favors the first interpretation of *ʾāmōn*. See also the divergent approach of Oppenheimer, *op. cit.*, p. 335. R. B. Y. Scott, *Proverbs-Ecclesiastes* ("Anchor Bible" [New York, 1965]), pp. 69–72, correctly rejects the attempts to hypostasize Hebrew Wisdom on the basis of alleged parallels from oriental mythology. Less convincing is his suggested vocalization *ʾōmēn*, which he renders "uniting, binding together"; see *VT*, X (1960), 213–23.

17. The latest edition, with a Hebrew retroversion, is by M. Noth, "Die fünf syrisch überlieferten apokryphen Psalmen," *ZATW*, XLVIII (1930), 1–23.

18. The texts are published by J. A. Sanders in "Two Non-Canonical Psalms in Q Ps^a," *ZATW*, LXXVI (1964), 57 ff., which should be supplemented by the suggestive study by Oppenheimer, *op. cit.*

19. In the opening section of *Midrash Berēšīt Rabbāh* on Gen. 1:1, we read: *Hatōrāh ʾōmeret ʾanī hāyithi kelī ūmānūthō šel hakkādōš bārūkh hūʾ*, "The Torah says, 'I was the instrument employed by the Holy One blessed be He [at creation].'" Here the identification of Hokmah and Torah has undoubtedly been influenced by Philonic ideas of the *Logos*. In the Jewish Prayer Book, the classical repository of rabbinic thought, Wisdom is identified with the Torah. Thus the service at the return of the Torah Scrolls to the Ark includes the verses in Prov. 4:2; 3:18, 17 (in this sequence) which praise Wisdom.

20. See J. C. Rylaarsdam, *Revelation in Jewish Wisdom Literature* (Chicago, 1946), *passim*, esp. pp. 99–104.

21. On the entire institution, see R. Gordis, "Primitive Democracy in An-

cient Israel," in *Alexander Marx Jubilee Volume* (New York, 1950), English Section, pp. 369–88.

22. Reading for the meaningless *velō⁾ yissā⁾ ⁾elōhīm nāpheš*, by a slight change, *velō⁾ yissā ⁾alehem nāpheš*. For the variety of interpretations of this verse and the evidence for my proposed emendation, see *KMW*, p. 350, n. 22.

23. See, for example, the Book of the Covenant (Exod., chaps. 21–23); the Holiness Code (Lev., chaps. 18–21); and in the Book of Leviticus, the laws of sacrifice (chaps. 1–5; note particularly 5:20–26), of leprosy (chaps. 13–14), and of ritual impurity (chap. 15).

24. Cf. Jer. 12:1 ff.; 31:28 ff.; Ezek. 18:1 ff.

25. See "SBWL," pp. 84 ff., and *KMW*, pp. 18 ff.

26. In its first meaning, *sophia* is applied to Hephaestus, the god of fire and the arts, to Athena, to Daedalus, the craftsman and artist, and to the Telchines, a primitive tribe who are represented under three aspects: (1) as cultivators of the soil and ministers of the gods; (2) as sorcerers and envious demons who had the power to bring on hail, rain, and snow, and to destroy animals and plants; and (3) as artists working in brass and iron. (Gen. 4:20–22 offers a suggestive parallel.) *Sophia* is used of such crafts as carpentry, driving a chariot, medicine, and surgery. It is used particularly of singing, music, and poetry (*Homeric Hymn to Mercury*, ll. 483, 511; Pindar *Odes* 1.187; Xenophon *Anabasis* I, 2, 8). On the usage of all three terms here discussed, see Liddell and Scott, *A Greek-English Lexicon*, *s.v.*

27. Cf. Pindar *Odes* 1.15; Euripides *Iphigenia in Tauris* l. 1238; Plato *Laws* 696c. See Liddell and Scott, *op. cit.*, *s.v.*

28. Cf. Pindar *Odes* 1. 5. 36; Aeschylus *Fragmenta* no. 320. See Liddell and Scott, *op. cit.*, *s.v.*

29. Cf. Xenophon *Memorabilia* I. 6, 13; Thucydides *History* 3. 38; Plato *Protagoras* 313c.

30. For a conspectus of oriental Wisdom, see J. Fichtner, *Die altorientalische Weisheitsliteratur in ihrer israelitisch-jüdischen Ausprägung* (Giessen, 1933). A briefer survey appears in *KMW*, pp. 8–13. The principal texts are available in Pritchard, *ANET.*

31. Cf. A. Erman, *The Literature of the Ancient Egyptians*, trans. A. M. Blackman (New York, 1927).

32. See W. G. Lambert, *Babylonian Wisdom Literature* (Oxford, 1960), p. 1. Lambert's hesitation to apply the term "Wisdom" to the second category is unjustified in view of the parallels we have adduced and the intimate organic relationship between the two types of Wisdom writings.

33. See *KMW*, p. 339 ff., for a full discussion of this significant passage, the meaning of which had not previously been fully understood.

34. In addition to the standard commentaries on Proverbs, see the analysis of the document in "SBWL," p. 106–7.

35. For a full study of the book, see *KMW* (2d ed.).

36. See chapter v.

37. This is the contention of P. Volz, *Hiob und Weisheit in den Schriften des alten Testaments* (Göttingen, 1921), and C. Westermann, *Der Aufbau des Buches Hiob* (Tübingen, 1956). The position is subjected to stringent but justifiable criticism by G. Fohrer in *VT*, VII (1957), 107–11.

38. For a complete discussion of the upper-class orientation of oriental and biblical Wisdom, see "SBWL."

39. The plural "widows" in such passages as Isa. 9:16; Jer. 15:8; 49:11; Ezek. 19:7 refers, of course, to the surviving spouses of many men. The same is true of Ps. 78:64b, where the exact phrase is used in reference to Israel as a collectivity.

40. Against P. Humbert, *Recherches sur les Sources égyptiennes . . .* (Neuchâtel, 1929).

41. See G. Hölscher's correct conclusion (Commentary, p. 7) that the author of Job was a Palestinian who had traveled widely, hence his familiarity with Egyptian flora and fauna, the Sinai desert, and the hail, ice, and snow of the north, probably the Lebanon region.

42. R. H. Pfeiffer, *Introduction to the Old Testament* (New York, 1941), p. 687.

43. See "SBWL," p. 89 ff., for a fuller discussion.

44. E.g., *Proverbs of Amenemope* (col. XXV, l. 496): "The strength of Ra is to him that is on the road" as an instance of a popular saying.

45. Thus, taking Prov. chap. 16 at random, we find JHVH used ten times, of which at least four are in stock phrases (vss. 5, 6, 7?, 20). On divine names in Wisdom, see Fichtner, *op. cit.*, p. 103 ff.; O. S. Rankin, *Israel's Wisdom Literature . . .* (Edinburgh, 1936), p. 39, note.

46. Even the Temple in Jerusalem is called *bēt ᵓelōhīm* not *bēt Adōnai* in Eccles. 4:17!

47. JHVH and *Adōnai* occur in the poetry of Job: (a) in 12:9, which is either an interpolation or, more probably, a reminiscence of Isa. 41:20c, *yad JHVH* being a stock phrase; (b) in 28:28, in which *yirat ᵓAdōnai* is again a typical phrase of the Wisdom schools (the entire chapter is an independent poem); and (c) in 38:1 and 40:1, in the superscriptions announcing the appearance of the Lord "from the whirlwind." Here the traditional association of the God of Israel with storm, thunder, and lightning, led to the use of His name. Cf. the theophanies in Exod. 19:16; Judg. 5:4–5; Isa. 64:1; Nah. 1:3–4; Hab. 3:3 ff.; Ps. 18:8 ff.; 29 *passim*; 144:5–6.

48. See W. O. E. Oesterley and T. H. Robinson, *Hebrew Religion* (London, 1930), p. 223; also Rankin, *op. cit.*, pp. 124–97.

49. Cf., e.g., Prov. 13:22; 14:26; 20:7; Ecclus. 44:10–11.

50. Cf. also Ecclus. 17:27; 14:14.

51. For a fuller treatment of these passages, see "SBWL," pp. 111–16.

52. While the last passage is attributed to Job in the Masoretic Text, it ob-

viously belongs to one of the Friends, probably Bildad, to whom it is assigned by Reuss, Duhm, Siegfried, Dhorme, and Hölscher. See the Comm., *ad loc.*

53. This distinction is clearly recognized by DG, I, 85–86.

54. On this rendering, which presupposes a minor emendation, reading *vayyāsar* (root *sūr*) instead of *vayyeʾsōr* (root *ʾasar*), and interpreting *Beth* in *bᵉmothneihem* as "from," as in Ugaritic, see the Comm., *ad loc.*

55. Failure to note this difference in attitude has led some scholars to delete considerable portions of chap. 12. Siegfried and Grill retain only vss. 1–3; Jastrow omits vss. 4c, 5 in part, 6c, 10, 12, 13, 17–19, 22, and 23. Volz transfers vss. 4–10, 13–25, and 13:1 to Zophar in chap. 11. Only Budde argued strongly in favor of the authenticity of the passage a half-century ago. See Comm., *ad loc.*

V: JOB AND NEAR EASTERN LITERATURE

1. See such proverbs as 5:7; 12:11, 12; 17:5; 32:8, 9; and as instances of rhetorical questions, 6:5, 6. See chapter xii on this stylistic trait in Job.

2. A complete list of the extant documents of oriental Wisdom may be found in J. Fichtner, *Die altorientalische Weisheitsliteratur in ihrer israelitisch-jüdischen Ausprägung* (Giessen, 1933). The principal texts are accessible in H. Gressmann, *Altorientalische Texte und Bilder zum A.T.* (2d. ed.; Berlin-Leipzig, 1926), pp. 25–29, 33–46; in A. Erman, *The Literature of the Ancient Egyptians*, trans. A. M. Blackman (New York, 1927), pp. 54–131; and in *ANET, passim.*

3. W. Kaufmann, *From Shakespeare to Existentialism* (New York, 1960), p. 152.

4. For the extensive literature on *Amenemope* since the publication of the text by E. A. W. Budge in 1923, see Fichtner, *op. cit.*, p. 4, n. 3; W. O. E. Oesterley, *The Book of Proverbs* (Philadelphia, 1929), esp. pp. xlvi ff. and liv; G. A. Barton, *Archaeology and the Bible* (7th ed.; Philadelphia, 1937), pp. 511 ff.; L. Finkelstein, *The Pharisees* (Philadelphia, 1938), I, 203 ff.; II, 678; *ANET,* p. 420. The view that the Egyptian text is derived from the Hebrew is maintained by H. O. Lange, in *Kgl. Danske Vidensk Selskab, Hist. fil. Med. XI,* 2 (125); W. O. E. Oesterley, in *ZATW,* XLV (1927), p. 23; R. O. Kevin, *The Wisdom of Amen-em-apt and Its Possible Dependence upon the Hebrew Book of Proverbs* (Philadelphia, 1931).

5. For a brief conspectus of oriental Wisdom, see *KMW,* pp. 8–13 and notes.

6. Most of the text is available in *ANET,* pp. 420–21.

7. The translated text (with bibliography) is available in *ANET,* pp. 441 ff.

8. See chapter iv for the social significance of such passages as Prov. 30:21–22; Eccles. 10:6–7.

9. See the translated text (with bibliography) in *ANET,* pp. 405–7, and in Erman, *op. cit.*, pp. 86–92.

10. The translated text (with bibliography) is to be found in *ANET*, pp. 407–10.

11. See Gressmann, *op. cit.*, pp. 28–29; *ANET*, p. 467.

12. See *KMW* on Eccles. 9:9 ff.

13. Cf. the remarks of Fichtner, *op. cit.*, p. 6, and W. G. Lambert, *Babylonian Wisdom Literature* (Oxford, 1960), p. 1.

14. W. G. Lambert, *op. cit.*, p. 1. He hesitates to apply the term "Wisdom" to Babylonian literature because: (a) he conceives of biblical Wisdom principally in terms of piety; and (b) he observes that "Wisdom" in Babylonian sources generally refers to skill in cult and magic lore. These considerations fall away in view of our discussion on the full semantic meaning of "Wisdom" in Hebrew and the dual concept of "lower" and "higher" Wisdom in all branches of oriental literature (chapters iii and iv).

15. See B. Meissner, *Babylonien und Assyrien* (Heidelberg, 1920–25), II, 424 ff.; E. Ebeling, "Reste Akkadischer Weisheitsliteratur," *Meissner Festschrift* (1928), I, 21 ff.

16. See Ebeling, in Gressmann, *op. cit.*, pp. 201–2.

17. See Meissner, *op. cit.*, p. 430; Th. Noeldeke, *Untersuchungen zum Ahiqar-Roman* (Berlin, 1913); A. E. Cowley, *Aramaic Papyri of the Fifth Century B.C.E.* (Oxford, 1923). The Aramaic text found in Elephantine has been translated by H. L. Ginsberg in *ANET*, pp. 427–30.

18. It is older than the new Assyrian and the new Babylonian copies in which the poem has reached us; cf. Fichtner, *op. cit.*, p. 6; Ebeling, *op. cit.*, p. 273. For the translation of the text see *ANET*, pp. 434 ff. A detailed and balanced discussion is to be found in E. F. Sutcliffe's excellent study, *Providence and Suffering in the Old and New Testaments* (London, 1953), pp. 27 ff. See also DG, I, xxxi–xxxii.

19. Lambert, *op. cit.*, p. 27.

20. For a translation of the text, see *ANET*, p. 437–38. For important and differing discussions of the meaning of the text, cf. Sutcliffe, *op. cit.*, pp. 34–38; Lambert, *op. cit.*, pp. 139 ff. Cf. also DG, I, xxiii, n. 2. On its alleged affinities with Eccles., see *KMW*, p. 348, n. 22, and references there.

21. So argue Stamm, Zimmern, Meissner, Gray, Speiser. Cf. Sutcliffe, *op. cit.*, pp. 37–38.

22. Cf. Lambert, *op. cit.*, p. 139.

23. Sutcliffe, *op. cit.*, pp. 36–38.

24. Lambert, *op. cit.*, p. 141.

25. For the text see *ANET*, pp. 438–40; Ebeling, *op. cit.*, pp. 287 ff. Cf. Sutcliffe, *op. cit.*, pp. 30–33; Lambert, *op. cit.*, pp. 15 ff.; and the basic study of P. Dhorme, "Ecclésiastes ou Job?" in *RB*, XXXII (1923), 1–23.

26. See Lambert, *op. cit.*, pp. 16–17.

27. On the plethora of interpretations of this difficult verse, see the Comm.

28. C. H. Gordon, *Ugaritic Handbook* (Rome, 1947), p. 138. In *ANET*, p.

140, the tenses are rendered differently by H. L. Ginsberg: "So I knew that alive was Puissant Baal! Existent the Prince, Lord of Earth."

29. Cf. Gordon, *op. cit.*, p. 138; C. Virolleaud in *Syria*, XII (1931), 212–13; *ANET*, p. 140. See S. L. Terrien in *Interpreter's Bible*, III, 1053, for an effort to find in the Job passage an echo of a revived (or reviving) God.

30. See Pfeiffer in *ANET*, p. 436. The lines occur at the end of Tablet II, reverse (ll. 54–55).

31. Lambert, *op. cit.*, p. 15.

32. *Gilgamesh Epic*, Tablet XI, l. 14 and ll. 32–48, in *ANET*, p. 73.

33. L. Ginzberg, *Legends of the Jews* (Philadelphia, 1909–38), I, 153 ff.; V, 174 ff., nn. 19, 20.

34. E. A. Wallis Budge, ed., *The Book of the Dead* (New York, 1956). A section of chapter 125 of the text is available in translation in *ANET*, p. 34–35.

VI: THE TALE OF JOB

1. B. *Baba Bathra* 15a: *Yethībh hahū° miderabbānan kammei derabh Šemu°el bar Nahmani veyethībh vek°amar Iyyōbh lō° hāyā velō° nibhrā °ella° māšāl hāyāh.*

2. In a post-talmudic responsum by R. Hai Gaon; cf. L. Ginzberg, *Legends of the Jews* (Philadelphia, 1909–38), V, 381, n. 3: *Iyyōbh lō° hāyāh velō° nibhra° °ellā° lemāšāl.*

3. For the moving legend that describes Job's role as an adviser of Pharaoh, see chap. xvi.

4. For a summary of the Haggadic material on Job, see A. Wjernikowski, *Das Buch Hiob nach der rabbinischen Agada* (Frankfurt, 1893). Briefer surveys are available in *JE*, VII, 193b–195a; Michael Guttmann, *Mafteah HaTalmud* (Budapest, 1917), II, 315–23; L. Ginzberg, *op. cit.*, II, 223–42; V, 381–90.

5. *Midrash Gen. Rabbah*, sec. 57: *Mai lō° hāyāh velō° nibhrā°? Bayyesūrīm °šenikhtebhū °ālāv. Velāmāh nikhtebhū °ālāv še°illū bā°ū °ālāv hāyāh yākhōl la°amōd bāhen.* ("What is the meaning of the statement 'Job never existed'?—In the calamities described as befalling him. Why then were they narrated? To indicate that had they befallen him, he would have been able to bear up under them.")

6. Cf. Jud. 6:3, 33; 7:12; 8:10.

7. *ANET*, pp. 18–22.

8. Cf. Gen. 10:23, where Uz is given as a brother of Aram.

9. In Jer. 25:23, Buz is referred to as an Arab tribe. In Gen. 22:31, Buz is described as a brother of Uz.

10. Josephus *Antiquities* I. 145, refers to Uz as a city near Damascus.

11. In Gen. chap. 36, especially vss. 4, 11.

12. Lam. 4:21.

13. The names may mean "God is fine gold" (so BDB). That it means "God crushes," as Terrien thinks (*Job: Poet of Existence* [New York, 1957], p. 69), is unlikely in the absence of the alleged root in Hebrew.

14. Gen. 29:29 a. e.; 36:27; Num. 22:5; I Chron. 1:42.

15. Num. 22:2.

16. I Kings 14:21.

17. So notably Pfeiffer, *IOT*, pp. 680–81. For a full discussion, see chapter xv.

18. Cf. Gen. 25:2 = I Chron. 1:32. The identification with the place name Suhu, on the Euphrates, was withdrawn by Delitzsch, who originally proposed it. Cf. DG, I, xxviii, and the Lexicons.

19. Gen. 22:21–22.

20. Cf. *Yebhārekhyāhu* (Isa. 8:2). The more common apocopated form, *Berekhiāh*, occurs for no less than six different characters, including the father of the prophet Zechariah (Zech. 1:1), the son of Zerubbabel (I Chron. 3:20), the father of Asaph (I Chron. 6:24; 15:17), and one of Nehemiah's chiefs (Neh. 3:4, 20; 6:18). The name has its Babylonian parallel in *Bariki-ili* (cf. J. Oppert, in *Journal Asiatique* [1887], 536–37).

21. See chapter ix.

22. J. A. Knudtzon, *Die El-Amarna-Tafeln* (Leipzig, 1915); W. F. Albright in *BASOR*, No. 83, p. 36; No. 89, p. 11.

23. Cf. *yillōd*, "born" (Exod. 1:22; II Sam. 5:14; 12:14 a. e.), and *šikkōr*, "drunken" (I Sam. 25:36, and often), which are passive in meaning, rather than *gibbōr*, "brave, strong," lit. "one who magnifies himself" (BDB). Another striking instance of folk etymology is afforded by the name of Moses, which is authentically Egyptian (*MESU* = "son, child"); cf. *Rameses* "son of Ra," *Tutmose*, "son of Tut." In the case of Moses, the theophoric element has been dropped as is frequent in biblical names. The theme of "the one drawing forth, the savior," is suggested by giving the name the form of an active participle. The interpretation in Exod. 2:10, "for from the water have I drawn him forth," represents a second folk etymology. If the name bore this meaning it would need to be revocalized as a participle passive *māšūi*, "the one drawn forth."

24. E. G. Kraeling, *The Book of the Ways of God* (New York, 1938), p. 15.

25. Ezek. 14:14, 16.

26. The first edition was published by Charles Virolleaud, *La Légende phénicienne de Danel* (Paris, 1936). The text is conveniently accessible in the translation of H. L. Ginsberg in *ANET*, pp. 149–50. For the bibliography, see S. Spiegel, "Noah, Daniel and Job," in *Louis Ginzberg Jubilee Volumes* (New York, 1945), English Section, pp. 310–11, n. 1; and Ginsberg, *ANET*, p. 149b.

27. It is noteworthy that the MT in Ezekiel spells the name *defectiva*, without a *yod*, *Dnʾel*, exactly as in the *Aqhat* epic, and not *plene*, *Dnyʾl*, as in the biblical book of Daniel. The variation in spelling was acutely noted by David Kimhi in his Commentary, *ad loc.*

28. See, e.g., H. H. Rowley, *The Faith of Israel* (London, 1956), p. 80, and the detailed bibliography there cited for the Persian influence on later Jewish

thought; see also, K. Kohler's *Jewish Theology* (Cincinnati, 1917), pp. 86, 189–95, which is still a very useful conspectus.

29. Cf. II Sam. 24:1 and I Chron. 21:1.

30. The prologue consists of chapters 1 and 2; the epilogue is to be found in 42:7–17. However, the passages 2:11–13 and 42:7–10 do not belong to this original stage of the tale but were added by the poet himself. See the text for details.

31. Cf. Job 19:13–19; 30:1.

32. *ʾElōhīm*, which is employed in the Pentateuch whenever a Gentile is involved (cf., e.g., Gen. 20:6 ff.), occurs in Job 1:1, 5, 8, 9, 22; 2:9, 10, in reference to Job, who is a non-Jew. When, however, the narrative mentions God independently, JHVH is used (1:7, 8, 9, 12; in the classic utterance 1:21; and in 2:1, 3, 4, 6, 7). *Bᵉnai ʾelōhīm* (1:6; 2:1) is a standard phrase (cf. Gen. 6:2) for "divine beings, angels," lit. "individual members of the *genus ʾelōhīm*, divinity, the numinous." Cf. *bᵉnai bāqār*, "members of the class 'cattle' "; *bᵉnai ʾādām*, "members of the class 'mankind.' " *ʾEš haʾelohim* (1:16) is a characteristic use of the divine name in a superlative, hence, "a mighty fire."

33. There are two exceptions, already noted above. In 12:9, JHVH appears in what is obviously a conventional phrase recalled by the poet from prophetic literature (Isa. 41:20). In 28:28, *Adonai*, "The Lord," occurs also in a stock phrase, *Yirat Adonai*, "the fear of the Lord." JHVH is used also in the superscriptions 38:1; 40:1, 3, 6. Here the appearance of the Lord "out of the whirlwind" is obviously based on the traditional theophany which associates the God of Israel with the storm, notably at Sinai (Exod. 20:16; Deut. 33:2e), but on other occasions as well (cf. e.g., Jud. 5:4–5; II Sam. 22:7–13; Nah. 1:3; Hab. 3:3–8).

34. On the linguistic character of the book and its bearing upon the date, see chapter xii and xv.

35. On the entire problem, see G. Fohrer in *VT*, VI (1956), pp. 24a ff.; Pfeiffer, *IOT*, pp. 668–69; Rowley, *op. cit.*, pp. 177–78.

36. So A. Schultens, *Liber Jobi* (1737), Preface, I, 34; G. Studer, *Jahrbücher für protestantische Theologie* (1875), I, 706 ff.; K. Kautzsch, *Das sogenannte Volksbuch von Hiob* (1900), pp. 69, 88; Pfeiffer, *IOT*, p. 669; B. D. Eerdmans, *Studies in Job* (1939), p. 5.

37. For this contention, W. B. Stevenson, *The Poem of Job* (London, 1947), pp. 21 ff.; J. Pedersen, *Israel* (London and Copenhagen, 1926), II, 531.

38. A. Alt in *ZATW*, N.F., XIV (1937), 265–68. While I believe Alt's view to be untenable, it is his merit to have underscored the fact that 42:7–10 is entirely distinct from 42:11–17. See the text for comment on the significance of this fact.

39. The term used here effectively disproves the view (of Alt, Duhm, and MacDonald; also accepted by E. Kraeling, *The Book of the Ways of God* [New York, 1938], p. 169) that the prose is a folk tale in which originally the Friends

urged Job to blaspheme his Maker—hence the Lord's castigation of them as "not speaking what is right" (42:7, 8). The word *nekhōnāh*, "right, correct, true" (Gen. 41:30; Ps. 51:12; 57:8; 78:37; 108:2; and esp. Deut. 13:15; 17:14), is a synonym of *ʾemet*, "true." It could be used in the negative to describe an unsatisfactory defense of God but is much too weak for blasphemy; for that the word is *nebhālāh*, "disgrace, contumely" (Gen. 34:7; Deut. 22:21), the root of which is used of the denial of God in the Book of Job itself (2:9), and elsewhere (e.g., Ps. 14:1 = 53:1; 74:22).

40. So J. Wellhausen, *Jahrbücher für deutsche Theologie* (1871), XVI, 555; K. Budde, *Das Buch Hiob*; T. K. Cheyne, *Job and Solomon* (1889), pp. 66–67, and in *EB* (1901), II, 2467–68; D. B. Macdonald in *JBL*, XIV (1895), 63 ff., and in *AJSL*, XIV (1897–98), 137 ff.; F. Delitzsch, *Das Buch Iob* (1902), p. 13; B. Duhm, *Das Buch Hiob erklaert*, pp. vii–viii; C. Siegfried, in *JE*, VII, 195; W. O. E. Oesterley and T. H. Robinson, *An Introduction to the Books of the O.T.* (New York, 1949), p. 173; A. Lods, *La Bible du Centenaire* (1947), III, xi, and *Histoire de la Littérature hébraïque et juive* (1950), pp. 671 ff.; A. M. Dubarle, *Les Sages d'Israël* (Paris, 1946), p. 67.

41. So Gray, in DG, p. xxxviii; P. Dhorme, *Le Livre de Job* (Paris, 1926), p. lxvii; H. Ranston, *The O.T. Wisdom Books and Their Teachings* (London, 1930), pp. 114, 172; J. E. McFadyen, *Introduction to the O.T.* (1909), p. 314; G. Hölscher, *Das Buch Hiob* (Tübingen, 1937), p. 4; H. Wheeler Robinson, *The O.T.: Its Making and Meaning* (Nashville, 1937), pp. 153–54; F. James, *Personalities of the O.T.* (New York and London, 1946), p. 194; and A. Bentzen, *Introduction to the O.T.* (2d ed.; Copenhagen, 1952), II, 175.

42. Thus, in the narrative of the prophet Balaam (Num. chaps. 22–24), he is granted permission by God before he leaves home (22:20) to answer the call of Balak. On his way, however, his life is threatened by an invisible angel with a sword (22:31). His life is saved by the prescience of his ass, and only after the angel is revealed to him is he granted permission to proceed. It is clear that two variant traditions (differing over when the divine permission was granted) have been placed in succession here.

In the Book of Samuel, David comes to the attention of King Saul and is brought to court because of his skill with the harp, which relieves Saul's melancholy (I Sam. 16:22). In the very next chapter, however, after David slays Goliath, neither the king nor Abner, his general, recognizes the lad (I Sam. 17:55 ff.), and only thereafter is David taken to the royal court. In the Arab chronicle *Kitab Alᶜaghan*, in the life story of a poet named Kais, the author informs us that because Kais contracted a marriage opposed by his parents he never saw them again. The very next line reads, "When Kais visited his parents."

43. On this last point, see n. 39 above.

44. Alfred Tennyson, *In Memoriam*, st. xcvi.

45. On this significant passage, which has been widely misunderstood and

hence subjected to needless and useless emendation, see Gordis, "Corporate Responsibility in Job: A Note on 22:28–30," in *JNES*, IV (1945), 54–55.

46. One recalls the discomfiture of Haman after he advises Ahasuerus on how to honor a deserving and loyal subject and finds that he must shower these dignities upon his arch-enemy, Mordecai (Esther, chap. 6).

47. Cf. Job 42:12–13 and the Comm., *ad loc.*

48. On the meaning of *šibhᶜānāh bānim* (42:13), see the Comm.

VII: JOB AND HIS FRIENDS:
THE FIRST TWO ROUNDS

1. *The Art of Reading* (Cambridge, 1920), Lecture X, pp. 172–95.

2. See his *The Cross in the O.T.* (London, 1955), pp. 39–40.

3. Job 4:12–21.

4. This is clear from the greater length and eloquence of the Job speeches. Thus in the first two cycles Job's speeches consist of twelve chapters, while the words of the Friends occupy only seven. In the third cycle the disproportion is even greater. In MT, Eliphaz and Bildad speak only 34 verses between them, and Zophar is entirely silent, while Job's words occupy 199 verses. This cycle, however, sustained grave dislocations (see chap. viii). Even when we set the material in order as well as we are able, Job's speeches are far more extensive than those of his opponents. Equally significant evidence of the author's sympathy with Job's position is the divine judgment on the Friends in Job 42:8. On this verse, which is part of one of the "jointures" (12:11–13; 42:7–10) written by the poet to connect the prose tale with the poetic dialogue, see chapter vi.

5. See the translation and the Comm. for the text and exegesis of 9:35.

6. Cf. *šᵉal, vᵉthōrekhā, lekā, sī᾽ ah* ("Ask thou, will teach thee, to thee, speak thou") in vss. 7, 8.

7. The distinction is clearly recognized by DG, I, 84–85.

8. See "SBWL," pp. 113–14, for a full discussion. Unfortunately, J. W. Gaspar, *Social Ideas in the Wisdom Literature of the Old Testament* (Washington, 1947), fails completely to reckon with this and other indications of a specific social milieu and orientation in Wisdom literature.

9. On the details of exegesis, notably my new interpretations of vss. 4, 6, 18, see the Comm. The total view of the passage is not affected by these details.

10. On the use of the Tetragrammaton in this citation from Isa. 41:20, see the Comm.

11. Job thus rejects both forms of immortality symbolized by the two trees in the Garden of Eden: the personal deathlessness conferred by the fruit of the Tree of Life, and the vicarious immortality of children which comes to man through sexual experience, the fruit of the Tree of Knowledge. On the meaning of the Paradise narrative in Genesis (chap. 3), see R. Gordis, "The Signifi-

cause of the Paradise Myth," *AJSL*, LII (1936), 86–94, and the evidence, newly supplemented from the Dead Sea Scrolls, in Gordis, "The Knowledge of Good and Evil in the O.T. and the Qumran Scrolls," *JBL*, LXXVI (1957), 123–38.

12. Thus Schlottmann's insistence that Job's speeches in the first cycle express Promethean defiance, and in the second, glorious hope, is an instance of *eisegesis*, "reading into the text," rather than *exegesis*, "reading out of the text."

13. The various studies of Kemper Fullerton, as well as the brilliant commentary by N. H. Tur-Sinai, suffer from this common methodological error.

14. I find purely arbitrary Baumgärtel's view, adopted by E. G. Kraeling (*The Book of the Ways of God* [New York, 1938], p. 198), that only the passages in which God is addressed in the second person are genuine, and that all references to Him in the third person are to be deleted as interpolations designed to soften the impact of Job's attack.

15. Cf., e.g., the Pentateuchal regulations in regard to murder (Num. 35:9 ff.; Deut. 19:6 ff.) or the role of the *gōʾēl* in commercial affairs (Lev. 25:25 ff.) and marital situations (Ruth 3:9, 12; 4:1 ff.).

16. This view has been advocated by S. L. Terrien in his "Commentary on Job" in *The Interpreter's Bible* (New York–Nashville, 1954), III, 1051–52, and in his *Job: Poet of Existence* (New York, 1957), p. 140. For a detailed criticism of his views and a presentation of the grounds for my position, see the Comm.

17. Cf. 9:4 ff.; 9:17 ff.; 10:16 ff.

18. Cf. 7:31; 10:9 ff.; 13:16; 14:13.

19. See his *Keter Malkhut*, "The Royal Crown," sec. 38, ll. 562–66 in *Selected Religious Poems of Solomon ibn Gabirol*, ed. Israel Davidson, trans. Israel Zangwill (Philadelphia, 1944), p. 118.

20. The manifold difficulties of this passage have produced a plethora of interpretations and emendations. For the earlier history of the interpretation of these verses, see J. Speer, *ZATW*, XXV (1905), 47 ff. An extensive selection of recent translations may be found in H. H. Rowley, "The Book of Job and its Meaning," *Bulletin of the John Rylands Library*, XLI (1958), p. 203, n. 5. By and large, the idea that Job is here referring to the afterlife is finding less and less favor among commentators. See, e.g., the Catholic scholar, E. F. Sutcliffe, in his excellent study *Providence and Suffering in the Old and New Testaments* (London, 1953), p. 117, n. 1., and see my Comm., *ad loc*. Against the enigmatic character of this passage is Job's clear rejection of this hope in 14:7 ff.

21. See the brief but illuminating summary of Rabbi Kuk's religious philosophy in J. B. Agus, *Guideposts of Modern Judaism* (New York, 1954), pp. 53–54.

22. This was acutely noted by J. A. Mason. On the relation between faith and ethics, see Gordis, *A Faith for Moderns* (New York, 1960), esp. chapter xiii.

23. On this rendering, which accepts the variant *veyištabbeḥū* for *veyiš-*

takkeḥū (the former supported by the Septuagint and some rabbinic sources), see Kittel, *Biblia Hebraica*, and *KMW, ad loc.*

24. Verse 22 may be rendered differently, as follows:
"Shall any one teach God knowledge,
And shall he judge the All High?"

(I.e., "Can any human being presume either to instruct or to judge God?") This rendering has the advantage of giving a better parallelism to the verse. For *rāmīm* as an epithet of God, compare the biblical and Canaanite use of *ᶜelyōn* (Num. 24:16; Deut. 32:8; II Sam. 22:14; Isa. 14:14; Lam. 3:35, 38; frequently in the Ps. 91:1, 9; 92:2, and often). Cf. also the very common title *gabhōᵓah*, "The All-High," in rabbinic literature—probably a development from the usage in Ps. 138:6. Note also the use of *rām vᵉnissāᵓ* in Isa. 57:15. The plural of *rāmīm* would be analogous to similar epithets for God, like *kᵉdōšīm*, (cf. Ehrlich on Hos. 12:1; Prov. 9:10). This latter usage we find also in Job 5:1, which is to be rendered:
Call out; is there one to answer thee?
And to whom rather than to God can you call?
See my Comm., *ad loc.*

VIII: THE END OF THE DEBATE:

THE THIRD CYCLE

1. Cf. such biblical passages as Isa. 29:15–16; Ezek. 8:12; 9:9; Mal. 3:14 ff.; Ps. 10:4, 11; 11:3; 14:1; 64:6, 10; 94:1–11; and see Sutcliffe, *Providence and Suffering in the Old and New Testaments* (London, 1953), pp. 82 ff.

2. B. *Moed Katan* 16b.

3. *Talmud Babli, Suk.* 45b: "The world cannot do with less than thirty-six saints who greet the Divine Presence daily." This legend, in variant form, is the basis of the deeply moving novel by André Schwarz-Bart, *The Last of the Just*, which deals with the Nazi holocaust.

4. See the writer's "Corporate Personality in *Job*: A Note on 22:29–30," in *JNES*, IV (1945), 54–55, for references and for the basis of my translation of the passage, which has been drastically and unnecessarily emended by scholars. See also Sutcliffe, *op. cit.*, chap. iv, "Corporate Responsibility," and the bibliography cited there.

5. Reading (with many moderns) *beḥeiqi*, by a slight change of one consonant, "in my bosom," instead of MT *meḥuqqi*, which can only be rendered "more than my allotted food."

6. After the introductory verse come the descriptions of the evildoer's actions (vss. 2–4), the suffering of the poor (vss. 5–8), the sinners (vs. 9), the poor (vss. 10–12), and the malefactors again (vss. 13–16). The succeeding sections seem to describe the destruction of the wicked (vss. 18–25).
It is possible that the bulk of the chapter is an independent poem, perhaps

a dialogue like that of the Babylonian *Pessimistic Dialogue of a Master and a Slave.* It is the last section (vss. 18–24) which offers the major difficulty, since it is not merely irrelevant but actually contradictory to Job's position. Some commentators (e.g., Terrien) have therefore suggested that this section is a part of Zophar's third speech. As will be indicated below, Zophar does not appear at present in the badly dislocated third cycle. It is clear, however, that a fragment of his address has survived in 27:13–23. This solution to the difficulties is based on the assumption that Zophar's speech was divided into several widely separated sections, one of which was placed here, before Bildad, who precedes Zophar everywhere else.

Another solution is to recognize in 24:18–24 a citation by Job of the contentions of the Friends that disaster ultimately overtakes the wicked (so also Tur-Sinai, RSV). This use of virtual quotation in argument and elsewhere, we have amply documented (see chapter xiii). Against this view Terrien raises the reasonable objection that the passage is not followed by any refutation by Job of this conventional doctrine.

On balance, I believe the assumption that Job is here quoting the Friends' position is preferable to the alternative of attributing the passage to Zophar. My reasons are these: (1) the style of 24:18–24 is of a piece with that of 24:1–17; (2) it is radically different from the style of 27:14–23 and cannot easily be articulated with it; (3) it is clear that the closing verse, 24:25, is appropriate in style and spirit to Job; and (4) in each section of the poetry, Job's speeches are characterized by this use of quotations of his opponents' views and his refutation of them (chaps. 12, 21, 41). See chapter xiii.

Terrien's objection to treating 24:18–24 as a quotation can therefore be met by the assumption that a few verses which originally contained Job's refutation of the Friends' position were lost, their original place being between 24:23 and 24:24. In further support of this assumption is the evidence that the third cycle sustained a loss of material in chapters 25–27, almost surely in Bildad's and Job's speeches (chaps. 25–27:12) and certainly in Zophar's speech (27:14 ff.).

7. See Isa. 27:1, where both serpents are used figuratively by the prophet, and cf. C. H. Gordon, *Ugaritic Manual* (Rome, 1955), Glossary Nos. 358, 379, 1439, for references to Ugaritic literature.

8. Nor is it satisfactory to assume that Job has now been "converted" to the position of the Friends (as Marshall argues), an assumption that is belied by all that follows and that transforms the God speeches and Job's final submission into the sorriest of anticlimaxes.

9. A convenient summary of no less than twelve such proposals is to be found in R. H. Pfeiffer, *IOT,* p. 671. Additional restorations are given by DG, I, 41, and H. H. Rowley, "The Book of Job and its Meaning," *Bulletin of the John Rylands Library,* XLI (1958), 188, n. 2. S. L. Terrien, *Job: Poet of Existence* (New York, 1957), p. 34, offers the following: Eliphaz (22:1–30),

Job (23:1–17; 24:25), Bildad (25:1–6; 26:5–14), Job (26:1–4; 27:1–12), Zophar (24:18–24; 27:13–23), Job (missing).

10. My reconstruction of Bildad agrees with that of Elzas; and of Zophar, with that of Graetz (cf. DG, I, 41).

11. On this rhetorical usage, see "QLU," and for this particular use, pp. 118 ff. See also chapter xii.

12. On this meaning of the verb *hithᶜanneg*, see the Comm.

13. On this meaning of *bᵉyad* (= *bᵉᶜad*), instead of "pro," see Gordis, "A Note on *Yad*," *JBL*, LXII (1943), 341–44, and references there, e.g. Ezek. 37:19.

14. See Terrien, *Job: Poet of Existence*, p. 186: "As has often been remarked, Job's oath of clearance reflects a standard of behavior which is unexcelled either in the Old Testament, the literature of the Ancient Near East and classical Greece, or in the New Testament, not excluding the Sermon on the Mount."

15. It has been assumed by most commentators that the entire chapter is to be interpreted as a series of oaths, and that each occurrence of the conjunction *ʾim* in the chapter must introduce the formula of the oath which is: "If I did thus and so . . . may this be my punishment." This schematic approach necessitates many deletions and transpositions of material. Cf. Yellin, Duhm, Hölscher, and Torczyner, among others. This procedure does not commend itself for several reasons: (1) it requires many extensive changes in the text; (2) the apodosis or conclusion of the alleged condition actually occurs only four or five times and is lacking ten times; (3) it is hardly likely that a long chapter containing 34 verses would follow the same unvarying formula throughout, in view of the great artistic gifts of the author.

A preferable view is to read the text without preconceptions. It then becomes clear that the conjunction *ʾim* is used here in three distinct ways, for which see chap. xiii, n. 47, and the translation in Part Two.

16. S. L. Terrien, *Job: Poet of Existence*, pp. 173–74.

17. This refrain may originally have stood also at the beginning of the poem.

18. See Pfeiffer, *op. cit.*, p. 672; Rowley, *op. cit.*, p. 191.

19. This view is shared by Dhorme, Chaine, Robert, Pfeiffer, Lods, Duesberg, and Rowley (doubtfully).

20. Calvin Thomas (ed.), *Faust* (Boston, 1894), Part I, Introduction; L. Lewisohn, *Goethe: The Story of a Man* (2 vols.; New York, 1949).

IX: ELIHU THE INTRUDER

1. Cf., e.g., Hebrew *zākēn*, Latin *senex* and *senator*, English *alderman*.

2. Thus the Mishnah (*Abot* 5:7) declares, "There are seven traits in a fool and seven in a wise man," and proceeds to list among them: "The wise speaks of the first matter first and of the latter afterwards." It then ignores this very

principle by describing the wise man first and the fool last. The reason for this violation of the logical order in ordinary discourse is inherent in human psychology: when the second element of two is mentioned, the association of ideas leads to an extended discussion of the last-named, after which the speaker returns to the first. This tendency is the basis for the rhetorical figure of chiasmus.

3. See Pfeiffer, *IOT*, p. 666, and the commentaries on this passage.

4. J. G. Eichhorn, *Einleitung in das Alte Testament* (3d ed.; Leipzig, 1803), III, 597–98; W. M. L. de Wette, *Introduction to the O.T.* (Boston, 1843), II, 558–59; P. Dhorme, *Le Livre de Job* (Paris, 1926), pp. lxxvii ff.; J. Goettsberger, *Einleitung in das Alte Testament* (Freiburg im Breisgau, 1928), p. 227; E. J. Kissane, *The Book of Job* (Dublin, 1939), p. xl; E. König, *Das Buch Hiob* (2d ed.; Gütersloh, 1929), pp. 466 ff.; N. H. Tur-Sinai, *The Book of Job* (Jerusalem, 1957), pp. xxxviii–xxxix; S. R. Driver, *Introduction to the Literature of the Old Testament* (9th ed.; New York, 1913), p. 429; Driver and Gray, *Commentary*, I, xl ff.; M. Buttenwieser, *The Book of Job* (New York, 1922); Oesterley and Robinson, *An Introduction to the Books of the Old Testament* (New York, 1949); and H. H. Rowley, "The Book of Job and its Meaning," *Bulletin of the John Rylands Library*, XLI (1958), pp. 173–74, who describes the authenticity of the Elihu chapters as "the first of the critical problems of the book."

5. So Helen Nichols, *AJSL*, XXVII (1910–11), 97 ff.; M. Jastrow, *The Book of Job* (Philadelphia, 1920), pp. 77 ff.; and W. A. Irwin, "The Elihu Speeches in the Criticism of the Book of Job," *JR*, XVII (1937), 37–47, all of whom assume several interpolators in the Elihu passages.

6. They include K. Budde, *Beiträge zur Kritik des Buches Hiob* (Göttingen, 1876), pp. 65 ff., and *Das Buch Hiob* (Göttingen, 1896), pp. xxiv ff.; and C. Cornill, *Introduction to the Canonical Books of the Old Testament*, trans. G. H. Box (New York, 1907), pp. 426 ff.; as well as other critics like Rosenmüller, Umbreit, Stickel, and Wildeboer. R. H. Pfeiffer, who originally maintained the authenticity of the Elihu chapters (*Le Problème du Livre de Job* [Geneva, 1915]), later changed his mind on the question (*ZATW*, N.F. [1926], p. 23–24); cf. his *Introduction to the Old Testament* (New York, 1941), pp. 673–74. Rowley ("The Book of Job and Its Meaning," p. 175) also cites W. S. Bruce, *The Wisdom Literature of the Old Testament* (London, 1904), pp. 22–23; H. M. Kallen, *The Book of Job as a Greek Tragedy Restored* (New York, 1918), pp. 31 ff.; L. Dennefeld, *Introduction à l'Ancien Testament* (Paris, 1934), p. 121, and *Revue Biblique*, XLVIII (1939), 163 ff.; P. Szcygiel, *Das Buch Job* (Bonn, 1931), pp. 24 ff.; B. D. Eerdmans, *Studies in Job* (Leiden, 1939), pp. 16–17; J. H. Kroeze, *Old Testament Studies* (1934), II, 156 ff.; A. M. Dubarle, *Les Sages d'Israël* (Paris, 1946), pp. 84 ff.; J. E. Steinmüller, *A Companion to Scripture Studies* (New York, 1944), II, 167; P. Humbert, *VT Supplements*, No. III (*Rowley Festschrift*, 1955), p. 150, as retaining the Elihu chapters. By and large, however, these scholars content themselves largely with the mere asser-

tion of the authenticity of chapters 32–37; a full re-examination of the problem is not undertaken.

7. See the trenchant observations of H. D. F. Kitto, *The Greeks* (Harmondsworth, 1951), p. 63: "This attribution (of the *Iliad* and the *Odyssey* to Homer) was accepted quite wholeheartedly until modern times, when closer investigation showed all sorts of discrepancies of fact, style and language both between the two epics and between various parts of each. The immediate result of this was the minute and confident division of the two poems, but especially of the *Iliad*, into separate layers of different periods, appropriately called 'strata' by critics who . . . imperfectly distinguished between artistic and geological composition. The study of the epic poetry of other races, and of the methods used by poets working in this traditional medium, has done a great deal to restore confidence in the substantial unity of each poem: that is to say, that what we have in each case is not a short poem by one original 'Homer' to which later poets have added more or less indiscriminately, but a poem conceived as a unity by a relatively later 'Homer' who worked over and incorporated much traditional material—though the present *Iliad* certainly contains some passages which were not parts of 'Homer's' design."

A similar change has taken place in the study of Dante's *Divine Comedy*. As Marc Slonim points out: "Critics in the 19th century saw the work as composed of dualisms. . . . The same critics either rejected Dante, the faithful son of the church, and extolled the great creator of images and characters—or the other way around. . . . Modern critics and scholars reject the theory of antinomies in the 'Commedia' and speak of its structural unity and harmonious proportions reflecting the perfect integration of its varied components." ("The Miracle of Dante," in the *New York Times Book Review*, Aug. 29, 1965, p. 6.)

8. See DG, I, xli–xliv, for a painstaking statistical summary of the stylistic differences. W. E. Staples, *The Speeches of Elihu* ("University of Toronto Studies, Philological Series," No. 8 [Toronto, 1924]), pp. 19 ff., and J. Herz, *Wissenschaftliche Zeitschrift der Karl Marx Universität* (Leipzig, 1953–54), III, 107 ff., find the Elihu speeches to be distinct from the dialogue on stylistic grounds.

9. Elihu uses *El* nineteen times, *Eloah* six times, *Shaddai* six times. In the rest of the book, *El* appears thirty-six times, *Eloah* thirty-five times, and *Shaddai* twenty-five times.

10. In the dialogue ᵓᵃnī occurs fifteen times, ᵓᵃnōkhī eleven times. In Elihu they occur respectively nine and twelve times. In the prose prologue, ᵓᵃnī occurs four times, ᵓᵃnōkhī not at all.

11. The prepositional forms with *yodh*, ᶜᵃlei (for ᶜal, "on"), ᶜᵃdei (for ᶜad, "toward"), ᵓᵉlei (for ᵓel, "to") occur only twice in Elihu, nineteen times in the poetic dialogue, thirty-five times elsewhere in the Old Testament.

12. Elihu does not use the enclitics *bᵉmō*, *kᵉmō*, *lᵉmō*, or such other poetic forms as *minnī*, *bᵉlī*, ᶜᵃlēmō. They occur eighteen times in the poetic dialogue.

13. DG, p. xlv. But *tāmīm* occurs in 12:4, which is dismissed unjustifiably as an addition to the text.

14. Thus the entire first stich in 36:2, *Kattar li zᵉᶜēr vaᵓaḥavvekā*, can, with a slight revocalization of the last word, be read as Aramaic! On the other hand, *zᵉᶜēr* occurs in Isaiah (28:10, 13), as does *mizᶜār* (10:25; 16:14; 24:6; 29:17). The verb *ḥāwāh* occurs in Ps. 19:8 and in Job 25:17, and the noun *ᵓaḥwāh* in Job 13:17. The verb *kathār* in the Aramaic-Syriac nuance of "wait, hope for," does not occur elsewhere in biblical Hebrew, but the root is to be found in the *piel* and *hiphil* in the sense of "surround" (*piel*, Judg. 20:43; Ps. 22:13; *hiphil*, Hab. 1:4), which F. Brown, S. R. Driver, C. A. Briggs, *A Hebrew and English Lexicon of the Old Testament* (Oxford, 1907), regard as basic to the meaning "wait." The uses in Ps. 142:8 and Prov. 14:18 are also probably denominatives from *keter* ("crown").

It should be noted that the list of Aramaisms in Job cited by E. Kautzsch (*Die Aramäismen im alten Testament* [Halle, 1902], p. 101) was severely criticized by T. Noeldeke in his review in *ZDMG*, LVII (1907), 412–20. Cf. DG, I, xlvi–xlvii.

A reconsideration of so-called biblical Aramaisms is in order, not only because of new epigraphic material, but because of a basic methodological error, the failure to recognize the three categories of biblical Aramaisms (which, incidentally, cannot always be distinguished): (1) words originally part of the Northwest Semitic vocabulary which were therefore indigenously Hebrew, but rare, while they became common in Aramaic and therefore *appear* as Aramaisms, as, e.g., *ᵓātāh*, "come" (Deut. 33:2); (2) words probably borrowed from Aramaic during the period of the First Temple due to geographical proximity with Syria, as, e.g., *šāwāh*, *Piel*, "make, produce" (Hos. 10:1); *tōbh*, "increase" (Hos. 8:3; 10:1); *rāᶜāh*, "chase" (Hos. 12:2); and (3) words borrowed during the hegemony of Aramaic as the *lingua franca* of the Near East, where it became the spoken tongue of the Jews, as, e.g., *sālaq*, "rise, go up" (Ps. 139:8).

15. DG, p. xli: "They are superfluous because they add nothing substantial to what the friends have said except in so far as they anticipate what Yahveh is to say."

16. As maintained, e.g., by Rowley, "The Book of Job and its Meaning," p. 173.

17. Cf. my "QLU," pp. 211–18. In 12:4–13:3, at the end of the first cycle, Job parodies the position of the Friends and dismisses it as irrelevant. In 21:19–34, at the end of the second cycle, he cites and refutes four arguments advanced by the Friends. In Job 42:3a, 4, he quotes twice from the words of the Lord (38:2, 3b; 40:7b), with minor variations, as is generally the case with quotations.

18. Cf. Psalms 14 and 53 and note the minor variations throughout this dittograph, except for the two penultimate verses (14:5–6; 53:4–5), which had evidently become largely illegible in some manuscript and "restored" in

two radically different forms in our Masoretic Text. So too, Job, chapter 24, seems to have sustained more textual damage than the surrounding material.

19. The judgments cited in the text are to be found respectively in Driver, *op. cit.*, p. 429; M. Buttenwieser, *The Book of Job* (New York, 1922), p. 85; J. T. Marshall, *Job and His Comforters*, p. 6; and C. Cornill, *Introduction to the Canonical Books of the O.T.* (New York, 1907), p. 428.

20. See his *Das Buch Hiob* (Göttingen, 1896), p. xxxv: "Ausdrücklich gelehrt wird es (sc. das Läuterungsleiden) von Elihu *und von ihm allein*" (my italics).

21. Pfeiffer, *op. cit.*, p. 673.

22. See *KMW* for a detailed study of the critical problems of the book.

23. *Encyclopaedia Britannica* (14th ed.), X, 473b.

24. The contradictions between the details in the prologue and the dialogue have long been noted. See the discussion in chapter vi, n. 42.

25. Cf. *Midrash Tehillim* on Ps. 123:1 (ed. Buber), p. 255a; cf. also *Pesikta de Rab Kahana*, p. 102b.

26. The distinction was acutely noted by Budde, *op. cit.*, p. xxxvi.

27. On this meaning of *rāṣāh*, see R. Gordis, "Leshon Ha-Miqraᵓ Le-ᵓ Or Leshon Ḥakhamim" ("Biblical Hebrew in the Light of Rabbinic Hebrew"), in *Sefer Tur-Sinai* (Jerusalem, 5720 = 1960), pp. 163–64, where it is applied to several passages in the Psalms (49:14; 50:18; 62:5). The traditional rendering of *rāṣāh* in this passage obviously does not affect the meaning of the first stich.

28. We may note the greater length and eloquence of Job's speeches and his final vindication by God, who condemns the Friends (42:7–8). The passage which links the dialogue and the prose epilogue (42:7–10), like its earlier counterpart (2:11–13), was written by the poet to link the already existing prose tale, which served as his framework, and the poetic dialogue, which he composed. See chapter vi.

29. See the author's "All Men's Book—A New Introduction to Job," in *Menorah Journal*, XXXVII (1949), 329 ff.; "The Temptation of Job—Tradition vs. Experience in Religion," in *Judaism* IV (1955), 195–208, reprinted in R. M. MacIver, ed., *Great Moral Dilemmas* (New York, 1956); his later book, *A Faith For Moderns* (New York, 1960), chap. x, esp. pp. 168 ff.; and chapter xi of the present work.

30. On the far-flung use of "allusiveness" and analogy in Semitic literature, see chapter xiv of the present work.

31. It occurs as *Ba-rik-ili*; see *Babylonian Expedition of the University of Pennsylvania*, Series A, IX, 52.

32. Cf. Elihu (with aleph as final letter) (I Sam. 1:1; I Chron. 12:20) and Elihu (without the aleph) (I Chron. 26:7; 27:18). N. H. Tur-Sinai calls it "an artificial differentiation" (*The Book of Job* [Jerusalem, 1957], p. 456–57). His elaborate theory on the difference between Barakhel and Elihu is unconvincing.

33. On these roles of Elijah in post-biblical literature, see L. Ginzberg, *Legends of the Jews* (Philadelphia, 1909–38), IV, 193–235; VI, 316–42. The belief that Elijah could resolve all difficulties is embodied in the folk etymology of the talmudic term, *tēkū* ("let it stand"), popularly interpreted as *tishbi yetareṣ kushyoth va-ʾabaᶜyoth*, "Elijah the Tishbite will answer all difficulties and questions."

X: THE LORD OUT OF THE WHIRLWIND

1. The first speech consists of 38:1–40:2, with Job's reply in 40:3–6; the second of 40:6–41:26, with Job's reply in 42:1–6. On the view which would reject the second speech of the Lord, in whole or in part, as unauthentic, see the Comm. and this chapter.

2. For an appreciative insight into this significant section, see Kraeling, *The Book of the Ways of God* (New York, 1939), p. 158, and James Strahan, *The Book of Job* (Edinburgh, 1913), p. 332.

3. Cf. the Babylonian creation myths and the Ugaritic epics conveniently assembled in *ANET;* and see H. Frankfort, *The Intellectual Adventures of Ancient Man* (Chicago, 1941); T. H. Gaster, *Thespis* (New York, 1950); and S. H. Hooke, *Middle Eastern Mythology* (Harmondsworth, 1963).

4. We thus reject the view (cf. Graves, Patai) that the poet describes imaginary monsters, a view to which some scholars have been tempted by discoveries of ancient oriental literary documents and artistic works.

5. This is the view of Vernes, Studer, Hempel, Baumgärtel, Volz, Finkelstein, and Kraeling. See Pfeiffer, *IOT*, p. 674, n. 7.

6. Driver, *Introduction*, p. 427. See also Rowley, "The Book of Job and Its Meaning," *Bulletin of the John Rylands Library*, XLI (1958), p. 190.

7. So argue Bickell, Dillmann, Duhm, Cheyne, Hölscher, Kraeling, and apparently, Terrien.

8. On the Septuagint of Job, cf. especially H. B. Swete, *Introduction to the O.T. in Greek* (Cambridge, 1914), pp. 255 ff.; B. J. Roberts, *The O.T. Text and Versions* (Cardiff, 1951), p. 184; the standard commentaries, esp. DG, I, lxxi ff.; D. H. Gard, *The Exegetical Method of the Greek Translator of the Book of Job* (Philadelphia, 1952); and H. M. Orlinsky, "Studies in the Septuagint of the Book of Job," in *HUCA*, XXVIII (1957), 53–74; XXIX (1958), 229–71; XXX (1959), 153–67; XXXII (1961), 239–68; XXXIII (1962), 119–51.

9. Cf. Pfeiffer, *op. cit.*, pp. 673–75, and Rowley, *op. cit.*, p. 190, for the long catena of scholars (Ewald, Dillmann, Cheyne, Weber, and Eissfeldt, among others) who delete these passages in whole or in part and then rearrange the remainder. On the other hand, Dhorme, Lefevre (in Pirot's *Supplément au Dictionnaire de la Bible*, IV [1949], 1081), H. W. Hertzberg (in *Festschrift Alfred Bertholet* [1950], pp. 253 ff.), and A. Lods (in *Histoire de la Littérature hébraïque et juive* [1950], pp. 678–79) retain both speeches.

10. See Pfeiffer, Rowley, and Terrien, among others.

11. For an illuminating parallel, see the discussion above on the variation in rhetorical form to be found in Job's "Confession of Integrity" (chap. 31).

12. The first speech uses the question form consistently until the section on the ostrich, which is not interrogative. This passage leads directly to the section on the horse (39:18—"She [i.e., the ostrich] mocks the horse and his rider"), in which the question form is again used (39:19). The second speech begins by asking Job ironically to assume the throne of God. Then comes the Behemot section (40:15 ff.), which is not couched in interrogative form. It is followed by the section on the Leviathan (40:25 ff.), which is again in question form. Thus the pattern in both speeches is question-statement-question.

13. The "original" text would then have been: God—chaps. 30–39; 40:2, 7–14; Job—40:3–5; 42:2–5 (see Pfeiffer, *op. cit.*, p. 675).

14. See S. L. Terrien, *Interpreter's Bible*, p. 1184, whose insight into the two Joban responses is superb and altogether convincing.

15. Pfeiffer, *op. cit.*, p. 674.

16. Chaim Zhitlowsky, *Job and Faust*, trans. Percy Matenko.

17. Pfeiffer, *op. cit.*, p. 689.

18. Cf., e.g., 38:25–26; 39:1 ff., 5 ff., 13–16; 40:19.

19. K. Fullerton, "The Original Conclusion of Job," *ZATW*, XXIV (1924), 116–36.

20. E. M. Good, *Irony in the Old Testament* (Philadelphia, 1965). See chapter vii, pp. 196–240.

21. *Ibid.*, p. 239. The quoted passages are not cited in the order in which they appear in Good's book.

22. *Ibid.*, p. 240.

23. Undoubtedly, as is the case with every reader of Job, Good is predisposed to his view of the book by his own theological position on man's innate and ineluctable guilt. See Good's comment on Paul, on Augustine and the Pelagian heresy, and on Luther's and Calvin's struggles against indulgences (*ibid.*, p. 197).

24. Cf. 9:1–13; 12:7–25; and my Comm., *ad loc.*

25. See his *Einleitung in die kanonischen Bücher des Alten Testaments* (2d ed.; Freiburg, 1891), p. 232. In later editions, this language is considerably toned down.

26. Cf. S. L. Terrien, *op. cit.*, and in his *Job: Poet of Existence* (New York, 1957).

27. Zhitlowsky, *op. cit.*

28. Terrien, *Job: Poet of Existence*, p. 241.

29. Cf., e.g., Num. 14:16 ff.; Deut. 32:27; Ezek. 20:9, 14, 22. The same theme is expressed in a long misunderstood passage in Hosea (4:15), on which see Gordis, "Studies in the Relationship of Biblical and Rabbinic Hebrew," in *Louis Ginzberg Jubilee Volumes* (New York, 1945), English Section, pp. 195–98.

30. Cf. B. *Megillah* 29a: *Rabbi Šimeon bar Yohai ᵓōmēr "Bō ᵓurᵉēh kammāh ḥabhibhin yisrāᵓēl liphenei hakādōš bārūkh hūᵓ šebekhol mākōm šegālū šekhinah gālethāh ᶜimmāhem.*" "Rabbi Simeon bar Yohai said, 'Come and see how beloved Israel is of the Holy One, blessed be He. Wherever Israel went into exile, the Divine Presence was exiled with them.'" The Talmud bases this idea on a biblical text, Deut. 30:3, "The Lord thy God will restore you to your former estate," which it interprets, "The Lord thy God will return with your captivity," since the verb *šābh* (lit. "return") is normally intransitive.

Cf. also the Midrash *Mekhilta de Rabbi Ishmael, Shirata,* sec. 3, 11.67 ff. (ed. Lauterbach, Vol. II, p. 27): *Kešeyāredu yisrāᵓēl lemiṣrayīm šekhīnāh yāredāh ᶜimmāhem . . . ᶜĀlū, ᶜālethāh šekhīnāh ᶜimmāhem. Yāredū lāyam šekhīnāh ᶜimmāhem yāṣᵉᵓū lammidbār šekhīnāh ᶜimmāhem ᶜad šehebhiᵓūhū ᶜimmām lebhet mikdāšō.* "When Israel went down to Egypt, the Divine Presence was with them. . . . When they came forth, the Divine Presence was with them. . . . When they went down to the sea, the Divine Presence went down with them. . . . When they went out into the wilderness, the Divine Presence was with them, *until they brought Him with them to His holy Temple.*" Scriptural proof for this homily is derived by rabbinic exegesis from the biblical passages Gen. 46:4; Exod. 14:19; 13:21.

Cf. also the striking variant in *Midrash Echah Rabbati, Petihta: ᶜAd šelōᵓ nigᵓalū yisrāᵓel mimmiṣrayīm hāyū yōšebhīm biphenei ᶜaṣmām ūšekhīnāh biphenei ᶜaṣmāh vekhevān šenigᵓalū naᶜasū hōmōnoiā ᵓaḥat vekhevān šegālū ḥāzerāh šekhīnāh biphenei ᶜaṣmāh veyisrāᵓel biphenei ᶜaṣmān.* "Until the Israelites were redeemed from Egypt, they sat by themselves and the Divine Presence was by itself. When Israel was redeemed, they became one union [Greek, *homonoia*]. But when Israel went into exile, the Divine Presence again became separated from Israel."

31. This idea is expressed biblically by the root *naḥam,* the most common meaning of which, "to comfort," would be literally "to cause (the mourner) to change (his state of mind)." That God does not "change" or "repent" of His previous attitude is expressed by this root in Num. 23:19; I Sam. 15:29; Ps. 110:4. On the other hand, because of God's fellowship with man, He is at times described as "repenting" His previous kindness (Gen. 6:6–7; I Sam. 15:11, 35; Jer. 18:10), or more frequently, as "repenting" His wrath (Exod. 32:12, 14; Jer. 18:8; 26:3, 13, 19; 42:10; Amos 7:3, 6; Joel 2:13; Jonah 3:10; 4:2; Zech. 8:14–15; I Chron. 21:15).

This meaning should be distinguished from *nāḥam,* a metaplastic form for *rāḥam,* which carries the meaning of "pity" (Judg. 2:18; Isa. 57:6; Ezek. 24:14; Ps. 90:13; 106:45). The root also has a third meaning, "avenge," parallel to *naqam* (cf. Isa. 1:24).

32. *Major Trends in Jewish Mysticism* (Jerusalem, 1941), pp. 7–10.

33. Rowley, *op. cit.,* p. 201.

34. On the evidence for this usage and its significance, see chapter xii.

35. In his essay "The Lantern Bearers," *The Travels and Essays of Robert Louis Stevenson* (New York, 1897), XV, 247.

36. Havelock Ellis, *The Dance of Life* (New York, 1923), p. 333.

XI: JOB AND THE MYSTERY OF SUFFERING

1. B. *Berakhot* 7a: *rāšāᶜ vetōbh lōʾ, ṣaddik verāᶜ lōʾ.*

2. The literature on the problem of suffering in the Bible is limitless. It is treated in (1) all systematic presentations of theology, like Millar Burrows, *Outline of Biblical Theology* (Philadelphia, 1946); W. Eichrodt, *Theologie des A.T.*, trans. J. A. Baker (5th ed.; Philadelphia, 1961), Vol. I; L. Kohler, *Theologie des A.T.* (3d ed.; Tübingen, 1953); P. Heinisch, *Theology of the O.T.*, trans. William Heidt (Collegeville, Minn., 1950); H. H. Rowley, *The Faith of Israel* (London, 1956); (2) works dealing with specific aspects of the theme, as, e.g., C. R. North, *The Suffering Servant in Deutero-Isaiah* (London, 1948); H. H. Rowley, *The Servant of the Lord and Other Essays* (London, 1952); (3) histories of Hebrew religion, as, e.g., W. O. E. Oesterley and T. H. Robinson, *Hebrew Religion: Its Origin and Development* (New York, 1930); I. G. Matthews, *The Religious Pilgrimage of Israel* (New York, 1947); W. A. L. Emslie, *How Came Our Faith* (New York, 1949); Yehezkel Kaufmann, *Toledot Haʾemunah Hayisreʾelit* ("History of the Faith of Israel" [8 vols.; Tel Aviv, 1937–56]), of which an excellent one-volume English abridgment by Moshe Greenberg, *The Religion of Israel* (Chicago, 1960), has appeared; (4) special studies, as, e.g., A. S. Peake, *The Problem of Suffering in the O.T.* (London, 1904, 1947); H. Wheeler Robinson, *Suffering Human and Divine* (New York, 1939), and *Inspiration and Revelation in the O.T.* (Oxford, 1946); E. F. Sutcliffe, *Providence and Suffering in the Old and New Testaments* (London, 1953); J. A. Sanders, *Suffering as a Divine Discipline in the O.T. and Post-Biblical Judaism* (Rochester, N.Y., 1955); (5) all commentaries on Job (for which see the bibliography); and (6) modern discussions of the problem of suffering that seek to relate biblical teaching to contemporary life and thought, e.g., John Hadham, *Good God* (Harmondsworth, 1940), and *God in a Time of War* (Harmondsworth, 1946); C. S. Lewis, *The Problem of Pain* (London, 1940); C. G. Jung, *Answer to Job* (London, 1964); R. Gordis, *A Faith For Moderns* (New York, 1960). My earlier treatment of the problem in Job may be found in "The Temptation of Job—The Conflict of Tradition and Experience," published in *Judaism*, IV (1955), 195–208, and in R. M. MacIver (ed.), *Great Moral Dilemmas* (New York, 1956).

3. See his *Kuzari*, trans. H. Hirschfeld (London, 1905), and I. Heinemann (Philadelphia, 1960), Book One, par. 25.

4. Cf. Sutcliffe, *op. cit.*, pp. 52–71, for an excellent treatment of the subject and for the literature (cited on p. 70). For the texts, cf. J. Kohler and F. E. Peiser, *Hamurabis Gesetz* (Leipzig, 1904), I; G. R. Driver and J. C. Miles, *The Assyrian Laws* (Oxford, 1935); F. Hrozny, *Code Hittite* (Paris, 1922). Much of the relevant material is available in *ANET*, *passim*.

5. Cf. also secs. 116, 209, 210, of the Code of Hammurabi for additional instances of the doctrine of family solidarity superimposed on the principle of *lex talionis*.

6. Cf. A. Marmorstein, *The Doctrine of Merits in the Old Rabbinical Literature* (London, 1920). In the *Amidah*, note the constant invocation of the patriarchs, a theme reaching its climax in the High Holy Day liturgy.

7. Cf. chapter viii of this work, and see Gordis, "Corporate Personality in Job," *JNES*, IV (1945), 54–55.

8. Amos' radical shift of viewpoint with regard to both Israel and Judah after his expulsion from Beth-El is the key to an understanding of the structure and content of the book. When it is recognized, no radical excision or reordering of the text is required. For a full presentation of the problem and a solution, see Gordis, "The Composition and Structure of Amos," in *Harvard Theological Review*, XXXIII (1940), 239–51.

9. The term *šᵉʾār* ("remnant") seems to be a coinage of Isaiah (10:19, 20, 22; 11:11, 16; 14:22; 17:3; 21:17; 28:5). It is used by the prophet in naming his son *Shear-Yashub* (7:3), "A remnant shall return." Elsewhere it occurs only in Zeph. 1:4 and in post-Exilic sources (Mal. 2:15; Esther 9:12–16; Ezra 3:5; 4:3, 7; Neh. 10:29; 11:1, 20; I Chron. 11:8; 16:41; II Chron. 9:29; 24:14).

The synonymous term *šᵉʾᵉrīth* occurs in Gen. 45:7, but its conceptual sense does not appear until the prophets, Amos (5:15, cf. 1:8; 9:12), Isaiah (37:32 = II Kings 19:31), and the latter's younger contemporaries, Micah (2:12; 5:6, 7) and Zephaniah (2:9; 3:13). In Jeremiah, Ezekiel, Haggai, and Zechariah, it is a basic element of prophetic teaching.

10. The Hebrew *bᵉšalekhet* is a *hapax legomenon* (aside from the proper noun in I Chron. 26:16, where it is the name of a gate of Jerusalem). It is rendered by most moderns, "when it is felled." However, this view of the clause is not defensible either syntactically or semantically. The root *šalakh* means "throw, fling," and is not appropriate for "felling, cutting a tree," which is expressed in biblical Hebrew by several common roots, *ḥatabh, ḥaṣabh, gazar, kaṣaṣ*, etc. I prefer the rendering of the medieval commentators (Rashi, Kimhi, and Karo), "autumn, the season of the falling of the leaves."

11. In MT *bydm*, the Mem is the enclitic, amply attested in Ugaritic and biblical Hebrew; cf., e.g., Isa. 10:1b, which, as Ginsberg has acutely pointed out, should be read *umikhtebhei(m)* ᶜamal kittēbhu, "documents of evil do they indite." Also Hos. 14:3e, which should be read *unešallemāh perī(m) sephāthēnū*, "we shall render Thee the fruit of our lips" (Gordis, "The Text and Meaning of Hosea XIV 3," in *VT*, V [1955], 88–90).

12. Cf., e.g., Hab. 2:1–8.

13. Cf. the Essenic sectarian *Commentary on Habakkuk* and the two full MSS of Isaiah found in Qumran. For the vast literature on the Dead Sea Scrolls see C. Burchard, *Bibliographie zu den Handschriften vom Toten Meer* (Berlin, 1957), and such later lists as A. Dupont-Sommer, *The Essene Writings*

from Qumran (Oxford, 1961), pp. 416–17, and the bibliographically rich papers on the Dead Sea Scrolls by H. H. Rowley (*Bulletin of the John Rylands Library*, 1949, *et seq.*).

14. See *Siphre, Deuteronomy*, sec. 346 (ed. M. Friedmann [Vienna, 1864], p. 144); *Midrash Shoher Tobh, on Psalm 123* (ed. S. Buber [Vilna, 1891], p. 509). Both Midrashic passages derive the same theological doctrine of God's dependency on man from Ps. 123:1: "Were it not for me [says the Psalmist], You would not be sitting in heaven."

15. On the Servant of the Lord in Deutero-Isaiah, cf. R. Levy, *Deutero-Isaiah* (Oxford, 1925); C. R. North, *The Suffering Servant in Deutero-Isaiah* (Oxford, 1948); H. H. Rowley, *The Servant of the Lord and Other Essays* (London, 1952), and the rich bibliography there cited.

16. On "the Day of the Lord," cf. Amos 5:18 ff.; Isa. 2:18 ff.; Zeph. 1:14 ff.; Mal. 3:19 ff.

17. Cf. Hos. 2:20–25; 3:1–5; Amos 9:11–15; Isa. 2:1–4; 9:1–6; 11:1–16; 21:23–25; Mic. 4:1–5, 6–14; Ezek. 37:1–14, 15–28; Zeph. 3:9 ff.; Zech. 14:1–21, in which national and universal motifs are inextricably interwoven.

18. Cf. Isa. 9:1–6; 11:1–16; Jer. 23:5 ff.; Zech. 3:8; 6:12.

19. See O. S. Rankin, *Israel's Wisdom Literature* . . . (Edinburgh, 1936), chap. ii, for a comprehensive survey of the role of the individual in biblical religion and law before Jeremiah and Ezekiel.

20. On the upper-class social views in Psalm 37, see "SBWL," p. 95.

21. I. Abrahams, *Permanent Values in Judaism* (New York, 1923), pp. 14, 23.

22. On this rendering of ṣela⁶, "wife," see the Comm.

23. Cf. Ps. 17:15; Isa. 25:8; 26:19; Dan. 12:1–3, on which see J. A. Montgomery, *Daniel* ("ICC" [New York, 1923]), pp. 471–72. For the entire subject cf. P. Volz, *Jüdische Eschatologie* (Tübingen, 1903); R. H. Charles, *A Critical History of the Doctrine of a Future Life* (London, 1899); E. F. Sutcliffe, *The Old Testament and the Future Life* (London, 1946); and for a briefer treatment, H. H. Rowley, *The Faith of Israel* (London, 1956), chap. vi.

24. For the Pharisaic opposition to the Sadducean standpoint, cf. M. *Sanhedrin* 10:1, "He who maintains that the resurrection of the dead does not derive from the Torah has no share in the world to come." The rabbis offer a variety of ingenious but far-fetched interpretations of biblical verses in order to find support in Scripture for their tenaciously held belief in the resurrection of the dead.

25. For a fuller analysis of these factors, cf. "SBWL," pp. 103–5.

26. On the upper-class orientation of Wisdom, which serves to explain why Wisdom literature persisted in maintaining the old view of Sheol even after the new idea of the afterlife had won its way into the thought of most Jewish groups, cf. "SBWL," pp. 101–6.

27. Cf. Job 14:7–22, esp. 12, 14. That the famous passage 19:23–27 does not imply a faith in life after death is today recognized by virtually every competent scholar. Cf., e.g., the Catholic writer, E. F. Sutcliffe, *Providence and*

Suffering . . . , p. 117, n. 1, and *idem, The Old Testament and the Future Life,* pp. 131–37.

28. Cf. Eccles. 3:18 ff.; 9:1 ff.; and *KMW, ad loc.*

29. This rendering is based upon the assumption that we have here a *tikkun sopherim,* a euphemistic change in the closing stich, the original reading being *kī lō khēn hū᾽ ᶜimmādī.* Cf. Ehrlich and my Comm., *ad loc.*

30. This most famous crux in the book is, of course, discussed in all the commentaries at length. For a convenient summary of the exegesis, see DG, I, 170–74; II, 126–33; as well as S. L. Terrien in *Interpreter's Bible,* III, 1050–57, and in *Job: Commentaire de l'Ancien Testament* (Neuchâtel, 1963), pp. 149–55, who ably expounds a divergent approach which I regard as totally unacceptable.

31. Cf. M. *Sotah* 5:5, the text of which, in translation, is quoted in chapter xvi.

32. That divine reward and punishment serve as instruments for moral pedagogy is the theme of Maimonides' classic treatment of the biblical doctrine of retribution in his *Introduction to the Commentary on the Mishnah* (Introduction to Sanhedrin, chapter x). He cites the relevant texts from rabbinic sources on the theme of serving God without desire for reward, thus effectively combining Job's and Elihu's insights.

33. M. *Abot* 4:15: *Ein beyadeinu lo᾽ miyissurei haṣaddikim velo᾽ mišalvath harᵉšāᶜim.*

34. Job 10:22.

XII: THE LANGUAGE AND STYLE OF JOB

1. "The Hero as Prophet," *On Heroes, Hero Worship and the Heroic in History* (New York, 1905), pp. 69–70.

2. On biblical poetry, cf. G. B. Gray, *The Forms of Hebrew Poetry* (London, 1915); R. Gordis, *Al Mibneh Hasirah Haivrit Haqedumah* ("On the Structure of Ancient Hebrew Poetry") in *Sefer Hasanah Liyehudei Amerikah* (New York, 5705 = 1944), pp. 136–59; T. H. Robinson, *The Poetry of the O.T.* (London, 1947). The attempts of E. Sievers and others to establish a quantitative meter for biblical poetry have not thus far succeeded. Cf. W. H. Cobb, *A Criticism of Systems of Hebrew Metre* (Oxford, 1905). The problem of biblical metrics is complicated by a consideration all too often overlooked: biblical poetry was not recited, but chanted, and the musical value that was given to any word or phrase which affected its stress and length is totally lost to us today.

3. Cf. the list of *hapax legomena* in F. Delitzsch, *Das Buch Iob* (Leipzig, 1864), p. 125.

4. Job 4:10–11; 18:8–9.

5. *Ibid.,* 10:22, for example.

6. *Ibid.,* 9:9; 38:31 ff.

7. *Ibid.,* 28:1–2; 28:15 ff.

8. *Ibid.,* 40:15 ff.; 40:25 ff.

9. *Ibid.*, 9:2 ff.; 14:15.

10. *Ibid.*, 28:1–10.

11. *Ibid.*, 16:12 ff., for example.

12. The repetition of the same vocable occurs also in Job 8:3 (*ʿiwwēt*); 11:7 (*māṣāʾ*); 15:31 (*šāwʾ*); 17:15 (*tiqwāh*), as well as in Eccles. 3:16 (*rešaʿ*) and 4:1 (*mᵉnaḥem*).

13. The Septuagint, intended for non-Semitic readers to whom parallelism was alien and who might find the repetition monotonous, tends to substitute a Greek synonym for one or the other stich in these cases. On the basis of this practice, modern scholars have often, and uncritically, assumed an error in the Hebrew text and exhibited their ingenuity by proposing a Hebrew synonym to replace the repeated root.

14. There is no need to document this phenomenon. For an illustration, cf. Hebrew *pardes* and Greek *paradeisos* from the Persian *pairi-daeza;* Hebrew *ʾapiryon* (Song of Songs 3:9) from Sanskrit *paryanka*, on which see Gordis, *Songs of Songs*, *ad loc*. The list can be extended indefinitely. In modern languages, cf. French *redingote* (from English *riding-coat*) and *bifteck* (from English *beefsteak*), to say nothing of thousands of technological terms that are today international.

15. Cf. the standard commentaries *passim*, esp. Delitzsch, Dhorme, Tur-Sinai, and Yellin.

16. This idea was suggested by the medieval scholar Abraham ibn Ezra, who was struck by the Arabisms in the book (cf. his Commentary on 2:11). On the theory of an Arabic origin, see chapter xv. Carlyle, whose praise of the Book of Job we have quoted, is not alone in being able to combine reverence for the Bible with prejudice against the people that produced it. He says: "Biblical critics seem agreed that our own book of *Job* was written in that (i.e., Arab) region of the world. *One feels indeed as if it were not Hebrew;* such a noble universalism different from noble patriotism or sectarianism reigns in it" (my italics). Carlyle's approach, which can scarcely be regarded as objective, is, unfortunately, not lacking even in modern scholarship.

17. Cf. DG, I, xlvi ff., for a careful tabulation and analysis of the Aramaisms, real and alleged.

18. See John Bright, *A History of Israel* (Philadelphia, 1959), pp. 210–58.

19. Cf. the standard collection of these texts by E. Sachau, *Aramäische Papyrus und Ostraken* (Leipzig, 1911), and the supplementary collection by E. G. Kraeling, *The Brooklyn Museum Aramaic Papyri* (New Haven, 1953), as well as the smaller collection by A. Ungnad, *Aramäische Papyrus aus Elephantine* (Leipzig, 1911).

20. Cf. the second-century Book of Daniel, which entered the biblical canon, and the later so-called *A Genesis Apocryphon*, or "Midrash on Genesis," found at Qumran, published by Y. Yadin (Jerusalem, 1956). Some early sections of the Mishnah are also given in Aramaic.

The complex question of when Hebrew ceased to be a spoken language in

Palestine is unsolved today. For the view that Hebrew remained a living tongue throughout the mishnic period, and a conspectus of the evidence, see E. Ben Yehuda, *Thesaurus Linguae Hebraicae, Prolegomena* (Tel Aviv, 1948), pp. 80–254. It is certain that Hebrew continued to be spoken in certain "pockets" of population as late as the third century c.e.

21. See E. Kautzsch, *Die Aramäismen im A.T.* (Halle am Saale, 1902), which was significantly criticized by Th. Noeldeke in *ZDMG*, LVII (1907), 412–20.

22. As, e.g., ᵓathah, "come" (Deut. 33:2; Mic. 4:8; Jer. 3:22; often in Deutero-Isaiah and Job); the *Lamed accusative*, as, e.g., after ᵓāhabh (Lev. 19:18, 34; II Sam. 3:30) or hārag (II Sam. 3:30; see BDB, p. 512a); *mālal*, "speak" (Gen. 21:7).

23. As, e.g., rāᶜāh, "chase, desire," parallel to rādaph (Hos. 12:2).

24. Cf. such use as bar, "son" (Prov. 31:2).

25. Cf. such idioms as ᵓim ᶜal hammelekh tobh (Esther 7:3; cf. Ezra 5:17), as against the classical Hebrew phrase tōbh bᵉᶜeinei (I Sam. 29:6), and the use of *in* as the masc. plur. ending, as in Prov. 31:3; Job 4:2; 24:22; 31:10; Dan. 12:13. Yet even this indubitably Aramaic ending occurs in such earlier texts as Judg. 5:10; Mic. 3:12; I Kings 11:33; II Kings 11:13; Ezek. 4:9; 26:18.

26. A striking illustration, and a rare one, is afforded by Ps. 139, where the opening verses contain at least four Aramaisms: lereᶜiy (vs. 2), ribhᶜiy (vs. 3), millāh (vs. 4), and ᵓessaq (vs. 8).

27. Cf. the verb hawah (15:17; 32:6, 10, 17; 36:2) and the noun ᵓahwāh (13:19), a root occurring in only one other passage outside Job (Ps. 19:2); the *in* masc. plur. ending as, e.g., hayyin (24:23), millin (4:2, and elsewhere). In 36:2a, we have an entire stich which is Aramaic in vocabulary: *Kathar li zᵉᶜer vaᵓahawwekkā.*

On the higher concentration of Aramaisms in the Elihu chapters (32–37), see chapter ix. On the bearing of the Aramaisms on the date of Job, see chapter xv.

28. On the need to recognize these two aspects of comparative philology, see Gordis, "Studies in the Relationship of Biblical and Rabbinic Hebrew," in *Louis Ginzberg Jubilee Volumes* (New York, 1945), English Section, pp. 173–75 *et seq.* This paper presents a substantial number of instances in which post-biblical Hebrew sheds welcome light on biblical usages. Additional examples are adduced in Gordis, "Lesōn Hamiqrā Leᵓōr Lešōn Hakhamīm," in *Sefer Tur-Sinai* (Jerusalem, 5720 = 1960), pp. 149–68.

29. Cf., e.g., hiqšāh in Job 9:4, on which see the Comm.

30. Cf. chapter xv.

31. For some of the often overlooked implications of the stylistic differences between prose and poetry and their bearing on the evaluation of different literary genres, cf. Gordis, "Qoheleth and Qumran—A Study in Style," *Biblica*, XLI (1960), 395–410, esp. 402 ff.

32. The one exception is the root *kibbel* (2:10) which occurs only in late biblical texts (Esther 4:4; 9:21, 23; Ezra 8:30; I Chron. 12:18; 21:11; II Chron. 29:16, 22; Prov. 19:20 cannot be dated with any assurance, but may be late), and frequently in the Mishnah. Though W. F. Albright believes he has discovered the root in a Canaanite gloss in the Tel-el-Amarna Letters of the fourteenth century B.C.E. (cf. *BASOR*, No. 89 [1943], 29 ff.), the exclusively late usage of the verb makes it a late word in Hebrew.

The use of *bērēkh*, "bless," as a euphemism (1:5, 11; 2:5, 9) occurs elsewhere only in I Kings 21:10, 13, and Ps. 10:3. It is likely that these are both late sources. Kings was obviously completed in the Exilic period and the acrostic form of the psalm suggests a late date (cf. R. Gordis, "Psalm 9–10: A Textual and Exegetical Study," in *JQR*, XLVIII (1957), 104–22.

33. Pfeiffer, *IOT*, p. 687.

34. Thus the "Song of the Sea" (Exod. chap. 15) is written basically in a 4:4 rhythm. However, it exhibits the following meter-patterns: 4:4 (vs. 1); 3:3 (vs. 2); 3:2 (vs. 3); 5:5 (vs. 4); 4:4 (vs. 5, giving *tehōmot* and *yᵉkhasyūmū* each two beats, and vss. 6–18). In the latter half of the song, monotony is avoided by varying the number of stichs per verse. Thus we have distichs (vss. 5, 6, 7, 10, 11, 13, 14, and 16, which contains a pair of distichs), tristichs (vss. 8, 9), as well as monostichs (vss. 12, 18).

The "Song of Deborah" (Judg. chap. 5) is basically in 3:3 meter but exhibits similar variations in meter and stichometry, as is the case with Isa. chap. 1. With regard to the "Allegory of Old Age" in Eccles., see *KMW*, p. 323, for a discussion of its varied meter.

On the use of variations in meter and stichometry, cf. "MHHH," pp. 142 ff. On variations in the accent of longer words or thought-units, cf. *op. cit.*, pp. 140–41.

35. Cf. C. H. Gordon, *Ugaritic Manual* (Rome, 1955), pp. 108–9, especially p. 108, n. 1: "Structurally different verses and strophes occur constantly within the same poem in Ugaritic. It is therefore unsound to attribute similar variety in the Bible to the blending of different poems. . . . All that is asked of those who maintain metric hypotheses is to state their metric formulae and to demonstrate that the formulae fit the texts. Instead, they emend the texts to fit their hypotheses. A sure sign of error is the constant need to prop up a hypothesis with more hypotheses." Cf. also G. D. Young in *JNES*, IX (1950), 124–33; W. F. Albright in *HUCA*, XXIII (1950–51), 1–39.

36. Gordon, *op. cit.*, p. 108, n. 1.

37. See "MHHH," pp. 143–44, and see nn. 41 and 42 below.

38. See n. 41 below.

39. Cf., e.g., Job 17:1.

40. This is achieved in a variety of ways:

(a) In a section containing distichs, the closing verse will end with a tristich, cf. Job, chaps. 10, 11, 19, 26. So also Ps. 13, 14, 16, 18, 19, 37, 47, 53, 55, 63, 73, 90, 94, 103, 104, 111, 119, 125, 129, 148.

(b) The closing stich will be extended by the use of more words or by longer ones. Job, chaps. 5, 17, 18, 21. So also Ps. 17, 21, 26, 41, 45, 71, 81, 91, 116.

(c) The composition or the section will change in the closing verse from a shorter to a longer meter, as in Ps. 19 (vs. 11), 24, 27, 34, 41–42, 51 (vs. 19), 82, 89.

(d) The meter may be lengthened in the closing stich only. Thus Job 18, basically in 3:3 meter, ends in 4:4. Cf. Ps. 4, 8, 10, 13, 15, 20, 47, 50, 52, 59, 62, 63, 66, 67, 84, 86, 123, 145. The ritual term *Hallelūyā* apparently served also to extend the meter of the closing stich, as in Ps. 113, 117, 146, 147.

(e) Two of these devices may be used simultaneously, as in Ps. 47. For a detailed examination of this important poetic usage, not hitherto adequately recognized, see "MHHH," pp. 144 ff.

41. Thus Job's opening soliloquy (chap. 3) exhibits the following rhythm pattern: 4:4 (vs. 3), 4:4:3 (vs. 4), 3:3:3 (vs. 5), 4:3:3 or 4:4:4 (vs. 6), 4:4 (vs. 7), 3:3 (vs. 8), 3:3:3 (vs. 9), 3:3 (vss. 10–16), 4:4 (vs. 17), 3:3 (vss. 18, 19), 4:3 (vs. 20), 3:3 (vs. 21, where two beats are to be assigned to either of the two longer words in stich b, *Vayaḥpᵉrūhū mimmatmōnīm*, and vs. 22, giving two beats to *hassemēḥīm*), 4:3 (vs. 24 and vs. 25, giving two beats to *vayeᵓetāyēnī*), 3:2 or 2:2:2:2 (vs. 26).

This chapter is more varied than is usually the case. Thus in chap. 4, the 3:3 meter predominates. The pattern is as follows: 4:4 (vs. 2), 3:3 (vss. 3, 4), 4:3 (vs. 5), 3:3 (vss. 6, 7, *zᵉkōr nāᵓ* is an anacrusis outside the meter), 4:4 (vs. 8, giving *yiqṣᵉrūhū* two beats), 3:3 (vs. 9), 4:3 (vs. 10), 3:3 (vss. 11, 12, 13, 14, 15), 3:3:3 (vs. 16), 3:3 (vss. 17, 18), 3:3:3 (vs. 19), 3:3 (vss. 20, 21).

42. Cf. "MHHH," pp. 143 ff., 148–49, where Deut. 33:11; Hos. 8:11; Ps. 4, 7–8; and Job 19:14, 15; 20:29, are adduced as instances of the proper use of metrics in textual criticism.

43. On the various patterns of parallelism, see "MHHH," pp. 151 ff.

44. *Loc. cit.*, for analysis of such examples of alternate parallelism as Hos. 5:3; Ps. 33:20, 21. This usage occurs also in prose, cf. Exod. 29:27; Deut. 22:25–27, as Ehrlich acutely noted. It is the key to the difficult passage in Eccles. 5:17–19. See *KMW, ad loc.*

45. *Loc. cit.*, for such instances of chiastic parallelism as Hos. 2:21–22; 8:14; Ps. 1:5, 6; Prov. 23:15, 16; Job 20:3; Lam. 2:13. For the structure and meaning of Job 29:25, see the translation and the Comm.

46. For an analysis of their basic role in poetry in general and in Job in particular, see chap. xiv.

47. For *zeugma*, cf. Job 4:10; 10:12. For *hendiadys*, cf. 5:15; 10:12; 25:2. (For other biblical examples, see "LMBH," pp. 263 ff.) For *hysteron proteron*, cf. Job 14:10; 16:9; 20:19, and other biblical examples in "LMBH," pp. 262 ff.

48. Cf. I. M. Casanowicz, *Paronomasia in the O.T.* (Boston, 1894); E. König, *Stilistik, Rhetorik, Poetik* (Leipzig, 1900); D. Yellin, *Kethabim Nibharim*

Letorat Hamelitzah Batanakh (Jerusalem 5699 = 1939). See also "LMBH," pp. 253–67, esp. pp. 255 ff., on paronomasia and *talhin*. It was noted by the medieval Hebrew grammarians Menahem ben Saruk, Jonah Abulwalid ibn Ganah, and Abraham ibn Ezra. Cf. Yellin, *op. cit.*, p. 67, note.

49. Thus, the noted Shakespearean scholar and Elizabethan linguist, Helge Kökeritz, "discovered several additional and more complicated puns that amused Shakespeare's contemporaries. *Some of them were not merely double but triple and even quadruple in meaning.*" (The italics are mine.) (Naboth Hedin in *American Swedish Monthly*, cited in the *New York Times*, March 28, 1964.)

50. The Arabic term means, among other things, "mode of speech, dialect, error in pronunciation, leading to a change in meaning or construction." Arab rhetoricians distinguished between (a) ʾistaḥdaʾm, lit. "use, serving, ministering," where "only one meaning is intended, and another, less common, is suggested by phonetic similarity" (i.e., *paronomasia*), and (b) *tawrīya*, "concealment," where "both meanings are intended" (i.e. *talhin*). Cf. Yellin, *op. cit.*, p. 87 and n. 7.

51. *Talhin* occurs in Job 3: 6–7, 22; 5:24; 7:6; 9:17; 12:6; 21:13; 22:25. For other examples see "LMBH," pp. 255–62.

XIII: THE USE OF QUOTATIONS IN JOB

1. See my brief discussion of this phenomenon in *KMW*, p. 256. Examples in the prophets are to be found in Isa., chap. 19, where the prophecy on Egypt (vss. 1–15) is amplified by a series of oracles, radically different in content from it and from one another, but linked by the opening phrase *bayom hahu*, "on that day" (vss. 16, 18, 19, 23, 24). In Micah, the key to an understanding of the passage 4:8–5:5 lies in recognizing that this is not a single prophecy but a collection of distinct oracles linked by the two similar sounding introductory words ʾattah, "you," and ʿattah, "now" (4:8, 9, 11, 14; 5:1). In Ecclesiastes, 7:1–14 is a heptad, a collection of seven utterances beginning with *tobh*, "good." See *KMW*, pp. 255 ff. For rabbinic examples, see the Mishnah *Eduyot, passim; Yadayim,* chap. 4; *Pesahim,* chap. 4.

2. On the treatment in the Versions of the alleged interpolations in Ecclesiastes, see "QLU," pp. 160 ff. On the admittedly complex problem of the Septuagint version of Job, see chapter xv. Our present LXX text contains additions from Aquila, Symmachus, and, principally, Theodotion. These additions were supplied because the original text presented a briefer recension of the book. The Sahidic version probably testifies to the pre-Origenic text of Job (Ciasca, against Burkitt). Nonetheless, "in the main the Hebrew, as far as the extent is concerned, represents an earlier text than the Greek" (DG, I, lxxvi, cf. pp. xlix, lxxi ff.). It should also be recalled that the Elihu speeches (chaps. 32–37), the authenticity of which has often been denied, are translated in LXX, and were included in the Greek version by 100 B.C.E. See chapter xv.

3. The rabbinic term *mikkan vaʿilakh*, "from this time henceforth," as

marking the end of prophetic inspiration is, of course, indefinite. It was equated with the period of Ezra, who was taken to be a contemporary of the last three prophets, Haggai, Zechariah, and Malachi, the last named often being identified with Ezra. The traditional rabbinic chronology drastically foreshortened the Persian period. On the manifold problems of the O.T. canon, see F. Buhl, *Canon and Text of the O.T.* (Edinburgh, 1892), pp. 1–78; M. L. Margolis, *The Hebrew Scriptures in the Making* (Philadelphia, 1922); R. H. Pfeiffer, *IOT*, pp. 50–70; S. Zeitlin, *An Historical Study of the Canonization of the Hebrew Scriptures*, in *PAAJR*, III (1932), 121–58.

4. Cf. G. A. Barton, *Ecclesiastes* ("ICC" [New York, 1908]); M. Jastrow, *The Gentle Cynic* (Philadelphia, 1919), pp. 245–55; Volz, *Hiob und Weisheit in den Schriften des A.T.* (Göttingen, 1921), p. 235; C. Siegfried, *Kommentar zu Koheleth* (1898); O. Eissfeldt, *Einleitung in das A.T.* (Tübingen, 1934), p. 558.

5. Siegfried omits 12:4–13:1; W. Grill (*Zur Kritik der Komposition des Buches Hiob* [Tübingen, 1890]) omits 12:4–13:2. DG delete 12:4–12 (I, 111). Volz leaves only five verses in Job's speech (12:2, 3, 11, 12; 13:13) and transfers the remainder (12:4–10, 13–25; 13:1) to Zophar in chap. 11 (*op. cit.*, pp. 39–40). Jastrow (*op. cit.*) omits vss. 4c, 5 in part, 6c, 10, 12, 13, 17–19, 22, 23, and 25. Ball removes vss. 4c, 6, 10 (doubtfully), and 13. Budde, on the other hand, argues forcefully against Grill and Siegfried's procedure (*Das Buch Hiob, ad loc.*; also *ThLz*, 1891, No. 2). Dhorme places vss. 11–12 before vs. 9.

6. The variety of views may be studied in the commentaries of Driver and Gray, Budde, Ball, Dhorme, and Tur-Sinai. For a discussion of the difficulties involved in these proposed excisions and emendations and my view of these passages, see the Comm. My translation is given in this chapter.

7. It is noteworthy that LXX omits only two verses and three stichs in chap. 12 (8b, 9, 18b, 21a, 23). In 21:19–34, LXX omits vss. 19b, 23, 28–33, and in many of these cases "the removal of the passages in the Greek destroys the poetical structure" (DG, lxxv). All in all, the evidence is clear that in contending with a difficult text like Job, the translator contracted his original and thus simplified his task.

8. For a recognition of the basic unity and integrity of Qoheleth, from varying points of view, cf. Ludwig Levy, *Das Buch Qoheleth* (Leipzig, 1912), pp. 57–59; D. B. MacDonald, *The Hebrew Philosophic Genius* (Princeton, 1936); H. W. Hertzberg, *Der Prediger* (Leipzig, 1932); M. Haller and K. Galling, *Die Fünf Megilloth* (Tübingen, 1940); R. Gordis, *The Wisdom of Ecclesiastes* (New York, 1945); J. J. Weber, *L'Ecclésiaste* (Paris, 1947); R. Gordis, *Koheleth—The Man and His World* (New York, 1951), and the earlier papers cited there in the bibliography.

9. A. Bentzen, *Introduction to the O.T.* (Copenhagen, 1948), I, 13.

10. The significant emphasis of Meir Weiss, *Hamiqra Kidemutho* ("The Literary Form of Scripture" [Jerusalem, 1962]), lies in his protesting against

the excessive categorizing of biblical poetry in terms of fixed patterns and in his highlighting the personal and unique elements in the literary unit under discussion. The value of his contribution is not impaired by the extreme lengths to which he goes in applying his method, which may impress the reader as unconvincing in certain instances.

11. See *KMW*, pp. 87–94, for an extensive discussion of this phenomenon, already proposed in *The Wisdom of Ecclesiastes* in 1945 and in earlier papers, cited in n. 12.

12. This insight was first proposed in "Quotations in Wisdom Literature," *JQR* (1939), pp. 123–47; also "Mabo Lesafrut Hahokmah" ("Introduction to Wisdom Literature" in Hebrew) in *Sefer Hashanah Liyehude Amerika* (New York, 1942), pp. 117–48. Cf. "The Heptad as an Element of Biblical and Rabbinic Style," *JBL* (1943), pp. 12–26; "The Social Background of Wisdom Literature" in *HUCA* (1943), pp. 77–118.

13. See "QLU," pp. 157–219, for extra-biblical parallels. On this usage of "virtual quotations," fundamental to the understanding of Ecclesiastes, see *KMW* (chap. xii), the Comm. *passim*, and N. H. Tur-Sinai, *The Book of Job* (Jerusalem, 1957), who cites my paper in *HUCA* (1949) in his *Book of Job, A New Commentary* (Jerusalem, 1957), Introduction, p. lii. He has applied this insight very significantly to the Song of Songs in his *Hălason Vehasepher; Kerekh Hasepher* (Jerusalem, 1950), pp. 351–88; cf. also my *Song of Songs* (New York, 1954) on 1:8; 8:14.

14. When my first paper on "virtual quotations" was read in December, 1948, at the Annual Meeting of the Society of Biblical Literature and Exegesis, Prof. S. N. Kramer cited some corroborative evidence from Sumerian and declared his conviction that more would be forthcoming. His ready acceptance of the thesis doubtless explains the relatively large number of instances thus far brought to light in Sumerian, but the phenomenon is also attested in other areas of oriental literature. New examples constantly appear.

The following conspectus of the passages discussed in "QLU," as well as some additional texts, should prove useful:

In *Sumerian*, the poem "Gilgames, Enkidu and the Nether World" (published by S. N. Kramer in *JAOS*, LXIV [1944], 7–23). Here the editor's recognition of the "virtual quotation," which was subsequently confirmed by a duplicate tablet, is crucial to the understanding of the text (cf. "QLU," pp. 178–79). Also "Gilgames and the Land of the Living," ll. 16–21 ("QLU," pp. 179–82). Again in the Paradise Myth, "Enki and Ninhursag," ll. 22–25 (cf. *ANET*, p. 38).

In *Akkadian*, "The Complaint on the Injustice of the World," ll. 69–71; ll. 215 ff. ("QLU," pp. 205 ff.) and "Gilgames Epic," Tablet VI, l. 74 (*ANET*, p. 84 and n. 106).

In *Egyptian*, "Admonitions of a Prophet," Second Poem ("QLU," p. 199–200).

In *Ugaritic*, in the Baal-Mot poem AB, II, l. 8 (cf. *ANET*, p. 138), on which the editor remarks, rather too casually, "A quotation without an introduction not unexampled" (n. 6).

In *rabbinic literature*, in the Mishnah: M. *Keth* 13:3; M. *Abot* 2:4; 4:4, 24; and in the Talmud, B. *Shab.* 23a, b; 30a; B. *Erub.* 54a; B. *Taan.* 23b; B. *Keth* 22b; B. *Kid.* 44a; B. *Baba Kamma* 56a; B. *Baba Metzia* 35a. (See "QLU," pp. 175-98.)

15. On the significance of these and other tasks that devolve upon the Semitic reader, see chapter xiv.

16. Thus, I believe that Tur-Sinai, whose brilliant commentary on Job, like all his studies, is deeply stimulating, tends to invoke the usage of "virtual quotations" where other interpretations are preferable.

17. Archer Taylor, *The Proverb* (Cambridge, 1931), pp. 34-43, 52-61, esp. pp. 6, 34, 52.

18. For this practice, see "QLU," p. 178.

19. Cf. *KMW*, chap. xii, and the Comm., *passim*.

20. Cf. Ps. 2:2-3; 22:8-9; 55:22-23; 109:5-20; also Obad. 1:7d.

21. Cf. Ps. 52:8, 9.

22. Cf. Ps. 75:10-11; 95:7 ff.; 22:27; 69:33.

23. Cf. Hos. 4:4; Isa. 28:9-12; Jer. 3:5. Chapter 53 of Isaiah is the speech of the "many nations," *goyim rabbim*, referred to in 52:15.

24. Cf. Hos. 5:15-6:4; 14:2-9; Jer. 2:25; 3:22-23; 6:4 ff.; 6:16-17; 8:18-23; Ps. 4:7; 32:6-7.

25. Cf. my *Song of Songs* (New York, 1954), Introduction, pp. 41-42, and Comm.

26. Cf. Gen. 26:7; Ps. 8:4 ff.; 10:4; 59:8; Job 15:21; 22:14.

27. Cf. Gen. 41:51-52; Exod. 18:4; I Sam. 1:20.

28. Cf. Ps. 30:9-12; 32:6-7.

29. Cf. Ps. 27:1-6; 22:23-32, on which see "QLU," pp. 187-88.

30. Cf. Ps. 44:21-22, on which see "QLU," pp. 190 ff. Several crucial passages in Job, discussed below, fall into this hitherto unrecognized category.

31. Cf. Eccles. 4:8, and frequently in rabbinic literature, on which see "QLU," pp. 194 ff.

32. Cf. Exod. 23:8; Ps. 34:12-15; Job 2:4; 17:5; Deut. 16:19.

33. This usage is particularly characteristic of Ecclesiastes; cf. the collection in Eccles. 7:1-18; 8:2-4; 8:11-14.

34. Cf. Prov. 26:4, 5; Eccles. 4:5, 6. On Job 12:12 ff.; 22:7-8; see below in the text.

35. On the basic meanings of the term, see O. Eissfeldt, *Der Maschal im A.T.*, Beiheft, *ZATW* (Giessen, 1913), pp. 1 ff.

36. *Be'ad* cannot mean "in place of," which would be expressed by *tahat* (Exod. 21:23-24; Lev. 24:18, 20) or by the *Beth pretii* (Deut. 19:2). It must be interpreted "on behalf of" (e.g., Isa. 8:19) with *yitten* understood, "(a man will give one) skin on behalf of (another) skin." That it means "upon, about,"

hence, "one skin lies upon another skin" (Schultens, Merx, Budde), is less likely, since this meaning of be'ad is restricted (even in Jonah 2:7; Ps. 3:4; 139:11) to verbs or nouns which mean "shutting off" or "protecting" (cf. Judg. 9:51; Job 7:7, and often). Torczyner's ingenious suggestion in his Hebrew commentary that b'ad is the Arabic ba'ada ("after, under"), and hence is equal to taḥat, should also be mentioned, even if it does not carry conviction. Much more attractive is his suggestion in his earlier German work (Das Buch Hiob [Vienna, 1920], p. 2) that the verse read originally 'or b'ad 'or yittēn iš vekhol 'ašer lō yittēn, though the change is not absolutely required.

37. The Hebrew word 'āwen, which occurs in both verses, is broader in meaning than the English term "trouble" by which it is rendered. It encompasses both "sin" and "punishment." Not nature, but man, is the source of evil in the world.

38. So Budde, Peake, DG, and my Comm.

39. ANET, p. 425b, and n. 12.

40. Render b'yādō "for him," not "in his hand." On b'yad as a phonetic equivalent of be'ad, cf. I Sam. 21:14; Ezra 37:19; Isa. 64:6; Job 8:4; 27:11; and Tel-el-Amarna Letters, No. 245, l. 35 (ba-di-u = ba-ya-di-ḥu); as well as the Ugaritic texts where be-yad is spelled bd. Cf. H. Torczyner in Samuel Krauss Jubilee Volume (Jerusalem, 5697 = 1937), pp. 1 ff.; R. Gordis, "A Note on Yad," in JBL, LXII (1943), 341 ff., and the literature there cited.

41. Duhm, Siegfried, Budde, and Hoelscher delete the verse; DG (I, 195) is unable to reach a satisfactory conclusion. Tur-Sinai moves the verse after 12–14. However, he does recognize its true intent.

42. So DG, ad loc.

43. Ehrlich and Dhorme correctly see that vs. 12 is essential to the text as the basis of Job's alleged standpoint in vs. 13, but they do not concern themselves with the technical form of vs. 12. The passage in Isa. 40:26–27, which Dhorme cites as a parallel, would be a striking illustration of the same connection of ideas were it certain that the verses in Isaiah belong together and not to two different passages, as is correctly indicated by the Masoretic division. Isa. 40:26 emphasizes the creative power of God, not His remoteness from man. The intent of the passage has been intuitively grasped by the medieval Jewish commentators, who are unaccountably neglected by modern students. Rashi interprets vs. 12 as a quotation (le'mor) "Saying." Ibn Ezra has the quotation begin with vs. 11 (ḥāsabhtā) "You thought."

44. Hᵃlō', "indeed" (lit. "does not"), often introduces a virtual quotation; cf. Ps. 44:22; Job 31:3, 4, 15. The presence of a verb of speaking in one verse (vᵉ'āmartā) and its absence in the other are well attested in this usage.

45. It is noteworthy that both verses are introduced by the conjunction Vav, "and, for." It indicates here a shift from the description of his actions to his thinking. On the use of the Vav in circumstantial clauses, indicating the concomitant conditions, modal, causal, or temporal, of the main action, cf. S. R. Driver, Hebrew Tenses (Oxford, 1892), secs. 156–60; BDB, s.v. Vav, sec.

I, k, p. 253a, b, and the frequent use of the analogous Arabic *Waw alḥali;* cf. W. Wright, *A Grammar of the Arabic Language* (London, 1874–75), Vol. 2, sec. 183.

46. Reading *mešō̂atho,* "His destruction" (cf. Zeph. 1:15; Job 30:3; 38:27), for the ungrammatical *missᵉᵓētho* of MT. The usual rendering, "And because of His majesty I could do nothing (evil)" is linguistically awkward and leaves unstated the most important idea in the verse, "evil." See Comm. for details. The recognition of the quotation here is not affected by the specific rendering adopted.

47. The use of *ᵓim* in Job, chap. 31, which occurs no less than 20 times, has occasioned much difficulty because of the effort by scholars to reduce all instances of its occurrence to one pattern. Hence many suggestions have been made to excise verses or to rearrange the chapter, but they have not met with any general assent. See DG (I, 261–62), who summarize these attempts and correctly caution: "It would be a great mistake to reduce all this variety to the monotonous repetition of a single scheme." But the implications of this just observation have not been kept in mind. There is no need for assuming that *ᵓim* throughout the chapter must always mean "if" (15 or 16 times without and four times with the imprecatory clause). Actually, the repetition of the same word in the Hebrew gives the passage great power, while the variety in meaning avoids monotony. Cf. *mah,* which occurs three times with two different meanings in Gen. 44:16: "*What* shall we say to my lord? *What* shall we speak. Or *how* shall we clear ourselves?" (AV), and in Lam. 2:13: "*How* shall I fortify you, *what* shall I liken unto you, O daughter of Jerusalem. *What* shall I compare unto you, and comfort you, O virgin daughter of Zion?" On this latter verse, cf. Gordis in *JThS,* XXIV (1933), 1962–63.

Similarly, in this long chapter (Job, chap. 31), two (or three) different uses of *ᵓim* occur: (1) "if," in the protasis of an ordinary conditional sentence (vs. 19); (2) "if," in a protasis where the apodosis constitutes the penalty for the sin contemplated. In these instances, "the punishment fits the crime," in accordance with the doctrine of *middāh kᵉneged middāh,* "measure for measure," which underlies the tenet of *lex talionis,* universal in ancient law (vss. 7–8, 9–10, 21–22, 38–40); (3) *haᵓim* (Latin *num*), the sign of a question expecting a negative reply and hence without an apodosis (vss. 5, 13, 16, 19, 24, 25, 26, 33). The interrogative *ᵓim lō* is equivalent to Latin *nonne,* the sign of a question expecting an affirmative answer (vss. 20, 31?).

Unfortunately, the power of the repeated particle is largely lost in translation since it must be rendered differently in different passages. Dhorme (p. 411) recognizes the use of both meanings of *ᵓim* here. He renders it as the interrogative in vss. 5, 13, 16, 24, 25, 26, 33, and as "if" in vss. 7, 9, 19, 31, 38. Similarly, Hölscher renders it as the interrogative in vss. 5, 13, 16, 19, 24, 25, 26, 33, and as "if" in vss. 2, 9, 21, 38.

48. I revocalize 31:15 slightly, following Targum in stich *a* and LXX in *b,* and read *Halō babbeten ꜥāsanī ꜥāsāhū vayyehunnenū bᵉreḥemᵓ eḥád.* So do most

moderns. Hölscher deletes this matchless affirmation of human equality—perhaps a tribute that virtue is forced to pay to vice. His commentary was published in Tübingen under the Nazis in 1937.

49. Cf. chapter viii above and the Comm. The various efforts at reconstruction are summarized in DG, I, xl, and Pfeiffer, *IOT*, p. 671. Briefly our restoration is as follows: Bildad, chap. 25; 26:5–14; Job, 2ɔ:1–4; 27:2–11; Zophar, 27:13–23; Job, chaps. 29–31. Zophar's speech is definitely fragmentary and Bildad's probably so. Chap. 28, the "Hymn to Wisdom," is an independent poem emanating from the same author or from his school.

50. These conclusions on vss. 2–6 and 13–23 are accepted by virtually all critics, as in the reconstructions of Kennicott, Stuhlman, Reuss, Hoffmann, Bickell, Duhm, Barton, and Dhorme, in spite of other divergences. A few critics like Siegfried, Laue, and Buttenwieser accept only the first conclusion and try to meet the second problem in other ways.

51. So Driver and Gray (doubtfully), Hoffmann, Bickell, Duhm, Barton.

52. Thus Kennicott, Stuhlman, Reuss, and Dhorme attribute these verses to Job, in spite of the obvious difficulties.

53. A somewhat similar view of this section was proposed by Hengstenberg in part and by Budde (in *ZATW* [1882], pp. 205–10, and in his Commentary). See Driver, *IOT* (9th ed.; New York, 1906), p. 422. That it was not more generally accepted may be attributed to the absence at the time of supporting evidence for this usage of virtual quotations.

For my rendering of this passage, see chapter viii. On the evidence for my independent interpretations at several points (notably on *yith'annag*, vs. 10; *b*e*yad*, vs. 11), cf. the notes and the Comm. The over-all approach to the passage as a whole is not affected by these exegetical details.

54. On this passage, see *KMW*, pp. 150, 230–31.

55. For the sentiment, cf. Deut. 32:7.

56. It is true that this passage occurs after 12:12, but it does not affect our view that 12:12–13 is a refutation of the Friends' glorification of age. As has been universally recognized, there is no logical progression of thought in the Friends' position in the dialogue, and hence the same point of view prevails throughout. Even in Job's words there is no change of outlook, only a heightening of the emotion and a corresponding rise and fall in the intensity of his conviction that he will be vindicated.

57. Siegfried and Duhm omit both verses—an easy escape from the difficulty, but one which does not (among other things) explain why the verses were interpolated in the first place. Some scholars take vs. 12 interrogatively, "Have the aged men wisdom, and length of days understanding?" (Volz, Ball). Others interpolate the interrogative particle *hakhi* before the verse (Hölscher) or prefix *lō*, "The aged have not wisdom" (Beer, Jastrow), thus deriving from the verse a denial of the wisdom of the old. On the other hand, Dhorme places vss. 11 and 12 after vs. 9, thus having Job affirm the wisdom of the aged. But this idea is irrelevant if not totally repugnant to Job, for he is the iconoclast

attacking the accepted wisdom of the past. In view of the constant invoking of age by the Friends, such a sentiment would be even more uncongenial to him. Among earlier commentators, Budde stands alone in recognizing that vs. 12 is a quotation of the traditional view, refuted in vs. 13. DG, I, 116–17, who quote this interpretation, do not accept it "because the antithesis is formally unexpressed." Instead they are forced to delete both verses as unauthentic. The evidence we have adduced of the frequent absence of such formal signs of quotations should be sufficient to modify this judgment.

58. See *ANET*, p. 425, col. 2, and nn. 25, 26. We have supplied the *verba dicendi* in the text.

59. In vs. 12a the aged are credited with *ḥokmāh*, in 12b with *tᵉbhūnāh*. That vs. 13 follows directly upon it as a refutation is clear from the fact that 13a attributes the same *ḥokmāh* to God, and 13b, the identical *tᵉbhūnāh*, but adds *gebhūrāh* and *ᶜeṣāh* respectively. It should be added that these four qualities are identical with the attributes of "the spirit of the Lord" given in Isa. 11:2.

Other evidence of the familiarity of the author of Job with the book of Isaiah occurs in the same chapter: 12:9 is a citation of Isa. 21:20c. Cf. also the table of parallels with Isa., chaps. 40–66, in DG, I, lxviii, and chap. xi above. Thus Job gives an earlier *terminus non post quem* for the uniting of the prophecies of Isaiah ben Amoz and Deutero-Isaiah than the reference to Isaiah in Ben Sira (48:24–25).

> With the spirit of might he foresaw the future
> And comforted the mourners of Zion;
> For all time he announced what was to be,
> And hidden things before they came.

The full texts of Isaiah found among the Dead Sea Scrolls also presuppose a preceding period of substantial length to allow for the uniting of both parts of the book.

60. On this important passage, which has also suffered greatly at the hands of commentators because of the failure to recognize the use of quotations, cf. the discussion in *KMW*, pp. 282–84.

61. The use of quotations in chap. 21 has been partially recognized. Thus, vs. 19a is taken as a quotation by Budde and by Driver and Gray, who follow the English version and prefix, "Ye say," and apparently by Ball (*Book of Job* [Oxford, 1922]). Verse 22 is similarly treated by Hitzig. The satiric intent of vss. 28–29 has been overlooked, and vs. 30 has proved another stumbling-block. See DG, I, 185, for an excellent conspectus of the interpretation of these passages. On the other hand, Yellin, *Hiqre Miqra-lyyob* (Jerusalem, 5687 = 1927), p. 52, renders vss. 19, 22, and 30 as quotations, but takes vs. 28 differently.

62. Cf. *šᵉal, vethōrekhā, lekha, siʾaḥ*.

63. The minor variations are natural in recapitulating an argument. *Maᶜalīm*

in 42:3a for *maḥsīkh* in 38:2. In 42:4a, *šᵉmaᶜ nā² vᵉ²anōkhi ²adabber* replaces
²ezōr nā khᵉgebher hᵃlāṣekhā in 38:3a as an introductory challenge. Were these
verses in chap. 42 interpolated from chap. 38, they would be repeated exactly.
That the verses are a quotation by Job is recognized by DG, I, 372, and now
by RSV.

64. The following biblical examples of indirect quotation without a *verbum
dicendi* or *cogitandi* may be given:

Isa. 52:14: When many were astonished at you,
> *Thinking that* his appearance is marred beyond human semblance.

(Note the second person ᶜ*ālekhā* followed by the third person *mar²ēhū*). The
nations continue to be quoted indirectly throughout the passage, 52:15–53:12
(note the third person).

Hos. 7:2a: *Ubhal yōmerū lilebhābhām kol rāᶜathām zākhartī,* ("They do not
think in their hearts *that* I remember all their wickedness.") The conjunction
is lacking before the indirect quotation.

Hos. 12:5c, d: *Beth²ēl yimṣā²ennū vešām yᵉdabbēr ᶜimmānū.* I regard these
two stichs as constituting the plea of the angel with whom Jacob wrestled.
In my opinion the verse is to be rendered as follows:

> He (Jacob) struggled with an angel and prevailed
> He (the angel) wept and made supplication to him,
> *Saying that* he would meet him in Beth El
> And there he would speak with him.

A full discussion of this fascinating and complex passage must be reserved for
another occasion. My early treatment of Hosea, chap. 12 ("Midrash in the
Prophets," *JBL*, XLIX (1930), 417–22) needs to be amplified in several significant respects.

Ps. 32:6–7: Here an indirect quotation (vs. 6b) is followed by a direct quotation of the psalmist's prayer, which is succeeded by God's direct response (vs.
8 ff.):

> For this every pious soul prays to Thee
> In a time of divine favor,
> *Asking that* the flood of great waters may not reach him,
> *Saying,* "Thou art my shelter, saving me from trouble,
> With songs of deliverance wilt Thou surround me."
> *And the Lord answers,*
> "I will guide and teach you the way to go,
> I shall place My eye upon you."

The proposed change of *²ēlāv* (him) to *²ēlai* (me) in vs. 6 is not difficult, but it
is not needed, in view of the well-attested usage of indirect quotation and the
principle of *difficilior lectio praestat.*

Ps. 69:5: Here the closing stich is generally rendered interrogatively, as,
e.g., in JPS (similarly in RSV):

They that hate me without a cause are more than the hairs of my head;
They that would cut me off, being mine enemies wrongfully, are many;
Should I restore that which I took not away?

The introduction of a question here is highly unlikely. What we have is a
indirect quotation without a *verbum dicendi.* The passage is better rendered

> More than the hairs of my head are my enemies without cause,
> My would-be destroyers are many, my foes without due reason,
> *Who say that* what I have not stolen, I must return!

65. Cited are a few instances that have come to my attention in my reading
Undoubtedly additional examples will come to light when the category i
recognized by scholars.

In the *Hammurabi Code,* sec. 96, the *verbum dicendi* before an indirect quo
tation is omitted:

> "If a seignior borrowed grain or money, and does not have the
> grain or money to pay it back, but has other goods, he shall give to
> his merchant whatever there is in his possession, (affirming) before
> witnesses that he will bring it, while the merchant shall accept it
> without making any objection" (*ANET,* pp. 169–70).

Here, the verb "affirming" is left to be supplied by the reader.

In the *Qoran, Sura* 16, vss. 58–59, an indirect quotation occurs without a
verbum dicendi: "And when any of them is told the news of the birth of a
female, his face becometh black, and he is deeply afflicted: he hideth himsel.
from the people, because of the ill tidings which have been told him; *considering
within himself* whether he shall keep it with disgrace, or whether he shall bury
it in the dust." The Sales translation here quoted supplies the words in italic
which are lacking in the Arabic original. The N. J. Dawood Version (Harmondsworth, 1932), p. 298, leaves it to be understood by the reader.

66. The emendations of *bī* to *bō* ("to him") in 19:28 and of *lākh* to *lī* ir
35:3 are to be rejected on the principle of *difficilior lectio praestat.*

67. Cf. DG and my Comm. for the various suggestions offered.

XIV: THE RHETORIC OF ALLUSION AND ANALOGY

1. On the development of Hebrew vocalization and its bearing on the his-
tory of the biblical text, cf. C. D. Ginsburg, *Intro. to a Massoretico-Critical Edi-
tion of the Hebrew Bible* (London, 1897); R. Gordis, *The Biblical Text in the
Making* (Philadelphia, 1937); D. N. Freedman and F. W. Cross, *Early Hebrew
Orthography* (New Haven, 1952); B. J. Roberts, *The O.T. Text and Versions*
(Cardiff, 1951); E. Wurthwein, *Der Text des A.T.* (Stuttgart, 1952).

2. They are *kādōš, kaddeš, kiddeš, kuddaš, kōdeš, kedeš,* and *kaddiš.*

3. I first called attention to the direct relationship between the existence of
a sacred text and the introduction of a vowel system in my study "Yihusei
Hakhethibh Vehanniqqud Balašon Ha-ivrith," in *Lešonenu,* 5696 = 1937, pp.
202–8.

4. See chapter xiii.

5. From the vast literature on this subject, cf. C. K. Ogden and I. A. Richards, *The Meaning of Meaning* (New York, 1930); Suzanne K. Langer, *Philosophy in a New Key* (Cambridge, 1951); and W. Kaufmann, *Critique of Religion and Philosophy* (New York, 1961).

6. On Buber, see in addition to his own voluminous writings, M. Friedman, *Martin Buber—The Life of Dialogue* (Chicago, 1955); M. Diamond, *Martin Buber: Jewish Existentialist* (New York, 1960). On Franz Rosenzweig, whose major work, *Der Stern der Erlösung* (Frankfurt, 1921), has not yet appeared in English, cf. J. B. Agus, *Modern Philosophies of Judaism* (New York, 1941); H. Bergmann, *Modern Jewish Thinkers* (New York, 1962); N. M. Glatzer, *Franz Rosenzweig—His Life and Thought* (New York, 1953). For a modern view of revelation, see e.g., R. Gordis, *A Faith for Moderns* (New York, 1960), chap. ix, pp. 150 ff. The divine "pathos" is viewed as the essence of God's relationship to man by A. J. Heschel, *The Prophets* (New York, 1962).

7. Cf. W. Kaufmann, *op. cit.*, pp. 93–94, and chap. xiv *passim*. On the theoretical issues underlying modern art, see the excellent survey by H. Read, *A Concise History of Modern Painting* (New York, 1959).

8. D. Yellin, *Hiqre Miqraɔ-Iyyob* (Jerusalem, 5687 = 1927), pp. 67–68.

9. For this evaluation of Poe, see J. Isaacs, *The Background of Modern Poetry* (London, 1951), pp. 19–20. It is quoted, together with Whitman's reference, in John Press's brilliant study, *The Chequer'd Shade—Reflections on Obscurity in Poetry* (London, 1958), p. 166, to which I am greatly indebted. Chap. viii, "Theme and Images," and chap. ix, "The Nature of Poetry," are particularly valuable.

10. George Steiner, in his essay on Shakespeare in the *New York Times Book Review*, April 19, 1964 (p. 5), illustrates his thesis with passages from Shakespeare that are virtually instances of *talḥin*.

11. For the following paragraphs on the New Criticism I have drawn upon M. Weiss, *Hamiqra Kidemutho* ("The Literary Form of Scripture") (Jerusalem, 1962), esp. pp. 9–44. The book as a whole is an interesting and largely successful effort to apply the principles of the New Criticism to biblical interpretation.

12. *Ibid.*, p. 20.

13. See P. Ker, *Form and Style in Poetry* (London, 1928), p. 141, for the various meanings of "form."

14. Weiss, *op. cit.*, p. 136. (The translation is mine.)

15. *Ibid.*, pp. 17–18.

16. *Ibid.*, p. 81.

17. See her important work, *Philosophy in a New Key*, cited above.

18. See the searching treatment of the subject by John Press (*op. cit.*), who carefully analyzes the various reasons for, as well as the long history of, "obscurity" in poetry.

19. For a discussion of the role of metaphor in religious discourse in general as illustrated by the connotations of the traditional religious phrase, "our Father, our King," cf. my book *A Faith for Moderns*, chap. viii, esp. pp. 133 ff.

20. E. M. Good, *Irony in the O.T.* (Philadelphia, 1965), chap. i, esp. p. 30.

21. *Ibid.*, p. 19.

22. *Ibid.*, pp. 32–33.

23. In Hab. 2:6, *ḥīdāh* is again parallel to *mᵉlīṣāh*. In medieval and modern Hebrew, *mᵉlīṣāh* means "poem, literary conceit," with no satiric overtones. Cf. I. Ben-Jehuda, *Thesaurus, s.v.*

24. Cf. the recent study of Yehezkel Kaufmann, *"Mešal Yōthām"* in *Molad* (Vol. 20, No. 163, pp. 25–32), and his *Commentary on Judges* (Jerusalem 5722 = 1962), *ad loc.* On the Riddle of Samson see Tur-Sinai, *Halašon Vehasepher; Kerekh Hasepher* (Jerusalem, 1950), pp. 89 ff.

25. Solomon's activity in both these areas is greatly elaborated upon in apocryphal and rabbinic literature. See L. Ginzberg, *Legends of the Jews*, IV, 130–42; VI, 282–88.

26. In his essay, "And Wanton Optics Roll the Melting Eye," quoted by Press, *op. cit.*, p. 41.

27. *Op. cit.*, n. 24 above, p. 13 (translation mine).

28. For a full discussion of the "Allegory of Old Age" and its interpretation, see *KMW*, pp. 328–39.

29. With Ehrlich reading in Ps. 48:8, *kᵉrūaḥ* instead of MT *bᵉrūaḥ*.

30. Pope thought that Shakespeare wrote "siege of troubles"; Lewis Theobald proposed "th'assay of troubles"; others suggested "seat."

31. See the excellent though brief treatment of mixed metaphors by Robert Gorham Davis in the *New York Times Book Review*, April 22, 1962 (p. 2), from which the quotation in the text is taken. Shakespeare's extreme use of mixed metaphors is discussed by Press, *op. cit.*, pp. 195 ff.

32. See the classical presentation by Shalom Spiegel, "On Medieval Hebrew Poetry," in *The Jews*, ed. L. Finkelstein (New York, 1949), pp. 528–66.

33. See his paper *Milešon Payyetanim* ("On the Language of the Medieval Poets") (New York, 1963).

34. The refrain is *vaʾamartem zebhaḥ pesaḥ*, "Ye shall say, 'This is the offering of Passover!'"

35. The Hebrew text and English versions of these *piyyutim* are conveniently available in the *Sabbath and Festival Prayer Book of the Rabbinical Assembly and the United Synagogue* (New York, 1951), pp. 180–81 and 210–11, as well as in all standard prayer books.

36. Cf. J. C. Rylaarsdam, *Revelation in Jewish Wisdom Literature* (Chicago, 1946), p. 40: "The book is allusive rather than explicit; its historical references can be grasped only by those who are familiar with them."

37. See S. Holmes in R. H. Charles, *Apocrypha and Pseudepigrapha of the Old Testament* (Oxford, 1913), I, 518–19.

38. The literature on the Dead Sea Scrolls is, of course, enormous. Most of the documents are conveniently accessible in A. M. Haberman, *Megillot Midbar Yehudah* (Tel Aviv, 1959), and in translation and notes in A. Dupont-Sommer, *The Essene Writings from Qumran* (Oxford, 1961).

39. Cf. chap. 13 *passim*. Such apothegms as 8:9, 12:11, and 14:1 may be quotations from traditional sources or they may be original with the author.

40. So Budde. See chap. xiii and my forthcoming Comm.

41. As in the allegories of Isaiah and Ezekiel, on which see my discussion above.

42. This translation rests in part upon some original interpretations of my own, the evidence for which will be found in the Comm.

43. For a detailed discussion of this passage and the various proposed solutions, see chapter viii, and especially n. 6.

44. The use of the pronoun *hēmāh*, "they," in vs. 13, which introduces a new and contrasting subject (the wicked) with no external mark of the transition, recalls the similar use of the pronoun *hūᵓ*, "he," which similarly introduces a new subject (the righteous) in 8:16.

45. See his *Collected Essays in Literary Criticism* (London, 1952), p. 98.

46. In his "Essay on Pope," quoted by Press, *op. cit.*, p. 212.

XV: THE AUTHOR: HIS PROVENANCE AND DATE

1. With regard to Aramaisms, cf. the lists in DG, I, xl, xlvi–xlvii; Dhorme, *Le Livre de Job* (Paris, 1926), pp. cxl–cxli; and the Commentaries. See the analysis of the various categories of Aramaisms in chapter xii.

2. On proposed Arabic cognates see Dhorme, *op. cit.*, pp. cxl–cxli, and the various Commentaries, *passim*.

3. Cf. his *Commentary on Job* at 2:11: *Vehakarobh ᵓeilai ki hu sepher methurgam ᶜal ken huᵓ kašeh bepherush kederekh kol sepher methurgam.*

4. *On Heroes, Hero Worship and the Heroic in History* (New York, 1905), p. 69.

5. E. Renan, *Le Livre de Job* (3d ed.; Paris, 1864), p. xvii.

6. F. H. Foster, "Is the Book of Job a Translation from an Arabic Original?" *AJSL*, XLIX (1932–33), 21–45.

7. Cf. his detailed discussion in his Comm., pp. xxx–xl.

8. The translation theory for Daniel was first proposed by C. C. Torrey in 1909. Cf. F. Zimmermann, *JBL*, LVII (1938), 255–72; (1939), 349–54; and H. L. Ginsberg, *Studies in Daniel* (New York, 1948), pp. 41–61. The theory of an Aramaic original for Daniel leans heavily on the difficult and unidiomatic style of the Hebrew, particularly in chaps. 11 and 12.

9. Cf. C. C. Torrey, "The Older Book of Esther," in *HThR*, XXXVII (1944), 33–38, and my critical observations in *JQR*, 1949, pp. 104–5.

10. The theory of an Aramaic original for Ecclesiastes was first tentatively suggested by F. C. Burkitt, "Is Ecclesiastes a Translation?" *JThS*, XXII

(1921), 23–26. It was adopted by F. Zimmermann and has been most passionately maintained by H. L. Ginsberg. The literature on the subject includes: F. Zimmermann, "The Aramaic Provenance of Qoheleth," in *JQR*, XXXVI (1945), 17–45; R. Gordis, "The Original Language of Qoheleth," in *JQR*, XXXVII (1946), 67–84; C. C. Torrey, "The Question of the Original Language of Qoheleth," in *JQR*, XXXIX (1948), 151–60; F. Zimmermann, "The Question of Hebrew in Qoheleth," *JQR*, XL (1949), 79–102; R. Gordis, "The Translation-Theory of Qoheleth Re-examined," in *JQR*, XL (1949), 103–16; H. L. Ginsberg, *Studies in Koheleth* (New York, 1950); R. Gordis, *KMW*, chap. vii; H. L. Ginsberg, *Koheleth* (a Commentary in Hebrew [Jerusalem 5721 = 1961]). Virtually no scholars except Zimmermann and Ginsberg have accepted the Aramaic origin theory for Ecclesiastes. Thus Albright (*Jewish Frontier*, January, 1952, pp. 30 ff.): "This position, which he [i.e., Gordis] holds against the theory of Zimmermann and H. L. Ginsberg that Koheleth is a translation from a lost Aramaic original, appears sound to the reviewer." The discovery of Qumran fragments of Ecclesiastes in Hebrew has given the theory its coup de grâce. Cf. J. Muilenberg, *BASOR*; Gordis, "The Significance of the Dead Sea Scrolls," in *Jewish Frontier*, April, 1957, p. 22; M. J. Dahood, "Qoheleth and Recent Discoveries," in *Biblica*, XXXIX (1958), 302–18.

11. See my observations on the style of the Dead Sea Scrolls in chapter xiv. The style of these sections in Daniel, like that of portions of Ezekiel, would repay investigation from this point of view.

12. Cf. R. H. Pfeiffer, *ZATW*, XLIV (1926), 13–25, and his *IOT*, pp. 680–81. Some eighteenth-century scholars, like Herder, Dessau, and Ilgen, had advanced a similar suggestion. See *IOT*, p. 680, n. 13.

13. Pfeiffer, *IOT*, pp. 159–67.

14. Cf. P. Humbert, *Recherches sur les Sources égyptiennes de la Littérature sapientiale d'Israël* (Neuchâtel, 1929).

15. On the relationship of Job and oriental Wisdom, see chapter v. On the extensive literature on Amenemope and Proverbs, see chapter v, note 4.

16. Cf. 38:39–40; 38:41–42; 39:5 ff.; 39:9 ff.; 39:13–14; 39:26 ff.; 40:15 ff.; 40:25 ff.

17. Cf. 7:12; 38:8 ff.; 38:21 ff.

18. Cf. 38:24, "What is the path in which the light is divided?"

19. Cf. 9:9; 38:31 ff.

20. Cf. 6:15 ff.; 39:5 ff.

21. Cf. 10:8 ff.; 39:1 ff.

22. Cf. 14:7 ff.

23. Cf. 18:8 ff.

24. Cf. "The Tale of Aqhat," *ANET*, pp. 149–55, and references there.

25. For the Ahiqar tale, cf. *ANET*, pp. 427–30, and the bibliographical references there.

26. On the universalistic emphasis in normative Judaism, both talmudic and medieval, and its relevant insights for contemporary world issues, the reader may be referred to R. Gordis, *The Root and the Branch: Judaism and the Free Society* (Chicago, 1962), esp. chap. ii, "Judaism—Its Character and Content."

27. Cf. "SBWL," pp. 89–91, and see above, chapter iv.

28. On the exegesis of this difficult verse, see my Comm.

29. Cf. the extensive collection of alleged parallels in Dhorme, *op. cit.*, pp. cxxi–cxxv.

30. See the very full and useful conspectus of views in Pfeiffer, *IOT,* pp. 675–78, and Rowley, "The Book of Job and Its Meaning," p. 197, n. 6.

31. Cf. B. *Baba Bathra* 14b, 15a: "Moses wrote his book and the section on Balaam and the book of Job." On the Hebrew texts and the Aramaic Targum of Job found in Qumran and not yet published, see W. H. Brownlee, *The Meaning of the Qumran Scrolls for the Bible* (Oxford, 1964), pp. 28, 81, 118.

32. See chapter xvi.

33. So Kleinert, Preiss, König, Baudissin, Schlögl, Beveridge, Gunkel, Pfeiffer, and Terrien.

34. So Cheyne, Dillmann, and Tur-Sinai (for the "Aramaic original," see his *The Book of Job—A New Commentary* [Jerusalem, 1957], pp. xxx–xxxix).

35. So Kuenen, Kittel, and G. Hoffmann, who date the book in the sixth century. Moore, Driver and Gray, Buttenwieser, Dhorme, Peale, and Bewer place it in the fifth century. The fourth century is favored by Cheyne, Budde, Jastrow, Eissfeldt, Finkelstein, Steuernagel, Meinhold, and Volz; the third century by Cornill and Holzmann. For reasons given below in the text, I believe that a third century date is too late.

36. Cf. I Chron. 21:1.

37. Cf. Wisdom of Solomon 2:24.

38. After Ben Sira mentions Ezekiel in his *Hymnus Patrum*, the Hebrew text has an incomplete line, which reads: *Vegam hizkīr ᵓet ᵓiyyōbh hammᵉkhalkel kol d.* . . . Cowley and Neubauer restore the lacuna as *darkē ṣedek*. M. M. Segal in *Sefer Ben Sira Hashalem* (Jerusalem 5713 = 1953), pp. 338–39 reads: *dābhār bᵉṣedek* or *dᵉbhārāv bᵉṣedek.* The Greek translation, prepared by Ben Sira's grandson (*ca.* 132 B.C.E.) renders the text as "He made mention of the enemy in the storm." When this Hebrew text was discovered in the Cairo Genizah at the turn of the nineteenth century by Solomon Schechter, he suggested that the word "enemy" (Hebrew *ᵓōyēbh*) was a textual error for "Job" (Hebrew *ᵓIyyōb*), both words being almost identical in Hebrew. R. Smend and R. H. Charles regard "in the storm" as an error for "among the prophets" (*nābāᵓ*, "flow," for *nābhiᵓ*, "prophet"). Segal suggests that only by mentioning Job in connection with Ezekiel could he include Job in his list of worthies, since the date of Job was unknown and even the place of the book in the canon was not yet fixed. Apropros of Schechter's suggestion, the Talmud B. *Baba Bathra* 16a contains a play on the two words: "He said to Him, 'Master of the Uni-

verse, perhaps a stormwind (*rūaḥ seārāh*) passed before Thee, and Thou didst mistake Job (*ʾiyyōbh*) for an enemy (*ʾōyēbh*)!' "

39. See chapter xvi on the canonization of Job.

40. The Church Father Eusebius (*Praeparatio Evangelica*, IX 25) extracts a passage from the Greek polymath Alexander Polyhistor (86–40 B.C.E.) citing the summary of the story of Aristeas, who refers to Elihu ben Barakhel by name. The passage is accessible in DG, I, lxv.

41. For the objection of the rabbis to Aramaic translations, see M. *Shabbat* 16:1; B. *Meg.* 3a. Their opposition to the Greek version was, of course, far greater: "The day the Torah was rendered into Greek was as evil for Israel as the day when the Golden Calf was fashioned."

42. For the religious and linguistic attributes of the Targums and the Ancient Versions, see the literature cited in chapter xvi, note 21.

43. Cf. Tos. *Shab.* 14:1; B. *Shab.* 115a; J. *Shab.* XVI, 15c top. The passage reveals the ultimate legitimization of written Targums, achieved not without opposition: "Rabbi Jose said, 'It happened with my father Halafta, who went to visit Rabban Gamaliel, the son of Rabbi in Tiberias. He found him sitting at the table of Johanan Hanazuph ("the one placed under the ban"). In his hand was the book of *Job* in an Aramaic translation, which he was reading. I said to him, "I remember your grandfather, Rabban Gamaliel, standing on the slope of the Temple mountain. They brought him a copy of a *Targum of Job* and he commanded the builder to place it under the masonry." Thereupon he, too, [i.e., the younger Rabban Gamaliel] commanded that the book be stored away and withdrawn from public use (*nignaz*, "hidden in the Genizah").' "

See W. H. Brownlee's discussion of this Aramaic Targum in *JJS*, VII (1956), 182–83. Churgin (*op. cit.*, pp. 87–88) believes that both these Targums on Job were identical and substantially the same as our present extant Targum. I do not share this view. It is far more likely that many different Targums, written and oral, were in circulation; witness the recently discovered Qumran Targum on Job, which is, incidentally, far more literal than the previously extant Targum.

XVI: THE LATER FORTUNES OF JOB IN THE CANON, THE VERSIONS, AND LEGEND

1. On the subject, see F. Buhl, *Canon and Text of the O.T.* (Edinburgh, 1892), pp. 3–32; H. E. Ryle, *Canon of the O.T.* (2d ed.; London, 1909); as well as the suggestive treatments of Max L. Margolis, *The Hebrew Scriptures in the Making* (Philadelphia, 1922), pp. 83–96, and S. Zeitlin, "An Historical Study of the Canonization of the Hebrew Scriptures," in *PAAJR*, III (1932), 121–58; G. F. Moore, *Judaism* (Cambridge, 1927), I, 240–47; Pfeiffer, *IOT*, pp. 50–70.

2. Buhl, *op. cit.*, p. 27.

3. According to the *locus classicus* in the Talmud, B. *Baba Bathra* 15b, the

order is: Ruth, Psalms, Job, Proverbs, Ecclesiastes, The Song, Lamentations, Daniel, Esther, Ezra, and Chronicles. In Jerome, the order is: Job, Psalms, Proverbs, Ecclesiastes, The Song, Daniel, Chronicles, Ezra, and Esther, while Ruth and Lamentations are included among the Prophets. The Masoretic work, *Ochlah Veochlah* (Nos. 111, 112, 127), gives the following as the Palestinian arrangement: Chronicles, Psalms, Job, Proverbs, Ruth, The Song, Ecclesiastes, Lamentations, Esther, Daniel, and Ezra. This order was the prevalent one among the Masoretes, and is therefore to be met in a variety of Spanish manuscripts and others, even in a Bible of C.E. 1009. Only the German manuscripts, according to the statements of Elijah Levita, placed the five Megillot (The Song, Ruth, Lamentations, Ecclesiastes, Esther) after Psalms, Proverbs, and Job, and before Daniel, Ezra, and Chronicles; and this arrangement has finally become the prevalent one in the printed editions. See Buhl, *op. cit.*, pp. 39 ff.

4. Cf. Buhl, *op. cit.*, pp. 25–27; Margolis, *op. cit.*, p. 88.

5. For the discussion and ultimate decision in favor of the Song of Songs and Ecclesiastes, see M. *Eduy.* 5:3; M. *Yad.* 3:5; Tos. *Yad.* 2:14. In B. *Meg.* 7a, R. Simeon ben Yohai, after declaring that the status of Ecclesiastes was disputed by the schools of Hillel and Shammai, continues, "but Ruth and the Song of Songs and Esther defile the hands [i.e., are canonical]." Esther continued to be discussed as late as the third century by the Babylonian Amora, Samuel (*loc. cit.*).

6. Cf. Tos. *Yad.* 2:13, "The books of Ben Sira and whatever books have been written since that time (*mikān va°īlākh*) do not defile the hands"; B. *Shab.* 100b. See also Moore, *op. cit.*, p. 243. Among the differences between the First and the Second Temple the Talmud lists "the absence of the Holy Spirit" (*rū°aḥ hakōdeš*) in the latter. Cf. B. *Yoma* 21b; J. *Taan.* II, 65a.

7. Cf. *Shab.* 30a, b: *Šedebhārāv sōteřīm zeh °et zeh.*

8. Cf. *Aboth de R. Nathan*, chap. 1, both versions (ed. Schechter, pp. 2, 3): *mipneī shehẽm mešālōt v°eīnān min hakethūbhīm.*

9. Cf. Tos. *Yad.* 2:14 (ed. Zuckermandl, p. 683); *Meg.* 7a: *mipneī šehī° hokmatho šel šelōmōh.*

10. Cf. *Pesikta de Rab Kahana*, piska 8 (ed. Buber, p. 61a); *Lev. Rab.* 28:1; *Koheleth R.* 3:1; Jerome, *Commentary on Ecc.* 12:13: *mipneī šemāṣe°ū bō debhārīm hamāttīm leṣad mīnūt.*

11. The view that the phrase *bō bayōm*, here as elsewhere in the Talmud, refers to the Council of Jamnia, lit. "the day when R. Eliezer ben Azariah was appointed as head of the Academy at Jamnia," is expressed in the Talmud (B. *Berakhot* 28a) and is followed by most modern scholars. This view, however, is doubted by Ch. Albeck (cf. his edition of the Mishnah, *Shishah Sidrei Mishnah, Seder Nashim* (Jerusalem, 1954), pp. 245, 384–85. He cites instances where the phrase is applied to other occasions.

12. The inability of the Mishnah to decide on the meaning of 13:15 derives from the fact that the text contains both variants, *lō°* (*lamed aleph*, "not")

and *lo* (*lamed vav*, "for him"). Both variants are preserved in our present Masoretic Text, the former in the *Kethib;* the latter in the *Qere*. For the significance of this ancient textual variation recorded in the Mishnah in establishing the character and the antiquity of the *Kethib-Qere* readings, cf. Gordis, *BTM*, pp. 50 ff.

13. Cf. M. *Sotah* 5:5.

14. See below in the text, and cf. the Targum and the Midrash, *passim.*

15. I am indebted to my son David, with whom I discussed this and many other aspects of Job, for stressing this new factor which is unique in biblical Wisdom.

16. On the LXX of Job, see H. B. Swete, *Introduction to the O.T. in Greek* (Cambridge, 1914), pp. 255 ff., and the basic treatment in DG, I, lxxi–lxxvi. Cf. also D. H. Gard, *The Exegetical Method of the Greek Translator of the Book of Job* ("*JBL* Monograph Series," Vol. 8 [1952]), which is strongly criticized by H. M. Orlinsky in his painstaking study, "Studies in the Septuagint of the Book of Job," *HUCA*, XXVIII–XXXIII (1957–62).

17. Cf. Swete, *op. cit.*, pp. 347, 350; DG, I, lxxiv, n. 1.

18. E. Hatch, *Essays in Biblical Greek* (Oxford, 1889), argues for the priority of the Greek. On the other hand, DG have effectively demonstrated the progressive contraction of the Greek translation (*loc. cit.*).

19. Cf. DG, I, lxxiii, n. 2.

20. According to J. Freudenthal, *Hellenistische Studien* (Breslau, 1875), pp. 136–41, Aristeas is the source of the identification in LXX of Job and Jobab.

21. Cf. the classic and still unsurpassed treatment of the methods of the Ancient Versions by S. D. Luzzatto, *Oheb Ger* (Vienna, 1830). Though Luzzatto was concerned with the Aramaic version of *Onkelos*, his observations apply with slight variations to all the Ancient Versions. On the method of the Targum, cf. P. Churgin, *Targum Kethubim* (New York, 5705 = 1945), pp. 98 ff. On the exegetical method of the Septuagint of the Pentateuch, cf. the works of Z. Frankel, as, e.g., *Ueber den Einfluss der palästinischen Exegese auf die alexandrinische Hermeneutik* (Leipzig, 1851). There are also valuable observations in the various studies of Chaim Heller on the Samaritan Pentateuch and the Pešita, etc., although some of his conclusions are open to question.

22. Cf. A. Mandl, *Die Peschitha zu Hiob* (Leipzig, 1892); E. Baumann, "Die Verwendbarkeit der Pesita zu Hiob für die Textkritik," in *ZATW*, 1898–1900.

23. Cf. W. Bacher, "Das Targum zu Hiob," in *MGWJ*, XX (1871), 208–23, 283–84; M. Lewin, *Targum und Midrasch zum Buche Hiob*, 1895; P. Churgin, *op. cit.*, pp. 87–116. In his interesting study, Churgin argues for the antiquity of our present Targum and identifies it with the Gamaliels' version.

24. Cf. the Targum on 14:12 (*lo yithᶜarō rāšiᶜayā*), "the wicked will not awake"; on 31:17 (*gehinnōm*); and on 38:18 (*gan ᶜēden*).

25. A brief *Midrash Iyyobh*, to which references are extant in medieval

works, was republished by S. Wertheimer in his *Leqet Midrashim* (Jerusalem, 1904). For the mass of rabbinic material on Job, cf. A. Wjernikowski, *Das Buch Hiob nach der rabbinischen Agada* (Frankfurt, 1893); M. Lewin in *JE*, s.v. *Job*, VII, 193–95; and the classic work of L. Ginzberg, *Legends of the Jews* (Philadelphia, 1913–38), II, 223–42, and the invaluable notes, V, 381–90.

26. For a brief presentation of the characteristics of rabbinic Aggadah, see R. Gordis, "Midrash—Its Method and Meaning," in *Midstream*, Summer, 1959, pp. 91–96.

27. Cf. B. *Baba Bathra* 15a: ᵓIyyōbh lo hāyāh velōᵓ nibhrāᵓ ᵓelā māšāl hāyāh.

28. Cf. *Midrash Gen. Rabbah*, sec. 57, except that *niheyāh* is substituted for *nibhrāᵓ*.

29. *Ibid.*: Sheᵓillu baᵓu ᶜālāv hāyāh yākhōl laᶜamōd bāhen.

30. In a Responsum of R. Hai Gaon quoted by Shuaib, ᵓIyyōbh lōᵓ hāyāh velōᵓ nibhrāᵓ ᵓelā lemāšāl. Cf. Ginzberg, *op. cit.*, V, 381, n. 3.

31. Cf. B. *Baba Bathra* 15b; *Targ. Jerusalem* on Job 2:9.

32. B. *Sotah* 11a; cf. B. *Sanh.* 106a.

33. Cf. J. *Sotah*, V, 8; B. *Baba Bathra* 15b.

34. Cf. B. *Baba Bathra* 15b; *Seder Olam* 21; and see Ginzberg, *op. cit.*, II, 228.

35. Cf. B. *Sotah* 11a; B. *Sanh.* 106a. The variant form of the legend is in *Sefer Hayashar*, sec. *Shemot*.

36. Cf. Ginzberg, *op. cit.*, V, 382.

37. Cf. B. *Baba Bathra* 16a.

38. This is the view of Rabbah, B. *Baba Bathra* 16a.

39. Cf. the statements of Raba and R. Johanan in B. *Baba Bathra* 16a, and Mid. *Tehillim* on Psalm 26 (ed. S. Buber, Vilna, 1890, p. 216); *Pesikta Rabbati*, *Ahare Mot* (ed. Friedmann, p. 190a). See Ginzberg, *op. cit.*, V, 389, n. 38.

40. The Greek text was first published by Cardinal Mai in Vol. VII of his *Scriptorum Veterum Nova Collectio* (Rome, 1833), edited from a single manuscript. For the literature, see Kaufmann Kohler, in *Semitic Studies in Memory of Dr. Alexander Kohut* (Berlin, 1897), pp. 264–338; M. R. James, in his *Apocrypha Anecdota* (2d series; Cambridge, 1897); K. Kohler in *JE*, VII, 200–202, s.v. *Testament of Job*; C. C. Torrey, *The Apocryphal Literature* (New Haven, 1945), pp. 140–45; R. H. Pfeiffer, *History of N.T. Times* (New York, 1949), pp. 70–72.

41. Torrey, *op. cit.*, p. 145, makes the brilliant suggestion that her name is originally *Ausitides*, "the woman from Ausitis or Uz," Job's native land.

42. Thus R. Akiba identifies Elihu with the heathen prophet Balaam, who is the enemy of Israel (J. *Sotah* V, 30d; cf. Ginzberg, *op. cit.*, V, 388).

43. Kohler equates this epithet with the Hebrew Ṣephōnī, from Ṣāphōn, "north." I suggest that it is an erroneous retroversion in the Greek of the Hebrew ṣiphᶜōnī, "asp, serpent"; cf. Isa. 11:8; 59:5; Jer. 8:17; Prov. 23:32.

44. The phrase occurs in the Epistle of James 5:11.

45. See his *Guide to the Perplexed*, trans. M. Friedlander (London, 1904, and often reprinted), Book III, chaps. 22–23. Rabbi Levi ben Gerson (Gersonides), born 1288, whose philosophic masterpiece is *Milḥamot Adonai* ("The Wars of the Lord"), presented a digest of his views on divine providence and omniscience and the nature of the human soul in his philosophic *Commentary on the Book of Job*, available in an English translation by A. L. Lassen (New York, 1946). A traditional approach to the problem of evil, mystical in character, is presented by Rabbi Moses ben Nahman (Nahmanides), born 1194, in his *Commentary on Job*, which, nevertheless, does not neglect the literal meaning of the text. The *Commentary* has been published with an introduction and valuable notes by Ch. D. Chavel in *Kithbhei Rabbenu Mose ben Nahman*, I (Jerusalem, 5723 = 1963), 19–28.

46. See Kant's "On the Failure of All Philosophical Attempts in the Matter of Theodicy."

Bibliography

TEXTS AND VERSIONS

The Hebrew Text

BAER, S., and F. DELITZSCH. *The Books of the Old Testament.* Leipzig, 1869–95.
GINSBURG, C. D. *Masoretic Bible.* London, 1st ed., 1894; 2d ed., 1926.
KITTEL, R. *Biblia Hebraica.* 4th ed.; Stuttgart, 1937. Edited by A. Alt and
O. E. Eissfeldt (Masoretic notes by P. Kahle. Job edited by G. Beer).

The Septuagint

SWETE, H. B. *The Old Testament in Greek.* Cambridge, 1887–94.
RAHLFS, A. *Septuaginta.* 2 vols. Stuttgart, 1935.

Aquila, Symmachus, Theodotion

FIELD, F. *Origenis Hexaplorum quae Supersunt.* Oxford, 1875.

The Vulgate

STIER, R., and K. G. W. THEILE. *Polyglotten-Bibel.* 4th ed. Bielefeld-Leipzig,
1875.

The Peshita

Kethabe Kadishe. Edited by S. Lee. London, 1823.

The Targum

Mikraoth Gedoloth. Vilna, 1912, often reprinted.

SOURCES

The Old Testament
The New Testament
The Apocrypha and Pseudepigrapha of the Old Testament. Edited by R. H. Charles. Oxford, 1913.
Works of Josephus ("Loeb Classics").
Mekilta de-Rabbi Ishmael. Edited by J. Z. Lauterbach. Philadelphia, 1933.
Sifre de be Rab. Edited by M. Friedmann. Vienna, 1864.
Mišnah. Vilna edition, frequently reprinted.
Tosefta. Edited by M. S. Zuckermandl. 2d ed. Jerusalem, 1938.
Aboth de Rabbi Nathan. Edited by S. Schechter. 2d printing. New York, 1945.
Babylonian Talmud. Vilna, 1928, frequently reprinted.
Jerusalem Talmud. Krotoschin, 1866.
Midraš Rabbah on the Torah and the Megilloth. Vilna edition, frequently reprinted.
Pesikta de Rab Kahana. Edited by S. Buber. 2d ed. Vilna, 1925.
Midraš Tehillim. Edited by S. Buber. Vilna, 1890.
Midraš ᵓIyyobh. Edited by S. A. Wertheimer. *Batei Midrašot.* 2d ed. Edited by A. Wertheimer. Jerusalem, 5713 = 1953.

COMMENTARIES

This list is arranged chronologically to afford a survey of the interpretation of Job. Modern commentaries nearly always include introductions to Job which discuss the salient problems of the book.

RASHI [RABBI SOLOMON ITZHAKI (1040–1105)].
SAMUEL BEN NISSIM MASNUTH. (12th cent.) *Mayan Gannim.* Edited by Salomon Buber. Berlin, 1889.
RAMBAN [RABBI MOSHE BEN NAHMAN or NAHMANIDES (1194–1270)].
RALBAG [RABBI LEVI BEN GERSHON or GERSONIDES (1288–1344)]. Translated by A. L. Lassen. New York, 1946.
MENDELSSOHN, MOSES. *Bible Commentary on Job.* Berlin, 1789.
RENAN, E. *Le Livre de Job.* 3d ed. Paris, 1864.
DELITZSCH, FRANZ. *Das Buch Iob.* Leipzig, 1864.
HITZIG, F. *Das Buch Hiob uebersetzt und ausgelegt.* Leipzig and Heidelberg, 1874.
SZOLD, BENJAMIN. *Sefer Iyyob.* Baltimore, 1886.
DILLMANN, A. *Hiob.* Leipzig, 1891.
BEER, G. *Der Text des Buches Hiob.* Marburg, 1895.
BUDDE, K. *Das Buch Hiob* ("Handkommentar zum Alten Testament"). Göttingen, 1st ed., 1896; 2d ed., 1913.
DUHM, B. *Das Buch Hiob erklaert.* Freiburg, 1897.
RABINOWITZ, A. Z., and A. OBRONIN. *Iyyob.* Jaffa, 5676 = 1916.
EHRLICH, A. B. *Randglossen zur hebräschen Bibel.* Vol. VI. Leipzig, 1918.

TORCZYNER, HARRY. *Das Buch Hiob*. Vienna-Berlin, 1920.

DRIVER, S. R., and G. B. GRAY. *A Critical and Exegetical Commentary on the Book of Job* ("International Critical Commentary"). 2 vols. New York, 1921.

BUTTENWIESER, M. *The Book of Job*. New York, 1922.

DHORME, P. *Le Livre de Job*. Paris, 1926.

YELLIN, D. *Hiqre Miqra—Iyyob*. Jerusalem, 5687 = 1927.

KÖNIG, E. *Das Buch Hiob*. 2d ed. Gütersloh, 1929.

SZCYGIEL, P. *Das Buch Hiob*. Bonn, 1931.

HÖLSCHER, G. *Das Buch Hiob* ("Handbuch zum Alten Testament"). Tübingen, 1937.

KISSANE, E. J. *The Book of Job*. Dublin, 1939.

TORCZYNER, N. H. *Sefer Iyyob*. Jerusalem, 5701 = 1941.

SNAITH, N. H. *The Book of Job*. London, 1945.

REICHERT, V. E. *Job* ("Soncino Bible"). Hindhead, Surrey, 1946.

HERTZBERG, H. W. *Das Buch Hiob*. Stuttgart, 1949.

JUNKER, H. *Das Buch Hiob*. Würzburg, 1951.

WEISER, A. *Das Buch Hiob*. Göttingen, 1951.

STEVENSON, W. B. *Critical Notes on the Hebrew Text of the Poem of Job*. Aberdeen, 1951.

STIER, F. *Das Buch Hiob*. Munich, 1954.

TERRIEN, S. L. Exegetical Commentary in *The Interpreter's Bible*. Vol. 3. New York–Nashville, 1954.

STEINMANN, J. *Le Livre de Job*. Paris, 1955.

TUR-SINAI, N. H. *The Book of Job—A New Commentary*. Jerusalem, 1957.

FREEHOF, S. B. *Book of Job—A Commentary*. New York, 1958.

HORST, F. *Hiob*. Neukirchen, 1960.

TERRIEN, S. L. *Job* ("Commentaire de l'Ancien Testament"). Neuchâtel, 1963.

POPE, MARVIN. *Job* ("Anchor Bible"). New York, 1965.

STUDIES IN JOB AND WISDOM LITERATURE

BACHER, W. "Das Targum zu Hiob," *MGWJ*, XX (1871).

BALL, C. J. *Book of Job*. Oxford, 1922.

BARTON, G. A. *Ecclesiastes* ("International Critical Commentary"). New York, 1908.

BAUMANN, E. "Die Verwendbarkeit der Pesita zu Hiob für die Textkritik," *ZATW*, XVIII–XX (1898–1900).

BUDDE, K. *Beiträge zur Kritik des Buches Hiob*. Göttingen, 1876.

BURKITT, F. C. "Is *Ecclesiastes* a Translation?" *JThS*, XXII (1921).

CARSTENSEN, R. N. *Job: Defense of Honor*. Nashville, 1963.

CHEYNE, T. K. *Job and Solomon*. New York, 1889.

DAHOOD, M. J. "Qoheleth and Recent Discoveries," *Biblica*, XXXIX (1958).

DHORME, P. "Ecclésiastes ou Job?" *RB*, XXXII (1923).

Dubarle, A. M. *Les Sages d'Israël.* Paris, 1946.

Ebeling, E. "Reste Akkadischer Weisheitsliteratur," *Meissner Festschrift,* I (1928).

Eerdmans, B. D. *Studies in Job.* Leiden, 1939.

Eissfeldt, O. *Der Maschal im Alten Testament.* Giessen, 1913.

Fichtner, J. *Die altorientalische Weisheitsliteratur in ihrer israelitisch-jüdischen Ausprägung.* Giessen, 1933.

Foster, F. H. "Is the Book of Job a Translation from an Arabic Original?" *AJSL,* XLIX (1932–33).

Froude, J. A. *The Book of Job.* London, 1854.

Fullerton, K. "The Original Conclusion of Job," *ZATW,* XXIV (1924).

Gard, D. H. *The Exegetical Method of the Greek Translator of the Book of Job* ("*JBL* Monograph Series," Vol. VIII). 1952.

Gaspar, J. W. *Social Ideas in the Wisdom Literature of the Old Testament.* Washington, 1947.

Ginsberg, H. L. *Koheleth* (a Commentary in Hebrew). Jerusalem, 5721 = 1961.

————. *Studies in Koheleth.* New York, 1950.

Good, E. M. *Irony in the Old Testament.* Philadelphia, 1965.

Gordis, R. "All Men's Book—A New Introduction to Job," *Menorah Journal,* XXXVII (1949).

————. "Corporate Personality in Job," *JNES,* IV (1945).

————. *Koheleth—The Man and His World.* New York, 1951.

————. "The Original Language of Qoheleth," *JQR,* XXXVII (1946).

————. "Qoheleth and Qumran—A Study in Style," *Biblica,* XLI (1960).

————. "Quotations as a Literary Usage in Biblical, Oriental and Rabbinic Literature," *HUCA,* XXII (1949).

————. "The Social Background of Wisdom Literature," *HUCA,* XVIII (1943).

————. *Song of Songs.* New York, 1954.

————. "The Temptation of Job—The Conflict of Tradition and Experience," *Judaism,* Vol. IV, No. 3 (1955).

————. "The Translation-Theory of Qoheleth Re-examined," *JQR,* XL (1949).

————. *The Wisdom of Ecclesiastes.* New York, 1945.

Grill, W. *Zur Kritik der Komposition des Buches Hiob.* Tübingen, 1890.

Humbert, P. *Recherches sur les Sources égyptiennes de la Littérature sapientiale d'Israël.* Neuchâtel, 1929.

Jastrow, Morris. *The Book of Job.* Philadelphia, 1920.

————. *The Gentle Cynic.* Philadelphia, 1919.

Jung, C. G. *Answer to Job.* London, 1964.

Kallen, H. M. *The Book of Job as a Greek Tragedy Restored.* New York, 1918.

Kautzsch, K. *Das sogenannte Volksbuch von Hiob.* Leipzig, 1900.

KEVIN, R. O. *The Wisdom of Amen-em-apt and Its Possible Dependence upon the Hebrew Book of Proverbs.* Philadelphia, 1931.

KOHLER, KAUFMANN. "The Testament of Job," *Semitic Studies in Memory of Dr. Alexander Kohut.* Berlin, 1897.

KRAELING, E. G. *The Book of the Ways of God.* New York, 1939.

LAMBERT, W. G. *Babylonian Wisdom Literature.* Oxford, 1960.

LEVY, LUDWIG. *Das Buch Qoheleth.* Leipzig, 1912.

MACDONALD, D. B. *The Hebrew Philosophic Genius.* Princeton, 1936.

MANDL, A. *Die Peschita zu Hiob.* Leipzig, 1892.

OESTERLEY, W. O. E. *The Book of Proverbs.* Philadelphia, 1929.

ORLINSKY, H. M. "Studies in the Septuagint of the Book of Job," *HUCA*, XXVIII–XXXIII (1957–62).

PFEIFFER, R. H. *Le Problème du Livre de Job.* Geneva, 1915.

RANKIN, O. S. *Israel's Wisdom Literature, Its Bearing on Theology and the History of Religion.* Edinburgh, 1936.

RANSTON, H. *The Old Testament Wisdom Books and Their Teachings.* London, 1930.

ROBINSON, H. WHEELER. *Suffering Human and Divine.* New York, 1939.

ROWLEY, H. H. "The Book of Job and its Meaning," *Bulletin of the John Rylands Library*, XLI (1958).

RYLAARSDAM, J. C. *Revelation in Jewish Wisdom Literature.* Chicago, 1946.

SANDERS, J. A. *Suffering as a Divine Discipline in the Old Testament and Post-Biblical Judaism.* Rochester, N.Y., 1955.

SEGAL, M. M. *Sefer Ben Sira Hashalem.* Jerusalem, 5713 = 1953.

SINGER, R. E. *Job's Encounter.* New York, 1963.

SPIEGEL, S. "Noah, Daniel and Job," *Louis Ginzberg Jubilee Volumes.* New York, 1945.

STAPLES, W. E. *The Speeches of Elihu.* Toronto, 1924.

STEVENSON, W. B. *The Poem of Job.* London, 1947.

STOCKHAMMER, MORRIS. *Das Buch Hiob: Versuch einer Theodizee.* Vienna, 1963.

STRAHAN, JAMES. *The Book of Job.* Edinburgh, 1913.

TERRIEN, S. L. *Job: Poet of Existence.* New York, 1957.

TORREY, C. C. "The Question of the Original Language of Qoheleth," *JQR*, XXXIX (1948).

VOLZ, P. *Hiob und Weisheit in den Schriften des Alten Testaments.* Göttingen, 1921.

WEBER, J. J. *L'Ecclésiaste.* Paris, 1947.

WESTERMANN, C. *Der Aufbau des Buches Hiob.* Tübingen, 1956.

WJERNIKOWSKI, A. *Das Buch Hiob nach der rabbinischen Agada.* Frankfurt, 1893.

ZHITLOWSKY, CHAIM. *Job and Faust.*

ZIMMERMANN, F. "The Aramaic Provenance of Qoheleth," *JQR*, XXXVI (1945).

———. "The Question of Hebrew in Qoheleth," *JQR*, XL (1949).

GENERAL BIBLIOGRAPHY

ABRAHAMS, I. *Permanent Values in Judaism.* New York, 1923.

ADLER, CYRUS, and ISIDORE SINGER (eds.). *The Jewish Encyclopedia.* 12 vols. 1903–6.

AGUS, J. B. *Guideposts of Modern Judaism.* New York, 1954.

———. *Modern Philosophies of Judaism.* New York, 1941.

ALBECK, CH. (ed.). *Shishah Sidrei Mishnah.* Jerusalem, 1954.

ALBRIGHT, W. F. *Archaeology and the Religion of Israel.* Baltimore, 1942.

BARTON, G. A. *Archaeology and the Bible.* 7th ed. Philadelphia, 1937.

BEN-JEHUDA, ELIEZER. *Thesaurus* ("Millon Halašon Haivrit Hayešanah vehahadašah"). 16 vols. Tel Aviv, n.d.

BENTZEN, A. *Introduction to the Old Testament.* 2d ed. Copenhagen, 1948.

BERGMANN, H. *Modern Jewish Thinkers.* New York, 1962.

BLANK, S. H. *Jeremiah: Man and Prophet.* Cincinnati, 1961.

———. *Prophetic Faith in Isaiah.* New York, 1958.

BRIGHT, JOHN. *A History of Israel.* Philadelphia, 1959.

BROWN, F., S. R. DRIVER, and C. A. BRIGGS. *A Hebrew and English Lexicon of the Old Testament.* Oxford, 1907.

BUDGE, E. A. WALLIS (ed.). *The Book of the Dead.* New York, 1956.

BUHL, F. *Canon and Text of the Old Testament.* Edinburgh, 1892.

BURCHARD, CH. *Bibliographie zu den Handschriften vom Toten Meer.* Berlin, 1957.

BURROWS, MILLAR. *Outline of Biblical Theology.* Philadelphia, 1946.

CARLYLE, THOMAS. *On Heroes, Hero Worship and the Heroic in History.* New York, 1905.

CASANOWICZ, I. M. *Paronomasia in the Old Testament.* Boston, 1894.

CHARLES, R. H. *A Critical History of the Doctrine of a Future Life.* London, 1899.

CHEYNE, T. K. *Encyclopedia Biblica.* 4 vols. New York, 1899–1903.

CHURGIN, P. *Targum Kethubim.* New York, 5705 = 1945.

COBB, W. H. *A Criticism of Systems of Hebrew Metre.* Oxford, 1905.

COOKE, G. A. *Ezekiel* ("International Critical Commentary"). New York, 1937.

CORNILL, C. *Introduction to the Canonical Books of the Old Testament.* New York, 1907.

COWLEY, A. E. *Aramaic Papyri of the Fifth Century B.C.* Oxford, 1923.

DAVIDSON, ISRAEL (ed.). *Selected Religious Poems of Solomon ibn Gabirol.* Philadelphia, 1923.

DENNEFELD, L. *Introduction à l'Ancien Testament.* Paris, 1934.

DE WETTE, W. M. L. *Introduction to the Old Testament.* Vol. II. Boston, 1843.

DIAMOND, M. *Martin Buber: Jewish Existentialist.* New York, 1960.

DRIVER, G. R., and J. C. MILES. *The Assyrian Laws.* Oxford, 1935.

DRIVER, S. R. *Hebrew Tenses.* Oxford, 1892.

———. *Introduction to the Literature of the Old Testament.* 9th ed. New York, 1913.

DUPONT-SOMMER, A. *The Essene Writings from Qumran.* Oxford, 1961.
EICHHORN, J. G. *Einleitung in das Alte Testament.* 3d ed. Leipzig, 1803.
EICHRODT, W. *Theologie des Alten Testaments.* Philadelphia, 1961.
EISSFELDT, O. *Einleitung in das Alte Testament.* Tübingen, 1934.
ELIOT, T. S. *Collected Essays in Literary Criticism.* London, 1952.
EMSLIE, W. A. L. *How Came Our Faith.* New York, 1949.
ERMAN, A. *The Literature of the Ancient Egyptians.* Translated by A. M. Blackman. New York, 1927.
FINKELSTEIN, L. (ed.). *The Jews—Their History, Culture and Religion.* 2 vols. New York, 1960.
———. *The Pharisees.* 2 vols. Philadelphia, 1938.
FRANKEL, Z. *Darkhei Hamishnah.* Leipzig, 1859.
———. *Ueber den Einfluss der palästinischen Exegese auf die alexandrinische Hermeneutik.* Leipzig, 1851.
FRANKFORT, H. *The Intellectual Adventures of Ancient Man.* Chicago, 1941.
FREEDMAN, D. N., and F. W. CROSS. *Early Hebrew Orthography.* New Haven, 1952.
FRIEDMAN, M. *Martin Buber—The Life of Dialogue.* Chicago, 1955.
GASTER, T. H. *Thespis.* New York, 1950.
GINSBERG, H. L. *Studies in Daniel.* New York, 1948.
GINSBURG, C. D. *Introduction to a Massoretico-Critical Edition of the Hebrew Bible.* London, 1897.
GINZBERG, L. *Legends of the Jews.* 7 vols. Philadelphia, 1913–38.
———. "The Place of Halacha in Jewish Research," *On Jewish Law and Lore.* Philadelphia, 1955.
GLATZER, N. M. *Franz Rosenzweig—His Life and Thought.* New York, 1953.
GOETHE, J. W. *Faust.* Edited by Calvin Thomas. Boston, 1894.
GOETTSBERGER, J. *Einleitung in das Alte Testament.* Freiburg-im-Breisgau, 1928.
GORDIS, ROBERT. "Al Mibneh Haširah Haivrit Haquedumah" ("On the Structure of Ancient Hebrew Poetry"), *Sefer Hašanah Liyehudei Amerikah.* New York, 5705 = 1944.
———. "The Bible as a Cultural Monument," *The Jews—Their History, Culture and Religion.* Edited by Louis Finkelstein. 2d ed. New York, 1960.
———. *The Biblical Text in the Making.* Philadelphia, 1937.
———. "The Composition and Structure of Amos," *HThR,* XXXIII (1940).
———. *A Faith for Moderns.* New York, 1960.
———. "The Knowledge of Good and Evil in the Old Testament and the Qumran Scrolls," *JBL,* LXXVI (1957).
———. "Lešon Miqra Leʾor Lešon Hekhamim" in *Sefer Tur-Sinai* (Jerusalem, 5720 = 1960).
———. "Lisegulloth Hameliṣah Bekhithebhei Haqodeš," *Sēpher Muggaš Likhebhod Doktor Mošeh Seidel.* Jerusalem, 5722 = 1962.
———. "Midrash—Its Method and Meaning," *Midstream* (Summer, 1959).
———. "A Note on Yad," *JBL,* LXII (1943).

———. "Primitive Democracy in Ancient Israel," *Alexander Marx Jubilee Volume*. New York, 1950.

———. "Psalm 9–10: A Textual and Exegetical Study," *JQR*, XLVIII (1957).

———. *The Root and the Branch: Judaism and the Free Society*. Chicago, 1962.

———. "The Significance of the Dead Sea Scrolls," *Jewish Frontier*, XXIV (April, 1957).

———. "The Significance of the Paradise Myth," *AJSL*, LII (1936).

———. "Studies in the Relationship of Biblical and Rabbinic Hebrew," *Louis Ginzberg Jubilee Volumes*. New York, 1945.

———. "Yihusei Hakhethibh Vehanniqqud Balašon Ha-ivrith," *Lešonenū* (5696 = 1937).

GORDON, C. H. *Before the Bible*. New York, 1963.

———. *Ugaritic Handbook*. Rome, 1947.

———. *Ugaritic Manual*. Rome, 1955.

GRESSMANN, H. *Altorientalische Texte und Bilder zum Alten Testament*. 2 vols. Berlin-Leipzig, 1926.

GUTTMANN, MICHAEL. *Mafteah HaTalmud*. Budapest, 1917.

HABERMAN, A. M. *Megillot Midbar Yehudah*. Tel Aviv, 1959.

HADHAM, JOHN. *Good God*. Harmondsworth, Middlesex, 1940.

HALLER, M., and K. GALLING. *Die Fünf Megilloth*. Tübingen, 1940.

HATCH, E. *Essays in Biblical Greek*. Oxford, 1889.

HEINISCH, P. *Theology of the Old Testament*. Collegeville, Minn., 1950.

HERTZBERG, H. W. *Der Prediger*. Leipzig, 1932.

HERZ, J. *Wissenschaftliche Zeitschrift der Karl Marx Universität*. Vol. III. Leipzig, 1953–54.

HESCHEL, A. J. *The Prophets*. New York, 1962.

HOOKE, S. H. *Middle Eastern Mythology*. Harmondsworth, Middlesex, 1963.

HROZNY, F. *Code Hittite*. Paris, 1922.

ISAACS, J., *The Background of Modern Poetry*. London, 1951.

JAMES, F. *Personalities of the Old Testament*. New York and London, 1946.

JAMES, M. R. *Apocrypha Anecdota*. 2d ser. Cambridge, 1897.

KAUFMANN, W. *Critique of Religion and Philosophy*. New York, 1961.

———. *From Shakespeare to Existentialism*. New York, 1960.

KAUFMANN, YEHEZKEL. *Commentary on Joshua*. Jerusalem, 5719 = 1959.

———. *Commentary on Judges*. Jerusalem, 5722 = 1962.

———. *The Religion of Israel*. Translated and abridged by Moshe Greenberg. Chicago, 1960.

———. *Toledot Haᵓemunah Hayisreᵓelit* ("History of the Religion of Israel"). 8 vols. Tel Aviv, 1937–56.

KAUTZSCH, E. *Die Aramäismen im Alten Testament*. Halle an der Saale, 1902.

KER, P. *Form and Style in Poetry*. London, 1928.

KITTO, H. D. F. *The Greeks*. Harmondsworth, Middlesex, 1951.

KNUDTZON, J. A. *Die El-Amarna-Tafeln*. 2 vols. Leipzig, 1915.

KOHLER, J., and F. E. PEISER. *Hamurabis Gesetz*. Leipzig, 1904.
KOHLER, K. *Jewish Theology*. Cincinnati, 1917.
KOHLER, L. *Theologie des Alten Testaments*. Tübingen, 1953.
KRAELING, E. G. *The Brooklyn Museum Aramaic Papyri*. New Haven, 1953.
LANGER, SUZANNE K. *Philosophy in a New Key*. 2d ed. Cambridge, Mass., 1951.
LEVINE, B. A. "The Netinim," *JBL*, LXXXII (1963).
LEVY, R. *Deutero-Isaiah*. Oxford, 1925.
LEWIS, C. S. *The Problem of Pain*. London, 1940.
LEWISOHN, L. *Goethe: The Story of a Man*. 2 vols. New York, 1949.
LIDDELL, H. G., and R. SCOTT. *A Greek-English Lexicon*. New York, 1883.
LIEBERMAN, S. *Greek in Jewish Palestine*. New York, 1942.
———. *Hellenism in Jewish Palestine*. New York, 1950.
LOWTH, R. *Praelectiones*. Oxford, 1753.
LUZZATTO, S. D. *Oheb Ger*. Vienna, 1830.
MAI, A. *Scriptorum Veterum Nova Collectio*. Rome, 1833.
MAIMONIDES, MOSES. *Guide to the Perplexed*. Translated by M. Friedlander. London, 1904, often reprinted.
———. Introduction to Sanhedrin, *Commentary on the Mishnah* (in most editions of the Talmud).
MARGOLIS, M. L. *The Hebrew Scriptures in the Making*. Philadelphia, 1922.
MARMORSTEIN, A. *The Doctrine of Merits in the Old Rabbinical Literature*. London, 1920.
MATTHEWS, I. G. *The Religious Pilgrimage of Israel*. New York, 1947.
MEISSNER, B. *Babylonien und Assyrien*. 2 vols. Heidelberg, 1920–25.
MONTGOMERY, JAMES. *Daniel* ("International Critical Commentary"). New York, 1923.
MOORE, G. F. *Judaism in the First Centuries of the Christian Era*. 3 vols. Cambridge, Mass., 1927–30.
NOELDEKE, TH. *Untersuchungen zum Ahiqar-Roman*. Berlin, 1913.
NORTH, C. R. *The Suffering Servant in Deutero-Isaiah*. Oxford, 1948.
OESTERLEY, W. O. E., and T. H. ROBINSON. *Hebrew Religion: Its Origins and Development*. New York, 1930.
———. *An Introduction to the Books of the Old Testament*. New York, 1949.
OGDEN, C. K., and I. A. RICHARDS. *The Meaning of Meaning*. New York, 1930.
PEAKE, A. S. *The Problem of Suffering in the Old Testament*. London, 1904, 1947.
PEDERSEN, J. *Israel: Its Life and Culture*. London and Copenhagen, 1926.
PFEIFFER, R. H. *History of the New Testament Times*. New York, 1949.
———. *Introduction to the Old Testament*. New York, 1941.
PRESS, JOHN. *The Chequer'd Shade—Reflections on Obscurity in Poetry*. London, 1958.
PRITCHARD, J. B. *Ancient Near Eastern Texts Relating to the Old Testament*. Princeton, 1950.
READ, H. *A Concise History of Modern Painting*. New York, 1959.
ROBERTS, B. J. *The Old Testament Text and Versions*. Cardiff, 1951.

ROBINSON, H. WHEELER. *The Cross in the Old Testament.* London, 1955.

————. *Inspiration and Revelation in the Old Testament.* Oxford, 1946.

————. *The Old Testament: Its Making and Meaning.* Nashville, 1937.

ROBINSON, T. H. *The Poetry of the Old Testament.* London, 1947.

ROSENZWEIG, FRANZ. *Der Stern der Erlösung.* Frankfurt, 1921.

ROWLEY, H. H. *The Faith of Israel.* London, 1956.

————. *The Servant of the Lord and Other Essays.* London, 1952.

RYLE, H. E. *Canon of the Old Testament.* 2d ed. London, 1909.

SACHAU, E. *Aramäische Papyrus und Ostraken.* Leipzig, 1911.

SCHOLEM, GERSHOM. *Major Trends in Jewish Mysticism.* Jerusalem, 1941.

SPIEGEL, S. *Milešon Payyetanim* ("On the Language of the Medieval Poets"). New York, 1963.

————. "On Medieval Hebrew Poetry," *The Jews.* Edited by L. Finkelstein. New York, 1949.

STEINMÜLLER, J. E. *A Companion to Scripture Studies.* 3 vols. New York, 1941–43.

SUTCLIFFE, E. F. *The Old Testament and the Future Life.* London, 1946.

————. *Providence and Suffering in the Old and New Testaments.* London, 1953.

SWETE, H. B. *Introduction to the Old Testament in Greek.* Cambridge, 1914.

TAYLOR, A. *The Proverb.* Cambridge, Mass., 1931.

TCHERIKOVER, V. *Hellenistic Civilization and the Jews.* Philadelphia, 1959.

TCHERNOWITZ, CH. *Toledot Hahalakhah.* 4 vols. New York, 1934–50.

TORREY, C. C. *The Apocryphal Literature.* New Haven, 1945.

————. "The Older Book of Esther," *HThR*, XXXVII (1944).

TUR-SINAI, N. H. *Halašon Vehasepher; Kerekh Hasepher.* Jerusalem, 1950.

UNGNAD, A. *Aramäische Papyrus aus Elephantine.* Leipzig, 1911.

VIROLLEAUD, CHARLES. *La Légende phénicienne de Danel.* Paris, 1936.

VOLZ, P. *Jüdische Eschatologie.* Tübingen, 1903.

WEISS, I. H. *Dor Dor Vedorshav.* 5 vols. Vilna, 1871–91.

WEISS, MEIR. *Hamiqra Kidemutho* ("The Literary Form of Scripture"). Jerusalem, 1962.

WERTHEIMER, S. (ed.). *Leqet Midrashim.* Jerusalem, 1904.

WRIGHT, W. *A Grammar of the Arabic Language.* London, 1874–75.

WURTHWEIN, E. *Der Text des Alten Testaments.* Stuttgart, 1952.

YADIN, Y. *A Genesis Apocryphon.* Jerusalem, 1956.

YELLIN, D. *Kethabim Nibharim Letorat Hamelitzah Batanakh.* Jerusalem, 5699 = 1939.

ZEITLIN, S. "An Historical Study of the Canonization of the Hebrew Scriptures," *Proceedings of the American Academy for Jewish Research*, III (1932).

Index

377